Journal of Semitic Studies Supplement 31

From Cairo to Manchester: Studies in the Rylands Genizah Fragments

Edited by

Renate Smithuis and Philip S. Alexander

Published by Oxford University Press
on behalf of the University of Manchester
2013

OXFORD
UNIVERSITY PRESS

Great Clarendon Street, Oxford OX2 6DP

Oxford University Press is a department of the University of Oxford.
It furthers the University's objective of excellence in research, scholarship,
and education by publishing worldwide in

Oxford New York

Athens Auckland Bangkok Bogotá Buenos Aires Cape Town
Chennai Dar es Salaam Delhi Florence Hong Kong Istanbul Karachi
Kolkata Kuala Lumpur Madrid Melbourne Mexico City Mumbai Nairobi
Paris São Paulo Shanghai Singapore Taipei Tokyo Toronto Warsaw

with associated companies in Berlin Ibadan

Oxford is a registered trade mark of Oxford University Press
in the UK and in certain other countries

Published in the United Kingdom
by Oxford University Press, Oxford

First published 2013

A catalogue for this book is available from the British Library

Library of Congress Cataloguing in Publication Data
(Data available)

ISSN 0022-4480
ISBN 978-0-19-870153-8

Subscription information for the *Journal of Semitic Studies* is available at the journal website:
jss.oxfordjournals.org

Printed in Great Britain by Bell & Bain Ltd, Glasgow

Table of Contents

The cover illustration is a Hebrew medical fragment with advice as to how to treat conjunctivitis (*ramad* in Arabic) – B 3591-1. (Reproduced by courtesy of the University Librarian and Director, The John Rylands Library, The University of Manchester).

Preface

The present volume is one of the outcomes of the Rylands Cairo Genizah Project. The overall aim of this project is to conserve, catalogue, digitize and interpret the 15,000 or so manuscript fragments which make up the Gaster Genizah collection in the John Rylands Library Manchester. This project has been running now for a number of years and has many more years to run. It began in earnest in 2003 with a pilot scheme to survey and evaluate the collection, funded by the Friedberg and Safra Foundations and by Mr Joe Dwek. The Principal Investigator was Philip Alexander, and the Postdoctoral Researcher Renate Smithuis. This led in 2006 to a successful application from the same two scholars, joined as co-applicant by Dr Stella Butler, then Head of Special Collections at the University of Manchester Library, to the Arts and Humanities Research Council for funding to digitize the whole collection and put it online with catalogue records. This resulted in the capture of digital images of all the fragments, and the publication of most of them (together with catalogue records) on a public access, searchable database, hosted on the University of Manchester library website.

The contextualizing side of the project was served by a series of workshops focusing on aspects of the Rylands Genizah collection, namely 'Scientific, Magical and Related Fragments' (30 April–1 May 2007), 'Prayer and Liturgical Poetry Fragments' (2–3 June 2008), and 'Manuscripts as Artefacts: The Evidence of the Genizah' (22–23 June 2009). The present volume emerges from those workshops. Its purpose is not only to publish a number of interesting manuscripts from the Rylands Genizah collection, but to try and characterize the entire collection in comparison and contrast to other Genizah collections, and the Genizah as a whole. Renate Smithuis offers a 'Short Introduction to the Genizah Collection in the John Rylands Library'. Despite the fact that considerable quantities of archival documentation exist, surprisingly little is known about how and when Gaster assembled his collection of Genizah fragments, or why precisely it ended up in two different libraries — the British Library in London, and the John Rylands Library in Manchester. Smithuis's essay shows how confusing and complex the picture is, and challenges some accepted 'verities' of the history of the Genizah.

This short introduction begins the task of trying to characterize the Rylands Genizah, and to explain why it is as it is. This theme is pursued in more detail in the following two essays. Philip Alexander and Renate Smithuis, 'Notes on Artefactual Aspects of the Rylands Genizah', attempts two things: (1) to create a descriptive framework for characterizing a collection such as the Rylands Genizah — a list of topics under which such collections should be described; and (2) to apply this to the collection at hand. The categorization of manuscript collections is under-theorized (standard distinctions between 'libraries' and 'archives', between 'literary texts' and 'documents', do not get us very far), but a framework is necessary if meaningful comparisons are to be made. This point is pursued in more detail in Smithuis and Alexander, 'Targum Manuscripts in the Rylands Genizah', by exploring a sub-category, representing a distinct literary genre, of the Rylands collection. There are numerous Targum manuscripts in the Rylands Genizah, but an analysis of them reveals some interesting patterns which, we believe, are indicative of the Rylands Genizah as a whole: they are palaeographically late, they probably represent only the 'official' Targums of Onqelos to the Torah, and Jonathan to the Prophets, and in the latter case only Haftarot, taken, at least in some cases, from Haftarot Books, rather than from complete manuscripts of the Prophets. There are no examples that we could find in the Rylands Genizah of paraphrastic Targums of the Palestinian variety, which are found in other Genizah collections.

The remaining essays in the volume focus on particular fragments or groups of fragments in the Rylands Genizah. Gideon Bohak, 'A New Genizah Fragment of the *Aramaic Levi Document*', supplements already known fragments in Oxford and Cambridge to give us less than half of this important text, copies of which were known to the community of the Dead Sea Scrolls. Ben Outhwaite and Friedrich Niessen, 'Between Cambridge and Manchester: Reuniting a Leaf of Maimonides' *Guide of the Perplexed* from the Cairo Genizah' is a republication, with revisions, of an article which first appeared in *Journal of Jewish Studies* in 2006. We thank its editors for allowing us to reprint the article. The lower third of the leaf is in Manchester, the upper two thirds in Cambridge — a striking illustration of how manuscripts in the original Genizah got dismembered and scattered round the world.

Two essays illuminate the contribution of the Rylands Genizah to the study of Hebrew poetry. Michael Rand, 'The Qillirian *Qᵉrôbâ* והיה אויב מתגבר in the Rylands Genizah', publishes a new recension which he discovered in the Rylands, of a *piyyûṭ* by Qillîr, and compares it with the already published recension, demonstrating that the Manchester text contains some valuable new readings. Michael Rand and

Jonathan Vardi, 'A Genizah Leaf from the *Dīwān* of Š^{e}mû'ēl Ha-Nāgîd', joins some fragments in the Rylands with Genizah fragments from elsewhere to reconstruct part of the collection of the great Andalusian poet of the Spanish Golden Age.

The subject-matter then turns more medical and scientific. Efraim Lev and Renate Smithuis provide 'A Preliminary Catalogue of the Medical and Para-Medical Manuscripts in the Rylands Genizah Collection together with the Partial Edition of two Medical Fragments (A 589 and B 3239)' — a substantial contribution to making the Genizah's treasures available to historians of medicine. As an appendix to this we have included an edition, by Efraim Lev and Zohar Amar, of an unpublished 'Medieval Judaeo-Arabic Glossary of Drugs' Names in the Taylor-Schechter Genizah Collection, Cambridge'. This manuscript, though not in the Rylands, complements so well the preceding essay that we deemed it worthwhile issuing them side by side. Gideon Bohak and Renate Smithuis, 'Four Amulets and an Exorcism from the Rylands Genizah Collection' illustrates the other side of medical practice — folk medicine. Three of the amulets are scorpion amulets, designed to guard their owners from scorpion stings, the fourth a spell to protect its owner from slander. There is nothing remarkable about these, but the final piece, the record of an exorcism from a woman of the ghost of her dead husband, is rare, if not unique.

Two studies on very different topics round off the volume. Geoffrey Khan in 'A Judaeo-Arabic Document from Ottoman Egypt in the Rylands Genizah Collection' demonstrates that the very lateness of the Rylands collection means that it contains valuable evidence for the history of the Arabic language in the eighteenth and nineteenth centuries. And Philip Alexander and Sagit Butbul offer an edition of fragments of a Judaeo-Arabic anti-Christian polemic similar, though not identical, to the *Qiṣṣat Mujādalat al-Usquf* ('Rylands Gaster Heb. Ms. 1623/3 and the *Qiṣṣat Mujādalat al-Usquf*'). These studies are only a taster for what awaits in the Rylands Gaster Genizah, but we hope they will whet scholars appetite to explore the collection further and publicize its contents.

The Rylands Cairo Genizah Project would have been impossible without the support of a large number of people and institutions. First our thanks must go to our funders, Joe Dwek, the Friedberg and Safra Foundations, the Arts and Humanities Research Council, and the British Academy. Second we would like to express our sincere gratitude to the staff of the Rylands Library, especially Stella Butler (a Co-Applicant in our grant from the AHRC), John Hodgson, Carol Burrows, Anne McClelland, Caroline Checkley-Scott, Steven Mooney, Jenny Curtis and Ben Green.

It was a pleasure to work with them and they did everything in their power to facilitate the project. The team we assembled to do the day-to-day work — Jamie Robinson and then Gwen Jones, the photographers, and Jane Donaldson and then Anna Hughes, the Catalogue Assistants, — were superb, and their obvious commitment to and pleasure in their work made life very easy for us.

Our debts to the wider scholarly community are varied and deep. Several visited our Genizah Unit to look at our manuscripts: here special mention must be made of Gideon Bohak and Sagit Butbul (the latter on a British Academy Visiting Fellowship). Some of the fruits of these visits are included in the present volume. The scholars who attended our workshops helped us enormously: Wout van Bekkum, Charles Burnett, Javier Castaño, Leigh Chipman, Uri Ehrlich, Edna Engel, Eleazar Gutwirth, Elisabeth Hollender, Zvi Langermann, Efraim Lev, Judith Olszowy-Schlanger, Ben Outhwaite, Peter Pormann, Michael Rand, Stefan Reif, Ortal-Paz Saar. There were scholars who always gave generously of their time and knowledge when we turned to them for advice. First of all, Ezra Chwat should be thanked here profusely. His help and advice as a cataloguer of subsections of the Rylands Genizah for the *Aleph* database of the Jewish National and University Library in Jerusalem have been invaluable. It was a pleasure and privilege to work with Dr Rabbi Julian Abel on the identification and description of numerous prayer fragments, and with Mark Cohen, Phillip Ackerman-Lieberman, Arnold Franklin, Roxani E. Margariti, Jessica M. Marglin, Luke B. Yarbrough and Oded Zinger of Princeton University on a selection of documentary material. Michael Rand's publications evince his ongoing interest in our collection. Special thanks must also go to Stefan Reif, Geoffrey Khan and above all Ben Outhwaite. The project would probably never have got off the ground, but for the promptings of Abraham David, and the preliminary work he did on the Rylands Genizah fragments many years ago. There are doubtless others who played a part over the past six years whose names have momentarily slipped our minds. We ask their indulgence. The collaboration, the networking which we established as a result of the project, has been a joy. Finally we are grateful for those who have contributed to the present volume, and thank them for their patience as its publication, for various reasons, was delayed.

Renate Smithuis
Philip Alexander
Centre for Jewish Studies
University of Manchester
February 2013

Short Introduction to the Genizah Collection in the John Rylands Library

Renate Smithuis
University of Manchester

'It is well known that the smaller the leaves are the older they are…'
(Moses Gaster)

The Origin of the Collection: Dr Moses Gaster

The John Rylands Library in Manchester holds about 15,000 fragments from the Cairo Genizah, which originally belonged to Rabbi Dr Moses Gaster (1856–1939).[1] Gaster became Sephardi Hakham of Britain (1887–1918) remarkably soon after his forced departure from his homeland Rumania in 1885. His career spanned several domains of society: deeply involved with Jewish religious, communal and political affairs, also of a transnational nature through his prominent role in the Zionist movement (Renton 2004), he devoted much of his professional life to academic study and teaching, which included an Oxford lectureship and running the Lady Judith Montefiore College in Ramsgate between 1888–96[2] during his early years in the United Kingdom (Alderman 2004; Schindler 1958). His voice was heard, and his influence noticed, throughout Anglo-Jewry and beyond. Delivering countless speeches and turning out newspaper articles and correspondence at great speed, Gaster moreover published a remarkably wide variety of academic papers and books encompassing ten languages,[3] which earned him honorary fellowships of, and leading roles in, various learned societies such as the Royal Asiatic Society (Alderman 2004). We can follow Gaster's life in the pages of the *Jewish Chronicle*, which allows us, e.g., insight into the lively academic scene of his time via regular updates on his talks together with the scholarly reactions they provoked.

1 The original estimate of the size of the collection in the region of 11,000 fragments was based on the total number of class-marks rather than of individual fragments.

2 Papers at University College London show that 1888 is the year in which Gaster was appointed principal of the College. It opened its doors to rabbinic seminarians in 1890 with actual courses starting in 1891. Haralambakis forthcoming in 2013.

3 For an overview see Schindler 1958: 23–40. For a major collection of his articles see Gaster 1925–28.

His biography, including a detailed evaluation of the significance of his scholarship for the development of Jewish Studies, remains to be written. This would be a very rewarding exercise, since the several voluminous archives of his correspondence, papers and other materials, found in the UK and further afield,[4] have hardly begun to be explored and are bound to yield a wealth of information regarding his intellectual endeavours as well as his role in modern Jewish history.[5]

A true bibliophile, Moses Gaster amassed a huge library of printed books and manuscripts, mainly in the fields of Hebraica, Judaica, and Romanian and Samaritan studies.[6] He tells about his obsession for collecting books in 'Die Geschichte meiner Bibliothek', a little personal memoir apparently written in the final decade of his life. The memoir remained unpublished during his lifetime, but was spotted by Brad Sabin Hill among the Gaster papers at the UCL (Gaster 1995: 16, 21). Perhaps it remained unpublished because the way in which Gaster describes his various book acquisition strategies there was deemed slightly too candid to be committed to print even in a magazine for seasoned bibliophiles. Thus he writes: 'I convinced people that when they keep books in their own house, sooner or later they are lost or consigned to oblivion (…) In order to avoid this literary barbarity, I induced people to donate their books to me, in effect to hand them over to the ordered care of my library (…) In gratitude for their giving me their books, I had the donors' names entered in the respective volumes' (Gaster 1995: 19).[7]

Similar to his personal archive, Gaster's printed books and manuscripts ended up in various parts of the world. The main current repositories for his manuscripts are:

---

4 The most important of these are the Gaster papers at University College London (337 boxes plus 22 volumes and 9 rolls, presently stored at the National Archive in Kew) and the Rylands (*c.* 20 boxes). For a list of the contents of thirteen boxes with Gaster's work in various stages of progress see Haralambakis 2012. More material can be found e.g. at Leeds University Library, the Muller Memorial Library at Yarnton (one box with newspaper cuttings about Gaster) and the YIVO Institute in New York (one box of stuff collected by Gaster, such as postcards, calendars etc. sent to him from Palestine). Haralambakis forthcoming in 2013.

5 The first steps in this direction have been taken by Dr Haralambakis, who has just spent a year at the Rylands studying the Gaster collection, focusing mostly on the archival material, and is continuing her studies in the academic year 2012-13 in Bucharest. It is to be hoped that a larger collaborative project, bringing together some modern Anglo-Jewish historians and experts on vital sub-sections of Gaster's academic activity, will be set up in due course. For an evaluation of Gaster's scholarly work, I think one should start with an examination of 'Gaster the palaeographer' in order to evaluate his competence in this field in comparison to his contemporaries as well as to modern standards. See further below.

6 For what it is worth, Bensusan 1936: 13 claims that Gaster had about 30,000 volumes in his library.

7 Compare also Philip Alexander's anecdote in the first note of the next Chapter.

the British Library (1,129 plus *c.* 3,000 Genizah fragments),[8] the John Rylands Library (*c.* 900 manuscripts and about 15,000 Genizah fragments) (Anonymous 1999: 38), the Romanian Academy in Bucharest, and the School of Slavonic and East European Studies in London. What is of interest here is that it was Moses Gaster himself who sold the first large chunk of his manuscript collection off to the British Museum (i.e. the collection which is now at the British Library) in 1925 (Gaster 1995: 16). According to letters found in the Library's archives, he approached the Department of Oriental Printed Books and Manuscripts of the museum in early 1924 offering them part of his collection of manuscripts for which he asked a sum of £10,000.[9] The sale was publicly announced a few years later, in 1927, but the deal was clinched in 1924.[10]

So why did he decide to sell these manuscripts at the time? They mainly consisted of Hebrew, among which were eighty Samaritan, manuscripts. By comparison, about fifteen years after his death in 1954, the remaining Hebrew manuscripts (*c.* 350) were sold to the John Rylands on the initiative of his eldest son Vivian Gaster, together with, notably, the larger part of his fine Samaritan collection (*c.* 350) and most of his Genizah fragments (Gaster 1995: 16; Anonymous 1999: 38).[11] By placing them in the British Museum Moses Gaster undoubtedly wanted a wider audience to be able to profit from his manuscripts, while keeping them still relatively close at hand for himself. But at the same time, from the point of view of self-interest, he might have calculated that the manuscripts and fragments would not yield any major new findings which he hadn't been able to publish himself. In other words, it seems reasonable to suppose that he wouldn't have parted with any manuscripts before having finished a more or less thorough investigation of each of them first. The Genizah fragments are probably a valid case in point here: it is more than likely that Gaster simply offered a sub-collection of *c.* 3,000 Genizah fragments to the British Museum rather than allowed members of that institution to pick and choose from among his entire Genizah collection.[12]

---

8 www.bl.uk/reshelp/findhelplang/hebrew/manuscripts/gastercoll/index.html

9 *c.* £300,000 today according to http://www.nationalarchives.gov.uk/currency/.

10 I would like to thank Ilana Tahan of the British Library for providing this information.

11 This is confirmed by archival correspondence between 'V.S. Gaster, Esq.' and the Librarian and Emeritus Professor of Semitic Languages Edward Robertson. Cf. Schindler 1958: 1, 22. For the announcement of the acquisition see Anonymous 1954: 2–6; see also 1958: 260–1.

12 Ilana Tahan assumes this to be the case as well. If we look at the most striking fragments identified so far among the Gaster Genizah fragments in the British Library, we note that most of them were made by S.D. Goitein among the documentary material (Goitein 1960a). His findings, though of obvious

There is some evidence in support of the assumption that Moses Gaster sold off part of his manuscripts strategically. Firstly, there was a time lapse of three years between the initial contact between Gaster and the British Museum and the public announcement of the sale. One reason for this was merely of a practical nature in that the British Museum paid the bill in three installments, the last being in 1926. But Ilana Tahan also states that the entire collection of manuscripts was deposited in the British Museum in 1924, except for some Samaritan and a few Hebrew manuscripts which Gaster had asked to keep a little longer because he was engaged in research on them. Secondly, in 1924 the British Library acquired some striking manuscripts about which Gaster had published previously and which thus, not least on the basis of his claims, represented attractive buys. A good case in point are the 'first and second Gaster Bibles' (Oriental 9879 and 9880, formerly Gaster's Codex 151 and Codex 150 respectively). Both are rare examples of early illuminated Bibles, of which Gaster had published a facsimile reproduction of one folio per manuscript in 1901. Today, Oriental 9879 (Codex 151) is considered the most precious of these manuscripts, a 'very rare early Hebrew Bible' which 'shows the influence of Islamic art in its decorative elements' produced in Egypt in the ninth/tenth century.[13] About Codex 150 Gaster had conjectured that it was produced for one of the 'Princes of the Exile' in Babylon in the ninth to tenth century, but nowadays it is believed to have been produced in eleventh- to early twelfth-century Egypt (Gaster 1901: 16). In the same publication with facsimile reproductions Gaster (1901: 23–52) described a Samaritan scroll of the Hebrew Pentateuch which I have not been able to track down in the catalogues (Crown 1998, Robertson 1962).

The year 1925 seems to have been a year in which Moses Gaster took stock of his life, especially of his intellectual achievements. It is well-known that he suffered from increasingly diminished eyesight, a problem which presumably started as early as the 1910s leading to total blindness (Schindler 1958: 20; Bensusan 1936: 13; Roth 1940).

---

importance, are not in the class of Genizah treasures the British Library has been able to identify so far among its other Genizah collections, especially in its Raffalovich collection of about 4,000 fragments which contains, e.g., a Judaeo-Arabic responsum in Maimonides' hand. Note also Goitein's opening remark (1960: 34, cf. 45) in this respect: 'As the Gaster collection has been wrapped in a shroud of mystery for a considerable time, exaggerated ideas about its contents have been entertained in various quarters.' Yet see Goitein 1958/59, where he does identify a responsum with an answer in Maimonides' hand (Or. 10578, fol. 50). Rowland Smith 1991: 21.

13 http://www.bl.uk/onlinegallery/sacredtexts/gasterbib.html and http://www.bl.uk/catalogues/illuminatedmanuscripts/record.asp?MSID=19287&CollID=96&NStart=9879. The other codices Gaster mentions in his article, namely 85, 149 and 152 are also found in the British Library as Or. 9883, 9881 and 9882 respectively.

In 1925, Gaster also made a start with a project to publish a collection of the major articles written by him during the previous fifty years. The three volumes, celebrating half a century of scholarly work, carry the dedication 'to my children at whose request I have gathered in these leaves' (Gaster 1925–28). And he managed to see through to the press his bold, pioneering study on *The Samaritans: Their History, Doctrines and Literatures*, which offers to the reader an expanded version of the Schweich Lectures on Biblical Archaeology he delivered in 1923 to the British Academy.

This is not to say that Gaster left all scholarly activity behind — this is clearly not the case. Another decade followed in which he managed to publish a remarkable amount of works, largely devoted to Samaritan literature, most markedly *The Asatir: The Samaritan Book of the 'Secrets of Moses'* (1927) and *The Samaritan Oral Law and Ancient Traditions* (vol. 1, *Samaritan Eschatology*, 1932). It is an interesting question how he managed to do so under the circumstances. It is clear he received vital help from people around him. One of them is his secretary for thirty-five years Bruno Schindler, who is known to have assisted him, for example, with publishing his *Exempla of the Rabbis* in 1924 and the three anthological volumes 1925–28 (Schindler 1958: 19).[14]

Moses Gaster's deeper scholarly interest in the Samaritans and the Cairo Genizah seem both to have been ignited around the turn of the century (Gaster 1923: foreword). However, it is quite obvious that the most intense and lasting of these interests concerned the first. Over his whole lifetime Gaster only published, as far as I am aware, three times on the Cairo Genizah (Gaster 1900a and b; 1901).[15] This stands

14 See the prefaces to the *Exempla* for an expression of gratitude to his daughter Henriette and Bruno Schindler, *Asatir* where he acknowledges the help of a certain B. Bamberger, and *Samaritan Eschatology* for thanks to, among others, one of his sons and Mr. M. Lutzki 'who kindly assisted me in the reading of these texts since my eyesight was failing'. Cf. Rowland Smith 1991: 23 on the latter. The Rylands keeps a large number of drafts of Gaster's articles and books which could throw further light on his method of working.

15 I have not had time to scan fully the Gaster 1925–28 volumes which unfortunately don't contain an index, let alone all of Gaster's academic publications, for possible references to Genizah fragments. I've merely looked at publications with 'Genizah' in the title as listed in Schindler 1958: 23–40. That he occasionally must have mentioned Genizah fragments in other publications as well is evidenced by the example below (Gaster 1917). I've tried to follow up to no avail Reif's lead (2000: 111, 118), where he claims that 'Fanciful expansions of biblical accounts, apocalyptic visions and mystical works were among the earliest midrashim acquired from the Genizah and quickly published by such equally colourful personalities as Solomon Wertheimer in Jerusalem and Moses Gaster in London', saying that Gaster's midrashic pieces were reprinted in Gaster 1925-28. Reif (2000: 238) mentions in passing that Moses Gaster was among the scholars who visited Cambridge University Library to view or study Genizah fragments also after Schechter's departure to the States in 1902.

in clear contrast to his sustained output in the field of Samaritan literature (Schindler 1958: 28–40). If we look again at Gaster's book on *Hebrew Illuminated Bibles of the IXth and Xth Centuries (Codices Or. Gaster, Nos 150 and 151); and A Samaritan Scroll of the Law of the XIth Century (Codex Or. Gaster, No. 350) together with Eight Plates of Facsimiles of these Manuscripts and of Fragments from the Geniza in Egypt* (1901), we see the two research interests come together, with his article on the Samaritan scroll in fact being his first known publication on Samaritan literature.

Gaster mentions evidence from the Cairo Genizah in a postscript to his article on Hebrew illuminated Bibles (1901: 20–1). After noting that 'many fragments of old Hebrew MSS. have come to light from the Genizah of the old Fostat close to Cairo', he goes on to boast that 'a large number of these fragments have come into my possession' (Gaster 1901: 20), characteristically without telling us anything as to how and where he obtained the manuscript fragments. He reports that he has discovered in his own Genizah collection a fragment of an illuminated Bible codex that is comparable to the ones he had discussed in the article. A reproduction of this fragment strikingly embellished with 'floral decorations and gold painting' is found at the back of the book (recto and verso) together with that of two more Genizah fragments (recto only) (Gaster 1901: 20–1, VI). The question is where these fragments ended up eventually — in the British Library, the Rylands or somewhere else? So far I've not been able to find any of them in Manchester.[16]

The two articles Gaster solely devoted to the Cairo Genizah both appeared in 1900. One of these (Gaster 1900a) was written for a *Gedenkbuch* in memory of his four years younger contemporary David Kaufmann (1852–1899), who had studied, as he himself had done, at the famous Jewish Theological Seminary at Breslau, and in the 1890s had managed to buy a Genizah collection, which went to the Hungarian Academy in Budapest after his death (Alderman 2004, Glickman 2011: 146). According to a recent study of the Library of the Hungarian Academy of Sciences,[17] David Kaufmann had hoped to acquire the entire Genizah of the Ben Ezra synagogue but Solomon Schechter had beaten him to it. Gaster's choice of topic is therefore apt enough, and after a brief but elegant eulogy he announces the publication, in the spirit of the deceased scholar, of 'ein Haüflein' of Genizah fragments from among the numerous fragments that are in his possession. He then describes how the fragments in his collection are rarely larger than a page, and more often smaller than that, and he

16 Ilana Tahan thinks it unlikely these fragments are at the British Library. But cf. Rowland Smith 1991: 23.

17 http://kaufmann.mtak.hu/index-en.html

has chosen a random handful of them which seemed particularly interesting to him. Gaster dates the fragments of the Cairo Genizah tentatively between the tenth and thirteenth centuries, i.e. the period which is presently considered that of the 'Classical Genizah', while estimating the date of his selected fragments as belonging to the eleventh or twelfth century at the latest with the first fragment being much older, indeed potentially 'viel älter als irgend eines der bisher bekannten datirten Documente' (Gaster 1925–28, II: 680–1) — in classic Gaster fashion.[18] Treading the unknown world of the Cairo Genizah, he clearly senses its great historical significance.

Before looking at the publication in detail, I had a strong suspicion that the twenty-two fragments Gaster transcribes and discusses in this article, like the other Genizah fragments on which he published, are not at the Rylands – if they were sold to a public institution, this was most likely to be the British Museum, for the simple 'strategic' reasons I mentioned earlier. Even though Gaster 1900a contains no images of the fragments of his choice, I managed to locate most of the fragments and they indeed turn out to be at the British Library. The vital clue was Klein's identification of Gaster's rare piece of Fragment-Targum to disparate verses from Deuteronomy 1:1–5:9 (V) with British Library, Or. 10794.8 (Klein 1986, I: 330-3; II, 89, Plate 148). All I had to do next was to browse through all the images of Or. 10794 using the excellent website of the Friedberg Genizah Project to note that of the twenty folios shown there as part of the classmark, as many as eighteen are discussed in Gaster's article. Later, I discovered that Goitein had located fragment XVII in the British Museum (Goitein 1960a: 43, 45). On the basis of my short descriptions of the remaining three fragments, Ezra Chwat was able to locate fragment XXI among the Gaster fragments of the British Library (Or. 10578S.12) — a piece of Mishnah Shabbat 2:2-3 (recto) and 2:5 (verso) with partial Tiberian vocalization and cantillation (Gaster 1925–28, II: 690). Unfortunately, I've not been able to spot the other two, but at least my main point is clear.[19] This is what has been found so far:

I Or. 10794.19 & Or. 10794.20[20]

---

18 See further below

19 So far I have managed to browse through Or. 10578S as well as the class-marks Gaster originally gave the fragments and by which the Gaster Genizah collection of the British Library can also be searched in the Friedberg database up to and including Gaster 1294, without any further results, though I might have overlooked something.

20 From Gaster's description it is clear that the Friedberg images of Or. 10794.20 should be reversed, i.e. what is now recto should become verso and *vice versa*. The same goes for Or. 10794.1 (XIX),

II	Or. 10794.20
III	Or. 10794.14[21]
IV	Or. 10794.10[22]
V	Or. 10794.8
VI	Or. 10794.7[23]
VII	Or. 10794.5
VIII	Or. 10794.6
IX	Or. 10794.4
X	Or. 10794.18
XI	Or. 10794.17
XII	-[24]
XIII	Or. 10794.9
XIV	Or. 10794.11
XV	Or. 10794.13
XVI	Or. 10794.12
XVII	Or. 10656.17
XVIII	Or. 10794.15
XIX	Or. 10794.1
XX	Or. 10794.16
XXI	Or. 10578S.12
XXII	-[25]

Or.10794.6 (VIII), Or. 10794.14 (III), Or.10656.17 (XVII), Or.10794.15 (XVIII) and Or. 10578S.12 (XXI).

21 Gaster suggests this is a 'very old' fragment on palaeographical and linguistic grounds (Gaster 1925–28, II: 681, 682–3). Targum Onqelos on Genesis 30:33 ff.

22 Recto: Targum Onqelos on Exodus 18.11–12. Verso: Gaster only transcribes lines 3–7 leaving out the Judaeo-Arabic which wasn't understandable to him. Draft of a court document which concludes with 'Mar<ḥešwan> (…) 1520 (the zero being uncertain here) in Fustat Miṣrayim on the Nile (…) our *'adôn*, our *nāgîd* our *nāgîd* (*sic*) <name lost> ?*ha-paṭṭišâ*'. Gaster understands the curious closing word on the document as an unusual title for a *nāgîd* (cf. *paṭṭiš* meaning hammer in Hebrew and Aramaic). He interprets the date as referring to 1209, thus assuming the date on the fragment to be rendered according to the Seleucid era. Ezra Chwat (see *Aleph* catalogue) believes the document alludes to Abraham Maimonides (1186–1237). Gaster's conclusion that this is one of the earliest *dated* Targum fragments is too rash, since in principle we don't know when that side of the fragment was written (Gaster 1925–28, II: 680, 683).

23 This is a piece of Targum Jonathan to Isaiah 19.15–18.

24 Gaster only seems to give the text found on the recto which includes the beginning of a treatise on the laws of benedictions (*hilkôt* b^{e}*rākôt*) by Isaac 'bir' Judah Ghiyyat, i.e. Isaac ben Judah ibn Ghiyyat (1038–89). Verso contains a nearly illegible poem. Paper; 1 leaf; 21 x 12 (Gaster 1925–28, II: 686).

25 According to Gaster this is a very small, accented Judaeo-Arabic fragment from among the oldest and most beautiful manuscripts from that period and region (Gaster 1925–28, II: 690).

The Friedberg database helpfully lists many of the publications which deal with some of these fragments, but somehow fails to make the link with Gaster's original article except for fragment XVII. The same goes for Ezra Chwat's recent identifications as found in the *Aleph* database, which can also be consulted via the Friedberg site.

Interestingly, at the very end of his article, Gaster mentions in passing that he possesses a parchment folio with an accented version of the Scroll of Antiochus, which he seems to count among his Genizah fragments (Gaster 1925–28, II: 690). Now, this leaf, which he mentions again in an article written in 1917, happens to be in the Rylands under classmark Gaster Heb. ms. 1774/1 (Gaster 1925–28, II: 1295–1329, esp. 1301–2).[26] It is somewhat doubtful whether the leaf was ever found in the loft of the Ben Ezra synagogue. Thus in his later article Gaster does not mention the exact provenance of the fragment. This only leaves Gaster's last article on the Cairo Genizah to be discussed: his contribution to the Ben Sira debate.

The Ben Sira Saga Revisited

Toward the end of his life, Gaster noted with satisfaction that his books and manuscripts were 'in safe [private] hands, or in larger libraries' (Gaster 1995: 21). For a long time now librarians at the Rylands and British Library have been frustrated at not being able to answer queries about the whereabouts of Gaster's Ben Sira fragment in their collections. This doesn't necessarily mean it isn't there, but so far it hasn't been found. The likelihood it eventually turns up at the British Library is very small indeed, since successive curators and plenty of researchers have tried to hunt down the elusive piece. The Gaster Genizah collection at the Rylands is of course larger but even so the chance of finding it in Manchester seems very slim as well. In the latest edition of the *Wisdom of Ben Sira*, the Gaster fragment is the only one to have a question mark against it instead of a classmark (Beentjes 1997: 17). Most likely it is still somewhere 'safe in private hands'. Fortunately, Gaster published the original fragment, which in fact consists of two conjoining fragments, with full transcription and plates (Gaster 1900b).

The Cairo Genizah's popular rise to fame was initially due to Solomon Schechter's discovery in 1896 of the first Hebrew Ben Sira fragment among its treasures. Two independent traveler-scholars, Agnes Lewis and Margaret Gibson, had bought some Genizah fragments on their most recent travel to Palestine and Egypt

26 Therefore, this fragment should be considered the exception which proves the rule, as it is clear that Gaster didn't part with this fragment in 1924.

and shown them to Schechter on their arrival back home in Cambridge. To his great excitement, he had spotted the fragment in question.[27] The twin sisters immediately announced this find in two academic newspapers, the *Atheneum* and *Academy*, where, interestingly, they mention Palestine as the place of purchase (Ben Zvi 2011: 66).[28] During that period more eminent scholars, already aware of the collection's great scholarly potential, were trying to get the funds together to buy the fragments that were left in the Ben Ezra synagogue and have them shipped to Europe. Yet it was due to Schechter's successful secret mission to Egypt that the Cambridge University Library managed to acquire the largest Genizah collection in the world.[29]

The story of the 'race to recover the lost leaves of the original Ecclesiasticus', and of the Cairo Genizah in general, is complicated and enigmatic (Jefferson 2009). As one of the less important players in the Genizah arena, Moses Gaster has hardly figured in this story so far. However, I'm convinced that some interesting details regarding the overarching story and Gaster's role in it will eventually come to light when the Gaster archives have been explored to the full.[30] Presently we don't even know the answer to simple questions like: Where and when exactly did Gaster acquire his fragments? Did he buy them in one or more batches? What's the exact story behind his discovery of the Ben Sira fragment?

The fact is that Moses Gaster was an extremely well-connected and influential figure in Anglo-Jewish circles after his arrival in England in 1885. His biography has some basic facts in common with Solomon Schechter (1847/50–1915): both born in Rumania, they moved to England (Schechter as the personal tutor of Claude Montefiore), married, and started lectureships — Gaster in Oxford and Schechter in Cambridge — around the same time. Apparently both enjoyed the regular company of fellow Jewish writers, a group of friends who had nicknamed themselves 'The Wanderers' (Glickman: 31–41; Reif: 2000: 47–54). Of course Moses Gaster knew

27 For an excellent biography of the two sisters see Soskice 2009.

28 My sincere thanks to Shlomo Leshem for providing me with Ben-Zvi's newspaper article and the relevant pages in Shurin 1964 mentioned below. Ben Outhwaite suspects that this early report about buying the Ben Sira in Palestine was deliberate misinformation, because it conflicts with what Margaret Gibson claims elsewhere.

29 For the full story see especially Reif 2000, Jefferson 2009 and 2010, Glickman 2011 and Hoffman and Cole 2011.

30 Gaster's correspondence and diaries seem the most logical to start with. Levi 1976 contains some good leads, such as his correspondence with the two Solomons (i.e. Wertheimer and Schechter). Cf. also Glickman 2011: 38. Dr Rebecca Jefferson has kindly informed me that she has not discovered anything of relevance in the archives of Elkan Nathan Adler at the JTS. So far I have done a limited amount of archival research only.

Elkan Nathan Adler (1861–1946), the younger half-brother of the Ashkenazi Chief Rabbi Hermann Adler (1839–1911) and original owner of the Genizah collection of the Jewish Theological Seminary in New York, very well. As they were both very active in Anglo-Jewish and Zionist affairs, they must have met each other on numerous occasions. Moreover, they shared several scholarly interests, the literature of the Samaritans being one of them. Thus, in 1908, they fought out a scholarly dispute over the Samaritan book of Joshua in the *Journal of the Royal Asiatic Society* but also more publicly in the *Times* and the *Jewish Chronicle*.[31] But how did Gaster relate to all the other figures involved in the selling and buying of Genizah fragments? Had he been in contact with the likes of Solomon Wertheimer, W.S. Raffalovich, Moses Shapira, or Count d'Hulst, for example?[32] In short, how exactly does Gaster fit into the Genizah story? In this context it is worth keeping the words in mind he wrote in 1931, boasting about his book acquisition techniques: 'In any case, much of that which was brought from the Orient to Europe in the last forty years is the result, directly or indirectly, of my initiative' (Gaster 1995: 19) — certainly a striking claim when we consider Solomon Schechter's achievement in the late 1890s!

Practically speaking, Moses Gaster could have acquired his fragments from dealers in London or have had people buy fragments for him from dealers in Jerusalem or Cairo.[33] It is a well-known fact that Gaster trained people to become book dealers on his behalf, some travelling as far as the Middle East for him (Gaster 1995: 19). In principle, he might also have bought Genizah fragments on his own travels to the Middle East — even have haggled at the Ben Ezra synagogue in person though somehow this seems less likely.

A baffling story linking Gaster and Solomon Wertheimer should be recounted in this context. In two different 'letters to the editor' published in the Hebrew dailies *Ha-Ṣôpēh* (20 October 1961) and *Ha-Ma'arîv* (30 January 1968), the son of the well-known Jerusalem scholar and bookseller, Moses Wertheimer, makes several striking

31 The Rylands preserves the original scrapbook (R148883) in which Gaster collected the relevant articles and newspaper clippings relating to the controversy, which also involved other scholars such as David Yellin. Crown 1998: 33.

32 Thus the Gaster Papers archive at the UCL contains correspondence of Raffalovich and Wertheimer. Wertheimer, Raffalovich and Shapira supplied the British Museum with fragments. Compare Gaster 1995: 19 for an example of a book dealer first trying to sell manuscripts to the British Museum and then to Gaster in London. Jefferson 2009: 128. On Wertheimer see below.

33 Or indeed elsewhere. Thus, to mention a random example, Elkan Nathan Adler, in his engaging account of the discovery of the Cairo Genizah, mentions Genizah fragments being sold at public auction in Cologne (Adler 1897: 672).

claims.[34] He tells us how on more than one occasion his father had told him that he had sold 'the first' page from the Hebrew Ben Sira to Moses Gaster who passed it on[35] to Schechter thus arousing the latter's interest in the Genizah; how Schechter had subsequently visited Wertheimer in Jerusalem to invite him along on his trip to Cairo; and, finally, how Schechter had travelled to Cairo by himself following Wertheimer's refusal (Shurin 1964: 91).[36] Clearly, this story contains apocryphal elements. It is curious Moses Wertheimer doesn't mention the crucial role of the twin sisters at all, instead attributing to Gaster (!) the origin of Schechter's resolve to go to Cairo. It seems somewhat unlikely that Schechter first went to see Wertheimer before travelling on to Cairo.[37]

Could there be *any* truth in the story? After all, Gaster must have been well aware of the Schechter-Margoliouth controversy over the true origin (Hebrew or Greek) of the Wisdom of Ben Sira, and he *was* in contact with Wertheimer.[38] If we imagine a hypothetical case where Schechter had become aware of Hebrew Ben Sira fragments in short succession, both via the twins and via Gaster, why should both Gaster and Schechter have kept their fragment under wraps while the discovery of the Gibson-Lewis fragment was immediately announced in the press? If we try to push this hard, we can think up a scenario where Schechter had heard from the sisters who their seller was (possibly Wertheimer),[39] and Gaster had told Schechter of his purchase of Genizah manuscripts, around the same time, from the same seller. When they found another Ben Sira fragment, Gaster had agreed to keep the discovery quiet until Schechter would have been able to go to Cairo to buy more. In this scenario Wertheimer most likely would have been unaware of the existence of the Hebrew Ben

---

34 My thanks to Mr Leshem, who kindly sent me scans of these letters.

35 Or sold — *m*^{e}*sārô* or *m*^{e}*kārô* depending on the letter one reads.

36 Cf. Soskice 2009: 242, 250, according to which Schechter invited the twins to come with him to Cairo. They joined him in the same city about a month after his arrival there.

37 For what it is worth, Ben Outhwaite has informed me that Schechter sailed on the SS Gironde from Marseilles to Alexandria. It is well-known that Schechter visited Palestine on his way back.

38 See Ben Zvi 2011:69 for an example of a letter from Wertheimer to Gaster. In fact, on p. 64 she claims that Gaster was among the people and institutions who bought Genizah fragments from Wertheimer, but she doesn't cite any proof for that statement. There is a letter from 1899 from Wertheimer to Gaster in which the first offers various early printed books and manuscripts for sale, but there is no mention of Genizah material there. Mr Leshem has kindly emailed me scans of this letter as well as correspondence between the two men, which are presently kept in London and further consist of a typed letter (1893) and a short disgruntled letter (1923), from Wertheimer to Gaster.

39 However, compare Soskice (2009: 232, 237), who mentions Cairo and the 'Plains of Sharon' (rather than Jerusalem) in Palestine as the two places where the sisters happened to buy manuscript fragments.

Sira fragments or have underestimated their importance.[40] With the risk of turning this too much into a detective story, I suggest one *could* discover a possible motive here for the (possibly) mysterious silence of Gaster and Schechter, namely an early effort by Schechter to play down Wertheimer's role in the history of the discovery of the Cairo Genizah in his eagerness to find honour for himself. But if this all *were* true, why should Gaster not have published his Ben Sira article much sooner rather than being one of the last of the early scholars to add a new chapter to the Ben Sira saga? I see two options here. Most likely, Gaster spotted the fragment among a *new* batch of fragments he bought in or just before 1900.[41] Alternatively, if his Ben Sira article did concern the rumoured Wertheimer fragment, Schechter must have left it to Gaster to publish it, while they considered it both prudent to wait several years in the hope not to raise Wertheimer's suspicion. All this is obviously *very* speculative and improbable, but I think it is worth trying to reason out a number of hypotheses, rather than ban a persistent family tradition straightaway to the world of fables.

Ignoring these unsolved riddles for the time being, let us consider the following general question: when did Gaster buy Genizah fragments for the first (and possibly only) time: before or after Schechter's successful trip to Cairo in 1897? For sure Gaster knew of Elkan Nathan Adler's travels to Cairo (in 1888 and 1896) and his actual acquisitions of Genizah fragments, which began in 1896 when Adler was allowed to enter the attic of the Ben Ezra synagogue and pull out a sack full of fragments. This was soon followed by his major purchase of about 6,000 items from the Bodleian Library brought there through the efforts of Archibald Sayce. The move of the Bodleian on the authority of Adolf Neubauer to sell these fragments to Adler was the more surprising since Neubauer and Arthur Ernest Cowley had recently managed to find nine Ben Sira leaves among the consignment of fragments from which they came (Adler 1897: 671–3, Jefferson 2010: 181–3).

If we ignore the earlier speculation regarding Gaster and Wertheimer as completely unfounded, the successive finds of Ben Sira fragments might well have sparked Gaster's interest to acquire his very own set of Genizah fragments. However, it is just as conceivable that he had already bought some before Adler did. After all, it was especially in the years of the complete rebuilding of the Ben Ezra synagogue

40 Of course Wertheimer was a distinguished scholar, who identified many important fragments, including an autograph letter to Maimonides by Jonathan of Lunel which is presently kept at the Bodleian. Ben Zvi 2011: 68. Thus he used to send itemized lists of Genizah fragments to libraries in order to try and sell them. Reif 2000: 71.

41 See further below

from 1889 onwards that fragments started pouring into the Egyptian and European antiquarian markets. It was during those years that one or other dealer might have pulled some of Gaster's fragments from among the 'rubbish heap' of Genizah fragments lying in the courtyard of the synagogue, for example (Jefferson 2009: 127).[42] The issue is somewhat academic though, since Gaster could have bought such a batch in principle just as well years after the event, say from a bookseller in London. We should, moreover, leave room for the possibility that he bought fragments recovered from the Genizah site in Cairo after Schechter's visit there.[43] Whatever the case, 1900 is obviously the *terminus ante quem* for Gaster's purchase of at least the first batch of his fragments. It is probably with this tangled history in mind when Stefan Reif (2010: 17–18) writes:

> Contrary to what is sometimes claimed, Schechter did not empty Cairo and its environs of all its Genizah material. American, Hungarian and French scholars also claimed their shares of the spoils and, in addition to fragments that made their way to other institutions in England, such as the British Museum (now British Library) and the John Rylands Library (now the John Rylands University Library of Manchester), both via the private library of Moses Gaster, and to the Selly Oak Colleges in Birmingham, substantial collections were acquired by Charles Freer of Detroit in 1908 (now at the Smithsonian Institution in Washington) and by Jack Mosseri, of the Cairo Jewish family, as announced by him in 1913.[44]

As a matter of fact, we can find the beginning of an answer to the above questions.

After Solomon Schechter made his exciting discovery of a Hebrew Ben Sira fragment in 1896, a string of scholars soon followed suit.[45] New discoveries were initially made really swiftly, starting with Neubauer and Cowley. They found nine more leaves after a frantic search among the Bodleian's Genizah riches that lasted nearly six weeks (Jefferson 2010: 181–2; Cowley and Neubauer 1897). We can keep a close track of the subsequent developments via the pages of the *Jewish Quarterly*

---

42 If Gaster acquired Genizah fragments before Adler and Schechter, the question is whether he fully understood where they came from at that point. Cf. Jefferson 2009: 125: 'The early collectors of this material, unaware of its exact provenance or keen to safeguard their access to it, did not divulge their sources.' Thus Neubauer published a number of 'Egyptian fragments' between 1892 and 1896 without giving any further information as to their exact source. See e.g. the last two issues of the *Jewish Quarterly Review* 1896.

43 See e.g. Reif 2000: 80: '(…) [Schechter] left behind much of the printed matter which he regarded, not fully with justification, as late and unimportant.'

44 Compare also Jefferson 2009: 132–3 regarding Count d'Hulst's role in handling the 'leftovers', such as through excavations in the direct vicinity of the Ben Ezra synagogue, and Jefferson 2010: 182–5.

45 For the most detailed account of the discovery of the Hebrew Ben Sira fragments see Reif 1996.

Review, which had recently been established by Israel Abrahams and Claude Montefiore as the English answer to the *MGWJ* and *ZDMG*. It is here that Schechter published a 'taster' for his 1899 edition, with Charles Taylor, of Ben Sira (1898) plus some additional finds in 1900b. And it is here that George Margoliouth (1899), a cousin of the famous 'thunderbolt from Oxford' (as Schechter once called his opponent in the Ben Sira controversy[46]), Elkan Nathan Adler (1900), and finally Moses Gaster (1900b) published their latest Ben Sira discoveries. In the meantime, Israel Lévi faithfully announced to a French readership all the latest finds of his British 'friends' in several issues of the *Revue des études juives* of which he was the editor, offering detailed studies of the texts as well.[47] In 1900, however, he was lucky enough to spot himself two Ben Sira fragments. It is worth quoting the opening sentences of the relevant article here in full (Lévi 1900: 1):

> Des marchands qui avaient vendu en Angleterre nombre de ballots de feuillets trouvés dans la *gueniza* (et peut-être dans le cimetière) du Caire, sont venus à Paris proposer le restant de leur lot, dont personne n'avait voulu. Sur ma prière, M. le baron Edmond de Rothschild, dont le zèle généreux pour les études juives ne saurait être trop loué, a bien voulu acheter ces pièces de rebut et en a fait don à la Bibliothèque du Consistoire israélite de Paris, me laissant le soin de les examiner à loisir. Je comptais fort peu y trouver des documents de valeur, mes confrères anglais ayant vraisemblablement écrémé cet amas de débris informes; je n'espérais pas du tout même y rencontrer de fragments de l'*Ecclésiastique* hébreu, qui est en ce moment à l'ordre du jour. Aussi grande a été ma surprise en découvrant deux feuillets de l'ouvrage de Ben Sira.

We get a nice insight here into the chaotic circumstances under which the Cairo Genizah fragments were sold by both named and unnamed antiquarians. In fact, we know from whom Lévi had bought because Adler happens to disclose this in the *Jewish Chronicle* of 11 March 1904, p. 29:

> He [Schechter] brought back more leaves [i.e. of Ecclesiasticus], and others were found by Israel Lévi, by Dr. Gaster, and by myself among the fragments that we had either bought, begged, or brought from Egypt. (...) I had been in Paris earlier in the week, and Mons. Lévi showed me a page of the text which he had bought from Goldstein and Raffalovich.

46 Schechter 1900a: 266.

47 Lévi 1896, 1897a–b, and so forth. See Reiterer 1998 for the remaining references. Compare also his republishing of the relevant texts with added French translation and commentary 1898–1901; with English translation and commentary 1904.

It should be considered entirely possible that Moses Gaster bought his batch of Genizah fragments just before Baron de Rothschild's successful purchases in Paris (and London in 1901?[48]), not least because of the comparatively poor state and small size of the fragments both bought — no more than a shapeless heap of skimpy leftovers in the eyes of Israel Lévi.[49] A random glance, via the Friedberg website, at images of the Genizah fragments kept at the library of the Alliance Israélite Universelle in Paris suggests that the collection might share some overall characteristics with that at the Rylands.[50]

We can conclude that 1900 was a fruitful year for the recovery of the original *Wisdom of Ben Sira*, notably the first time that fragments from the anthological manuscript C were found by Schechter, Lévi and Gaster in close succession (Beentjes 1997: 16-18).[51] In his article, Gaster doesn't say a word about the circumstances under which he bought (or even just spotted somewhere?) his two conjoining Ben Sira fragments, certainly in comparison to Adler, who usually happily discloses this kind of information (Adler 1897: 669; 1900: 466). In typical fashion, Gaster claims to have found fragments from the oldest Hebrew Ben Sira manuscript so far, since 'it is more archaic than the others, and is the only one, except B, written in uncials or square type', placing the manuscripts as a whole no earlier than the end of the tenth or the beginning of the eleventh century. However, the palaeographical arguments he adduces to prove his point are not particularly sound (Gaster 1900b: 688–91).[52] Time and again, Gaster has been criticized for assigning too readily too great an antiquity to his manuscripts.[53]

48 This is claimed by the director of the library of the Alliance Israélite Universelle in Paris, Mr Malthete, on http://www.genizah.org/VideoTapedPresentations.aspx.

49 Lévi's description is clearly too disparaging, if one looks at the actual AIU collection. This might be due to the fact he saw the fragments in pre-conserved state. In fact, the Rylands fragments tend to look scrappier than those at Paris. This should not surprise us since we know Gaster as a typically 'greedy', not too choosy book collector (Gaster 1995). Note also the fact that the Cambridge librarian Jenkinson generally considered the fragments Raffalovich had to offer 'a very rubbishy lot' (Jefferson 2010: 192–3).

50 To give a few examples: generally speaking, similar to the Rylands collection, there seems to be quite a lot of clearly late material (see e.g. series VII.F). Series XII is a series with a mixture of insignificant and nicer looking Arabic fragments similar to the Rylands Arabic series. Thus the two conjoined pages of XII.74 remind one of some of the nicer Arabic medical fragments in the Rylands collection. However, see also the previous note.

51 See further below

52 Beentjes 1997: 5 doesn't resolve the question of its most likely date of composition but tentatively describes manuscript C as '(much?) older [than the twelfth century]'.

53 Compare Rosen and Yassif 2002: 274: 'Gaster had the lamentable habit of dating the texts he discovered and published to impossibly early periods — perhaps in order to magnify the importance of his discoveries' with some striking examples. See also e.g. Alexander 1993: 793–9; Anderson and Giles 2005: 267.

We find such criticism already among his learned contemporaries (Neubauer 1894: 577, Adler 1908: 1143).

A Piece of Information that Nearly Went Unnoticed

Before reaching a preliminary conclusion regarding the possible origin(s) of Moses Gaster's Genizah fragments, I should quote at length a curious anecdote Gaster tells us at the end of a postscript to his article on Hebrew illuminated Bible manuscripts (1901: 21–2):

> One small incident may now be mentioned in conclusion.
>
> It so happened that I had left these MSS. with Messrs Vincent Brooks, Day and Co., for some length of time in order to prepare the facsimiles. They had been with the firm upwards of two years, when I suddenly was seized with the fear that they were exposed to the danger of being destroyed by fire. So strong was that feeling, that I went straight to the place with the intention of getting the MSS. back. On the way I allowed myself to be persuaded that I was needlessly exciting myself, and I left the MSS. where they were. This happened on the Friday before Easter, 1898. On Monday morning the first item which struck my eyes when opening "The Times" newspaper, was the report that the premises of Messrs Vincent Brooks, Day and Co., had been burned down in the night of Sunday to Monday. The MSS. had been placed in a safe in the office of the building, and the access was almost impossible. For two days the fate of the MS. (*sic*) was uncertain. But when we were able to penetrate the safe, to our great delight the MSS., round which the fire must have played, were found intact. I trust that this has been the last ordeal to which they have been exposed in their long life of close upon one thousand years, and that a place may soon be found where they remain safe from danger as far as human foresight can devise.

Vincent Brooks, Day and Co. (or Day and Son according to Wikipedia) was a well-known firm in London specialized in lithography, responsible for printing the famous caricatures in *Vanity Fair* magazine. The same online source indeed mentions the big fire on Sunday 10 April 1898. The firm must have been a logical choice for Gaster to bring his specimens of illuminated Bible manuscripts (including a few Genizah fragments) to, with an eye on having them reproduced in his bibliophile publication of 1901. It is clear from the acknowledgements underneath the plates that he had the lithographic work eventually done by another firm, Martin Hood & Larkin. Now, the tantalizing morsel of information here is obviously Gaster's statement regarding the manuscript fragments' being housed at the firm 'upwards of two years', which implies that he must have been in the possession of at least some Genizah fragments as early as spring 1896 at the very latest.[54] We should probably take Gaster at his word. A possible explanation is that he had bought a first batch of fragments in England from a dealer who had claimed they originated from Cairo.[55] Another possibility suggests itself that Gaster had bought a first batch from Solomon Wertheimer in Jerusalem. However, this doesn't reduce the likelihood that Gaster bought some more fragments in or just before 1900 as well, especially when considering his quest to track down a Ben Sira fragment in fierce competition with fellow scholars. Indeed it should be considered highly unlikely that Gaster wouldn't have spotted his Ben Sira fragment until 1900 in a bunch of fragments he had bought around 1896 *if* indeed it had been found there.[56]

The Rylands Fragments – a 'Very Rubbishy Lot'?

It must be said — the Rylands Genizah collection, mainly consisting of small, single page[57] manuscript fragments, looks distinctly unimpressive in comparison to most Genizah collections.[58] It would therefore not come as a surprise if Gaster had acquired some of the 'waste' or 'rubbish' 'of very little value' at which various librarians in Cambridge and Oxford had turned up their noses.[59] It is worth looking into the history of the recovery of some of these smaller fragments. In the final pages of her masterly article on a 'Genizah secret', Rebecca Jefferson describes how, in the wake of Schechter's visit to Cairo, Count d'Hulst was trying to retrieve more Genizah fragments for Neubauer in Oxford, especially by excavating the direct vicinity of the Ben Ezra synagogue. In 1898 the archaeologist announced that he had dug up enough

54 Note how Gaster's wish to find safe storage space for his precious manuscripts would be fulfilled only after another quarter of a century, though, as I mentioned before, the odd thing is that we don't know the present whereabouts of these particular Genizah specimens, one of which should contain some striking gold-leaf paint.

55 As noted before, around 1886 the precise origin of 'Egyptian fragments' became only gradually known to scholars. Jefferson 2009: 125, 131, 138.

56 In principle, we could consider even a further possibility here, namely that Wertheimer sold to Gaster a Ben Sira fragment for which he could, by now, have asked a good price. The pecuniary hardship of Wertheimer is well known. Cf. Ben Zvi 2011: 68.

57 Cf. Jefferson 2010: 188 regarding the average of respectively 2.5 and 6.5 leaves per item found in the Genizah manuscript consignments offered to the Bodleian by Sayce and Wertheimer.

58 Certainly in comparison to the Bodleian Genizah collection which was carefully handpicked by people like Greville John Chester but also Count d'Hulst before Schechter had even appeared on the scene (Jefferson 2010).

59 Compare Goitein 1960a: 35: 'The Gaster Collection as a whole is a gleaning which remained after the rich harvest, which fell to the earlier collectors of papers from the Cairo Geniza.'

manuscript fragments to fill sixteen big grain sacks. He dispatched these to Oxford in four large wooden packing cases, which reached their destination but subsequently left the library again under mysterious circumstances — clearly the librarians of the Bodleian lost interest in the excavated fragments after actually seeing them.[60] Now, what happened to all these fragments, of which Jefferson estimates there might have been about 10,000–15,000 in total (Jefferson 2010: 171, 185–6)? Was Gaster perhaps involved in a deal with the Bodleian?[61] The answer is no — they were sold to Elkan Nathan Adler instead (Jefferson 2010)![62]

Fragments retrieved through excavation were undoubtedly among the most severely damaged. After all, a substantial part of these had been thrown out from the Genizah chamber into the courtyard during the reconstruction work on the Ben Sira synagogue in 1889-92, never to be returned there again, but instead remaining stuck under heaps of rubble.[63] It is clear that also after the Bodleian's loss of interest in excavated fragments, leading to them being sold on to Adler in March 1899, Count d'Hulst continued to retrieve fragments for other interested parties (Jefferson 2010: 186–7). Thus it is very well possible that the batch Moses Gaster probably bought in or just before 1900 had originally been dug up from the grounds around the Ben Ezra synagogue by the same Count d'Hulst.[64] This is even more likely when we consider the history of Ben Sira fragment discoveries from 1900 onwards. Adler's latest Genizah purchase from the Bodleian was undoubtedly the source for his discovery in 1900 of two more Ben Sira pieces (from manuscript A) and probably also the source for Joseph Marcus' find, in 1931, of another piece (from manuscript E) among the ENA fragments at the Jewish Theological Seminary, not least because both report the

60 Bodley's Librarian Nicholson evaluates them as follows in a deleted passage from a draft letter to D'Hulst dated 25 November 1909: '(...) the fragments dug up for us, under your kind supervision turned out to be of very little value indeed by comparison; in fact, had they been offered to us for the same money they cost to recover (...) I don't think we should ever have *dreamt* of giving it' (Jefferson 2009: 133–5, 141–2). See also Jefferson 2010: 187, quoting a library report of 1899: 'It was found that a very large proportion of the manuscript scraps dug up were quite without value to a Library so extremely rich in Hebrew MSS. as the Bodleian.'

61 This possibility also occurred to me in view of Jefferson's detail that in 1903 Count d'Hulst contacted the Bodleian apparently for the first time since 1898, to offer a *Samaritan Pentateuch* for sale.

62 Admittedly, Jefferson 2010: 191 leaves room for the possibility that Adler was not the only buyer, though she also writes that 'it seems likely that Adler purchased almost everything that d'Hulst had excavated' from the Bodleian.

63 Jefferson 2010: 185 relates how d'Hulst discovered that 'a large part of the courtyard of the synagogue ha[d] been covered about one meter high with the same papers.'

64 The same goes for Lévi's Ben Sira fragments.

fragments to be in very poor condition (Marcus 1931, Jefferson 2010: 193). It has also been suggested that there might be a connection between d'Hulst's excavations and the Ben Sira fragments discovered by Schechter and Schirmann from 1900 onwards (Jefferson 2010: 193–4).[65]

To sum up, Moses Gaster seems to have bought Genizah fragments at least twice: the first time early on in or before 1896 when rumours about the exact provenance of 'Egyptian' fragments were only starting to become more specific, and a second time in or just before 1900, probably from a seller with links to d'Hulst,[66] if not from d'Hulst himself, due to the small size and bad state of preservation of the fragments. Future exploration of Gaster's archives will hopefully present us with a clearer picture.

Character and Structure of the Rylands Genizah Collection

The two main characteristics of the Rylands Genizah collection are the relatively small size of its fragments and the remarkable lateness of a comparatively large part of the collection. This description stands in marked contrast to the quotation from Moses Gaster's Ben Sira article with which my article started. To be fair to Gaster, it is quoted slightly out of context (Gaster 1900b: 689).[67] I suggested earlier that a possible explanation for the small size and comparatively bad state of preservation of the fragments might be that they were excavated rather than taken from the Genizah chamber as such. After all, Count d'Hulst tells us repeatedly about the rubbish mounds mixed with manuscript material found in the courtyard and garden around the Ben Ezra synagogue. It is clear that after the radical renovation of the synagogue in the years between 1889 and 1892 many manuscripts were either just left outside or hastily buried on its premises while only a proportion of the fragments were put back in the attic of the Ben Ezra synagogue. In a simplistic way we can perhaps imagine

65 To these we may also tentatively add Scheiber's discovery. The relevant fragments are T-S 12.727 (Schechter 1900), T-S 12.867 (old classification NS 194.114), AS 213.4 (all manuscript C), T-S 12.871 (formerly NS 193.107) and T-S NS 38a.1 (from manuscript B). The latter fragments represent discoveries reported by Schirmann 1957/58 and 1959/60 and Scheiber 1982. Note how these later discoveries tend to come from the New Series which should be distinguished from the main Taylor-Schechter collection and includes a large number of relatively small manuscript fragments in a bad state of preservation (Schirmann 1957/58: II, 440, cf. Jefferson 2010: 194).

66 E.g. Reginald Q. Henriques or Raffalovich (Jefferson 2010: 183, 191, 192–3).

67 What Gaster seems to say there is the smaller the format, the older the manuscript usually is. However, this is a problematic paleographical statement as well.

how the top of the pile with the most recent manuscripts in the Genizah chamber had ended up bottom in the courtyard where they had been mixed with soil and building materials. This brings us to the second characteristic of the Rylands Genizah collection: the remarkable lateness of much of its material, a characteristic it shares, for example, with the Mosseri collection. Jacques Mosseri was the last to appear on the scene, unearthing more fragments between 1909–12 and taking from the attic the very last, mostly printed material that had been ignored by all previous visitors, including Schechter and Count d'Hulst (Jefferson 2009: 134, 141).

The earliest dated fragment in the Rylands Genizah collection discovered so far is Rylands Genizah fragment 2, which on one side contains a copy of the beginning of the book of Jeremiah and on the reverse a rare colophon written by Sahlan in the Egyptian town of Ghaifa near Bilbais in *c.* 954 CE. What makes the parchment fragment even more special is the fact that the date is expressed according to a calendar starting from the destruction of the Temple.[68] Some of our parchment material is undoubtedly older than this. We have plenty of material from the period of the Classical Genizah (tenth to thirteenth centuries, especially eleventh–twelfth centuries), including, for example, various autographs of Maimonides (1135–1204) and a touching letter of a son to his father sent from Tyre to Egypt in the eleventh century (L 213).[69] But when we consider all those Rylands fragments which contain a date, mostly letters and documents, it turns out that the majority are from either the eighteenth or nineteenth century.[70] Our latest dated piece (A 960) is a divorce bill made up in Bombay as late as 8 March 1879. Goitein mentions the *gēṭ* as the most recent document he has ever encountered in the Cairo Genizah:

> The cause for the complete chaos in which the Geniza papers are found is to be sought, to my mind, in the fact that the Geniza was in living use during the whole time of its existence. I remember having seen in it a bill of divorce made out in Bombay as late as 1879, and, as it is unlikely that a document of such a character was disposed of in far away Cairo immediately after the legal act attested by it, it is not impossible that it landed in the Geniza only a few days before Solomon Schechter arrived in Cairo ready to carry off its entire contents (Goitein 1960b: 93; see also 1967–93, I: 9, 397).

68 For a further analysis see Wallenstein 1957–8 and 1959a: 310–14.

69 See Beit-Arié 1974, David 1991 and 1992/93, Hopkins 1984/85 and 1994 (in the latter he mentions the wrong classmark B 1019 — it should be A 1019), Rhezavi 1993: 198, 209, 216, Goitein 1971 and Ben Outhwaite's article in this volume.

70 Cf. Gaster 1900a who dates his fragments of the Cairo Genizah tentatively between the tenth and thirteenth centuries.

Goitein is probably right in saying this, but at the same time we should not forget that some material which is counted among the Rylands Genizah collection today might, in fact, not stem from the Ben Ezra synagogue, or even Cairo, at all — either because genuine Genizah material was adulterated with non-Genizah fragments by dealers who sold it to Gaster, or because Gaster had acquired some pieces separately which eventually got swept up with the genuine Cairo Genizah material.[71] An obvious case in point is the Slavonic manuscript B 2951. This is unlikely to have ever been anywhere near Cairo. Gaster, of course, had huge interest in Slavonic literature, and is likely to have acquired it with his other Slavonic purchases.[72] Similarly the horoscopes for 7 January 1861 and 19 March 1863 on Ar. 345 have a Nablus connection, and may have come to Gaster from his Samaritan sources.[73] However, there is little reason to question the provenance of the bulk of the Rylands Genizah.[74] Hopefully, the later strata of the Cairo Genizah will eventually get the scholarly attention they deserve (cf. Jefferson 2010: 189).[75]

Let me add a brief word on the languages and scripts represented in the Rylands Genizah collection. Apart from Hebrew, Aramaic, Judaeo-Arabic and Arabic fragments we find various nice examples of Judaeo-Spanish. So far we have identified only one tiny Yiddish fragment (B 6619) plus a Yiddish line on an Aramaic prayer fragment (A 65), while one piece, officially found in the Arabic series (Ar. 400), is in

---

71 On the problem of genuine Genizah material getting mixed up with material from other sources see e.g. Ben-Shammai: 43. Compare also Ben-Shammai's questionable claim on p. 44 that Gaster's Genizah collection is an example of a collection stemming from other *genizot* than the one found in the Ben Ezra synagogue.

72 Compare also the Samaritan fragments G 1 and G 2. However, the possibility of Genizah fragments in Samaritan script should not be excluded. Curiously, Robertson mentions three Samaritan Genizah fragments of an Arabic-Samaritan book of Joshua in his catalogue of Samaritan manuscripts (1962, II: 230), which Gaster annotated as follows: 'Found among the Fragments of the Genīzah of Cairo and recognised by me on the 26th March, 1909.' Cf. Rowland Smith 1991: 23 and Crown 1998: 200.

73 For a discussion of this fragment see Goldstein and Pingree 1978, who assume the text is Egyptian simply because it belongs to the 'Rylands Genizah'. Only recently Zvi Langermann noticed the occasion for which one of the horoscopes has been drawn up, namely for the 'entry of Hilmi Bey into Nablus'. Langermann presented this finding as part of his paper for the workshop on scientific, magical and related fragments in the Rylands Genizah held in Manchester 30 April–1 May 2007.

74 However, consideration may be given to the following. On the basis of his experience with cataloguing the Gaster Genizah material in the British Library, Ezra Chwat estimates that of the 3,279 items there only about two thirds can confidently be qualified as Genizah. He bases his guess on the percentage of late material, which is relatively high when compared to qualified 'pure' Genizah collections, while in terms of content there is a disproportionately high amount of post-Lurianic Kabbalah (email communication).

75 Geoffrey Khan is one of the notable exceptions here. See his article in this volume.

fact in Ottoman Turkish. We have various fragments with Roman script on them, such as several Spanish ones as well as two fragmentary French invitations written in 'Le Caire' in an elegant curly hand, one of which mentions the couple Moïse Mousseri (1855–1933) and Henriette Nahmias (1868–1943). Coptic script is occasionally used for numerals, for instance on otherwise Judaeo-Arabic fragments (e.g. B 2220; for a few actual Coptic texts see B 6033).

Presently, the Rylands Genizah collection is made up of a bewildering number of series.[76] It is unclear what the origin of most of these series is. Either they were created after the arrival of Gaster's fragments at the Rylands or they somehow existed already before that time.[77] The bulk of the fragments are contained in the complementary A and B series (i.e. class-marks A 1-A 1921 and B 1921-B 8737). With a few exceptions, these are all paper fragments. The name of the two series might be related to the way the fragments were originally stored (in two boxes?), also because toward the end of both series the fragments become very tiny. Gaster's collection of Genizah fragments arrived at the Rylands Library in a number of tin trunks and boxes.[78] The A and B series must have formed part of the earliest subdivision just as probably did the parchment series (P 1-P 1358),[79] since there are three boxes with residue fragments from precisely these series.[80]

Apart from the P series we can explain the names of a few more series as abbreviations of a relevant word, namely the L series (L 1-L 292) consists of *large* fragments, while the C series (C 1-C 185) contains *calculatory* fragments. In addition to the A, B, P, L and C series, we have the G series (G 1-G 101), a 'Gaster Printed' fragments series (Gaster Printed 1-Gaster Printed 653), a 'Gaster Hebrew' fragments series (Gaster Hebrew 1-Gaster Hebrew 350) and an Arabic series (Ar. 1-Ar. 840),

---

76 See below for a table surveying these.

77 A library report written by F. Taylor (23 June 1965) mentions that 'on arrival the Genizah fragments were placed in folders and assigned temporary numbers (P --), so that scholars could refer to them without delay.' As early as 1956, Díez Macho writes how the Rylands Genizah collection consists of 1,358 Hebrew and Aramaic parchment fragments, 8,600 Hebrew and Aramaic paper fragments, and more than 600 Arabic paper fragments, indicating that a basic classification into, at least, a P (= parchment) series (P 1-P 1358), and probably an A and B series as well as an Arabic series (Ar. 1-840), must have existed at this time. Díez Macho obviously overlooks the fact that a lot of the Hebrew and Aramaic paper fragments are in fact in Judaeo-Arabic. Aramaic fragments are in the minority.

78 This is according to the library correspondence of 1953–4. The library's annual report of 1954 mentions thirty-three boxes.

79 See the note above.

80 The 'residue A', 'residue B' and 'residue P' fragments have not undergone any conservation work yet.

without it being clear why we should, in fact, have a separate 'Gaster Hebrew' (and for that matter G) series.

The situation with the P series requires some explanation. Not all the class-marks, running from P 1 to P 1358, are currently in use but rather only about eight hundred. This is because about forty percent of the fragments from this series ended up in respectively the 'Rylands Genizah fragments' (Rylands Genizah (fragment) 1-Rylands Genizah (fragment) 52), 'Additional fragments' (AF 1-AF 454), and 'Bible Gaster' series (Bible Gaster 1-Bible Gaster 83).[81] Apparently, this is (at least partially) due to the fact that one or more unsupervised scholars pulled fragments in their field of interest out of the P series without keeping track of the folder they came from.[82] More specifically, in 1965 the Rylands librarian Frank Taylor reports how hundreds of fragments of biblical interest were pulled out of their folders by a 'Mr Weiss' (probably Dr Weis),[83] who put them in another box (or boxes) with the intention of cataloguing the biblical fragments and giving them new class-marks, leaving the empty folders on the side. It is likely that most of these fragments ended up in a box with about 400 fragments, which were eventually cleaned and restored by Mr Wilson, a conservator at the library. Nowadays these fragments are numbered AF 54-AF 454.

Possibly the 'Rylands Genizah (fragment)' series was created to restore some of the damage done by Dr Weis. Thus annotations relating to fragments nos. 34–41 in the box with these fragments explicitly state that they stem from 'the boxes of Mr Weiss'. However, it seems more likely that the series was created to put some striking pieces together as it contains various manuscripts Wallenstein and Díez Macho had mentioned in their publications and which the Manchester-based Wallenstein had

81 Note the particularly confusing nomenclature here: a 'Rylands Genizah fragments' series? It is unclear why someone should have come up with such a generic name for a series which consists of merely fifty-two fragments, and then perhaps have come up with the idea of an 'Additional' series, which originally consisted of fifty-three class-marks AF 1- AF 53 (see further below).

82 Originally, the P series was stored, in makeshift fashion, in small-sized paper folders, each of which contained an average of three fragments, with their preliminary class-marks written on the outside of the folder, without it being specified which fragment inside the folder had which class-mark precisely. Presently each fragment has been assigned its own melinex folder and class-mark. When the series will be catalogued, each cataloguing record should mention the batch the fragment originally belonged to, while taking into account the information found in Díez Macho 1956. I'm not aware of any further publications on fragments from the P series.

83 'Mr Weiss' is presumably P.R. Weis, Nathan Laski Senior Lecturer in Post-Biblical Jewish Studies in the Department of Near Eastern Studies at the University of Manchester (till 1972) and author of *Mishnah Horayoth: Its History and Exposition* (1952) and *Midrashic Selections* (1955).

furthermore identified for the library (nos. 1–4 plus 49 and 5–33 respectively),[84] while it includes toward the end several fragments identified by Nehemyah Allony in 1965 (nos. 44–7 and 50–1). The eighty-four fragments of the 'Bible Gaster' series must originally have had P numbers too. Interestingly, these fragments were taken out of sequence and identified by Dr Talmon and Dr Baars as early as 1959, so that Dr Weis might simply have been bold enough to follow their example.

The final two series, Glass (Glass 1-Glass 17) and a selection of Gaster Hebrew manuscripts, found between Gaster Heb. ms. 1441/1 and Gaster Heb. ms. 2111/9, have not been properly conserved yet, with the exception of Gaster Heb. ms. 1764 which has recently undergone conservation as part of a pilot project. The seventeen fragments mounted in glass, of which some pieces have cracked, are a curious lot. One would expect these to have been rather special to the person who mounted them, but in fact they contain some absolutely tiny fragments (Glass 2 and Glass 12) and other fragments which don't immediately suggest great historical importance — quite to the contrary.[85] The Genizah fragments found in scrapbooks, which, confusingly, form part of the main sequence of *c.* 350 Gaster Hebrew manuscripts in the Rylands, might all have been taped in there by Gaster. The method he used to do so is extremely crude: the sellotape has obviously damaged the fragments, while the reverse of the fragments is often either partially or fully hidden from sight. The question arises whether they might be closely related to the Gaster Genizah material at the British Library, for Goitein (1960: 35–6) already observed with respect to the latter:

> The material is at present still preserved in the form in which it was turned over to the Museum: the fragments are fastened to pages of copybooks and often are covered with thin paper, as was done by E.N. Adler with his collection, which is now in the Jewish Theological Seminary in New York. This procedure, intended to protect the originals, had most unfortunate results. The covering paper in the course of the years has become in many places colored and impenetrable, and being adhesive, it cannot be removed without endangering or destroying the script beneath it. Immediate expert treatment is highly advisable.

Some scrapbooks explicitly say they contain Genizah fragments, while others don't. Some of the fragments are annotated by Gaster. The original hand-written catalogue of his collection of Hebrew and Samaritan manuscripts only refers to a limited number of items containing Genizah material, especially to some of the scrapbooks

84 Wallenstein 1957–8, 1959a–b; Díez Macho 1956

85 Cf. Rowland Smith 1991: 21.

but also to a few additional sets of fragments which he kept separate from the rest of his Genizah collection for some reason, perhaps because they derived from another acquisition. At this stage it is not clear which scrapbooks (probably) contain Cairo Genizah fragments and which (probably) not. In the online image collection and catalogue we have not attempted to distinguish between genuine and non-genuine Genizah manuscripts, but photographed and catalogued everything, leaving it to others to decide on its provenance.

Cataloguing and Digitising the Rylands Genizah Collection

Before the Rylands Cairo Genizah project started in 2003, there were hardly any tools for researchers to access the collection, not even a full, if rudimentary, hand-list. Past research basically depended on a few scholars visiting the collection, who in fact managed to pull out some significant pieces from among the fragments, such as autographs by Maimonides. Actual cataloguing of the Rylands Genizah fragments happened only piecemeal. The most important of these early efforts occurred at the end of the 1980s and beginning of the 1990s, when Dr Abraham David of the Jewish National and University Library in Jerusalem visited the Rylands library to make a basic classification according to subject of various Rylands Genizah series and, furthermore, to describe in detail several hundreds of individual fragments. Dr Alexander Samely's unpublished *A Preliminary Catalogue of the Hebrew Manuscripts in the John Rylands University Library* (1997), on the other hand, doesn't consider Gaster's collection of Genizah fragments.

The situation has changed dramatically: to date all fragments have been digitised (though a very small number, awaiting further conservation, will need to be re-digitised). While the majority of these have been catalogued, over 26,000 images (i.e. the recto and verso side of more than 13,000 fragments) are presently found with their catalogue descriptions live on the web (http://enriqueta.man.ac.uk/luna/servlet/), the rest of the images pending online publication, as follows:

Name series	Class-marks[86]	Images with basic catalogue records online	Catalogued online[87]
A series	A 1-A 1921	Yes	Yes
Additional Fragments series	AF 1-AF 454	Yes	No
Arabic series	Ar. 1-840[88]	About thirty fragments only, mainly medical fragments	Idem
B series	B 1922-B 8738	Yes	-B 1922-B 7015 systematically -B 7016-B 8738 sporadically (ca. 5%), including all Bible fragments
Bible Gaster fragments series	Bible Gaster 1- Bible Gaster 83	Yes	Yes
C series	C 1-C 185	Yes	No
G series	G 1-G 101	Yes	G 21 and G 63 only
Gaster Hebrew manuscripts series	Gaster Heb. ms. 1441/1-Gaster Heb. ms. 2111/9[89]	Gaster Heb. ms. 1774/1 only	Idem
Gaster Hebrew fragments series	Gaster Hebrew 1-Gaster Hebrew 350	Yes	No
Gaster Printed fragments series	Gaster Printed 1-Gaster Printed 653	Yes	No
Glass series	Glass 1- Glass 17	Yes	No
L series	L 1-L 292	Yes	About one-fifth of the class-marks
P series	P 1-P 1358[90]	Yes	A few fragments only
Rylands Genizah fragments series	Rylands Genizah (fragment) 1-Rylands Genizah (fragment) 52	Yes	A few fragments only

The Rylands Cairo Genizah project went through two phases. For the first three years (2003–6) the project was mainly funded by the Friedberg and Safra foundations. During this period the emphasis was on cataloguing the Rylands Genizah material, which was done by the writer of this article on site in Manchester as well as, intermittently, by Dr Ezra Chwat at the Jewish National and University Library in Jerusalem, who worked from microfilm. Dr Chwat was (and is) employed for part of

86 This column shows how the fragments should ideally be referred to in publications in order to avoid confusion.

87 Many of these fragments have been catalogued in great detail, while others have, by necessity, only been roughly described so far in the hope that the relevant records will be updated with more detailed cataloguing information in future.

88 This series needs to go online most urgently (more than 1,800 cataloguing records in total), as the fragments were catalogued by Dr Sagit Butbul between 1 September 2008 and 31 January 2009.

89 It should be noted that only a number of class-marks between 1441 and 2111 refer to Genizah fragments. These fragments are awaiting proper conservation and numbering. Expectations are that eventually this series will produce in the region of 1,200 cataloguing records.

90 Note that about 40% of the class-marks in this series are empty (see explanation above).

his time by the Friedberg Foundation, who are in the process of creating an image, cataloguing and bibliographic database for all Genizah collections worldwide as part of the Friedberg Genizah project (www.genizah.org). His catalogue descriptions were made in Hebrew in the 'Aleph' catalogue of the JNUL (http://aleph.nli.org.il), which in turn are embedded in the Friedberg database. For the duration of the project, Dr Chwat and I have been working closely together, while I have been able to integrate systematically his findings into the Rylands online image collection and catalogue.[91]

Digitization of the Rylands Genizah fragments happened relatively late into the project. Halfway through the first part of the Rylands Cairo Genizah project, I was asked by the library to take part in a pilot digitization project, whereby a selection of one hundred Genizah fragments would go online via the LUNA image collection and catalogue the Rylands library had just acquired. Due to the sophistication of the system, we decided to apply to the Arts and Humanities Research Council (AHRC) for funding for a bigger three-year project (2006–2009) led by Professor Philip Alexander and Dr Stella Butler — an application which was successful. The new grant allowed the university to employ, besides a full-time research assistant, a full-time cataloguing assistant and part-time photographer, and to acquire the necessary high spec equipment. The late introduction of an online system had as unfortunate result an enormous duplication of work, which the cataloguing assistant, however, helped to relieve significantly.

The fact that all these images and cataloguing records are now online opens up further possibilities for collaboration between parties involved in making the Cairo Genizah fragments accessible on the web. This can practically be done by, for instance, providing live links to interrelated fragments or descriptions of the same fragment allowing a user of one Genizah website simultaneously to visit another. A case in point is Rylands fragments B 6119 and B 7638 and Halper 89 kept at the University of Pennsylvania Libraries in Philadelphia (http://sceti.library.upenn.edu/genizah/), which all come from the same Talmud manuscript and now have been interlinked. Another example is the collaboration between the Rylands and Princeton University, where Professor Mark Cohen and his team have set up a Genizah website to disseminate knowledge about Goitein's archive and for transcriptions of documentary Genizah fragments with commentary. They have included transcriptions with commentary of a selection of documentary fragments from the Rylands on their website which could thus be cross-linked with the images in our database, e.g. A 75,

91 See the Preface to this book for further acknowledgements

A 316, A 337, and so forth (http://www.princeton.edu/~geniza/). In future, more such projects could be set up, e.g. with the Bodleian library (http://genizah.bodleian.ox.ac.uk/). The most important collaboration, which has just started, will be between the Rylands and the Friedberg Genizah project. In due course, our images and catalogue descriptions will also be found in their union catalogue. This is a great step forwards.[92]

References

Adler, Elkan Nathan. 1897. 'An Eleventh Century Introduction to the Hebrew Bible: Being a Fragment from the Sepher ha-Ittim of Rabbi Judah ben Barzilai of Barcelona', *Jewish Quarterly Review* 9/4, 669–716

—— 1900. 'Some Missing Chapters of Ben Sira', *Jewish Quarterly Review* 12/3, 466–80

—— 1908. 'The Samaritan Book of Joshua', *Journal of the Royal Asiatic Society* October, 1143–7 (with Gaster's reply on 1148–56)

Alderman, Geofrey. 2004. 'Gaster, Moses (1856–1939): Scholar and Rabbi', *Oxford Dictionary of National Biography.* (Oxford) (January 2011 online edition http://www.oxforddnb.com/view/article/33351, accessed 13 Aug 2012)

Alexander, P.S. 1993. 'Gaster's *Exempla of the Rabbis*: A Reappraisal', in G. Sed-Rajna (ed.), *Rashi 1040-1990: Hommage à Ephraïm E. Urbach* (Paris). 793–805

Anderson, R.T. and T. Giles. 2005. *Tradition Kept: The Literature of the Samaritans.* (Peabody, Massachusetts)

Anonymous. 1954. 'Notes and News', *Bulletin of the John Rylands Library Manchester* 37/1, esp. 2–6

—— 1958. 'Notes and News', *Bulletin of the John Rylands Library of Manchester* 40/2, esp. 260–1

—— 1999. *A Guide to Special Collections.* (Manchester)

Beentjes, P.C. 1997. *The Book of Ben Sira in Hebrew: A Text Edition of All Extant Hebrew Manuscripts and a Synopsis of All Parallel Hebrew Ben Sira Texts.* (Leiden/New York/Köln)

Beit-Arié, Malachi. 1974. 'A Maimonides Autograph in the Rylands Gaster Genizah Collection', *Bulletin of the John Rylands University Library of Manchester* 57/1, 1–6

Ben-Shammai, Haggai. 2010. 'Is "the Cairo Genizah" a Proper Name or a Generic Noun? On the Relationship between the *Genizot* of the Ben Ezra and the Dār Simḥa Synagogues', in B. Outhwaite and S. Bhayro (eds), *"From a Sacred Source": Genizah Studies in Honour of Professor Stefan C. Reif* (Leiden/Boston). 43–52

Bensusan, S.L., 1936. 'Moses Gaster', in B. Schindler (ed.), *Occident and Orient* (London). 9–14

Ben Zvi, Sara Jo. 2011. 'Whose Geniza?', *Segula* June, 60–70

Cowley, Arthur E. and Adolf Neubauer. 1897. *Ecclesiasticus XXXIX, 15 to XLIX, 11.* (Oxford)

Crown, Alan David. 1998. *A Catalogue of the Samaritan Manuscripts in the British Library.* (London)

92 When using the LUNA image collection-cum-catalogue, scholars are strongly advised to download the older Insight version (JVA client) from http://www.library.manchester.ac.uk/searchresources/imagecollections/usinglunainsight/installingthejvaclient/, because it allows them to browse each data field and thus see exactly what's there and search the catalogue systematically. The online version http://enriqueta.man.ac.uk/luna/servlet/ then becomes a very useful second way of accessing the same images and catalogue descriptions.

David, Abraham. 1991. 'An Unknown Autographic Genizah Fragment of Maimonides' Code (Mishneh Torah) in the John Rylands University Library of Manchester', *Bulletin of the John Rylands University Library of Manchester* 73, 3–5

—— 1992/93. 'קטע גניזה בלתי ידוע *ממשנה תורה* לרמב"ם (אוטוגראף)', *Alei Sefer* 17 (1992-93), pp. 109–11

Díez Macho, Alejandro. 1956. 'Nuevos manuscritos importantes, bibliocos o liturgicos en Hebreo o Arameo', *Sefarad* 16, 1–22

Gaster, Moses. 1900a. 'Geniza-Fragmente', in M. Brann and F. Rosenthal (eds), *Gedenkbuch zur Erinnerung an David Kaufmann*. 3 vols, (Breslau), vol. 1, 222–44; reprinted in Gaster 1925–28, II: 679–90 (German part) and III: 205–15 (Hebrew part)

—— 1900b. 'A New Fragment of Ben Sira', *Jewish Quarterly Review* 12:4, 688–702; reprinted in Gaster 1925–28, I: 184–98

— 1901. *Hebrew Illuminated Bibles of the IXth and Xth Centuries (Codices Or. Gaster, Nos 150 and 151); and a Samaritan Scroll of the Law of the XIth Century (Codex Or. Gaster, No. 350) together with Eight Plates of Facsimiles of these Manuscripts and of Fragments from the Geniza in Egypt*. (London); reprinted from *Proceedings of the Society of Biblical Archaeology* 1900, 226–69 (without the Plates)

—— 1917. 'A Codex of the Bible According to the Massora of Ben Naphtali and the Oriental Tradition', *Proceedings of the Society of Biblical Archaeology*, 73–84, 141–51, 172–83; reprinted in Gaster 1925–28, II: 1295–1329.

—— 1924. *Exempla of the Rabbis*. (London and Leipzig)

—— 1925. *The Samaritans: Their History, Doctrines and Literatures* (*The Schweich Lectures 1923*). (London)

—— 1925–8. *Studies and Texts in Folklore, Magic, Medieval Romance, Hebrew Apocrypha and Samaritan Archaeology*. 3 vols, (London)

—— 1927. *The Asatir: The Samaritan Book of the 'Secrets of Moses'*. (London)

—— 1932. *The Samaritan Oral Law and Ancient Traditions* (vol. 1 *Samaritan Eschatology*). (London)

—— 1995. 'The Story of my Library' (translated by Brad Sabin Hill), *The British Library Journal* 21, 16–22

Glickman, Mark. 2011. *Sacred Treasure – the Cairo Genizah: The Amazing Discoveries of Forgotten Jewish History in an Egyptian Synagogue Attic*. (Woodstock, Vermont)

Goitein, Solomon Dov. 1959. 'Unpublished Autograph Responsa by Maimonides', *Tarbiz* 28 (1958/59), 190–6 (in Hebrew)

—— 1960a. 'Geniza Papers of a Documentary Character in the Gaster Collection of the British Museum', *Jewish Quarterly Review* 51/1, 34–46

—— 1960b. 'The Documents of the Cairo Geniza as a Source for Mediterranean Social History', *Journal of the American Oriental Society* 80, 91–100

—— 1967-93. *A Mediterranean Society: the Jewish Communities of the Arab World as Portrayed in the Documents of the Cairo Geniza*. 6 vols, (Berkeley)

—— 1971. 'An Eleventh-Century Letter from Tyre in the John Rylands Library', *Bulletin of the John Rylands Library of Manchester* 54/1, 94–102

Goldstein, Bernard and David Pingree. 1978. 'The Astronomical Tables of al-Khwārizmī in a Nineteenth Century Egyptian Text', *Journal of the American Oriental Society* 98/1, 96–9

Haralambakis, Maria. 2012. *Boxlist of Moses Gaster's Working Papers at the John Rylands Library*. http://www.manchesterjewishstudies.org/storage/Gaster%20boxlist.pdf

—— Forthcoming in 2013. 'A Survey of the Gaster Collection at the John Rylands Library', *Bulletin of the John Rylands University Library of Manchester* 89/2

Hoffman, Adina and Peter Cole. 2011. *Sacred Trash: The Lost and Found World of the Cairo Geniza*. (New York)

Hopkins, Simon. 1984/85. 'Two New Maimonidean Autographs in the John Rylands University Library', *Bulletin of the John Rylands Library of Manchester* 67/2, 710–35

—— 1994. 'A New Autograph Fragment of Maimonides's *Epitomes* of Galen (*De Locis Affectis*)', *Bulletin of the School of Oriental and African Studies* 57, 126–32

Jefferson, Rebecca. 2009. 'A Genizah Secret: The Count d'Hulst and Letters Revealing the Race to Recover the Lost Leaves of the Original Ecclesiasticus', *Journal of the History of Collections* 21:1, 125–42

—— 2010. 'The Cairo Genizah Unearthed: The Excavations Conducted by the Count d'Hulst on Behalf of the Bodleian Library and their Significance for Genizah History', in B. Outhwaite and S. Bhayro (eds), *"From a Sacred Source": Genizah Studies in Honour of Professor Stefan C. Reif* (Leiden/Boston). 171–99

Klein, Michael. *Genizah Manuscripts of Palestinian Targum to the Pentateuch*. 2 vols, (Cincinnati, 1986)

Lévi, Israel. 1896. 'Découverte d'un fragment d'une version hébraïque de l'Ecclésiastique de Jésus, fils de Sirach', *Revue des études juives* 32, 303–4

—— 1897a. 'La sagesse de Jésus, fils de Sirach: découverte d'un fragment de l'original hébreu, *Revue des études juives* 34, 1–50, 294–6

— 1897b. 'Quelques notes fur Jésus ben Sirach et son ouvrage', *Revue des études juives* 35, 29–47

—— 1898–1901. *L'Ecclésiastique ou la sagesse de Jésus, fils de Sira: texte originale hébreu*. 2 vols, (Paris)

—— 1900. 'Fragments de deux nouveaux manuscripts hébreux de l'Ecclésiastique', *Revue des études juives* 40, 1–30 and 255–7

—— 1904. *The Hebrew Text of the Book of Ecclesiasticus*. (Leiden)

Levi, Trude. 1976. *Gaster Papers: A Collection of Letters, Documents, etc., of the Late Haham Dr. Moses Gaster, 1856–1939*. (London)

Marcus, 1931. 'A Fifth MS. Of Ben Sira', *Jewish Quarterly Review* 21/3, 223–40

Margoliouth, George. 'The Original Hebrew of Ecclesiasticus XXXI. 12–31, and XXXVI. 22-XXXVII. 26', *Jewish Quarterly Review* 12 (1899), 1–33

Neubauer, A. 1894. 'Two Monographs by Dr. M. Gaster', *Jewish Quarterly Review* 6/3, 570–7

Reif, Stefan C. 1996. 'The Discovery of the Cambridge Genizah Fragments of Ben Sira: Scholars and Texts', in P.C. Beentjes (ed.), *The Book of Ben Sira in Modern Research* (Proceedings of the First International Ben Sira Conference 28-31 July 1996 Soesterberg, Netherlands, Berlin/New York). 1–22

—— 2000. *A Jewish Archive from Old Cairo: The History of Cambridge University's Genizah Collection*. (Cambridge)

Reiterer, Friedrich V. 1998. *Bibliographie zu Ben Sira*. (Berlin/New York)

Renton, James. 2004. 'Reconsidering Chaim Weizmann and Moses Gaster in the Founding-Mythology of Zionism', in M. Berkowitz (ed.), *Nationalism, Zionism and Ethnic Mobilization of the Jews in 1900 and Beyond* (Leiden/Boston). 129–51

Rhezavi, Yehuda. 1993. 'צרור איגרות בקולמוסו של הרמב"ם', *Sinai* 111, 193–216

Robertson, Edward. 1962. *Catalogue of the Samaritan Manuscripts in the John Rylands Library, Manchester*, vol. 2 – the Gaster manuscripts (Manchester)

Rosen, T. and E. Yassif. 2002. 'The Study of Hebrew Literature of the Middle Ages: Major Trends and Goals', in M. Goodman (ed.), *The Oxford Handbook of Jewish Studies* (Oxford). 240–94

Roth, Cecil. 1940. 'Moses Gaster', *The Jewish Historical Society of England – Transactions* 14, 247–52

Rowland Smith, Diana. 1991. 'Genizah Collections in the British Library', in D. Rowland Smith and P.S. Salinger (eds), *Hebrew Studies* (London). 20–5

Schechter, Solomon. 1898. 'Genizah Specimens', *Jewish Quarterly Review* 10/2, 197–206

—— 1900a. 'The Hebrew Text of Ben Sira: The British Museum Fragments of Ecclesiasticus', *Jewish Quarterly Review* 12/2, 266–72

— 1900b. 'A Further Fragment of Ben Sira', *Jewish Quarterly Review* 12/3, 456–65

Schechter, Solomon and Charles Taylor. 1899. *The Wisdom of Ben Sira: Portions of the Book Ecclesiasticus from Hebrew Manuscripts in the Cairo Genizah Collection.* (Cambridge)

Scheiber, A. 1982. 'A Leaf of the Fourth Manuscript of the Ben Sira from the Geniza', *Magyar Könyvszemle* 98, 185

Schindler, Bruno. 1958. 'Some Personal Recollections of Dr. Moses Gaster' and 'List of Publications of Dr. M. Gaster', in B. Schindler (ed.), *Gaster Centenary Publication* (London). 19–21, 23–40

—— (ed.). 1936. *Occident and Orient.* (London)

—— 1958. *Gaster Centenary Publication.* (London)

Schirmann, J. 1957/58. 'A New Leaf from the Hebrew "Ecclesiasticus" (Ben Sira), *Tarbiz* 27, II–III, 440–3 (in Hebrew)

—— 1959/60. 'Additional Leaves from Ecclesiasticus in Hebrew', *Tarbiz* 29, 125–34 (in Hebrew)

Shurin, A. 1964. קשת גיבורים: דמויות באופק היהודי של דור אחרון. (Jerusalem)

Soskice, Janet. 2009. *Sisters of Sinai: How Two Lady Adventurers Found the Hidden Gospels.* (London)

Wallenstein, Meir. 1957-58. 'A Dated Tenth Century Hebrew Parchment Fragment from the Cairo Genīzah in the Gaster Collection in the John Rylands Library', *Bulletin of the John Rylands Library Manchester* 40, 551–8

—— 1959a. 'Two Fragments from the Cairo Genizah in the John Rylands Library, Manchester', *Sinai* 45, 302–14 (in Hebrew)

—— 1959b. 'A Unique Kol-Nidrê Piyyut', *Bulletin of the John Rylands University Library of Manchester* 41/2, 488–500

Weis, Pinkas R. 1952. *Mishnah Horayoth: Its History and Exposition.* (Leiden)

—— 1955. *Midrashic Selections.* (Manchester)

Notes on the Artefactual Aspects of the Rylands Genizah

Philip Alexander and Renate Smithuis
University of Manchester

Collections as Artefacts

Librarians and archivists have long recognized that *collections* of books and manuscripts constitute artefacts in their own right, with cultural and historical significance. They are more than the sum of their parts, and have their own distinctive character in comparison and contrast with other collections. What is the nature of the Rylands Genizah as a collection? How are we to delineate its distinctive character? With what other collections should we compare it in order to capture its peculiar traits? These questions are complex. We offer in this and the following chapter some notes towards an answer.

1 Genealogy

The obvious place to start is with the genealogy of the collection. Where did it come from, and how did it end up in Manchester? The basic facts have been covered above in Chapter 1, 'Short Introduction to the Genizah Collection in the John Rylands Library'. For our purposes here the following are the key points. The Rylands Genizah was assembled by a single collector, the Romanian Jewish scholar Moses Gaster (1856–1939), who spent the later part of his life in England. In 1914 Gaster's daughter, Phina Emiley, married Neville Laski, elder son of Nathan Laski, a Manchester cotton merchant, prominent in civic and Jewish communal life in the city. This forged a link between Gaster and Manchester, and it was because of this link with the Laskis that money was able to be raised locally to bring a part of Gaster's library to the Rylands.[1] Gaster is an intriguing figure who played a significant role in

1 The extent to which Gaster was known and revered in Manchester is reflected in the fact that there was a lodge of the B'nai Berith in the city named after him — the Dr Moses Gaster Lodge. In 1992 it was merged with the Cissie Laski Lodge and Whitefield Women's Lodge to form the Manchester B'nai B'rith Lodge. Before the merger one of the writers of this chapter (Alexander), after a talk to the lodge (at their request) about the Gaster books and manuscripts in the Rylands, was introduced to an elderly

Jewish scholarship, in Jewish communal politics in England, and in the Zionist movement in the first half of the twentieth century. There appears to be no major biography of him. An evaluation of his place in all three spheres is long overdue.[2]

The Rylands acquisitions were only a part of Gaster's considerable library, which has ended up scattered in various parts of the world. In 1925 the British Library bought 1,129 of Gaster's codices in Hebrew script, including texts in Yiddish and Judaeo-Greek.[3] They also acquired eighty Samaritan manuscripts and around 3,000 Genizah fragments. The Samaritan manuscripts have been catalogued, but the Genizah fragments and Hebrew codices have not, though Gaster's own handlist of the latter survives.[4] In 1936, a few years before his death, Gaster arranged for the bulk of his Romanian manuscripts and some printed books (around 750 items) to be sold to the Romanian Academy of Sciences in Bucharest. The rest of his library was disposed of piecemeal after his death, mostly in the 1950s. In 1952 the School of Slavonic and East European Studies in London purchased many of his books in Romanian and other European languages, dealing with a wide range of topics, such as language, literature, folklore, history and politics, and including one of the largest collections of books on Jews in Romania ever assembled by a single individual.[5] University College London created an archive of his papers. The largest Gaster archive in the world, it comprises 337 boxes plus twenty-two volumes and nine rolls. The contents include correspondence, invitations to dinner parties, pamphlets, photo albums, newspaper cuttings, sermons, notes and drafts of various scholarly and popular pieces.[6] Most of Gaster's Judaica books were bought by the bookseller Bamberger & Wahrmann of Tel-Aviv. Some of them were sold individually, but the majority found a home at the

---

Manchester GP who had personally known Gaster, and who told him a story of how, sitting in Gaster's study one day, he had asked Gaster how he had come by so many marvellous books and articles. Gaster allegedly replied, 'Some I bought, some I begged, some I borrowed, and some I stole'!

2 There are two short entries on him in the *Oxford Dictionary of National Biography Online*, the older by A.M. Hyamson, the more recent by Geoffrey Alderman. Both Hyamson and Alderman are historians of English Jewry and gave the basic facts of Gaster's life in context, but they have little to say about his intellectual biography. This is beginning to be addressed by Dr Maria Haralambakis in the Manchester Gaster Project. What follows relies heavily on her research.

3 Besides Hebrew, there are manuscripts in other Jewish languages in Hebrew script, e.g. Yiddish, Judaeo-Italian, Judaeo-Spanish, Judaeo-Arabic, Judaeo-Persian, Judaeo-Greek and Judaeo-Turkic. See the preface in Hill 1995.

4 Gaster's original handlist of his codices survives, but it is very brief and uninformative (Gaster 1995). The Samaritan codices are included in Crown 1998.

5 For a brief survey, with a strong focus on the oldest printed books in the collection, see Deletant 1975.

6 Information based on the handlist made by Vanessa Freedman, Hebrew and Jewish Studies Librarian at UCL.

University of California in Los Angeles. YIVO New York acquired several hundred items of an archival character – postcards, wall-calendars, letters of appeal in Hebrew, Yiddish, Judaeo-Arabic, French, English and German, sent to Gaster by all sorts of charitable institutions in Palestine (e.g. schools, orphanages and hospitals), between 1900 and the early 1920s (the end of the Ottoman period and the beginning of the British Mandate).[7] The library of the University of Leeds acquired several Gaster manuscripts, in Greek, Hebrew, Romanian and Church Slavonic.

The Rylands Gaster material dates back to the 1950s. The manuscripts, including *c.* 350 codices in Hebrew script, *c.* 350 codices in Samaritan, and *c.* 15,000 Genizah fragments arrived in January 1954 (Anonymous 1954).[8] Printed books and archival material followed in 1958, including important correspondence between Gaster and the Samaritan leadership in Nablus (Anonymous 1958). Of all the Gaster collections in the various libraries, the one in the Rylands is the most diverse. In terms of volume, it takes up *c.* thirty metres of shelving. The Rylands Gaster Samaritan manuscripts have been catalogued, and an un-published catalogue of the Hebrew codices is available for consultation within the library.[9] The Genizah fragments are in process of being catalogued through the Rylands Genizah Project. The archival material remains uncatalogued, though a start has been made on it by Maria Haralambakis (2012).

In attempting to characterize the Rylands Genizah this history is important. As a collection it exists in its own right, because it now resides under one roof in the John Rylands Library Manchester, but it also exists as a subcollection of the Gaster manuscripts in Manchester, which are in turn a subcollection of the original Gaster library. Particularly important for our present purposes is the fact that the Rylands holds only part of the total Gaster Genizah collection, one sixth being in the British Library. But at the same time the Rylands Genizah exists as a subcollection of the original Genizah, most of which was once housed in the Ben Ezra synagogue of Old Cairo. There is an intriguing symmetry between these two broader contexts of the Rylands Genizah – the original Genizah and Gaster's library. Neither exists any longer as a physically unified collection: both are scattered in various parts of the world. Gaster's total library, including his papers, was almost as diverse in content as the Cairo Genizah, and contained a huge variety of manuscripts and documents,

7 Gaster was a member of the honorary presidium of YIVO, together with Albert Einstein and Sigmund Freud (Hill 2006: 1617).

8 The Hebrew and Samaritan codices and Genizah fragments were bought, and the miscellaneous sequence was presented as a gift.

9 Robertson 1962. The in-house catalogue of the codices in Hebrew script is by Alexander Samely.

ranging from high-status cultural texts, to everyday trivia — letters and notes and scribbles of various kinds — in many languages. Gaster created his own 'Genizah', and his apparent inability to destroy anything that arrived in his study in written form seems to have been shared by the people who steadily filled the storeroom in Cairo.

Did any kind of acquisition policy guide Gaster's manuscript purchases? The analysis offered in the 'Introduction' above suggests he was largely an opportunistic buyer. An element of opportunism is certainly evident in his Samaritan acquisitions — some of the most important in his library. At the beginning of the twentieth century the Samaritan community in Nablus was very small and struggling for survival. In 1906 they sent a delegation to London to sell manuscripts. This seems to have been when Gaster first met them. He invited them to his house, and took time to get on friendly terms with them. The hospitality paid off: over several years Gaster exchanged many letters with them, bought some of their manuscripts for modest sums, and got texts copied for him by their scribes. In the case of the Genizah fragments, as noted above ('Introduction'), he probably bought them from dealers in two lots, the first around 1896, and the second around 1900, but many of them were too small and in too poor a condition for him to have known in any detail what he was buying. Though there was probably a large element of happenstance to Gaster's manuscript collecting, it is also true that it relates in a broad way to the intellectual concerns manifested in his published work. It reflects to a significant degree his mind. He had a strong interest in marginal, non-normative movements within Judaism, and with non-normative texts, beliefs and practices. He was one of the earliest to challenge the Wissenschaft des Judentums cosy picture of Judaism as a 'religion of reason', by highlighting its 'irrational' magical, mystical traditions. He avidly collected Jewish amulets and other examples of what he himself called Jewish 'superstition'. He was massively interested in popular culture as manifested in folklore. In many ways he anticipates Gershom Scholem. He has not received the credit he deserves, partly because he lacked Scholem's meticulous scholarship (he was infuriatingly slapdash at times, and prone to making exaggerated claims for the antiquity and importance of his own manuscripts), and partly because Scholem (pointedly?) ignores him, or, when he deigns to take notice, the reference notably low key. Gaster's published work relies heavily on his own manuscript collection, at least on his codices, and this correlation between his published work and his manuscripts suggests that everything was not down to chance. His own intellectual concerns seem generally to have informed his manuscript buying.[10]

It is unclear whether the fragments and codices were divided between the Rylands and the British Library according to some rational plan. The British Library acquired its batch first, and one might expect that it would, therefore, have got the pick of the crop, but that assumption is thrown into doubt by the simple fact that many obviously interesting and important items have ended up in the Rylands. The analysis offered in the 'Introduction', however, strongly suggests that it was Gaster who made the choice as to what should go to the British Library. He remained in total control of the process, and he selected manuscripts in which he no longer had an active interest, from which he no longer expected to make headline-grabbing discoveries. Lurking in the Gaster archives may be documents that could answer questions as to how, from whom and when Gaster purchased his manuscripts, and what motivated him to sell. The history of his library has still to be written.[11]

2 Physical Condition

In addition to its genealogy, the Rylands Genizah can be characterized in terms of its physical condition. One of the first things that strike any user of the collection is that the fragments on the whole are small, and tend to be in a rather poor state of preservation. When fragments of the same manuscript are found in other collections, they are usually in a somewhat better physical state. A partial explanation for this can be found in the history of the Gaster collection. When the Second World War broke out the Gaster family decided to keep the manuscripts still in their possession in a safe, which was located in a cellar in central London. The area was blitzed and the water used to put out the fires flooded into the cellar and damaged some of the manuscripts. The damage is particularly obvious in the notebooks into which some of the fragments have been pasted — whether by Gaster himself, or by the dealer(s) from whom he bought them, is unclear (though that Gaster himself was responsible is, perhaps, more likely, because they contain annotations in his hand). But war-damage will not explain everything. In the 'Introduction' the tentative hypothesis was advanced that at least the second batch of Genizah fragments, acquired by Gaster

10 The alternative, that he was an opportunistic *scholar*, that is to say that the purchase of the manuscripts propelled him in certain scholarly directions, may have an element of truth in it, but only in the sense that it confirmed his predilections. His amulet-collecting and his folklore interests seem to have been a matter of pure choice.

11 Brad Sabin Hill, the leading authority on the subject, is preparing a major study of Gaster's library.

around 1900, originated in the excavations which Count d'Hulst had carried out in 1898 in the rubbish heaps in the garden and courtyard of the Ben Ezra synagogue, where manuscripts from the synagogue Genizah had been dumped during the synagogue refurbishment between 1889 and 1892. These manuscripts, which had become mixed up with soil and builders' rubble were in an even worse state than those that had come directly from the storeroom. And there is a final factor to be borne in mind. The fragments belong to heavily used, worn out manuscripts, some of which have been repaired (a point to which we shall return later). In other words a lot of damage occurred *before* the manuscripts were deposited in the Genizah. A major reason for them being deposited there was the fact that there were worn out, and no longer serviceable.

It is instructive to compare the condition of the Rylands Genizah with that of the Bodleian Genizah. Superficially both collections are small, and consist, apparently, of random fragments, but there the similarity seems to end. The Bodleian pieces are choice and give the impression of having been hand-picked. They tend to be old, 'clean' and well preserved, and they have been carefully (perhaps too carefully!) bound into volumes, probably when they came into the Bodleian: they are certainly described in the Neubauer-Cowley catalogue (1886-1906, II) in terms of their present composite volumes.[12]

3 Content

The Rylands Genizah can also be characterized as a collection in terms of its content. To do this properly we would need to ascertain the proportions of the whole of it that fall into certain literary and documentary categories and subcategories and compare these with the proportions of other Genizah subcollections and of the Genizah as a whole. Till we have a complete database for the Genizah we are not really in a position to do this definitively, but a number of more impressionistic observations can be made. The Rylands fragments tend to be late and written on paper. A sizeable proportion is documentary, and many are in Judaeo-Arabic. These late Judaeo-Arabic texts are potentially of importance for the later developments of that language — developments which have been little studied, the lion's share of attention having been devoted to the classical period.[13] Where we do have literary texts they tend to be

12 Jefferson 2009 stresses the rivalry between Neubauer and Schechter to discover the Genizah, and extract its contents for their respective libraries in Oxford and Cambridge. For the possibility that the Bodleian collection was right from the start subject to some sort of selection see Jefferson 2010.

13 See Geoffrey Khan's article below.

copies of high status religious works, most of which are well known, and liturgical poetry. This pattern is well illustrated by fragments of the Targumim. We will analyse in detail the data on these in chapter three. To summarize here: a fair number of Targum fragments survive in the Rylands Genizah but the vast majority come from either Onqelos to the Torah or Jonathan to the Prophets, and in the latter case probably only from passages that served as Haftarot. In other words, only manuscripts with liturgical significance are found (the identification of the two fragments relating to the Writings is very uncertain). Above all we seem totally to lack copies of the 'deviant' Palestinian Targumim to the Torah or to the Prophets which feature in other collections (e.g. Cambridge and JTS). All this is consonant with the general lateness of Rylands Genizah: the collection comes from a time when greater uniformity of practice predominated, and non-normative Targumim had simply disappeared. But, somewhat paradoxically, this ought to mean that the Rylands fragments came out of the Genizah early, since one would have expected them to have been near the top of the pile. It should be noted in passing that we are not convinced that all the Rylands fragments are actually from Cairo.[14] In the online database we have not attempted to distinguish between genuine and non-genuine Genizah manuscripts, but photographed and catalogued everything, leaving it to others to decide on its provenance.

4 Typology

The Rylands Genizah contains only one part of the original Cairo Genizah. What was the nature of the Cairo Genizah itself as a collection? Though it no longer exists as a physical entity in one place, the question is important, because the answer will determine how we relate Rylands to the complete Genizah, as part to whole, and how we interpret the significance of the Genizah in historical and cultural terms.[15] So what kind of assemblage was it? One way of tackling this question is by comparison and contrast. The Genizah is not the only collection of written texts to have come down to us from the middle ages and antiquity. We have a number of others, which reflect in various ways the individuals and the communities that created them. The Dead Sea Scrolls come immediately to mind – often described as the 'library' of the Qumran community. We have the Vindolanda tablets from the Roman town of Vindolanda on

14 See the 'Introduction', p. 22.

15 It is the Genizah *as a whole* that testifies directly to the history of the community that created it. The subcollections do so only indirectly. They testify more to the history of *collecting*. The creation of the various subcollections in England, for example, have much to tell us about the mentality of late Victorian England. The Genizah as a whole obviously does not.

Hadrian's wall. We have the Herculaneum papyri. We have various palace archives from Mesopotamia and Middle East (e.g. Ebla, Mari, Amarna, Ugarit). We have the Oxyrhynchus papyri. We have libraries surviving from the medieval Christian (e.g. Mount Athos and St Catharine's) and Muslim (e.g. Chinguetti and Mashad) worlds. And so on. There would be much to be gained by drawing up a typology of such collections and seeing where the Genizah fits in. And scholars working on the diverse collections can profitably share expertise. For example, in the case of the Herculaneum papyri, the Vindolanda tablets and the Dead Sea Scrolls sophisticated techniques of imaging have been used which could be applied, if funds permitted, to the Genizah as well.[16] The various collections pose many similar problems of conservation and interpretation, and comparison is a powerful heuristic tool in determining their meaning and significance.

Where would the Cairo Genizah fit into a typology of such collections? The answer is complex. Collections of manuscripts are normally divided into two broad types: archives and libraries. Archives are collections of everyday documents — inventories, memoranda, letters, wills, deeds of sale, contracts and the like. Libraries are collections of literary texts. The degree to which archives and libraries embody *intention*, that is to say, were assembled deliberately, according to a plan, to serve a specific purpose, differs from case to case. Some archives were clearly put together because the documents they contained (contracts, records of payments, etc.) needed to be preserved: they were in some sense still active, and someone might want to consult them; but in other cases, they might represent a rather random assemblage of material from which no one had bothered to throw away the redundant items. The same goes for libraries. The Herculaneum papyri, for example, contain no documentary material, and seem to represent a conscious policy of assembling a collection of literary works of Epicurean philosophy. But other libraries are much more random in character. The Cairo Genizah held both documents and literary material but it is neither an archive nor a library. The documents it contained were not being stored potentially to be accessed at some future date: rather they were stored to forget about them, ultimately to destroy them. Similarly the literary texts were not put in the Genizah so that they could be consulted in the future. Quite the reverse: they were put there to take them

16 One thinks, in the case of the Dead Sea Scrolls, of the imaging techniques developed by Greg Berman, formerly of NASA. However we should never lose sight of the question of whether the outcomes will justify the expenditure of time and resources. In the case of the Scrolls the improved readings of the Genesis Apocryphon were certainly impressive and significant, but in other cases the yield has been sometimes disappointing and meagre.

out of circulation. Of the collections of manuscripts named earlier the Cairo Genizah in many ways seems typologically closest to Oxyrhynchus — though Oxyrhynchus is larger.[17] Both are the random deposits of a geographically defined community over a considerable stretch of time: in the case of Oxyrhynchus it was the community living in the small Egyptian town of the same name between the first and sixth centuries CE; in the case of the Genizah, it was the Jewish community of Cairo between the tenth and nineteenth centuries. In so far as they embody intention, both represent the intention to discard and destroy their contents: they are the 'rubbish dumps' of their respective communities; and both contain an array of texts ranging from the most banal, everyday 'shopping lists' to literary works of the highest status.

Once we classify the Genizah in this way, we begin to understand one important aspect of its cultural and historical significance. It gives us an insight into the production, circulation and consumption of written texts within the Cairo Jewish community, into that community's levels and uses of literacy. We should not assume, however, that it correlates exactly with the situation on the ground. There is one type of material which seems notably under-represented, particularly in Rylands Genizah, viz., expensive or *de luxe* copies of major literary works. A contrast with Europe suggests itself. In the case of the latter the surviving literary output is dominated by impressive and expensive codices (e.g. the great Hebrew Bible manuscript, Erfurt 1). Where are the remnants of such works in the Genizah? No sooner is the question posed than an answer presents itself — an answer which hints at the dangers of treating the Genizah as an *exhaustive* record of book production in the Jewish community of Old Cairo. Such works were less likely to have ended up in the Genizah. The Genizah was for old, worn-out books. Expensive and precious tomes would have been treated with great care and passed on. The picture for Europe is distorted in the opposite way because, on the whole, we don't have much material from there comparable to the mundane, everyday documents or the rough-and-ready private copies of high status works typical of Cairo, though the balance may be to some degree redressed by the material emerging from the so-called 'European Genizah'.[18] So to complete the picture of book consumption in Egypt we would need

17 Reputedly around half a million items, only ten percent of which are literary. For a readable and authoritative overview see Parsons 2007.

18 It should be noted, however, that, because the fragments were used for binding books, large and strong pieces of material were favoured, and these were likely to have come from high status books. Thus the Genizah Italiana seems to be made up entirely of folio parchment fragments, and so, by definition, consists of remnants of *de luxe* editions of high status texts. By way of contrast, some more mundane, everyday documents on paper *are* emerging from Spanish bindings. The website *Books within Books* –

to add in the more expensive copies of high status texts which never got into the Genizah, but which were more carefully preserved and are now housed in various libraries throughout the world.[19]

5 Formal and Material Aspects of the Manuscripts

Finally it is possible to characterize the Rylands Genizah in terms of the formal and material aspects of its constituent manuscripts. Each individual manuscript is an artefact in its own right which contributes to the character of the collection as a whole. Understandably the study of the Genizah has been dominated by interest in the texts. Scholars have expended most of their efforts on deciphering the writing: if it turned out to represent a copy of a known work, they were keen to compare it with existing copies; if it was hitherto unknown — better still! But manuscripts are more than the writing on the page. They are *in toto* cultural artefacts and their non-textual aspects are important as well. This point is well taken in the study of Western Latin manuscripts, and in Malachi Beit-Arié it has a learned advocate in the field of Jewish studies.[20] We will now run through a checklist of significant 'non-verbal' aspects of the Rylands Genizah manuscripts, with some comments on each.

5.1 Materials

The two main materials used to support the writing in the Rylands Genizah are parchment and paper, with the latter predominating. Within the Genizah as a whole this appears also to be the case, though we also find occasionally cloth and possibly papyrus. Parchment was the earlier writing surface, but after the introduction of paper

---

Hebrew Fragments in European Libraries (www.hebrewmanuscript.com) is planning to publish a catalogue of all the fragments discovered to date. See also Hollender 2011.

19 There are codices of Egyptian provenance in the Bodleian, the JNUL and Petersburg (Firkovitch). Gaster 151 (BL Oriental 9879) is an early *de luxe* copy of the Bible produced in Egypt in the ninth/tenth century, but there is no reason to think it comes from the Cairo Genizah (see above 'Introduction' p. 4). For the purposes of the analysis envisaged here we would need to identify manuscripts which were *written* in Cairo, or, even if written elsewhere, were *owned* by Cairene Jews. The evidence for this will have to be colophons, owners notes inserted in the manuscripts, or clear external attestation that the manuscripts were written or at some point owned in Cairo. It is not easy to distinguish an Egyptian manuscript on purely palaeographical/codicological grounds from other manuscripts of the Oriental group, written, e.g., in Syria or Palestine. Nor, it should be noted, is palaeography a sure guide to *where* a manuscript was written. The surviving Maimonides autographs illustrate the latter problem. Though they are commonly classified as exemplifying Sephardi script, few, if any, were written in Spain.

20 See his classic monograph Beit-Arié 1993a.

it continued to be used for Torah Scrolls and Ketubbot. The invention of printing reinforced the use of paper, because, although it is possible to print on parchment, and it was occasionally done, paper is the more convenient surface.

Under materials we should include not only the surfaces on which the writing has been done, but the ink in which it has been executed. There are sophisticated, non-intrusive ways of analysing the chemical composition of inks. This has been attempted in the case of the Dead Sea Scrolls (Nir-el and Broshi 1996a, b), and certain Western Latin manuscripts, but we do not know of any work in this area on the Genizah fragments. Three types of ink are used in the Dead Sea Scrolls: carbon-ink, metal-gall ink, and cinnabar (for rubrics). Both carbon and metal-gall ink were still widely in use in the middle ages, but which is found in the Genizah manuscripts? A possible indication that metal-gall inks were sometimes employed is the fact that in some Genizah manuscripts the ink has eaten away the material, leaving only a hollow outline of the letters.[21] This phenomenon is found both in parchment and paper, but occurs, in our experience, only when metal-gall inks are used. Analysis of the inks, like everything else, comes down in the end to a question of resources, and to whether or not the potential results justify the expenditure.

5.2 Script and Handwriting

Under this heading comes first and foremost the classic concerns of palaeographers with the evolution of scripts, the distinction of cursive, semi-cursive, documentary, and formal hands, the identification of regional styles. This is obviously important for the Genizah which contains samples of scripts extending over many centuries. There are important articles by Malachi Beit-Arié (1989) and Edna Engel (1999) on the subject.[22] The presence of a range of regional styles (Occidental, Oriental and

21 See, e.g., P 30; P 214; P 411; P 1152; P 1161; P 1164; P 1179; P 1222; P 1235 — all parchment, but a striking paper example is B 1010.

22 Engel proposes to distinguish three additional submodes of writing — proto-square, semi-square, and proto-semi-square — to add to the standard square, semi-cursive, and cursive. Interesting is her comment that 'most of the documents produced until the thirties of the eleventh century, either in the Orient or Spain, were written in square script. Probably due to the increasing need for an un-square script, a new process emerged, reaching its peak by the establishment of two formal modes: the semi-cursive and the cursive.' Presumably the emergence of the cursive forms corresponds with a greater use of writing for everyday purposes. In the longer historical perspective Engel's analysis raises some ticklish questions. Hebrew had already developed both cursive and semi-cursive letter-forms (in many cases similar to those found in the middle ages!) in Second Temple times, as witnessed by the Dead Sea Scrolls, and some of these persisted into late antiquity, as the Aramaic incantation bowls show. Was there, then, a *reversion* to square script in the early Middle Ages, followed by an *independent*

Byzantine) within the Genizah is potentially significant. It might suggest that the make-up of the Cairo Jewish community was rather cosmopolitan, or it might point to some sort of 'book-exchange', manuscripts copied in one region finding their way by gift or purchase to another.

Distinctions can be drawn between manuscripts not only in terms of styles and modes of writing but also in terms of the competence with which these are executed. By competence we mean the skill, professionalism and care shown by the writer of the text. In principle one could distinguish three broad levels of competence: (1) that of professional scribes; (2) that of ordinary, educated people; (3) that of children or other learners. Measuring competence is not easy, but the possibility is worth raising. One interesting aspect of the Rylands Genizah is how few manuscripts are careful, professional copies. The Genizah manuscripts seem to indicate that ordinary people had confident and serviceable handwriting, which, however, did not reach the standards of a professional scribe. This might seem at first sight unremarkable, but we must remember that throughout antiquity handwriting was not a skill that educated people cultivated. Basically they learned their letters for the purposes of being able to read, but once they could read they ceased to practise their letters. They could write, but if they wanted something written, even a personal letter, they tended to call on the services of a professional scribe. Even great scholars often had rather messy writing (one thinks of Maimonides, at least when he was drafting). Students of the Greek papyri are well used to copies of texts with rather poor handwriting being textually very correct, while beautifully written copies may be full of mistakes and textually poor. The former are often seen 'scholars' copies', the latter as copies made by professional scribes who transcribed rather mechanically, and often did not have a high level of grammatical and linguistic knowledge. The Genizah may indicate, at least within the Jewish community of Cairo, a more widespread exercise by ordinary people of writing-skills than in late antiquity. It must be said, however, that because

---

evolution of semi-cursives and cursives out of this in the eleventh century, which happen to look rather like the corresponding modes of writing in Second Temple times? Engel usefully distinguishes between 'styles' (Occidental, Oriental, Byzantine) and 'modes' (square, semi-cursive, cursive). But this leaves something out. We would add 'handwriting' (the idiosyncratic use by an individual of a particular style and mode), and competence (the skill and professionalism with which the writer executes a particular style and mode). On this final point see above. So one could describe a particular piece of writing as follows: script – Hebrew; style – Oriental; mode – cursive; competence – non-professional; and then detail some of its handwriting idiosyncracies. In Latin the form of writing used for administrative and legal documents was markedly different from that used for copying literary works. This systematic generic difference is not found in Hebrew.

of their small size and generally poor state of preservation the Rylands Genizah manuscripts can contribute less to the discussion of writing than some other subcollections.

5.3 Scribal Practices

The manuscripts can also be described in terms of the scribal practices they show. By scribal practices we mean how those who wrote the texts prepared the material to receive the writing (ruling, margins, etc.), how they marked corrections, how they bound the sheets up into codices – the whole area generally known as codicology, though it covers the writing of scrolls as well as codices. A useful checklist of the kind of things to look for can be found in Emanuel Tov's *Scribal Practices of the Dead Sea Scrolls* (2004). One general point seems clear: documentary texts and texts written by amateurs for their private use were not prepared as carefully as literary texts written by professional scribes. In fact in many cases they don't seem to have been prepared at all: the writers did not bother even to rule them, but simply wrote what they had to write, usually in a cursive hand. This observation may seem unsurprising but it is worth making. It is not as obvious as at first sight it appears to be. The eyes and hands of scribes were better trained, and it is perfectly conceivable that they would have needed less than amateurs the 'crutch' of ruling to keep their lines straight, However, it does seem to be the case that it was the professional scribes who ruled, and this is often clearly borne out by the quality of the handwriting.

It is a cardinal assumption in codicology that scribal practices differ from region to region, and these regional variations can be useful in confirming the provenance of a given manuscript. The Genizah manuscripts might help to establish whether there were distinctive Egyptian practices. The general impression one gets is of astonishing uniformity across space and time. Many of the basic scribal practices in evidence in the Genizah seem to differ surprisingly little from those we find in the Dead Sea Scrolls.

An interesting question is how scribes copied codices. Copying on a scroll is relatively simple. You simply start copying on to your sheets (assuming you are working with parchment), numbering them or using catchwords as you go, and then stitch them together. In ancient times, if you were copying on to papyrus it was even simpler, because the scroll came already made up. You copied your text into it, and then cut it off from the roll. But copying codices was more complicated. In the case of *pinakes* there was no problem: you copied into an already made up notebook. But these seem to have been used only for working notes. There is evidence that any scholar worth his salt kept notebooks into which he copied excerpts from texts which interested him as they became (temporarily) available. The Talmud refers to such a notebook as a *Siprā dᵉ-'aggādātā*.[23] The existence of these notebooks among our medieval Hebrew manuscripts has, perhaps, not received the attention it deserves. It means that when we find a fragment of text from a high status religious work written in a non-professional hand we cannot assume that it comes from a complete copy of that work, or even a copy of a substantial portion of it. It could just as easily have come from an excerpt contained in a scholar's notebook. Formal codices of high status religious works, however, were not copied into already made up volumes. What seems to have happened is that a copyist created fascicules of predetermined size (by tacking together a number of sheets) and copied into those, the sequence of fascicules being indicated in some way, to allow the volume to be made up (Beit-Arié 1988, 1993b). The Genizah has, undoubtedly, a part to play in elucidating these questions, but, as with handwriting, the contribution specifically of the Rylands subcollection is reduced by the fact that its fragments are small and rather badly preserved. For example it does contain quite a number of bifolia, but as far as we can see they add little or nothing to our knowledge of how codices were created.

5.4 Formats and Size

There are three main formats in which manuscripts are found: (1) scrolls; (2) codices; and (3) single sheets. There are a few fragments of scroll in Rylands Genizah: e.g. A 1108, B 2404, B 5049 all come from one scroll, and B 3104 and B 8129 from another, both written by Abraham ben Isaac ibn al-Baqara (who flourished in the eleventh century), and containing text from the Talmud. Talmud written on scrolls is somewhat puzzling. In the middle ages the only high status religious texts normally written on scrolls were the Torah and Megillat Esther. The use of the codex for high status texts was probably a Christian innovation, or at least they popularized it,[24] but one would assume that the codex was the standard format among Jews for all types of text, save the two mentioned, by the eleventh century. And it is surely somewhat puzzling that we do not find more traces of decommissioned Torah Scrolls in the Genizah (the only possible example in the Rylands is, apparently, the tiny fragment A 333).

---

23 E.g., b. Ber. 23a, 23b; b. Git. 60a. The term probably denotes a notebook with written content. The notebook itself may have been known as *dipᵉrā'ôt*, plural of *dipᵉrâ* (Greek *diphterai*; cf. Latin *membranae*) or as a *pinqās* (Greek *pinax*) (Jastrow 304a, 1165b). The use of the term *qunṭrēs* for a notebook is a medieval development.

24 See the classic study by Roberts and Skeat 1983, more recently: Hurtado 2006.

Single sheets would have been used not only for everyday documents such as letters (several hundreds in the Rylands in Hebrew [e.g. A 1016, A 1092], Judaeo-Arabic [e.g. A 19, A 120], and Judaeo-Spanish [A 1184]), but also important legal texts such as *K^e^tubbôt* (e.g. A 460, A 904, A 918, B 2078, B 3085, B 4925) and *Giṭṭîn* (e.g. B 5541).

Fragments of codices abound in the Genizah, with some rare traces of stitching and binding. One curious fact about the Rylands Genizah is that a sizeable number of its codices seem to have been very small, certainly in comparison to the generality of Hebrew manuscripts known from Europe. In a paper presented to a workshop on Prayer and Liturgical Poetry held at the Rylands in 2008, Elisabeth Hollender demonstrated that the majority of the Rylands corpus of liturgical and piyyutic fragments comes from very small codices, in modern terms roughly decimo-sexto in size or less! Two examples: (1) A 611, a fully vocalized manuscript of the Passover Haggadah. On the recto (A 611-1) the list of the last seven of the ten plagues, from *'ārôb* to *makkat b^e^kôrôt*, is visible, and the beginning of the Rabban Gamliel section. There is very little text missing from the ends of the lines, and yet the fragment is only 10.5 cm wide. The original cannot have been much more than 12.0 cm. (2) A 29-7+8 (see Plates), a fragment of the well-known poem *Eliyāhû ha-Nābî*, commonly recited at home after the Havdalah service. It is preserved to its full height of 9.2 cm. It was a tiny booklet with embellished headings. This phenomenon is not confined to strictly liturgical material, but found in legal and scientific texts as well. B 6314 is a case in point. This contained a fragment of *Hilkôt Ḥāmēṣ u-Maṣṣâ* from the *Mishneh Torah* of Maimonides. The recto displays section 9.22 and the verso 9.24. Despite the very small size of the fragment (9.2 x 5.6) not much text is missing. The original cannot have been much more than 15.0 cm high and 12.0 cm wide. The odd thing is that the letters in proportion to the page are large. In general, though this is by no means universal, small letters suggest a small manuscript, but this is not true in this case. It would be totally impractical to copy the whole of the *Mishneh Torah* on this scale, so one must assume that what we have here is a small booklet which extracted from Maimonides' code just the laws of *ḥāmēṣ* and *maṣṣâ*. The usefulness of this in preparing for Pesaḥ is obvious.

There is an intriguing parallel to this phenomenon of small manuscripts at Qumran. A surprising number of the manuscripts there come from what Emanuel Tov calls 'miniature scrolls'. What is the significance of this phenomenon? Certainly small manuscripts save material and consequently expense, and have a certain aesthetic appeal, but this surely cannot be the whole story. The size must be related to practicality and ease of handling in the situation in which they were envisaged to be used, and this is consonant with the damage to the manuscripts, which often suggests hard use. It is surely significant that the small size correlates so strongly with liturgical texts. In the Christian world we find, both before and after the invention of printing, that it is liturgy more than any other genre that generates small formats, and the reason is obvious: people wanted to have their prayerbooks in their hand during public or private devotions. The small size was related to ease of carrying. But there is a problem here. How were they carried? It has been suggested that the miniature scrolls from Qumran, when carried, would have been placed in the fold of the dress above the belt known in Greek as the *kolpos*. But did Arab dress have a *kolpos*? In the Byzantine world and the Latin West in the middle ages the practice was to carry books in a book-satchel tailored to fit the volume and hung on a strap from the neck, or from the belt. A number of these book-satchels survive, and they are shown in carvings and illuminations (Waterer 1968 [1969]).[25] But was this the custom also in the Arabic-speaking world? One conclusion we can reasonably draw from the prevalence of miniature codices is that it points to widespread private ownership of books and the widespread consumption of written texts in everyday life.

5.5 Repair and Reuse

One striking feature of the Rylands Genizah, and of the Genizah as a whole, is the evidence it presents of the hard, continuous use of manuscripts, and the recycling of their material when their life was deemed to have come to an end. There are examples of repair, aimed at prolonging the text's life. They range from the crude, as in A 36, a copy of Targum Onqelos, where a piece of rough cloth has been clumsily used to join two torn bits of manuscript together, to the painstaking and skilful, as in B 3108, a page from the Cremona printed edition of the Zohar (1559), which suffered damage on its outer edge (see Plates). The damage was neatly trimmed into the shape of a large triangle, extending from the outer edge deep into the page, and a patch of new paper carefully pasted in. The missing words of the text were then restored by hand in a script which attempts to match in size and form the letters of the printed text. The

25 Girdle-books were worn in the Latin West as a fashion accessory, to indicate the wearer's status and literacy, or even as amulets to ward off harm, but it is hard to see any of these reasons as applying to the Genizah miniature codices. We are grateful to Caroline Checkley-Scott of the John Rylands Library for informing us about book-satchels, and showing us examples from Egypt (Coptic) and Ethiopia.

work, which must surely have been done by a trained scribe, is so well executed as momentarily to deceive the eye.

A rather different example of renewing rather than discarding a text is provided by manuscripts originally with supralinear pointing, to which Tiberian vowels have subsequently been added. Where Tiberian vowels have been supplied they are usually sporadic and rather crudely done, suggesting a do-it-yourself effort by the owner of the manuscript. Rather than pay for a new copy of the text with the up-to-date pointing the owner took his old copy and modernised it himself.[26]

Evidence for re-use takes various forms. Blank material within a manuscript is not infrequently requisitioned for notes and memoranda which have nothing to do with the content of the volume. This may have happened in some cases after a codex was disbound and turned into scrap, but it may also have occurred while the codex was still intact, a page or a piece actually being torn from the book! B 3078 contains on the recto (B 3078-1) the text of Targum Onqelos to Leviticus 23:40–3 and on the verso (B 3078-2) a text in a different hand (possibly Maimonides'), which, though we have not managed to decipher it, is clearly not Onqelos. The implication seems to be that someone used a blank space in an Onqelos manuscript to write a note, though why there should have been a blank in a copy of Onqelos to Leviticus at this point is a bit of a puzzle. B 2349 recto (B 2349-1) contains a note written by a student to his teacher Rav Ḥabibai asking him about the meaning of the biblical words *šēš* and *tašbēṣ* (cf. Ex. 28:4-5). The handwriting is a very confident cursive, and the piece illustrates communication between student and teacher in a Beit Midrash setting. It is interesting that the student did not pose his question, which only amounts to a few lines, verbally to his teacher, but wrote it down. The beginning of the teacher's reply is preserved, and seems to have opened with an apology, perhaps for a delay in answering. This is written on the back of a totally different text (B 2349-2) which seems to be about metempsychosis (*gilgûl ha-nᵉšāmôt*) and sacrifice (see Plates). This is a well-known problem. What has happened to the soul of Aaron? Has it been reincarnated in the present generation, and what would the priestly status be of the individual who had received Aaron's soul? What is the sacrificial status of an animal that has received the soul of a human? The writing is again a flowing, confident cursive, and may be a responsum or treatise on *gilgûl*. The top and side margins are ruled, but this ruling is not replicated on the other side (B 2349-1). The two texts are totally unconnected as to content, and are written at right angles to each other (B

26 See Chapter 3 below.

2349-1 in 'landscape', and B 2349-2 in 'portrait'). B 2349-2 is surely the earlier text. It refers to Rabbi Ovadya Bertinoro (lines 2 and 8), so must be at least sixteenth century.

We have examples of palimpsests. A well-known case is P 49, which joins to Taylor-Schechter 16.326. The underwriting is a Christian Palestinian version of 1 Thess. 3:1–13, the overwriting a passage from Yerushalmi ʿEruvin.[27] The parchment Bible Gaster 15 also looks like a palimpsest, though we cannot identify the underwriting. The fact that *Jews* reused *Christian* manuscripts in this way may point to some sort of trade in scrap. Parchment manuscripts, which can be quite successfully cleaned, were recycled after they were no longer needed in their original form, and traded as cheap writing material. Who would have rubbed off the underwriting? Possibly the trader. Old books would be sold to a dealer, who would then add value to them by disbinding them, rubbing off the handwriting as best he could, and selling the sheets.

The recycling of manuscripts raises some interesting questions regarding attitudes towards religious texts. The very existence of the Genizah is often seen as evidence for high respect among the Jews of Cairo for the written word, but some forms of reuse suggest there were limits to this. Manuscripts were torn and doodled on in ways which suggest a very functional attitude towards them. A lot may have depended on the status of the text in question. The text on *gilgûl* in B 2349-2 may have been regarded as of little intrinsic sanctity — simply the notes of some scholar; but Onqelos was surely a text of some standing, and to casually use it for a scribbled note, as in B 3078-2, especially if the Rambam was the author of that note, is a little surprising. We should not forget the state in which the manuscripts existed within the Genizah was anything but dignified. They were subject to attack by insects and rodents. And during the rebuilding of the Ben Ezra synagogue between 1889 and 1892 large quantities of the 'holy' texts from the Genizah were, apparently, unceremoniously dumped outside.[28] The whole cultural attitude of the Jews of Cairo towards 'holy' texts as physical objects needs to be rethought, and the ways in which they were reused should be seen as part of the evidence. One thing is clear, and it is that many of the texts were in very active use: they were, in some cases, literally used to destruction, and that simple fact tells its own story.

---

27 Smith Lewis 1900; Baars 1960; Sokoloff and Yahalom 1978; Ginzberg 1909: fragments 95, 100–1.

28 Where some of them were rescued by Count d'Hulst: see Jefferson 2009, and further the 'Introduction' to the present volume. On the architectural history of the Ben Ezra synagogue see Lambert *et al.*, 2001.

5.6 Reconstruction

The study of the physical and material aspects of the fragments forms the basis for any attempt to reconstruct the texts, fill lacunae and generally reverse the ravages of time. By way of an addendum to the foregoing analysis we would like to say a few words on this subject. Coming from the study of the Dead Sea Scrolls, one is immediately struck by how little reconstruction is attempted on the Genizah manuscripts. In the case of the Scrolls it is regularly attempted, sometimes to excess. Some have claimed to recover whole scrolls from a few handfuls of fragments, or to reconstruct whole columns from a few lines. Reasons for this difference of scholarly practice spring to mind. The first has to do with resources: there are many more scholars working on the Scrolls than on the Genizah, and there is a desire in the case of the Scrolls, which often contain hitherto unknown texts, to squeeze out of them the maximum amount of information they can yield. But the differences in format between the texts in the respective collections may also have something to do with it. The patterns of decay in the case of scrolls are now rather well understood, and they help reconstruction. One can, for example, by observing the pattern of decay in a scroll sometimes work out the diameter of the turn of the scroll at a given point, and from this make a rough calculation as to how much of the scroll remained between this point and the end. Anyone who has worked on the Scrolls knows the phenomenon of the 'pile' — a series of overlapping fragments of the same shape but decreasing size which can be a help in reconstructing and arranging the fragments in the correct order. Maybe the pattern of decay in the cases of codices is not so helpful in this regard, though even a little reflection will make it obvious that they too must have decayed to a pattern. An obvious aid to the reconstruction of codices is bifolia, which, if they don't constitute the innermost bifolium of the quire, may enable us to calculate how many folios are missing in between — provided, of course, the text is already known. Clearly a lot of time and resources can be expended for limited results (this is certainly an issue in the case of the Scrolls), but it surprising how little reconstruction is attempted in the case of the Genizah, e.g., calculation of line length and page size from surviving fragment(s), again in the case of a known work. There is a real danger of being too logocentric in our approach to manuscripts, too fixated on the written text. We need to adopt a more forensic approach, which treats the whole fragment — its shape and size, the patterns of its decay, its physical condition, the way it was written, its handwriting, as well as its text — as evidence for its historical and cultural meaning. The study of manuscripts as artefacts, just as much as the study of them as texts, provides important evidence for interpreting their cultural and historical significance. It illuminates how one particular, clearly defined community in a known locality at a certain period of time produced and consumed texts. The implications of the Genizah in this area are potentially vast. It illustrates levels of literacy both in terms of reading and writing in the context of both everyday life and the practice of religion. It throws light on book collecting and library-building, and on the book trade (the business of professionally copying and circulating high-status texts), as well as many other facets of the intellectual and material life of the Jews of medieval and early modern Cairo.[29]

Conclusion

In conclusion we would stress that these notes are preliminary and tentative. They offer, hopefully, not only the beginnings of an account of what is typical about the Rylands Genizah, but, equally importantly, they raise the questions that need to be answered, more fully and definitively than we can manage at the present, to create such an account. In particular much statistical analysis and 'number crunching' remains to be done, but this will have to await the creation of a complete, searchable database not only for the Rylands collection but for the Genizah as a whole.

References

Anonymous. 1954. 'Notes and News', *Bulletin of the John Rylands Library Manchester* 37/1, esp. 2–6

— 1958. 'Notes and News', *Bulletin of the John Rylands Library Manchester* 40/2, esp. 260–1

Baars, Willem. 1960. 'A Palestinian Syriac Text of the Book of Lamentations', *Vetus Testamentum* 10, 224–7

Beit-Arié, Malachi. 1988. 'How Hebrew Manuscripts Are Made', in L.S. Gold (ed.), *A Sign and a Witness – 2000 Years of Hebrew Books and Illuminated Manuscripts* (New York/Oxford). 35–46

— 1989. 'The Contribution of the Fustat Genizah to Hebrew Palaeography', *Pe'amim* 41, 32–40 (in Hebrew)

— 1993a. *Hebrew Manuscripts of East and West: Towards a Comparative Codicology*. (The Panizzi Lectures 1992; The British Library: London)

— 1993b. *The Makings of the Medieval Hebrew Book*. (Jerusalem)

Crown, Alan D. 1998. *A Catalogue of the Samaritan Manuscripts in the British Library*. (London)

Deletant, Dennis. 1975. 'A Survey of the Gaster Books in the School of Slavonic and East European Studies Library', *Solanus: Bulletin of the Slavonic and East European Group of SCONUL* 10, 14–23

---

29 Note the existence of library lists among the Genizah manuscripts (Frenkel 1999). The starting point for such cultural analysis remains Goitein 1967–1993: on libraries, see vol. 5, 4, 80; on booklists, see vol. 2, 206, 248; vol. 5, 3–4, 425; on bookselling, see vol. 1, 64, 196, 334–5, 382; vol. 2, 189, 515, 560, 597; vol. 5, 457; on books as valuable objects, see vol. 1, 259 (collateral); vol. 1, 266 and vol. 4, 311 (as heirlooms). The one subject about which Goitein seems to say little or nothing is book-production!

Engel, Edna. 1999. 'Styles of Hebrew Script in the Tenth and Eleventh Centuries in the Light of the Dated and Datable Genizah Documents', in Friedman (ed.), *A Century of Geniza Research* (Tel Aviv). 365–412

Frenkel, Miriam. 1999. 'Book Lists as a Source from the Cultural and Social History of the Jews in Mediterranean Society', in Friedman (ed.), *A Century of Geniza Research* (Tel Aviv). 333–50

Friedman, Mordechai A. (ed.). 1999. *A Century of Geniza Research.* (Tel Aviv)

Gaster, Moses. 1995 (with a preface by Brad Sabin Hill). *Handlist of Gaster Manuscripts Held Mostly in the British Library (Formerly British Museum) London, and in the John Rylands Library, Manchester.* (London)

Ginzberg, Louis. 1909. *Yerushalmi Fragments from the Genizah. Text with Various [sic] Readings from the Editio Princeps.* (New York) (repr. Hildesheim 1970 and Jerusalem 1974)

Goitein, Solomon Dov. 1967–93. *A Mediterranean Society: The Jewish Communities of the Arab World as Portrayed in the Documents of the Cairo Geniza.* 6 vols, (Berkeley)

Haralambakis, Maria. 2012. *Boxlist of Moses Gaster's Working Papers at the John Rylands Library.* http://www.manchesterjewishstudies.org/storage/Gaster%20boxlist.pdf

Hill, Brad Sabin. 1995. *The Gaster Collection of Rumanian Printed Books Held in the Library of the School of Slavonic and East European Studies.* (London, 1995)

— 2006. 'The YIVO Collection of "Moses Gaster Papers"', *YIVO News*

Hollender, Elisabeth. 2011. '"Genizot Germania": A Projected Comprehensive Electronic Catalogue of Hebrew Fragments from Bindings of Books or Archival Files in German Libraries and Archives', in R. Leicht and G. Freudenthal (eds), *Studies in Steinschneider: Moritz Steinschneider and the Emergence of the Science of Judaism in the Nineteenth Century* (Leiden). 531-45

Hurtado, Larry W. 2006. *The Earliest Christian Artifacts: Manuscripts and Christian Origins.* (Grand Rapids, MI)

Jefferson, Rebecca J.W. 2009. 'A Genizah Secret: The Count d'Hulst and Letters Revealing the Race to Recover the Lost Leaves of the Original Ecclesiastes', *Journal of the History of Collections* 21/1, 125–42

— 2010. 'The Cairo Genizah Unearthed: The Excavations Conducted by the Count d'Hulst on Behalf of the Bodleian Library and their Significance for Genizah History', in B. Outhwaite and S. Bhayro (eds), *"From a Sacred Source": Genizah Studies in Honour of Professor Stefan C. Reif* (Leiden/Boston). 171–99

Lambert, Phyllis et al. 2001. *Fortifications and the Synagogue: The Fortress of Babylon and the Ben Ezra Synagogue, Cairo.* (Montreal)

Neubauer, Adolf and Arthur E. Cowley. 1886–1906. *Catalogue of the Hebrew Manuscripts in the Bodleian Library.* 3 vols, (Oxford)

Nir-el, Yoram and Magen Broshi. 1996a. 'The Black Ink of the Dead Sea Scrolls', *Dead Sea Discoveries* 3, 157–67

— 1996b. 'The Red Ink of the Dead Sea Scrolls', *Archaeometry* 38, 97–102

Parsons, Peter J. 2007. *City of the Sharp-Nosed Fish.* (London)

Roberts, Colin H. and Theodore C. Skeat. 1983. *The Birth of the Codex.* (London)

Robertson, Edward. 1962. *Catalogue of the Samaritan Manuscripts in the John Rylands Library Manchester*, vol. 2 – the Gaster Manuscripts. (Manchester)

Smith Lewis, Agnes 1900. *Palestinian Syriac Texts from Palimpsest Fragments in the Taylor-Schechter Collection.* (London) (repr. Piscataway, NJ, 2005)

Sokoloff, Michael and Joseph Yahalom. 1978. 'Christian Palimpsests from the Cairo Geniza', *Revue d'histoire des texts* 8, 109–22

Tov, Emanuel. 2004. *Scribal Practices and Approaches Reflected in the Texts Found in the Judaean Desert.* (Leiden)

Waterer, John W. 1968 [1969]. 'Irish Book-Satchels or Budgets', *Medieval Archeology* 12, 70–82

Plate 1: A 29-7, the liturgical poem *Eliyāhû ha-Nābî* in miniature. (Reproduced by courtesy of the University Librarian and Director, The John Rylands Library, The University of Manchester)

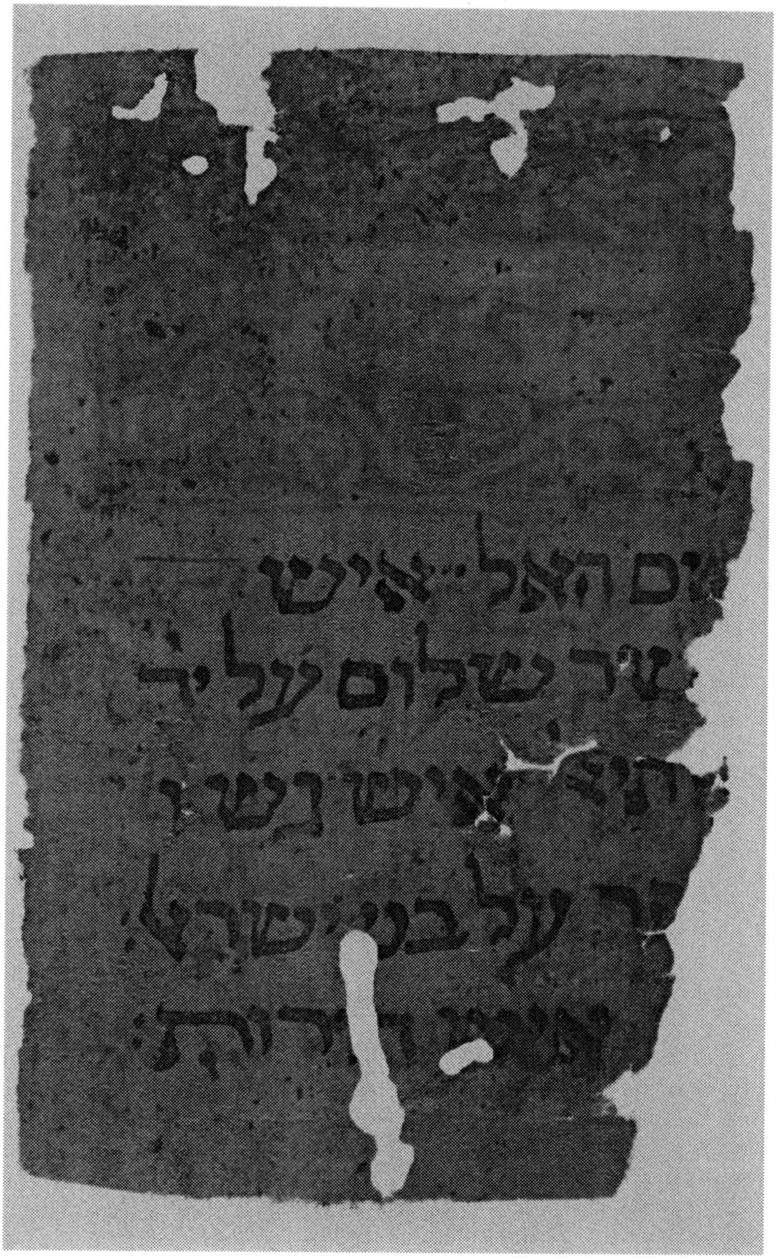

Plate 2: A 29-8, the liturgical poem *Eliyāhû ha-Nābî* in miniature. (Reproduced by courtesy of the University Librarian and Director, The John Rylands Library, The University of Manchester)

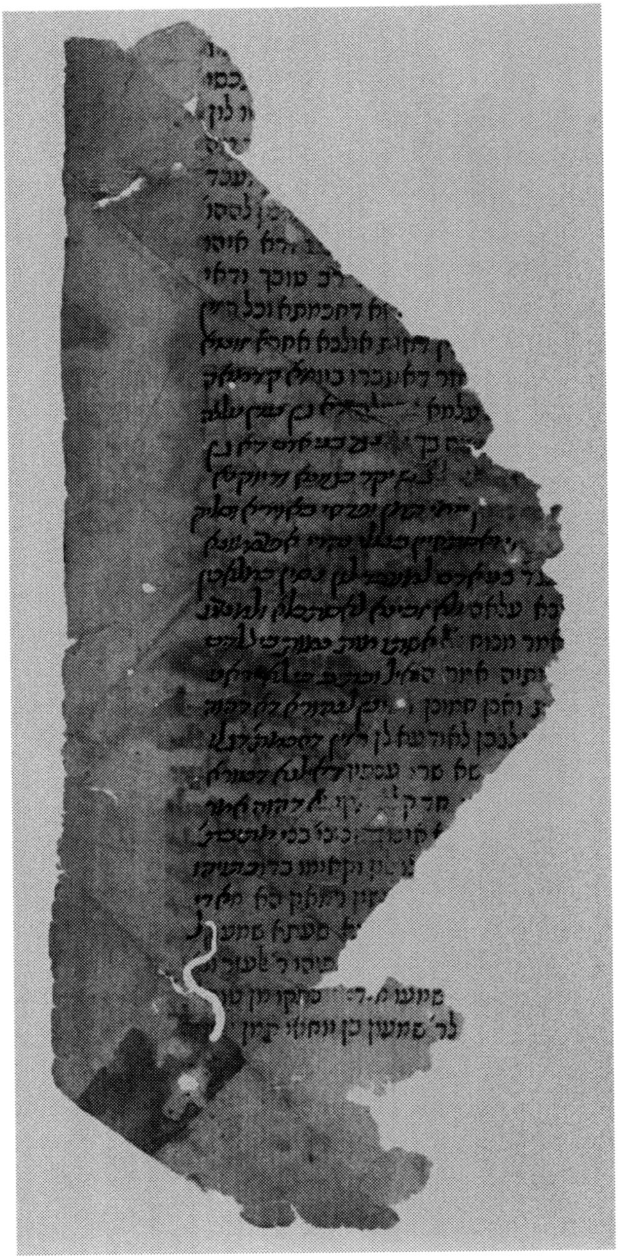

Plate 3: B 3108-1, carefully restored page from a printed Zohar. (Reproduced by courtesy of the University Librarian and Director, The John Rylands Library, The University of Manchester)

Plate 4: B 3108-2, carefully restored page from a printed Zohar. (Reproduced by courtesy of the University Librarian and Director, The John Rylands Library, The University of Manchester)

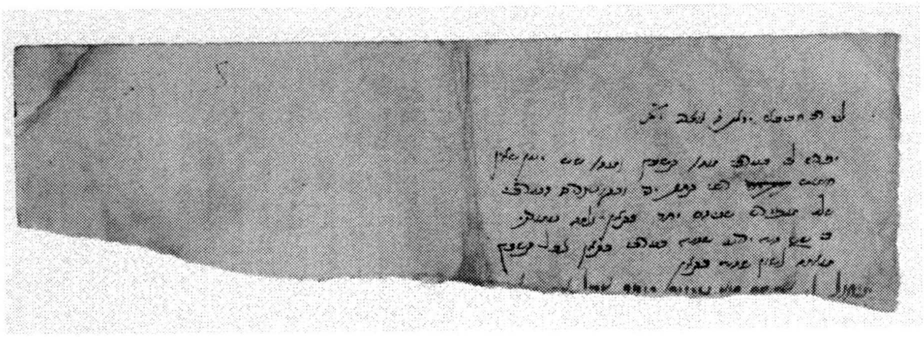

Plate 5: B 2349-1, note from a student to his teacher. (Reproduced by courtesy of the University Librarian and Director, The John Rylands Library, The University of Manchester)

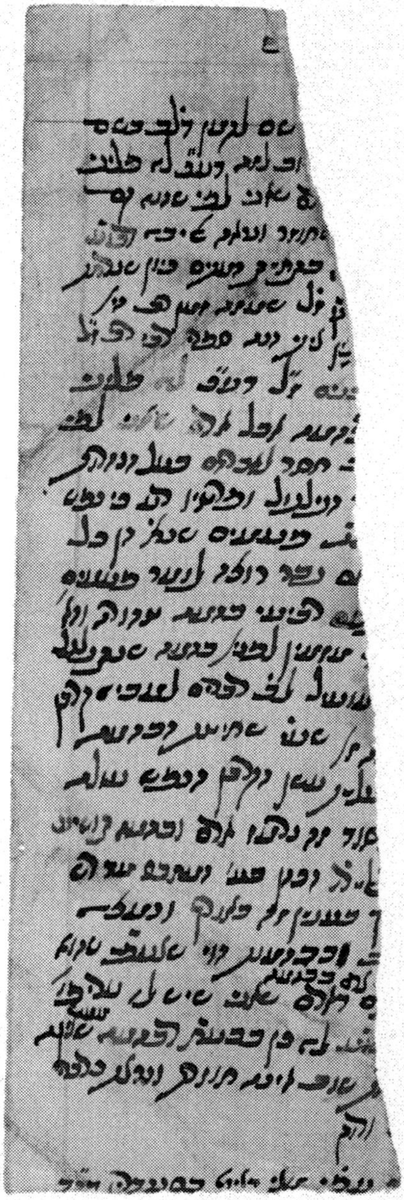

Plate 6: B 2349-2, on metempsychosis. (Reproduced by courtesy of the University Librarian and Director, The John Rylands Library, The University of Manchester)

Targum Manuscripts in the Rylands Genizah

Renate Smithuis and Philip Alexander
University of Manchester

The Rylands Genizah as a Subcollection of the Cairo Genizah

In Chapter 2 of the present volume we argued that collections of manuscripts can be seen as artefacts in their own right, with their own distinctive character, in comparison and contrast to other manuscript collections. In the case of the Cairo Genizah the situation is complex. An original collection, housed in a synagogue in Old Cairo, has now been scattered to various locations across the world, and spawned a set of subcollections. These new collections can be characterized not only in their own right, and in relation to each other, but in relation to the original, mother collection, which no longer exists physically in one place, but is in process of being reassembled in cyberspace.

The purpose of this chapter is to carry forward the analysis of the character of the Rylands Genizah by examining one literary genre of text found within it, namely Targum. Targum is a useful genre to investigate, since there is a significant number of fragments of it not only in the Rylands Genizah, but in the other Genizah subcollections as well. Analysing the Rylands Targum manuscripts will generate a set of hypotheses about the character of the Rylands subcollection, which can be tested in respect of other data.

We noted in Chapter 2 that there was evidence to suggest that not all the Rylands Genizah actually originated in the Cairo Genizah, and strictly speaking we ought to enclose 'Genizah' in this instance in scare quotes. The Rylands 'Genizah' material has been seeded by items from other sources. This does not negate our analysis but, actually, enhances it. The bulk of the Rylands material is unquestionably from Old Cairo, and that allows us to construe the non-Ben Ezra element as 'contamination'. The extent of this contamination, which is found also in other Genizah subcollections, can be regarded as one aspect of the character of the Rylands collection. The basic premise we are working on is that whatever its source, and whatever principles or lack of them lay behind its creation, what we are loosely calling the Rylands Genizah now exists as a physical archive under one roof, and that means it can be described and characterised. The purpose of this chapter is to explore further a methodology for doing this.

Preliminary Catalogue of the Rylands Targum Manuscripts

We begin with a preliminary listing of all the Targum manuscripts in the Rylands Genizah. The description of the fragments follows basically the method established by the editors of the catalogues of the Cambridge Genizah collections. The descriptions are per side of fragment, rather than per fragment, as this makes it easier to correlate with the images in the online database. Measurements give the vertical dimensions first followed by the horizontal, and are in centimetres. The catalogue is, to the best of our current knowledge, exhaustive for fragments A 1-B 7000 and Bible Gaster 1-83, though there may well be fragments we have missed, and there may be fragments which we have misidentified. It represents work in progress.

1a. A 36-1 (together with A 36-2,3,4; A 37-1,2; A 194-1,2; join between A 36-1,2,3,4 and A 37-1,2; A 36-1,2 consists of two fragments held together by a piece of cloth – an early repair). Targum Jonathan to the Prophets: 1 Samuel 15:30–2 and, upside down, Ezekiel 36:35–6. Sections from the *Hapṭārôt* for the Sabbaths preceding and following Purim (*Pārāšat Zākôr*, *Pārāšat Pārâ*). Languages: Hebrew lemmata and Aramaic alternating. Vocalisation: Tiberian (Hebrew), Babylonian (Aramaic). Accents (Hebrew). Paper (and cloth for the repair). Recto. 8.4 x 18.1. 8 lines.

1b. A 36-2 (together with A 36-1,3,4; A 37-1,2; A 194-1,2; join between A 36-1,2,3,4 and A 37-1,2; A 36-1,2 consists of two fragments held together by a piece of cloth – an early repair). Targum Jonathan to the Prophets: Ezekiel 36:18-20 and, upside down, Ezekiel 45:12–13. Sections from the *Hapṭārôt* for the Sabbaths following Purim and preceding the second day of Nisan (*Pārāšat Pārâ*, *Pārāšat ha-Ḥodeš*). Languages: Hebrew lemmata and Aramaic alternating. Vocalisation: Tiberian (Hebrew), Babylonian (Aramaic). Accents (Hebrew). Paper (and cloth for the repair). Verso. 8.4 x 18.1. 6 lines.

1c. A 36-3 (together with A 36-1,2,4; A 37-1,2; A 194-1,2; join between A 36-1,2,3,4 and A 37-1,2). Targum Jonathan to the Prophets: 1 Samuel 15:29–30. Section from the *Hapṭārâ* for the Sabbath preceding Purim (*Pārāšat Zākôr*). Languages: Hebrew lemmata and Aramaic alternating. Vocalisation: Tiberian (Hebrew), Babylonian (Aramaic). Accents (Hebrew). Paper. Recto. 3.8 x 2.8. 4 lines.

1d. A 36-4 (together with A 36-1,2,3; A 37-1,2; A 194-1,2; join between A 36-1,2,3,4 and A 37-1,2). Targum Jonathan to the Prophets: Ezekiel 36:17–18. Section from the *Hapṭārâ* for the Sabbath following Purim (*Pārāšat Pārâ*). Languages: Hebrew lemmata and Aramaic alternating. Vocalisation: Tiberian (Hebrew), Babylonian (Aramaic). Accents (Hebrew). Paper. Verso. 3.8 x 2.8. 4 lines.

1e. A 37-1 (together with A 36-1,2,3,4; A 37-2; A 194-1,2; join between A 36-1,2,3,4 and A 37-1,2). Targum Jonathan to the Prophets: 1 Samuel 15:28–32. Section from the *Hapṭārâ* for the Sabbath preceding Purim (*Pārāšat Zākôr*). Languages: Hebrew lemmata and Aramaic alternating. Vocalisation: Tiberian (Hebrew), Babylonian (Aramaic). Accents (Hebrew). Paper. Recto. 12.4 x 5.2. 13 lines.

1f. A 37-2 (together with A 36-1,2,3,4; A 37-1; A 194-1,2; join between A 36-1,2,3,4 and A 37-1,2). Targum Jonathan to the Prophets: Ezekiel 36:16–19. Section from the *Hapṭārâ* for the Sabbath following Purim (*Pārāšat Pārâ*). Languages: Hebrew lemmata and Aramaic alternating. Vocalisation: Tiberian (Hebrew), Babylonian (Aramaic). Accents (Hebrew). Paper. Verso. 12.4 x 5.2. 13 lines.

1g. A 194-1 (together with A 36-1,2,3,4; A 37-1,2; A 194-2). Targum Jonathan to the Prophets. Ezekiel 36:36; 45:9. Sections from the *Hapṭārôt* for the Sabbaths following Purim and preceding the second day of Nisan (*Pārāšat Pārâ, Pārāšat ha-Ḥodeš*). Liturgical information in large letters. Languages: Hebrew lemmata and Aramaic alternating. Vocalisation: Tiberian (Hebrew), Babylonian (Aramaic). Accents (Hebrew). Paper. Recto. 10.8 x 8.4. 9 lines.

1h. A 194-2 (together with A 36-1,2,3,4; A 37-1,2; A 194-1). Targum Jonathan to the Prophets: Ezekiel 45:11–14. Section from the *Hapṭārâ* for the Sabbath preceding the second day of Nisan (*Pārāšat ha-Ḥodeš*). Languages: Hebrew lemmata and Aramaic alternating. Vocalisation: Tiberian (Hebrew), Babylonian (Aramaic). Accents (Hebrew). Paper. Verso. 10.8 x 8.4. 9 lines.

2a. A 204-1 (together with A 204-2). Targum Onqelos and Saadya's Tafsīr: Numbers 1:34-5. Languages: Hebrew lemmata with Aramaic and Judaeo-Arabic alternating. Vocalisation: Tiberian (Hebrew, Aramaic). Accents (Hebrew). Paper. Recto. 14.2 x 9.5. 14 lines.

2b. A 204-2 (together with A 204-1). Targum Onqelos and Saadya's Tafsīr: Numbers 1:36-7. Languages: Hebrew lemmata with Aramaic and Judaeo-Arabic alternating. Vocalisation: Tiberian (Hebrew, Aramaic). Accents (Hebrew). Paper. Verso. 14.2 x 9.5. 15 lines.

3a. A 565-1 (together with A 565-2). Targum Onqelos: Exodus 28:31–3 (+ 28:30 in the left margin). Marginal correction. Languages: Hebrew lemmata and Aramaic alternating. Vocalisation: Tiberian (Hebrew, Aramaic). Paper. Recto. 7.3 x 11.4. 8 lines.

3b. A 565-2 (together with A 565-1). Targum Onqelos: Exodus 28:35-7. Languages: Hebrew lemmata and Aramaic alternating. Vocalisation: Tiberian (Hebrew, Aramaic). Paper. Verso. 7.3 x 11.4. 7 lines.

4a. A 664-1 (together with A 664-2,3,4,5,6). Targum Onqelos and Saadya's Tafsīr; Genesis 21:16–17. Languages: Hebrew lemmata (visible on A 664-5,6) with Aramaic and Judaeo-Arabic alternating. Paper. Recto. 7.7 x 5.8. 5 lines.

4b. A 664-2 (together with A 664-1,3,4,5,6). Targum Onqelos and Saadya's Tafsīr: Genesis 21:22–3. Languages: Hebrew lemmata (visible on A 664-5,6) with Aramaic and Judaeo-Arabic alternating. Paper. Verso. 7.7 x 5.8. 5 lines.

4c. A 664-3 (together with A 664-1,2,4,5,6). Targum Onqelos and Saadya's Tafsīr: Genesis 21:28–9. Languages: Hebrew lemmata (visible on A 664-5,6) with Aramaic and Judaeo-Arabic alternating. Paper. Recto. 8.2 x 10.6. 5 lines.

4d. A 664-4 (together with A 664-1,2,3,5,6). Targum Onqelos and Saadya's Tafsīr: Genesis 22:1. Hebrew liturgical information on line 1. Languages: Hebrew lemmata (visible on A 664-5,6), Aramaic and Judaeo-Arabic alternating. Paper. Verso. 8.2 x 10.6. 5 lines.

4e. A 664-5 (together with A 664-1,2,3,4,6). Targum Onqelos and Saadya's Tafsīr: Genesis 22:5–6. Languages: Hebrew lemmata with Aramaic and Judaeo-Arabic alternating. Paper. Recto. 7.8 x 11.8. 5 lines.

4f. A 664-6 (together with A 664-1,2,3,4,5). Targum Onqelos and Saadya's Tafsīr: Genesis 22:9–10. Languages: Hebrew lemmata with Aramaic and Judaeo-Arabic alternating. Paper. Verso. 7.8 x 11.8. 4 lines.

5a. A 711-1 (together with A 711-2). Content unidentified, possibly a liturgical poem. Languages: Hebrew. Paper. Recto. 6.4 x 7.5. 9 lines.

5b. A 711-2 (together with A 711-1). Targum Onqelos: Exodus 14:28. Languages: Hebrew lemmata and Aramaic alternating. Paper. Verso. 6.4 x 7.5. 7 lines.

6a. A 855-1 (together with A 855-2; A 1098-1,2). Targum Onqelos and Saadya's Tafsīr: Genesis 4:1–3. Languages: Hebrew lemmata with Aramaic and Judaeo-Arabic alternating. Vocalisation: Tiberian (Hebrew, Aramaic). Accents (Hebrew, Aramaic). Paper. Recto. 19.0 x 13.7. 14 lines.

6b. A 855-2 (together with A 855-1; A 1098-1,2). Targum Onqelos and Saadya's Tafsīr: Genesis 4:3–6. Languages: Hebrew lemmata with Aramaic and Judaeo-Arabic alternating. Vocalisation: Tiberian (Hebrew, Aramaic). Accents (Hebrew, Aramaic). Paper. Verso. 19.0 x 13.7. 14 lines.

6c. A 1098-1 (together with A 855-1,2; A 1098-2). Targum Onqelos and Saadya's Tafsīr: Genesis 5:7–10. Languages: Hebrew lemmata with Aramaic and Judaeo-Arabic alternating. Vocalisation: Tiberian (Hebrew, Aramaic). Accents (Hebrew, Aramaic). Paper. Recto. 19.0 x 13.0. 14 lines.

6d. A 1098-2 (together with A 855-1,2; A 1098-1). Targum Onqelos and Saadya's Tafsīr: Genesis 5:10–13. Languages: Hebrew lemmata with Aramaic and Judaeo-Arabic alternating. Vocalisation: Tiberian (Hebrew, Aramaic). Accents (Hebrew, Aramaic). Paper. Verso. 19.0 x 13.0. 14 lines.

7a. A 1000-1 (together with A 1000-2). Targum Onqelos: Leviticus 24:21–3. Languages: Hebrew lemmata and Aramaic alternating. Vocalisation: Tiberian (Hebrew, Aramaic). Accents (Hebrew, Aramaic). Paper. Recto. 6.5 x 14.2. 5 lines.

7b. A 1000-2 (together with A 1000-1). Targum Onqelos: Leviticus 25:5–6. Languages: Hebrew lemmata and Aramaic alternating. Vocalisation: Tiberian (Hebrew, Aramaic). Accents (Hebrew, Aramaic). Paper. Verso. 6.5 x 14.2. 4 lines.

8a. A 1106-1. Targum Onqelos: Exodus 19:23 (lines 1-2), 19:25-20:2 (lines 3-6). Languages: Aramaic (no Hebrew lemmata visible). Vocalisation: Tiberian. Paper. Recto. 8.0 x 6.0. 6 lines.

8b. A 1106-2. Blank. Paper. Verso. 8.0 x 6.0.

9a. A 1295-1 (together with A 1295-2). Targum Onqelos and Saadya's Tafsīr: Genesis 4:26 (left); 5:5–7 (right). Languages: Hebrew lemmata with Aramaic and Judaeo-Arabic alternating. Vocalisation: Tiberian (Hebrew, Aramaic). Accents (Hebrew). Paper. Bifolium, recto. 8.7 x 12.4. 10 lines on each folio.

9b. A 1295-2 (together with A 1295-1). Targum Onqelos and Saadya's Tafsīr: Genesis 5:1-2 (right); 5:3–5 (left). Languages: Hebrew lemmata with Aramaic and Judaeo-Arabic alternating. Vocalisation: Tiberian (Hebrew, Aramaic). Accents (Hebrew). Paper. Bifolium, verso. 8.7 x 12.4. 10 lines on each folio.

10a. A 1420-1. Targum Onqelos: Deuteronomy 2:14. Languages: Hebrew lemmata and Aramaic alternating. Paper. Recto. 3.8 x 5.2. 3 lines.

10b. A 1420-2. Blank. Paper. Verso. 3.8 x 5.2.

11a. A 1466-1. Targum Onqelos: Leviticus 22:7. Languages: Hebrew lemmata and Aramaic alternating. Paper. Recto. 5.6 x 13.6. 2 lines.

11b. A 1466-2. Blank. Paper. Verso. 5.6 x 13.6.

12a. A 1621-3 (together with A 1621-4; A 1621-1,2 from different manuscript). Targum Onqelos: Exodus 39:43–40:3. Languages: Hebrew lemmata (on verso A 1621-4) and Aramaic (on recto A 1621-3) alternating. Vocalisation: Tiberian (Hebrew, Aramaic). Accents (Hebrew, Aramaic). Printed on paper. Recto. 2.5 x 2.1. 4 lines.

12b. A 1621-4 (together with A 1621-3; A 1621-1,2 from different manuscript). Targum Onqelos: Exodus 40:19–20. Languages: Hebrew lemmata (on verso A 1621-4) and Aramaic (on recto A 1621-3) alternating. Vocalisation: Tiberian (Hebrew, Aramaic). Accents (Hebrew, Aramaic). Printed on paper. Verso. 2.5 x 2.1. 4 lines.

13a. A 1649-1 (together with A 1649-2). Targum Onqelos and Saadya's Tafsīr: Genesis 49:11. Languages: Hebrew lemmata with Aramaic and Judaeo-Arabic alternating. Vocalisation: Tiberian (Hebrew, Aramaic). Paper. Recto. 4.7 x 4.3. 2 lines.

13b. A 1649-2 (together with A 1649-1). Targum Onqelos and Saadya's Tafsīr: Genesis 49:16. Languages: Hebrew lemmata with Aramaic and Judaeo-Arabic alternating. Vocalisation: Tiberian (Hebrew, Aramaic). Paper. Verso. 4.7 x 4.3. 2 lines.

14a. A 1681-1 (together with A 1681-2; B 1994-1,2; B 5115-1,2). Targum Onqelos and Saadya's Tafsīr: Exodus 30:5-6. Languages: Hebrew lemmata with Aramaic and Judaeo-Arabic alternating. Vocalisation: Tiberian (Hebrew), Babylonian (Aramaic). Accents (Hebrew). Paper. Recto. 8.7 x 5.6. 9 lines.

14b. A 1681-2 (together with A 1681-1; B 1994-1,2; B 5115-1,2). Targum Onqelos and Saadya's Tafsīr: Exodus 30:16-18. Languages: Hebrew lemmata with Aramaic and Judaeo-Arabic alternating. Vocalisation: Tiberian (Hebrew), Babylonian (Aramaic). Accents (Hebrew). Paper. Verso. 8.7 x 5.6. 8 lines.

14c. B 1994-1 (together with A 1681-1,2; B 1994-2; B 5115-1,2). Targum Onqelos and Saadya's Tafsīr: Exodus 7:16-7, 7:19-20. Languages: Hebrew lemmata with Aramaic and Judaeo-Arabic alternating. Vocalisation: Tiberian (Hebrew), Babylonian (Aramaic). Accents (Hebrew). Paper. Recto. 16.2 x 18.8. 2 columns, 15 lines each.

14d. B 1994-2 (together with A 1681-1,2; B 1994-1; B 5115-1,2). Targum Onqelos and Saadya's Tafsīr: Exodus 7:21-3, 7:26-7. Languages: Hebrew lemmata with Aramaic and Judaeo-Arabic alternating. Vocalisation: Tiberian (Hebrew), Babylonian (Aramaic). Accents (Hebrew). Paper. Verso. 16.2 x 18.8. 2 columns, 15 lines each.

14e. B 5115-1 (together with A 1681-1,2; B 1994-1,2; B 5115-2). Targum Onqelos and Saadya's Tafsīr: Genesis 39:4–5. Languages: Hebrew lemmata with Aramaic and Judaeo-Arabic alternating. Vocalisation: Tiberian (Hebrew), Babylonian (Aramaic). Accents (Hebrew). Paper. Recto. 5.0 x 5.5. 5 lines.

14f. B 5115-2 (together with A 1681-1,2; B 1994-1,2; B 5115-1). Targum Onqelos and Saadya's Tafsīr: Genesis 39:12–13. Languages: Hebrew lemmata with Aramaic and Judaeo-Arabic alternating.

Vocalisation: Tiberian (Hebrew), Babylonian (Aramaic). Accents (Hebrew). Paper. Verso. 5.0 x 5.5. 5 lines.

15a. B 1932-1 (together with B 1932-2). Targum Onqelos: Leviticus 4:35–5:4 (left), 6:2–6 (right). Interlinear and marginal corrections. Languages: Hebrew lemmata and Aramaic alternating. Vocalisation: partial Tiberian (Aramaic). Paper. Bifolium, recto. 13.3 x 34.7. 11 lines on each folio.

15b. B 1932-2 (together with B 1932-1). Targum Onqelos: Leviticus 5:8–12 (right), 5:17–23 (left). Interlinear and marginal corrections. Languages: Hebrew lemmata and Aramaic alternating. Vocalisation: partial Tiberian (Aramaic). Paper. Bifolium, verso. 13.3 x 34.7. 11 lines on each folio.

16a. B 2083-1 (together with B 2083-2). Targum Onqelos: Exodus 24:9–12 (left), 25:6–11 (right). Marginal correction. Languages: Hebrew lemmata and Aramaic alternating. Vocalisation: Tiberian (Hebrew, Aramaic). Accents (Hebrew, Aramaic). Paper. Bifolium, recto. 18.1 x 26.5. 13 lines on each folio.

16b. B 2359-2 (together with B 2359-1). Targum Onqelos: Deuteronomy 5:12–14 (right), 5:17–19 (left). Languages: Hebrew lemmata (on recto B 2359-1) and Aramaic alternating. Vocalisation: Tiberian (Aramaic). Paper. Bifolium, verso. 9.9 x 22.6. 6 lines on each folio.

18a. 2696-1 (together with B 2696-2). Targum Onqelos: Genesis 22:6–7. Languages: Hebrew lemmata and Aramaic alternating. Vocalisation: partial Tiberian (Hebrew, Aramaic). Paper. Recto. 7.4 x 6.3. 6 lines.

18b. 2696-2 (together with B 2696-1). Targum Onqelos: Genesis 22:11–12. Languages: Hebrew lemmata and Aramaic alternating. Vocalisation: partial Tiberian (Hebrew, Aramaic). Paper. Recto. 7.4 x 6.3. 6 lines.

19a. B 2802-1 (together with B 2802-2). Targum Onqelos and Saadya's Tafsīr: Genesis 16:3 (left), 17:19 (right). Languages: Hebrew lemmata (visible on left side verso B 2802-2) with Aramaic and Judaeo-Arabic alternating. Vocalisation: Tiberian (Aramaic). Paper. Bifolium, recto. 12.7 x 15.4. 5 lines on each folio.

19b. B 2802-2 (together with B 2802-1). Targum Onqelos and Saadya's Tafsīr: Genesis 16:4–5 (right), 17:17–19 (left). Languages: Hebrew lemmata (visible on left side only) with Aramaic and Judaeo-Arabic alternating. Vocalisation: Tiberian (Aramaic). Paper. Bifolium, verso. 12.7 x 15.4. 7 lines on each folio.

20a. B 2941-1 (together with B 2941-2). Targum Onqelos: Leviticus 4:13–20. Languages: Hebrew lemmata and Aramaic alternating. Vocalisation: sparse Tiberian (Hebrew, Aramaic). Paper. Recto. 13.0 x 17.3. 11 lines.

20b. B 2941-2 (together with B 2941-1). Targum Onqelos: Leviticus 4:25–30. Interlinear correction. Languages: Aramaic with Hebrew lemmata. Vocalisation: sparse Tiberian (Hebrew, Aramaic). Paper. Verso. 13.0 x 17.3. 11 lines.

21a. B 3014-1 (together with B 3014-2). Targum Onqelos and Saadya's Tafsīr: Genesis 50:21–3. Languages: Aramaic and Judaeo-Arabic alternating (no Hebrew lemmata visible). Paper. Recto. 10.5 x 8.4. 6 lines.

21b. B 3014-2 (together with B 3014-1). Targum Onqelos and Saadya's Tafsīr: Genesis 50:25–6 (lines 1–4). Languages: Aramaic and Judaeo-Arabic alternating (no Hebrew lemmata visible). Paper. Verso. 10.5 x 8.4. 5 lines.

22a. B 3078-1 (together with B 3078-2). Targum Onqelos: Leviticus 23:40–3. Languages: Hebrew lemmata and Aramaic alternating. Paper. Recto. 5.5 x 7.7. 7 lines.

22b. B 3078-2 (together with B 3078-1). Judaeo-Arabic text, possibly in the handwriting of Maimonides. Paper. Verso. 5.5 x 7.7. 4 lines.

23a. B 3167-1 (together with B 3167-2). Targum Onqelos: Exodus 1:11–18. Languages: Hebrew lemmata and Aramaic alternating. Vocalisation: partial Tiberian (Hebrew, Aramaic). Paper. Recto. 19.3 x 13.5. 16 lines.

23b. B 3167-2 (together with B 3167-1). Targum Onqelos: Exodus 1:18–2:5. Languages: Hebrew lemmata and Aramaic alternating. Vocalisation: partial Tiberian (Hebrew, Aramaic). Paper. Verso. 19.3 x 13.5. 16 lines.

24a. B 3187-1 (together with B 3187-2). Targum Jonathan to the Prophets: 1 Samuel 12:14 (lines 1–5). The text on the last two lines is not from the next verse in Samuel. The identified verse is from the *Hapṭārâ* of *Qoraḥ* (Numbers 16:1-18:32). Language: Aramaic (no Hebrew lemmata visible). Paper. Recto. 10.3 x 13.8. 7 lines.

24b. B 3187-2 (together with B 3187-1). Unidentified Hebrew text, starting with the opening words of the second verse of *Ḥuqqat* (Numbers 19:1–22:1), the *pārāšâ* following *Qoraḥ* (see recto). Language: Hebrew. Paper. Verso. 10.3 x 13.8. 8 lines.

25a. B 3611-1 (together with B 3611-2). Targum Onqelos: Exodus 30:18–23. Languages: Hebrew lemmata and Aramaic alternating. Paper. Recto. 11.2 x 10.6. 10 lines.

25b. B 3611-2 (together with B 3611-1). Targum Onqelos: Exodus 30:29–34. Languages: Hebrew lemmata and Aramaic alternating. Paper. Verso. 11.2 x 10.6. 9 lines.

26a. B 4038-1 (together with B 4038-2). Targum Onqelos: Numbers 28:28? (left), 29:4–7 (right). Marginal correction (Numbers 29:5). Languages: Hebrew lemmata and Aramaic alternating. Vocalisation: Tiberian (Hebrew, Aramaic). Paper. Bifolium, recto. 15.2 x 13. 13 lines on each folio.

26b. B 4038-2 (together with B 4038-1). Targum Onqelos: Numbers 29:8–10 (left), unidentified (right). Languages: Hebrew lemmata and Aramaic alternating. Vocalisation: Tiberian (Hebrew, Aramaic). Paper. Bifolium, verso. 15.2 x 13. 13 lines on each folio.

27a. B 4542-1 (together with B 4542-2; B 4543-1,2; B 4822-1,2; B 4932-1,2; B 5249-1,2). Targum Onqelos: Exodus 12:17–19. Languages: Hebrew lemmata (visible on recto B 4543-1) and Aramaic alternating. Paper. Recto. 12.6 x 7.5. 10 lines.

27b. B 4542-2 (together with B 4542-1; B 4543-1,2; B 4822-1,2; B 4932-1,2; B 5249-1,2). Targum Onqelos: Exodus 12:22–5. Languages: Hebrew lemmata (visible on recto B 4543-1) and Aramaic alternating. Paper. Verso. 12.6 x 7.5. 11 lines.

27c. B 4543-1 (together with B 4542-1,2; B 4543-2; B 4822-1,2; B 4932-1,2; B 5249-1,2). Targum Onqelos: Exodus 12:7–10. Languages: Hebrew lemmata and Aramaic alternating. Paper. Recto. 10.6 x 7.4. 7 lines.

27d. B 4543-2 (together with B 4542-1,2; B 4543-1; B 4822-1,2; B 4932-1,2; B 5249-1,2). Targum Onqelos: Exodus 12:13–15. Languages: Hebrew lemmata (visible on recto B 4543-1) and Aramaic alternating. Paper. Verso. 10.6 x 7.4. 8 lines.

27e. B 4822-1 (together with B 4542-1,2; B 4543-1,2; B 4822-2; B 4932-1,2; B 5249-1,2). Targum Onqelos: Exodus 11:5–7. Languages: Hebrew lemmata and Aramaic alternating. Paper. Recto. 8.5 x 6. 7 lines.

27f. B 4822-2 (together with B 4542-1,2; B 4543-1,2; B 4822-1; B 4932-1,2; B 5249-1,2). Targum Onqelos: Exodus 11:10–12:3. Languages: Hebrew lemmata and Aramaic alternating. Paper. Verso. 8.5 x 6. 8 lines.

27g. B 4932-1 (together with B 4542-1,2; B 4543-1,2; B 4822-1,2; B 4932-2; B 5249-1,2). Targum Onqelos: Exodus 12:28–9. Languages: Hebrew lemmata (visible on recto B 4543-1) and Aramaic alternating. Paper. Recto. 5.4 x 4. 6 lines.

27h. B 4932-2 (together with B 4542-1,2; B 4543-1,2; B 4822-1,2; B 4932-1; B 5249-1,2). Targum Onqelos: Exodus 12:33–5. Languages: (visible on recto B 4543-1) and Aramaic alternating. Paper. Verso. 5.4 x 4. 6 lines.

27i. B 5249-1 (together with B 4542-1,2; B 4543-1,2; B 4822-1,2; B 4932-1,2; B 5249-2). Targum Onqelos: Exodus 11:4–6. Languages: Hebrew lemmata and Aramaic alternating. Paper. Recto. 12.0 x 5.7. 10 lines.

27j. B 5249-2 (together with B 4542-1,2; B 4543-1,2; B 4822-1,2; B 4932-1,2; B 5249-1). Targum Onqelos: Exodus 11:9–12:3. Languages: Hebrew lemmata and Aramaic alternating. Paper. Verso. 12.0 x 5.7. 10 lines.

28a. B 4745-1 (together with B 4745-2). Targum Onqelos and Saadya's Tafsīr: Genesis 9:12–13. Languages: Hebrew lemmata with Aramaic and Judaeo-Arabic alternating. Vocalisation: Tiberian (Hebrew, Aramaic). Paper. Recto. 6.0 x 7. 5 lines.

28b. B 4745-2 (together with B 4745-1). Targum Onqelos and Saadya's Tafsīr: Genesis 9:15–16. Languages: Hebrew lemmata with Aramaic and Judaeo-Arabic alternating. Vocalisation: Tiberian (Hebrew, Aramaic). Paper. Verso. 6.0 x 7. 6 lines.

29a. B 4871-1 (together with B 4871-2). Targum Onqelos: Deuteronomy? (verses unidentified, text includes אמוראה). Languages: Aramaic (no Hebrew lemmata visible). Vocalisation: Tiberian (Aramaic). Paper. Recto. 7.9 x 6.6. 9 lines.

29b. B 4871-2 (together with B 4871-1). Targum Onqelos: Deuteronomy 3:2–3. Languages: Aramaic (no Hebrew lemmata visible). Vocalisation: Tiberian (Aramaic). Paper. Verso. 7.9 x 6.6. 9 lines.

30a. B 4874-1 (together with B 4874-2). Targum Onqelos: Deuteronomy 34:5–6. Languages: Hebrew lemmata and Aramaic alternating. Vocalisation: Babylonian (Hebrew, Aramaic). Accents (Hebrew). Parchment. Recto. 7.2 x 3.4. 8 lines.

30b. B 4874-2 (together with B 4874-1). Targum Onqelos: Deuteronomy 34:8. Languages: Hebrew lemmata and Aramaic alternating. Vocalisation: Babylonian (Hebrew, Aramaic). Accents (Hebrew). Parchment. Verso. 7.2 x 3.4. 8 lines.

31a. B 4884-1 (together with B 4884-2). Targum Onqelos: Leviticus 2:1–2 (left), 3:13–14 (right). Languages: Hebrew lemmata and Aramaic alternating. Vocalisation: Tiberian (Aramaic). Accents (Aramaic). Paper. Bifolium, recto. 19.1 x 13.4. 10 lines on each folio.

31b. B 4884-2 (together with B 4884-1). Targum Onqelos: Leviticus 2:4–6 (right); 3:9 (left). Languages: Hebrew lemmata and Aramaic alternating. Vocalisation: Tiberian (Aramaic). Accents (Aramaic). Paper. Bifolium, verso. 19.1 x 13.4. 9 lines on each folio.

32a. B 5277-1 (together with B 5277-2). Targum Onqelos: Genesis 12:16–13:2. Languages: Hebrew lemmata and Aramaic alternating. Paper. Recto. 11.7 x 5.3. 12 lines.

32b. B 5277-2 (together with B 5277-1). Targum Onqelos: Genesis 13:7–9. Languages: Hebrew lemmata (visible on recto B 5277-1) and Aramaic alternating. Paper. Verso. 11.7 x 5.3. 14 lines.

33a. B 5295-1 (together with B 5295-2). Targum Onqelos: Numbers 22:4. Sparse vocalisation. Languages: Hebrew lemmata and Aramaic alternating. Vocalisation: Tiberian (Aramaic). Paper. Recto. 7.3 x 8.0. 5 lines.

33b. B 5295-2 (together with B 5295-1). Targum Onqelos: Numbers 22:8. Languages: Hebrew lemmata (visible on recto B 5295-1) and Aramaic alternating. Paper. Verso. 7.3 x 8.0. 6 lines.

34a. B 5535-1 (together with B 5535-2). Targum Onqelos: Numbers 28:3–5. Languages: Hebrew lemmata and Aramaic alternating. Paper. Recto. 6.2 x 5.8. 6 lines.

34b. B 5535-2 (together with B 5535-1). Targum Onqelos: Numbers 28:8–9. Marginal correction. Languages: Hebrew lemmata and Aramaic alternating. Paper. Verso. 6.2 x 5.8. 6 lines.

35a. B 5601-1 (together with B 5601-2). Targum Onqelos and Saadya's Tafsīr: Genesis 6:9. Languages: Hebrew lemmata with Aramaic and Judaeo-Arabic alternating. Vocalisation: partial Tiberian (Hebrew, Aramaic). Paper. Recto. 5.1 x 5.0. 4 lines.

35b. B 5601-2 (together with B 5601-1). Targum Onqelos and Saadya's Tafsīr: Genesis 6:12. Languages: Hebrew lemmata with Aramaic and Judaeo-Arabic alternating. Vocalisation: partial Tiberian (Hebrew, Aramaic). Verso. 5.1 x 5.0. 4 lines.

36a. B 5782-1 (together with B 5782-2). Targum Onqelos and Saadya's Tafsīr; Deuteronomy 16:18–19. Languages: Hebrew lemmata with Aramaic and Judaeo-Arabic alternating. Vocalisation: Tiberian (Hebrew). Accents (Hebrew). Paper. Recto. 14.1 x 11.6. 12 lines.

36b. B 5782-2 (together with B 5782-1). Blank. Paper. Verso. 14.1 x 11.6.

37a. B 5831-1 (together with B 5831-2; B 5832-1,2; B 5833-1,2; B 5834-1,2; B 5835-1,2; B 5836-1,2; B 5837-1,2). Targum Jonathan to the Prophets: 2 Samuel 6:15–17. Languages: Hebrew lemmata (visible on verso B 5831-2) and Aramaic alternating. Paper. Recto. 7.2 x 4.9. 7 lines.

37b. B 5831-2 (together with B 5831-1; B 5832-1,2; B 5833-1,2; B 5834-1,2; B 5835-1,2; B 5836-1,2; B 5837-1,2). Targum Jonathan to the Prophets: 2 Samuel 6:20-1. Languages: Hebrew lemmata and Aramaic alternating. Paper. Verso. 7.2 x 4.9. 7 lines.

37c. B 5832-1 (together with B 5831-1,2; B 5832-2; B 5833-1,2; B 5834-1,2; B 5835-1,2; B 5836-1,2; B 5837-1,2). Targum Jonathan to the Prophets: 2 Samuel 7:13–15. Languages: Hebrew lemmata and Aramaic alternating. Paper. Recto. 7.2 x 4.7. 7 lines.

37d. B 5832-2 (together with B 5831-1,2; B 5832-1; B 5833-1,2; B 5834-1,2; B 5835-1,2; B 5836-1,2; B 5837-1,2). Targum Jonathan to the Prophets: 2 Samuel 7:20–2. Languages: Hebrew lemmata (visible on recto B 5832-1) and Aramaic alternating. Paper. Verso. 7.2 x 4.7. 7 lines.

37e. B 5833-1 (together with B 5831-1,2; B 5832-1,2; B 5833-2; B 5834-1,2; B 5835-1,2; B 5836-1,2; B 5837-1,2). Targum Jonathan to the Prophets: 2 Samuel 7:2–5. Languages: Hebrew lemmata and Aramaic alternating. Paper. Recto. 7.2 x 4.9. 7 lines.

37f. B 5833-2 (together with B 5831-1,2; B 5832-1,2; B 5833-1; B 5834-1,2; B 5835-1,2; B 5836-1,2; B 5837-1,2). Targum Jonathan to the Prophets: 2 Samuel 7:8–9. Languages: Hebrew lemmata (visible on recto B 5833-1) and Aramaic alternating. Paper. Verso. 7.2 x 4.9. 7 lines.

37g. B 5834-1 (together with B 5831-1,2; B 5832-1,2; B 5833-1,2; B 5834-2; B 5835-1,2; B 5836-1,2; B 5837-1,2). Targum Jonathan to the Prophets: 2 Samuel 8:7–10. Languages: Hebrew lemmata and Aramaic alternating. Paper. Recto. 7.2 x 4.6. 7 lines.

37h. B 5834-2 (together with B 5831-1,2; B 5832-1,2; B 5833-1,2; B 5834-1; B 5835-1,2; B 5836-1,2; B 5837-1,2). Targum Jonathan to the Prophets: 2 Samuel 8:12–14. Languages: Hebrew lemmata and Aramaic alternating. Paper. Verso. 7.2 x 4.6. 7 lines.

37i. B 5835-1 (together with B 5831-1,2; B 5832-1,2; B 5833-1,2; B 5834-1,2; B 5835-2; B 5836-1,2; B 5837-1,2). Targum Jonathan to the Prophets: 2 Samuel 7:25–7. Languages: Hebrew lemmata (visible on verso B 5835-2) and Aramaic alternating. Paper. Recto. 7.0 x 4.8. 6 lines.

37j. B 5835-2 (together with B 5831-1,2; B 5832-1,2; B 5833-1,2; B 5834-1,2; B 5835-1; B 5836-1,2; B 5837-1,2). Targum Jonathan to the Prophets: 2 Samuel 8:1–3. Languages: Hebrew lemmata and Aramaic alternating. Paper. Verso. 7.0 x 4.8. 7 lines.

37k. B 5836-1 (together with B 5831-1,2; B 5832-1,2; B 5833-1,2; B 5834-1,2; B 5835-1,2; B 5836-2; B 5837-1,2). Targum Jonathan to the Prophets: 2 Samuel 6:2–4. Languages: Aramaic, no Hebrew lemmata visible. Paper. Recto. 7.1 x 5.4. 6 lines.

37l. B 5836-2 (together with B 5831-1,2; B 5832-1,2; B 5833-1,2; B 5834-1,2; B 5835-1,2; B 5836-1; B 5837-1,2). Targum Jonathan to the Prophets: 2 Samuel 6:8–10. Languages: Aramaic, no Hebrew lemmata visible. Paper. Verso. 7.1 x 5.4. 6 lines.

37m. B 5837-1 (together with B 5831-1,2; B 5832-1,2; B 5833-1,2; B 5834-1,2; B 5835-1,2; B 5836-1,2; B 5837-2). Targum Jonathan to the Prophets: 2 Samuel 9:1–4. Languages: Hebrew lemmata and Aramaic alternating. Paper. Recto. 7.4 x 4.5. 7 lines.

37n. B 5837-2 (together with B 5831-1,2; B 5832-1,2; B 5833-1,2; B 5834-1,2; B 5835-1,2; B 5836-1,2; B 5837-1). Targum Jonathan to the Prophets: 2 Samuel 9:7–10. Languages: Hebrew lemmata and Aramaic alternating. Paper. Verso. 7.4 x 4.5. 7 lines.

38a. B 5846-1 (together with B 5846-2). Targum Jonathan to the Prophets: Ezekiel 36:37–37:1. Languages: Hebrew lemmata and Aramaic alternating. Vocalisation: Tiberian (Aramaic). Paper. Recto. 17.1 x 9.7. 15 lines.

38b. B 5846-2 (together with B 5846-1). Targum Jonathan to the Prophets: Ezekiel 37:2–6. Languages: Hebrew lemmata and Aramaic alternating. Vocalisation: Tiberian (Aramaic). Paper. Verso. 17.1 x 9.7. 13 lines.

39a. B 6241-1 (together with B 6241-2). Targum Onqelos: Genesis 11:9. Languages: Hebrew lemmata and Aramaic alternating. Paper. Recto. 4.4 x 6.0. 5 lines.

39b. B 6241-2 (together with B 6241-1). Targum Onqelos: Genesis 11:15. Languages: Hebrew lemmata and Aramaic alternating. Paper. Verso. 4.4 x 6.0. 5 lines.

40a. B 6262-1 (together with B 6262-2). Targum Onqelos: Deuteronomy 2:14–16. Languages: Aramaic (no Hebrew lemmata visible). Paper. Recto. 7 lines.

40b. B 6262-2 (togther with B 6262-1). Faint traces of writing but text illegible. Paper. Verso. 8.1 x 6.0.

41a. B 6533-1 (together with B 6533-2). Targum Onqelos: Leviticus 1:10–11. Languages: Aramaic (no Hebrew lemmata visible). Vocalisation: Tiberian. Paper. Recto. 5.5 x 3.7. 2 lines.

41b. B 6533-2 (together with B 6533-1). Targum Onqelos: Leviticus 2:17. Languages: Aramaic (Hebrew lemmata visible). Vocalisation: Tiberian. Paper. Verso. 5.5 x 3.7. 2 lines.

42a. B 6782-1 (together with B 6782-2). Targum Onqelos: Genesis 1:7–11. Languages: Hebrew lemmata and Aramaic alternating. Paper. Recto. 9.2 x 9.9. 10 lines.

42b. B 6782-2 (together with B 6782-1). Targum Onqelos; Genesis 1:14–17. Languages: Hebrew and Aramaic. Paper. Verso. 9.2 x 9.9. 11 lines.

43a. B 6888-1 (together with B 6888-2). Targum Onqelos: Leviticus 25:54–6:1. Languages; Hebrew lemmata (line 4) and Aramaic alternating. Vocalisation: Tiberian (Hebrew) + Rafe. Paper. Recto. 8.9 x 12.8. 5 lines.

43b. B 6888-2 (together with B 6888-1). Targum Onqelos: Leviticus 26:3–5. Languages: Hebrew lemmata (?) and Aramaic alternating. Vocalisation: Tiberian (Hebrew?). Paper. Verso. 8.9 x 12.8. 5 lines.

44a. B 6914-1 (together with B 6914-2; B 6915-1,2). Targum Onqelos: Genesis 1:11–14. Languages: Hebrew lemmata and Aramaic alternating. Vocalisation: Tiberian (Aramaic). Paper. Recto. 3.9 x 4.6. 4 lines.

44b. B 6914-2 (together with B 6914-1; B 6915-1,2). Targum Onqelos: Genesis 1:19–20. Languages: Hebrew lemmata and Aramaic alternating. Vocalisation: not visible. Paper. Verso. 3.9 x 4.6. 4 lines.

44c. B 6915-1 (together with B 6914-1,2, B 6915-2). Targum Onqelos: Genesis 1:11–13. Languages: Aramaic (no Hebrew lemmata visible). Vocalisation: Tiberian (Aramaic). Paper. Recto. 7.1 x 3.7. 6 lines.

44d. B 6915-2 (together with B 6914-1,2; B 6915-1). Targum Onqelos: Genesis 1:18–20. Languages: Hebrew lemmata (no Aramaic visible). Paper. Verso. 7.1 x 3.7. 4 lines.

45a. B 7000-1 (together with B 7000-2). Targum Onqelos: Leviticus 23:15–21. Languages: Hebrew lemmata and Aramaic alternating. Paper. Recto. 15.5 x 10.9. 19 lines.

45b. B 7000-2 (together with B 7000-1). Targum Onqelos: Leviticus 23:21–30. Languages: Hebrew lemmata and Aramaic alternating. Paper. Verso. 15.5 x 10.9. 19 lines.

46a. L 105-1 (together with L 105-2; L 106-1,2). Targum Onqelos and Saadya's Tafsīr: Numbers 10:5–22. Languages: Hebrew lemmata with Aramaic and Judaeo-Arabic alternating. Paper. Recto. 29.0 x 19.7. 34 lines.

46b. L 105-2 (together with L 105-1; L 106-1,2). Targum Onqelos and Saadya's Tafsīr: Numbers 10:22–11:3. Marginal correction/note. Languages: Hebrew lemmata with Aramaic and Judaeo-Arabic alternating. Paper. Verso. 29.0 x 19.7. 34 lines.

46c. L 106-1 (together with L 105-1,2; L 106-2). Targum Onqelos and Saadya's Tafsīr: Numbers 3:38–4:1. Marginal corrections. Languages: Hebrew lemmata with Aramaic and Judaeo-Arabic alternating. Paper. Recto. 28.9 x 18.2. 34 lines.

46d. L 106-2 (together with L 105-1,2; L 106-1). Targum Onqelos and Saadya's Tafsīr: Numbers 4:1–16. Marginal corrections. Languages: Hebrew lemmata with Aramaic and Judaeo-Arabic alternating. Paper. Verso. 28.9 x 18.2. 39 lines.

47a. Bible Gaster 15-1 (together with Bible Gaster 15-2,3,4,5,6). Targum Onqelos: Genesis 35:9–12. Languages: Hebrew lemmata and Aramaic alternating. Parchment (palimpsest?). Recto. 13.3 x 8.7. 14 lines.

47b. Bible Gaster 15-2 (together with Bible Gaster 15-1,3,4,5,6). Targum Onqelos: Genesis 36:6–7. Languages: Hebrew lemmata and Aramaic alternating. Parchment (palimpsest?). Verso. 13.3 x 8.7. 14 lines.

47c. Bible Gaster 15-3 (together with Bible Gaster 15-1,2,4,5,6; join between Bible Gaster 15-3/4 and Bible Gaster 15-5/6). Targum Onqelos: Genesis 36:12–14. Languages: Hebrew lemmata and Aramaic alternating. Parchment (palimpsest?). Recto. 9.0 x 8.7. 9 lines.

47d. Bible Gaster 15-4 (together with Bible Gaster 15-1,2,3,5,6; join between Bible Gaster 15-3/4 and Bible Gaster 15-5/6). Targum Onqelos: Genesis 36:36–9. Languages: Hebrew lemmata and Aramaic alternating. Parchment (palimpsest?). Verso. 9.0 x 8.7. 9 lines.

47e. Bible Gaster 15-5 (together with Bible Gaster 15-1,2,3,4,6; join between Bible Gaster 15-3/4 and Bible Gaster 15-5/6). Targum Onqelos: Genesis 36:14–15. Languages: Hebrew lemmata and Aramaic alternating. Parchment (palimpsest?). Recto. 6 lines.

47f. Bible Gaster 15-6 (together with Bible Gaster 15-1,2,3,4,5; join between Bible Gaster 15-3/4 and Bible Gaster 15-5/6). Targum Onqelos: Genesis 36:39–40. Languages: Hebrew lemmata and Aramaic alternating. Parchment (palimpsest?). Verso. 6 lines.

48a. Bible Gaster 29-1 (together with Bible Gaster 29-2). Targum Onqelos and Saadya's Tafsīr: Numbers 31:54–32:1. Languages: Hebrew lemmata with Aramaic and Judaeo-Arabic alternating. Vocalisation: Babylonian (Hebrew and Aramaic). Parchment. Recto. 10.0 x 17.4. 6 lines.

48b. Bible Gaster 29-2 (together with Bible Gaster 29-1). Targum Onqelos and Saadya's Tafsīr: Numbers 32:6–8. Languages: Hebrew lemmata with Aramaic and Judaeo-Arabic alternating. Vocalisation: Babylonian (Hebrew and Aramaic). Parchment. Verso. 10.0 x 17.4. 7 lines.

49a. Bible Gaster 81-1 (together with Bible Gaster 81-2). Targum Onqelos: Deuteronomy 34:3–4 (right) and 34:5–6 (left). Languages: Hebrew lemmata and Aramaic alternating. Vocalisation: Babylonian (Hebrew, Aramaic); sporadic Tiberian (?). Parchment. Recto. 7.4 x 10.6, 2 columns, 8 lines each.

49b. Bible Gaster 81-2 (together with Bible Gaster 81-1). Targum Onqelos: Deuteronomy 34:7–8 (right) and 34:9–10 (left). Languages: Hebrew lemmata and Aramaic alternating. Vocalisation: Babylonian (Hebrew, Aramaic); sporadic Tiberian (?). Parchment. Verso. 7.4 x 10.6. 2 columns, 8 lines each.

The following fragments should possibly be included in the catalogue but their identification as Targumic is far from certain:

50a. B 2333-1 (together with B 2333-2). Arabic translation of Targum Song of Songs (??): Song 2:16; 3:3. Hebrew lemmata (visible right line 9, left line 5) and Judaeo-Arabic alternating. Paper. Recto. 9.2 x 14.9. 2 columns, 12 lines on right, 11 lines on left.

50b. B 2333-2 (together with B 2333-1). Arabic translation of Targum Song of Songs (??): Song 4:5. Hebrew lemmata (visible right line 9) and Judaeo-Arabic alternating. Verso. 9.2 x 14.9. 2 columns, 12 lines on each.

51a. B 4159-1 (together with B 4159-2; B 4160-1,2). Targum of the Writings (?): 2 Chronicles 34:15–20. Languages: Hebrew lemmata and Aramaic with Hebrew alternating. Vocalisation: sporadic Tiberian (Hebrew, Aramaic). Paper. Recto. 9.6 x 6.8. 15 lines.

51b. B 4159-2 (together with B 4159-1; B 4160-1,2). Targum of the Writings (?): 2 Chronicles (?) Languages: Hebrew lemmata and Aramaic alternating. Vocalisation: sporadic Tiberian (Aramaic). Paper. Verso. 9.6 x 6.8. 14 lines.

51c. B 4160-1 (together with B 4159-1,2; B 4160-2). Targum of the Writings (?): 2 Chronicles (?) Marginal note. Languages: Aramaic (no Hebrew lemmata visible). Paper. Recto. 10.3 x 6.7. 16 lines.

51d. B 4160-2 (together with B 4159-1,2; B 4160-1). Targum of the Writings (?): 2 Chronicles (?) Languages: Aramaic (no Hebrew lemmata visible). Paper. Verso. 10.3 x 6.7. 14 lines.

52a. B 5314-1 (together with B 5314-2; B 5315-1,2). Unidentified text. Languages: Hebrew lemmata with Aramaic and Judaeo-Arabic alternating (?). Paper. Recto. 4.9 x 10.9. 6 lines.

52b. B 5314-2 (together with B 5314-1; B 5315-1,2). Unidentified text. Hebrew lemmata visible on B 5314-1 and B 5315-1. Languages: Hebrew lemmata (visible on B 5314-1 and B 5315-1 (?)) with Aramaic and Judaeo-Arabic alternating (?). Paper. Verso. 4.9 x 10.9. 4 lines.

52c. B 5315-1 (together with B 5314-1,2; B 5315-2). Unidentified text. Languages: Hebrew lemmata (Isaiah 10:22 on line 12) with Aramaic and Judaeo-Arabic alternating (?). Paper. Recto. 9.8 x 11. 12 lines.

52d. B 5315-2 (together with B 5314-1,2; B 5315-1). Unidentified text. Languages: Hebrew lemmata (Isaiah 18:5 on line 5) with Aramaic and Judaeo-Arabic alternating (?). Paper. Verso. 9.8 x 11. 5 lines.

53a. B 5353-1 (together with B 5353-2). Unidentified text. Marginal note. Languages: Hebrew lemmata with Aramaic and Judaeo-Arabic alternating (?). Vocalisation: Tiberian (Hebrew). Accents (Hebrew). Paper. Recto. 9.4 x 9.5. 9 lines.

53b. B 5353-2 (together with B 5353-1). Unidentified text. Marginal note. Languages: Hebrew lemmata with Aramaic and Judaeo-Arabic alternating (?). Vocalisation: Tiberian (Hebrew). Accents (Hebrew). Paper. Verso. 9.4 x 9.5. 9 lines.

Index of Scriptural Verses

The following are the verses of Scripture represented by these Targum fragments:

Genesis	
1:7–11	B 6782-1
1:11–14	B 6914-1
1:11–13	B 6915-1
1:14–17	B 6782-2
1:18–20	B 6915-2
1:19–20	B 6914-2
4:1–3	A 855-1
4:3–6	A 855-2
4:26	A 1295-1
5:1–2	A 1295-2
5:3–5	A 1295-2
5:5–7	A 1295-1
5:7–10	A 1098-1
5:10–13	A 1098-2
6:9	B 5601-1
6:12	B 5601-2
9:12–13	B 4745-1
9:15–16	B 4745-2
11:9	B 6241-1
11:15	B 6241-2
12:16–13:2	B 5277-1
13:7–9	B 5277-2
16:3	B 2802-1
16:4–5	B 2802-2
17:17–19	B 2802-2
17:19	B 2802-1
21:16–17	A 664-1
21:22–23	A 664-2
21:28–29	A 664-3
22:1	A 664-4
22:5–6	A 664-5
22:6–7	B 2696-1
22:9–10	A 664-6
22:11–12	B 2696-2
35:9–12	Bible Gaster 15-1
36:6–7	Bible Gaster 15-2
36:12–14	Bible Gaster 15-3
36:14–15	Bible Gaster 15-5
36:36–9	Bible Gaster 15-4
36:39–40	Bible Gaster 15-6
39:4–5	B 5115-1
39:12–13	B 5115-2

49:11	A 1649-1
49:16	A 1649-2
50:21–3	B 3014-1
50:25–6	B 3014-2

Exodus

1:11–18	B 3167-1
1:18–2:5	B 3167-2
7:16–17	B 1994-1
7:19–20	B 1994-1
7:21–3	B 1994-2
7:26–7	B 1994-2
11:4–6	B 5249-1
11:5–7	B 4822-1
11:9–12:3	B 5249-2
11:10–12:3	B 4822-2
12:7–10	B 4543-1
12:13–15	B 4543-2
12:17–19	B 4542-1
12:22–5	B 4542-2
12:28–9	B 4932-1
12:33–5	B 4932-2
14:28	A 711-2
19:23–20:2	A 1106-1
24:9–12	B 2083-1
24:13–16	B 2083-2
24:18–25:4	B 2083-2
25:6–11	B 2083-1
28:?28	B 4038-1
29:4–7	B 4038-1
29:8–10	B 4038-2
28:30–3	A 565-1
28:35–7	A 565-2
30:5–6	A 1681-1
30:16–18	A 1681-2
30:18–23	B 3611-1
30:29–34	B 3611-2
39:43–40:3	A 1621-3
40:19–20	A 1621-4

Leviticus

1:10–11	B 6533-1
2:1–2	B 4884-1
2:4–6	B 4884-2
2:17	B 6533-2
3:9	B 4884-2
3:13–14	B 4884-1
4:13–20	B 2941-1
4:25–30	B 2941-2

4:35–5:4	B 1932-1
5:8–12	B 1932-2
5:17–23	B 1932-2
6:2–6	B 1932-1
22:7	A 1466-1
23:15–21	B 7000-1
23:21–30	B 7000-2
23:40–3	B 3078-1
24:21–3	A 1000-1
25:5–6	A 1000-2
25:54–26:1	B 6888-1
26:3–5	B 6888-2
Numbers	
1:34–5	A 204-1
1:36–7	A 204-2
3:38–4:1	L 106-1
4:1–16	L 106-2
10:4–22	L 105-1
10:22–11:3	L 105-2
22:4	B 5295-1
22:8	B 5295-2
28:3–5	B 5535-1
28:8–9	B 5535-2
Deuteronomy	
2:14	A 1420-1
2:14-16	B 6262-1
3:2-3	B 4871-2
5:2-6	B 2359-1
5:12–14	B 2359-2
5:17–19	B 2359-2
5:22	B 2359-1
16:18–19	B 5782-1
34:3–4	Bible Gaster 81-1
34:5–6	Bible Gaster 81-1
34:5–6	B 4874-1
34:7-8	Bible Gaster 81-2
34:8	B 4874-2
34:9–10	Bible Gaster 81-2
1 Samuel	
12:14	B 3187-1
15:28–32	A 37-1
15:29–30	A 36-3
15:30–2	A 36-1
2 Samuel	
6:2–4	B 5836-1
6:8–10	B 5836-2

6:15–17	B 5831-1
6:20–1	B 5831-2
7:2–5	B 5833-1
7:8–9	B 5833-2
7:13–15	B 5832-1
7:20–2	B 5832-2
7:25–7	B 5835-1
8:1–3	B 5835-2
8:7–10	B 5834-1
8:12–14	B 5834-2
9:1–4	B 5837-1
9:7–10	B 5837-2
Ezekiel	
36:16–19	A 37-2
36:17–18	A 36-4
36:18–20	A 36-2
36:35–6	A 36-1
36:36	A 194-1
36:37–37:1	B 5846-1
37:2–6	B 5846-2
45:9	A 194-1
45:11–14	A 194-2
45:12–13	A 36-2
2 Chronicles	
34:17–20	B 4159-1
Song of Songs	
2:16	B 2333-1
3:3	B 2333-1
4:5	B 2333-2

An Edition of Three Rylands Targum Manuscripts

To put some flesh on the bare bones of this Catalogue we present editions of three Rylands Genizah Targum manuscripts. These are typical of the collection as a whole. Indeed, from the fact that these are among the more substantial pieces, it will be apparent how small the Rylands fragments are.

The editions use the following conventions:

] edge of the fragment

[edge of the fragment

... missing word(s) (if dots are unattached to a word)

... missing letter(s) (if dots are attached to a word)

[ ] insecure reading

[..] illegible

/ / interlinear and marginal notes are put between forward slashes

? placed in front of an insecure reading

We have ignored vocalisation, where it occurs, as immaterial to our present purposes. Verse numbers have been added for ease of reference. The alternative readings in the footnotes refer either to Sperber 1959–73 or to Derenbourg 1893 depending on the language involved. These are not meant in any sense as a critical apparatus, but simply to establish the relationship of our texts to standard texts of both Onqelos and Saadya's Tafsīr. The texts of Onqelos and the Tafsīr are highly stable, but by no means absolutely fixed. The purpose of the comparison is to show that, although our manuscripts differ from standard texts, they are still within the parameters of the traditions we know as 'Onqelos' and 'Saadya's Tafsīr'. This is important particularly for the Targum of the Pentateuch. None of the Rylands Genizah Targums we have looked at manifest the paraphrastic characteristics that are indicative of the Palestinian Targums of the Pentateuch. We will return to this point later.

I

Catalogue 15a-15b

B 1932-1 (left), Targum Onqelos to Leviticus 4:35–5:4

1 יעדי כמא יעדי תרבא דאמרא / דמתעדא תרב אימר[1] / מנכסת קדשיא[2]
2 ויסיק כהנא יתהון למדבחא על קרבניא[3] דיהוה[4]
3 ויכפר עלוהי כהנא על חובתיה דחב וישתביק ליה ·
4 5:1 ונפש · ואנש ארי תחוב / יחוב[5] / וישמע קל מ[י]מא / מומי[6] /
5 והוא סהיד או חזא או ידע אם לא יחוי[7] ויקבל[8] חוב[י]ה / ?יה / 2
6 או · או אנשא[9] ד[..] קרב בכל מדעם מסאב או ברחשת / בנבלת[10] /

---

1 The interlinear note corresponds with the reading in Sperber.

2 קודשיא

3 קורבניא

4 דיוי

5 The interlinear note corresponds with the reading in Sperber accept for the vocalisation.

6 The interlinear note corresponds with the reading in Sperber.

7 Vocalisation differs from Sperber's.

8 ויקביל

9 אנשא ד[..] קרב [קרב] אנש דיקרב

7 [..]א מסאבתא או ברחשת[11] בעירא מסאבתא[12] או

8]שת / [..]בלת[13] / רחיש מסאב ויתכסי / ויהי מכסא[14] / מניה והוא מסאב וחב :

9] 3 יקרב בס[וא]בת[15] א[נ]שא לכל סאובתיה[16] [ד]יסתאב

10] [..]דע וחוב[17] 4 · או · או [

11][ב]שא או ל[א][

B 1932-2 (right), Targum Onqelos to Leviticus 5:8–12

1 וימלוק ית רישיה מקבל[18] קדליה ולא יפריש · 9 והזה ·

2 וידי מדמא דחטאתא[19] על כתל[20] מדבחא ודישתאר

3 בדמא [יתמצי] ליסודא דמדבחא / חטאתא[21] / הוא · 10 ואת · וית תנינא

4 יעביד עלתא כד[חזי] ויכפר עלוהי כהנא מחובתיה

5 דחב וישתבק[22] ליה · 11 ואם · ואם לא תדביק

6 ידיה לתרין שפנינין או לתרין בני יונה וייתי ית

7 קרבניה[23] דחב חד מן עשרא[24] בתלת סאין ס[ו]ל[ת..]

8 לחטתא לא ישוי עלה משחא ולא יתן[25] עלה ל[

9 ארי חטאתא[26] הוא[27] · 12 והב[יאה] · וייתנה[28] לו[ת] [

10][מ]ץ כהנא מנה[29] מ[ל][

11]בחא על [ק][

B 1932-2 (left), Targum Onqelos to Leviticus 5:17–23

1 חדא / חד[30] / מכל פקודיא דיהוה[31] דלא כשרין לאתעבדא ולא

---

10 The interlinear note corresponds with the reading in Sperber. בנבלת is repeated a second time in the margin.

11 בנבלת

12 מסאבא in the margin, which corresponds to the reading in Sperber.

13 The interlinear note corresponds with the reading in Sperber.

14 The interlinear note corresponds with the reading in Sperber.

15 בסאובת

16 סובתיה

17 וחב

18 מקביל

19 דחטתא

20 כותל

21 / חטאתא / הוא] חטתא היא

22 וישתביק

23 קורבניה

24 עסרא

25 יתין

26 חטתא

27 היא

28 וייתינה

29 מינה

2 ידע וח[ו]ב[32] ויקבל[33] חוביה · 18 והביא · וייתי דכר שלים
3 מן ענא בפורסניה לאשמא לות כ[ה]... ויכפר
4 עלוהי כהנא על חובתיה[34] דחב / שלותיה דאשתלי והוא[35] / ולא[36] ידע וישתביק ליה :
5 19 אשם · אשמא הוא על חובתיה דהוא אשמא יקריב
6 קדם יהוה[37] · 20 וידבר · ומליל יהוה[38] עם משה
7]מימר · 21 נפש · אנש ארי יחוב וישקר שקר במימרא[39]
8] [וי]כדב[40] בחבריה בפקדנא[41] או בשתפות ידא
9] או עש[ק] ... ...[ב]ריה · 22 או · או א... [
10] ...ע על שקרא על ... ...ל̇
11] 23 והיה · וי[הי] [

B 1932-1 (right), Targum Onqelos to Leviticus 6:2–6

1 ית אהרן וית בנוהי למימר דא אוריתא דעלתא ה[..א]
2 עלתא דמ[ת]...דא על מדבחא כל ליליא עד צפרא
3 ... ...בחא תהי יקדא ביה | 3 ולבש ...לבש
4 [כ]ה[נ]... לבושין דבוץ ומכנסין דבוץ ילבש על [ב]סריה
5 [..] ית קטמא[42] דתיכול אשתא[43] ית עלתא על מדבחא
6 ויש...[נ]יה בסטר מדבח... 4 ופשט ...שלח ית לבושו[הי]
7 וילב[ש] ל[ב]ושין אחרנין[44] ...ק ית קטמא[45] למברא למ[ש]...
8 לאתר ד[כי] 5 ואשתא[46] על מדב[ח]א תהי יקדא ביה [ל][
9 ת... ...ר עלה כהנא ... בצפר [
10] ויסק[47] עלה [ע]ל[ן][48]
11] 6 ... תהי י[קד][

---

30 The interlinear note corresponds with the reading in Sperber.
31 דיוי
32 וחב
33 ויקביל
34 חובתיה דחב crossed out.
35 The interlinear note corresponds with the reading in Sperber.
36 לא
37 יוי
38 יוי
39 Sperber omits. In margin it reads: ק[ד]ם.
40 ויכדיב
41 בפוקדנא
42 דשנא
43 אישתא
44 אוחרנין
45 דשנא
46 ואישתא
47 ויסיק
48 תרבי

II
Catalogue 22a

B 3078-1, Targum Onqelos to Leviticus 23:40–3

קדם אדני[49] אלהכון שבעה יומ[

ותחגון[50] יתה חגה לשמיה [רא][41 2

3 [בכל][51] שנה קים עלם לדריכון]

4 תחג[ון][52] יתיה · 42 בסכת וג' ב[..][

5 שבעה יומין [כל[53] כל] יצי[ב][

6]לין[54] ... 43 [למ]ען ידעו]

7][דע][

III
Catalogue 46a-d

L 105-1, Targum Onqelos and Saadya's Tafsir to Numbers 10:5–22.

1]זלין[55] פי אל מש[רק] 6 ותקעתם ותיתקעון[56]

2]א יבבתא יתקעון

3]ל בהא אל עסאכר אל נאזלין[57] פי אל גנוב

4] 7 ובהקהל[58] ובמיכנש[59] ית [כ..]תא[60] תיתקעון[61] ולא

5] תגלבו 8 ובני ובני אהרן כהניא

6][דריכ]ון : ובני[62] הרון אל אימא יצרבו[63]

7]לכם : 9 וכי וארי תיעלון לאגחא

8]ור[צ]תא[64] וייעול דוכרניכון[65] לטבא

9] חרב עלי[66] אעדאיכם פי בלדכם

---

49 יוי

50 ותחגון ... [רא]] ותיחגון יתיה חגא קדם יוי

51 [בכל] שנה] בשתא

52 תיחגון

53 [כל כל]] כל

54 Absent in Sperber

55 אלנאזלה

56 ותתקעון

57 אלנאזלה

58 ובהקהיל

59 ובמכנש

60 קהלא

61 תתקעון

62 בנו

63 יצרבון

64 בחצוצרתא

65 דוכרנכון

10] בקתם[67] בין ידי אללה רב[כ]ם[68]
11 10]תכון[69] ובמועדיכון וברישי ירחיכון
12]ל[70] ניכסת[71] קדשיכון[72] ויהון לכון
13]ם אעיאדכם ורוס אשהורכום[73]
14]כם פתכון[74] לכם דכרא בין ידי רבכם
15 11][ת]א תנייתא בירחא תניינא[75] בעשרין[76]
16][ת]א : ולמא[77] כאן פי אל כנה[78] אל
17] אל [..]אם ען מסכן אל שהאדה :
18] 12 דסיני ושרא עננא במדברא
19]הם מן בריה סיני וסכן אל גמאם
20 13]מרא דייי[79] בידא דמשה : פכאן
21] 14 ויסע ונטל טיקס משריית[80] בני
22] [..] עמ[י] נדב : תם[81] רחל מרכז עסכר
23] [גישה] נחשון בן[82] עמי נדב : 15 ועל ועל חילא
24] [..] ועלי גיש סבט ישׂשכ' נתנאל
25] 16 [..] דשיבט[א][83] [..]בני זבולון[84] אליאב בר חילון[85] : ועלי גיש
26] [..] [..]אב ב[..] חלון 17 והורד ומיתפרק[86] משכנא ונטלין בני גרשון
27] [..] תם פצל אל מסכן פירחל[87] בני[88] גרשון ובני מררי

---

66 Derenbourg omits [עלי אעדאיכם.

67 בוקתם

68 רבבם

69 The preceding letters do not belong to this part of the text due to faulty restoration work on the fragment.

70 The preceding letters do not belong to this part of the text due to faulty restoration work on the fragment.

71 נכסת

72 קודשיכון

73 שהורכם

74 פיכון

75 תנינא

76 בעסרין

77 פלמא

78 אלשהר

79 דיוי

80 משרית

81 באן

82 אבן

83 דשבטא

84 זבולן

85 חילן

86 ומתפרק

87 פרחל

88 בנו

28] 18 [..]סע [..]ל טי[ק]ס משריית[89] ראובן לחיליהון ועל חיליה אליצור

29] [..] [..]ל מרכז עסכר ראובן לגיושהום[90] ועלי גישה אליצור

30] [..]19 [..]טא דבני שמעון שלומיאל[91] בר צורי שדי : ועלי

31] [..] [..]אל בן צורישדי : 20 ועל ועל חילא שבטא[92] דבני

32] [..] [..]ש סבט [..] אליסף בן דעוא[ל] : 21 ונסעו ונטלין

33] [..] [..]מקימין ית משכנא עד מיתיהון : תם רחלו[93]

34] [..] אלי מגי[ה]ם : 22 ונסע ונטיל טיקס

L 105-2, Targum Onqelos and Saadya’s Tafsīr to Numbers 10:22–11:3

1 משריית[94] בני אפרים [..]]

2 עסכר בני[95] אפרים ל[..] ועלי [..]]

3 23 דבני מנשה גמליאל[96] בר [..]]

4 24 ועל חילא שבטא[97] דבני]

5 בן גדעונ[י] 25 ונסע ונטיל טיקס מ]

6 חיליה אחי עזר בר עמ[י] שדי]

7 ליגיושהם[98] ועלי גישה אחי עז[ר]]

8 26 בן[99] עכרן : ועלי גיש סבט בני[100]]

9 27 אחירע בר עינן : ועלי גיש סבט]

10 28 בני ישראל לחיליהון ו נטלו]

11 29 ויאמר ואמר משה לח[ו]ב[ב][101]]

12 דאמר ייי[102] יתיה א[תין] לכון[103]]

13 על ישראל : קאל מוסי לח[..]]

14 קאל אללה איאה אעטיה[104] לכם תע[א]]

15 30 ויאמר ואמר ליה לא איזיל [אל]הון]

---

89 משרית

90 לגיושהם

91 שלמיאל

92 דשבטא

93 רחל

94 משרית

95 Derenbourg omits.

96 גמילאל

97 דשבטא

98 לגיושהם

99 בר

100 Derenbourg omits.

101 לחבב. The following letters do not belong to this part of the text due to faulty restoration work on the fragment.

102 יוי

103 The following letters do not belong to this part of the text due to faulty restoration work on the fragment.

104 אעטיה לכם תע[א]] אעטיכם פתעאל

16 ומולדי : 31 ויאמר ואמר]
17 במידברא[105] וגבורן דאי[ת..]]
18 פאנך[106] תעלם[107] טול מקאמנא פי]
19 32 עימנא[108] ויהי טבא ההוא דיוטיב]
20 כיר אן[109] יחסן אללה בה אלינא נחסן אלי[ך]]
21 33 דייי[110] מהלך תלתה יומין / [..]ארון קיימא ... נ[ט]יל ...הון ...ך תלתה יומין[111] / לאתקנא ל...]
22 ג'[112] איאם וצנדוק עהד[113] אללה יסיר בין [א]יד[ה]ם[114]]
23 34 וענן וענן יקרא דייי[115] מטיל עילווה[ו]ן [בי]ממא [..]]
52 4 עליהם נהארא ענד[116] רחולהם מן אל ע[..] [..] 35 ויהי]
25 משה איתגלי[117] יייי ויתבדרון סנאך ויערקון [..] מ[..] [..]]
26 רחול[118] אל צנדוק אן יקול מוס[י] קום יא רב [..]]
27 מן בין ידיך : 36 ובנחה ובמישרוהי[119] הוה אמר [..]]
28 דישראל וענד נזולה[120] [י]קול ר[ו]ד[121] יא ר[..] [..]]
29 11:1 והוה עמא כד מסתפקין[122] ביש קדם [..]]
30 אשתא[123] קדם יייי[124] ושיציאת בסיפי משריתא ...]
31 אללה פסמע אללה דלק ואשתד גצבה פאש[..][125] [..]]
32 עסכר 2 ויצעק וצוח עמא על[126] משה [..]]
33 פצרך אל קום אלי מוסי פדעי [..]]
34 3 שמיה דאתרא ההוא [..] אישתא [..]]

105 במדברא

106 באנך

107 תעלם אן פי

108 עמנא

109 Derenbourg omits.

110 דיוי

111 We have not included the first three lines of the marginal note that read as follows: [וא]רון קיימא מהליך הון[..]. Apparently, they represent a first abortive attempt to correct the parablepsis, after which the correct text follows.

112 תלאתה

113 עהד אללה] עהדה

114 ידיהם

115 דייי ... עילווה[ו]ן] דיוי מטל עלויהון

116 ענד רחולהם] אדא רחלו

117 איתגלי יייי] אתגלי יוי

118 רחיל

119 ובמישרוהי הוה] ובמשרוהי

120 נזולה אן

121 רד

122 מסתקפין

123 אישתא מן

124 יוי

125 ואשתעלת

126 על משה] למשה

L 106-1, Targum Onqelos and Saadya's Tafsīr to Numbers 3:38–4:1

] משכן זימנא[127] מדינחא משה
] וחילוני דיקרב יתקטיל : ואל
] פי אל... מוסי והרון ו...
] / ומחאפ[בני [..] / [..] [..]ס אלי דלק פ[ל]יק[..] 39 כל
] לזרעייתהון[128]
] [..] עדד אל ליואניין אלדי[129]
] ד[כ]ר מן אבן שהר וצאעדה[130]
] 40 ... כל בוכרא[131] דיכריא לבני ישראל
] קאל אללה למוסי עד כל בכר
]הם 41 ולקחת ותקריב
] דליואי חלף כל
]רפת[ה]ם בדל כל בכר מן בני
] מן בהאים בני איסראיל[132]
] 42 בבני ישראל : ועדהם מוסי
43]הי והוו כל בוכריא דיכריא[133]
] ותרין אלפין ומאתן[134] ושבעין
] [..]א[..]א[135] אתנין ועשרין
] 44 [..] : וכלם[136] אללה למוסי[137]
] 45 בבני ישראל [ו]ית בעירא דליואי
] אל ליואניין בדל כל[138] בכר מן
] לי אנא אללה שרפתהום[139]
] 46 מבוכרא[140] דבני ישראל
]זאידין עלי אל ליואניון[141] מן בכור בנ[י]
] 47 [..]הא בסלעי קודשא תיסב עשרין[142]

---

127 זימנא מדינחא] זמנא מדנחא
128 לזרעיתהון
129 אלדין
130 פצאעדה
131 בוכרא דיכריא] בכוריא דכריא
132 אסראיל
133 דכריא
134 מאתן
135 אסמאיהם כדלך
136 תם כלם
137 מוסי
138 Derenbourg omits [כל ... מן
139 שרפתהם
140 מבכוריא
141 אלליואניין
142 עסרין

25] [..][..מו]מא[143] פצה במתאקיל אל קדש[144] כל

26] [..] 48 ולבנוהי פורקן דיתירין[145] על

27] [..] פדא אלפאצלין עליהום[146] : 49 ויקח

28] [..][..]קי ליואי : פאכד מוסי פצה אל

29] [..] 50 מאת מן בוכרייא[147] דבני ישראל

30] [..] סילעין[148] בסילעי קדשא מן

31] [..] מיאה[149] וכמסה וסתין[150] מתקאלא במתקאל

32] [..] 51 [..]אהרון[151] ולבנוהי על מימרא דיייי[152] כמא

33] [..] אל[153] פדא אלי הרון ובניה עלי קול אללה כמא

34] [..] 4:1 [..ם][154] אהרון למימר : וכלם[155] אללה למוסי[156]

L 106-2, Targum Onqelos and Saadya's Tafsīr to Numbers 4:1–16

1 והרון קאילא 2 נשא קבילו[157] ית ח[

2 ארפעו[158] גמלה בני קהת מן ב[

3 3 [..] תלתין שנין ולעילא ועד בר חמשין ש[

4 [..] מן אבן תלאתין[159] סנה פצאעד[א] [

5 פ[..]ה[160] כבא אל מחצר 4 זאת ...א[161] [

6 כדמה בני קהת פי כבא אל [

7 5 במיטל משריתא ויפרקון י[ת] [

8 פידכל[162] הרון ובניה[163] ענד רחי[

9 6 ונתנו [ו]יתנון עלוהי חופאה [/ ויפרסון לבוש /

---

143 [..מו]מא ... במתאקיל] גמגמה מנהם במתקאל

144 קדס

145 דיתירין על] דיתיריא דבהון

146 עליהם

147 בכוריא

148 סילעין ... קדשא] סלעין בסלעי קודשא

149 מאיה

150 וסתון

151 לאהרן

152 דיוי

153 Derenbourg omits [אל פדא.

154 [..ם] אהרון] משה ולאהרן

155 תם כלם

156 מוסי

157 קביל

158 ארפעא

159 תלתין

160 צנאעה פי

161 דין

162 וידכל

163 ובנוה

10 וישוון א[ריח][

11 גמלתה מן[164] אסמאנגון[165] ויצ[/ אקואבה /

12 7 לבוש דתיכלא[166] ויתנון עלו[

13 ניסוכא[167] ולחמא תדירא ע[

14 נגון ויגעלו עליה[168] אל קצאע [

15 יכון עליה[169] : 8 ופרשו ויפ[

16 ססגונא וישוון ית אר[

17 בגטא[170] מן[171] גלוד אל[172] דארש / ויצלחון[173] אקואבה / [

18 9 דישמשון[174] יתיה[175] בהון בקו[דש...][176] [

20 10 דימשך[177] ססגונא ויתנון על[178] [

21 / ועל מדבחא [דד]הב[א] יפרסון לבוש דתיכלא[179] ו...ון יתיה בחופאה דימשך[180] ססגונא ושוו[181]
ית אריחוהי[182] /

22 12 פי אל קדש פיגעלוהא פי [

21 ויגעלוהא[183] עלי אלדהוק[184] : 13 ודשנו [

22 לבוש ארגונא[185] : וירמדו [

23 14 ויתנון עלוהי ית כל מנוהי דישמ[

24 וית מגריפתא[186] וית מזרקיא כל מני [

25 וישוון אריחוהי : ויגעלו עליה גמיע [..] [

26 ואל מגארף ואל כראנב וגמיע[187] אני[..] [

---

164 Derenbourg omits.

165 אסמאנגון פוקה

166 תכלא

167 נסוכא

168 עליהא

169 עליהא

170 בגשא

171 Derenbourg omits.

172 Derenbourg omits.

173 ויצלחון אקואבה] ויצלחו אקואבהא

174 Some text is missing before this word, for the verse is long and this is already the end of the verse.

175 לה

176 Sperber omits. Subsequently, the complete verse in Judaeo-Arabic is missing.

177 דמשך

178 The verse in Judaeo-Arabic is again missing.

179 תכלא

180 דמשך

181 וישוון

182 The complete verse in Aramaic is written in the margin. Subsequently, the verse in Judaeo-Arabic is missing as well as the next verse in Aramaic.

183 ויצנעוהא

184 אלדהק

185 ארגון

186 מגרופיתא

27 דהוקה[188] / אקואבה / : 15 וכלה וישיצי אהרן ובנוה... ...כסאה ית [..] [
28 במיטל משריתא ובתר כין ייעלון בני [..] [
29 ימותון אילין[189] מטול בני קהת במשכן זימנא[190] [..] [
30 קדס וגמיע אואניתה[191] ענד רחיל אל עסכר [..] [
31 ידנו אלי[192] אל קדס ולא[193] יהלכון הדה צפה [..] [
32 16 ודמסיר אל[194] עזר בר אהרון[195] כהנא משחא דא[..] [..] [
33 ומנחתא תדירא ומשחתא[196] דרבותא [..] [
34 ווכאלת[197] אל עזר בן[198] הרון אל אמאם על[..][199] דהן אל א[..] [..] [

This text is followed by four barely legible lines in the bottom margin of the page, of which the first two lines turn out to correspond with the above missing parts of verse 9:

9 [..]ן לבוש דתיכלא[200] ויכסון [..] [
בהון ויאכדו[201] [..]אב[202] אל אסמאנגון ויגט[..][203] [..] [

The last two lines are difficult to decipher.

Characteristics of the Rylands Genizah Targum Manuscripts

1. The first general characteristic that will strike any user of the Rylands Genizah Targum manuscripts is their generally small size and poor state of preservation. Even with the more substantial pieces, the text is often rubbed and hard to decipher. This makes identification sometimes difficult and tentative, and so introduces a substantial element of uncertainty into any analysis. Our Catalogue can be improved, but frankly

187 וסאיר
188 Derenbourg omits.
189 דין
190 זמנא
191 אניתה
192 מן
193 ולא יהלכון] פיהלכון
194 אל עזר] לאלעזר
195 אהרן
196 ומשחא
197 ווכאלה
198 אבן
199 Derenbourg omits.
200 תכלא
201 וליאכדו
202 [..]אב אל] תוב
203 פיגטו

we doubt if further expenditure of effort on decipherment will add much to the sum of our knowledge. If these had been fragments of Dead Sea Scrolls, then extended toil and reconstruction might pay dividends, since we may be dealing there with hitherto unknown texts of a very early date, but all the indications are that our corpus represents late copies of already well-known texts.

2. The vast bulk of our Targums are either Onqelos to the Pentateuch or Jonathan to the Prophets. In other words they are copies of the 'official' Targums of both these divisions of the Hebrew Bible. We could not find a single clear example of the more paraphrastic type of Targum representative of the so-called Palestinian Targums to the Pentateuch or the Targumic Toseftas to the Prophets.[204] Even in the tiniest fragments we usually found evidence, either direct or circumstantial, that we were most likely dealing with Onqelos and Jonathan. The contrast with the Targum manuscripts in some other Genizah subcollections, where Palestinian Targums *are* well represented, is striking and surely significant (Klein 1986).[205]

3. The vast bulk of our Targums cover the Pentateuch or Haftarot. Some of the manuscripts of the Prophets seem to be from anthologies of Haftarot, and not from complete versions of a biblical Prophetic book. This is definite in the case of the interrelated fragments A 36, A 37, A 194. In the case of the two possible Targums of the Writings (2 Chronicles in Catalogue 51a and 51b, and Song of Songs in Catalogue

---

204 The Palestinian Targum is marked not only by paraphrase, but also by great textual diversity. It survives in a number of different forms. Codex Neofiti 1 is usually regarded as the sole extant example of a complete Palestinian Targum, but the lateness of the one surviving copy (early sixteenth century) should never be forgotten (Díez Macho 1968–79). The Fragment Targum is the remnant of a once complete Palestinian Targum, from which the interesting paraphrastic bits were extracted in the Middle Ages (Klein 1980). Pseudo-Jonathan is a Palestinian literary Targum compiled in the early Islamic period from older sources and augmented. Like Neofiti 1 it now exists in only one very late manuscript. It testifies indirectly to the paraphrastic character of the Palestinian Targum tradition (Clarke 1984). The Prophetic Toseftot are, like the Fragmentary Targum to the Torah, remnants of a once complete, more paraphrastic Palestinian Targum to the Prophets (Rimon Kasher 1996). Finally we have the numerous fragments of Palestinian Targumim from the Cairo Genizah, which often differ textually from each other and from the other Palestinian Targumin (Klein 1986).

205 The main repositories are the Cambridge, JTS, Bodleian and Petersburg subcollections. There *is* a substantial fragment of a Palestinian Targum to Deuteronomy 1:1–5:9 (= Fragment Targum?) in the British Library Gaster Genizah collection (MS Or. 10794, fol. 8), and so there may be others there. We must be careful, therefore, not to extrapolate from our preliminary findings with regard to the Rylands Gaster Genizah to the original Gaster Genizah collection as a whole. The fragment is well known because it was published by Gaster himself in 1900. See the edition by Klein (1986, I: 330–3; II, 89–91, Plate 148).

50a and 50b), the identifications are desperately uncertain. If 50a+50b is indeed a Judaeo-Arabic version of Targum Song of Songs, then it would have some interest, but it is not easy to correlate its text with the Targum, and it may be some sort of commentary or paraphrase of the Song of Songs.[206] The focus on the parts of Tanakh that played a major liturgical role, and on their corresponding Haftarot, suggests that the fragments are related to the Shabbat lectionary cycle in synagogue, but we must be careful how we construe this relationship. It does not mean that they were necessarily aids to the oral delivery of the Targum during the synagogue service. The history of the oral delivery of the Targum in synagogue is complicated. As is evident from the numerous references to it in rabbinic literature, the Targum seems to have been orally recited in synagogues throughout the talmudic era, in both Eretz Israel and Babylonia, but this practice was increasingly neglected in the middle ages, as more and more Jews in the Muslim world went over to Arabic as their vernacular, and Aramaic became a scholarly language, even less generally understood than Hebrew.[207] For those in Christian Europe Aramaic had *never* been a vernacular, except, perhaps, in some communities in very early times, and so the recitation of Targum was probably *never* customary in European synagogues. Interest in Targum continued, however, partly because Targum was a useful repository of traditional exegesis of value to *daršānîm* and scholars, and partly because some may have continued to adhere to the rabbinic injunction to prepare in private in advance the weekly Torah lection by going over it twice in the Hebrew and once in the Targum.[208] The very occasional liturgical notes in some of our manuscripts are consonant with this use. It is probable that all our manuscripts date from a time when Targum was no longer recited in synagogue. Some fifty copies of Targum within our corpus strikes us as quite high, and testifies, surely, to the fact that Targum continued to be valued, at least among scholars.

---

206 The highly paraphrastic Targum of the Song of Songs was translated into a number of Jewish languages (Alexander 2002; see also 2003).

207 The oral recitation of the Targum in synagogue has been customary in Yemenite synagogues down to modern times, but it is impossible to say whether this is a continuous survival from hoary antiquity or a medieval innovation in the light of the practice presupposed in the Talmud, as the Yemenite Jewish community increasingly rabbinized. All things considered the latter is the more likely possibility.

208 See b. Ber. 8a–8b: 'R. Huna b. Judah says in the name of R. Ammi: A man should always complete his *Pārāšiyyôt* together with the congregation, twice in the Hebrew and once in the Targum, and even [such verses as] *'Aṭārôt* and *Dîbon* (Num. 32:3), for if one completes his *Pārāšiyyôt* together with the congregation, his days and years are prolonged.' It is interesting that this tradition is preserved in the Bavli. The Targum seems to have played a particularly central role in the religious life of Babylonian Jews.

4. The ways in which the Targum is presented are varied. While in every case the Targum alternates with the biblical lemmata, a verse at a time, the lemmata are presented sometimes in abbreviated form (with only the opening word or phrase of the verse), and sometimes in full. They are differentiated from the Targum either by a dot, a *sôp pāsûq*, or by the use of bigger, bolder letters. Some of the texts are totally unvocalised, some have partial vocalisation, some are fully vocalised. Lemmata, when presented in full, may be vocalised either with supralinear (Babylonian) or Tiberian points, or with both. Where both systems occur side by side it is reasonable to suppose that the Babylonian vocalisation is the earlier, and that the Tiberian was added later, after the Tiberian had become standard. Both Tiberian and Babylonian vocalisation is found also in the Targum texts, though a significant number of our texts have Tiberian for the lemma and Babylonian for the Targum, thus further highlighting the difference between Scripture and Targum. A trajectory is detectable here running from supralinear vocalisation for both Scripture and Targum *through* Tiberian for Scripture and supralinear for Targum *to* Tiberian for both Scripture and Targum. Accents are occasionally supplied to the Hebrew, and sometimes even to the Aramaic! The presence of vocalisation and accentuation would seem to indicate a concern to pronounce the text correctly, and, perhaps, to read it aloud. A small but significant proportion of our manuscripts adds Saadya's Tafsīr, verse-by-verse, after the Targum. There are also plenty of manuscripts in the Rylands Genizah, not listed in the Catalogue above, where we find only Bible + Tafsīr, with the Targum being ignored. A trajectory can be traced here running from Bible + Targum *through* Bible + Targum + Tafsīr *to* Bible + Tafsīr. Saadya's Tafsīr originated as an Arabic Targum designed to meet the needs of the growing numbers of Jewish speakers of Arabic. We know of no evidence, however, that the Tafsīr was ever used in synagogue like the old Targum.

5. The vast majority of our fragments are on paper, with a very few on parchment. This is consonant with the general impression we have of their lateness, and with the fact that most are in non-professional hands. We have not attempted to say anything about scripts or handwriting in the Catalogue. It would undoubtedly have been an advantage to have been able to date the hands, but we did not feel able to do so. We have reservations that the palaeography of the Genizah has advanced far enough to allow secure datings to be made on the basis of the letter-forms alone, and this problem is compounded by the fact that, as already noted, our fragments are small and often poorly preserved, and corroborating codicological evidence is thus almost

entirely lacking. However, one can say with considerable confidence that very few of these fragments were written by professional scribes (a marked exception is B 1994). The handwriting is often quite crude and inelegant. This suggests to us that the majority of these copies of the Targum were made by scholars for their private use.

Conclusion

The conclusion we draw from this analysis of the dominant traits of the Targum manuscripts in the Rylands Genizah is that we are dealing here on the whole with a late assemblage of texts, which has not been carefully selected to preserve only substantial and choice items, but created rather opportunistically and randomly. It remains to be seen whether or not this characterisation of this particular genre would apply to the Rylands subcollection as a whole, in contrast, for example with the Bodelian subcollection, which is about the same size, but which contains more early, well preserved and choice items. Our initial impressions are that it would.[209]

References

Alexander, Philip S. 2002. 'Notes on some Targums of the Targum of the Song of Songs', in Paul V.M. Flesher (ed.), *Targum and Scripture: Studies in Aramaic Translations and Interpretation in Memory of Ernest G. Clarke* (Leiden). 159–74

—— 2003. *The Targum of Canticles translated, with a Critical Introduction, Apparatus, and Notes.* (The Aramaic Bible 17A; The Liturgical Press: Collegeville, MN)

Clarke, Ernest G. 1984. *Targum Pseudo-Jonathan to the Pentateuch: Text and Concordance*. (Hoboken, NJ)

Derenbourg, Joseph. 1983. *Version arabe du Pentateuque de R. Saadia ben Iosef Al-Fayyoûmî.* (Paris)

Díez Macho, Alejandro. 1968–79. *Neophyti 1: Targum Palestinense Ms de la Biblioteca Vaticana*. 6 vols, (Madrid)

Gaster, Moses. 1900. 'Geniza-Fragmente', in M. Brann and F. Rosenthal (eds), *Gedenkbuch zur Erinnerung an David Kaufmann*. 3 vols (Breslau), vol. 1, 222–44

Kasher, Rimon. 1996. *Targumic Toseftot to the Prophets*. (Jerusalem)

Klein, Michael L. 1980. *The Fragment Targums of the Pentateuch according to their Extant Sources*. 2 vols, (Rome)

— 1986. *Genizah Manuscripts of Palestinian Targum to the Pentateuch*. 2 vols, (Cincinnati)

Sperber, Alexander (ed.). 1959–73. *The Bible in Aramaic based on Old Manuscripts and Printed Texts*. 4 vols, (Leiden)

209 See further Chapter 1 above.

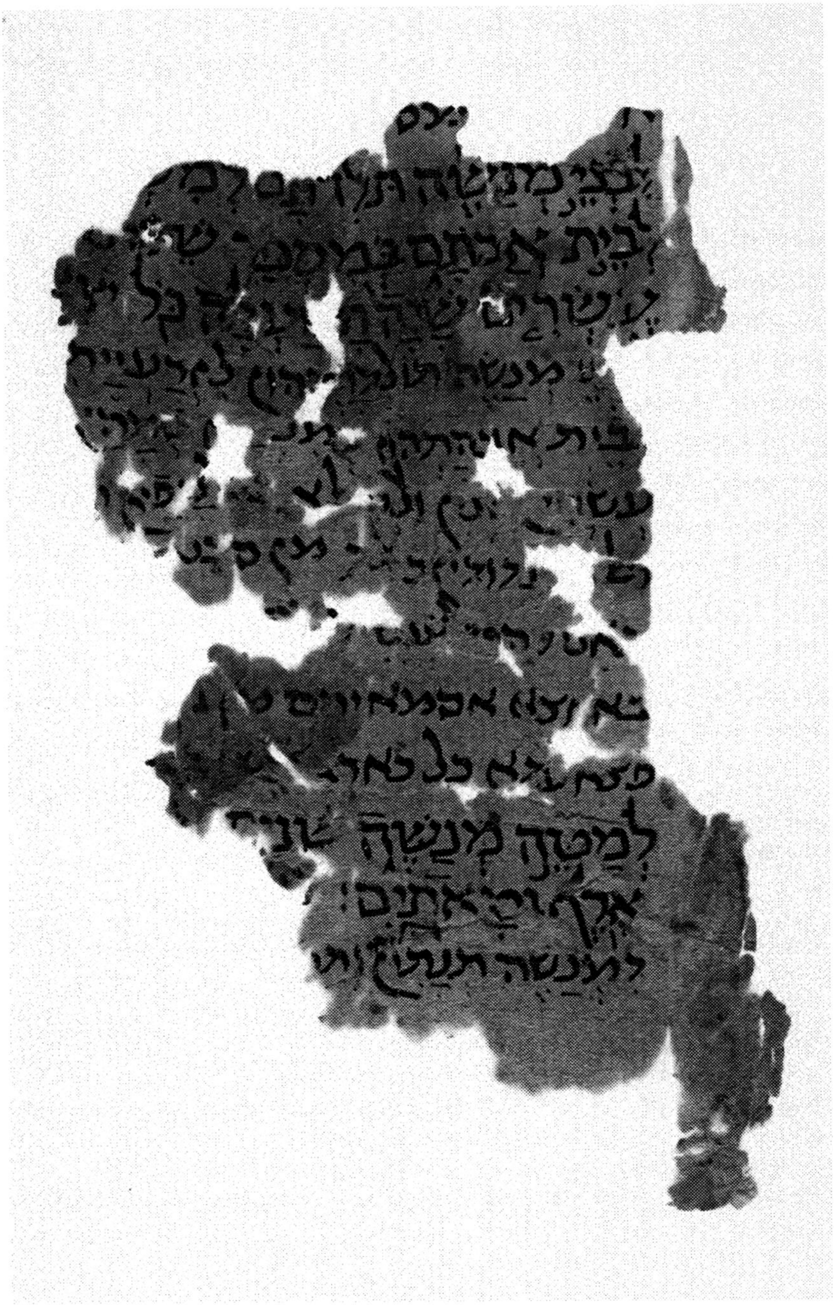

Plate 1: A 204-1, Hebrew Bible, Targum Onqelos and Saadya's Tafsīr, Num. 1:34-5. Catalogue 2a. (Reproduced by courtesy of the University Librarian and Director, The John Rylands Library, The University of Manchester)

Plate 2: B 1932-1, Targum Onqelos, Lev. 4:35-5:4 (left) and 6:2-5 (right). Catalogue 15a and edition I above. (Reproduced by courtesy of the University Librarian and Director, The John Rylands Library, The University of Manchester)

Plate 3: B 1994-1, Hebrew Bible, Targum Onqelos and Saadya's Tafsīr, Exod. 7:16-7 and 7:19-20. Catalogue 14c. (Reproduced by courtesy of the University Librarian and Director, The John Rylands Library, The University of Manchester)

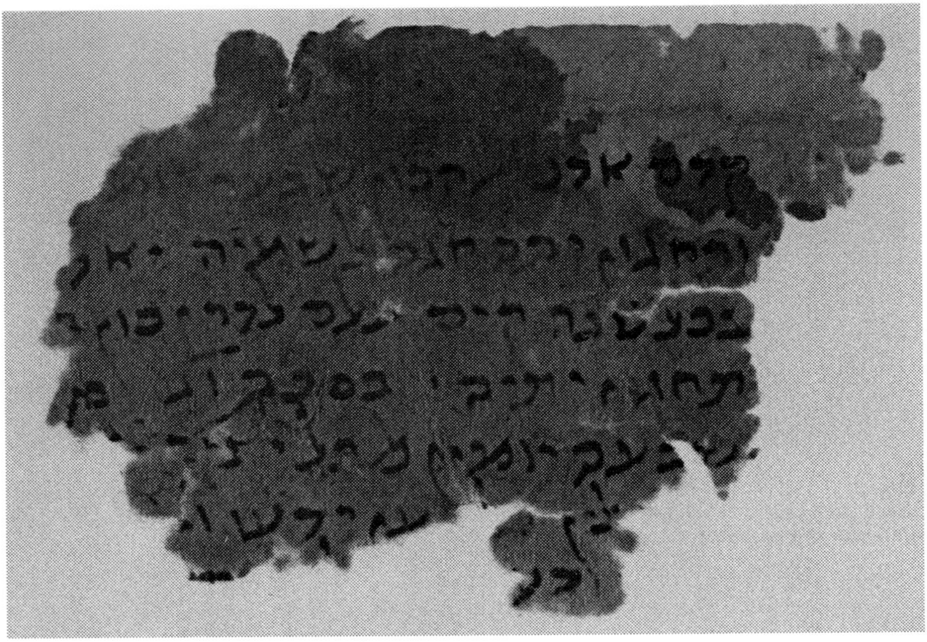

Plate 4: B 3078-1, Targum Onqelos, Lev. 23:40-3. Catalogue 22a and edition II above. (Reproduced by courtesy of the University Librarian and Director, The John Rylands Library, The University of Manchester)

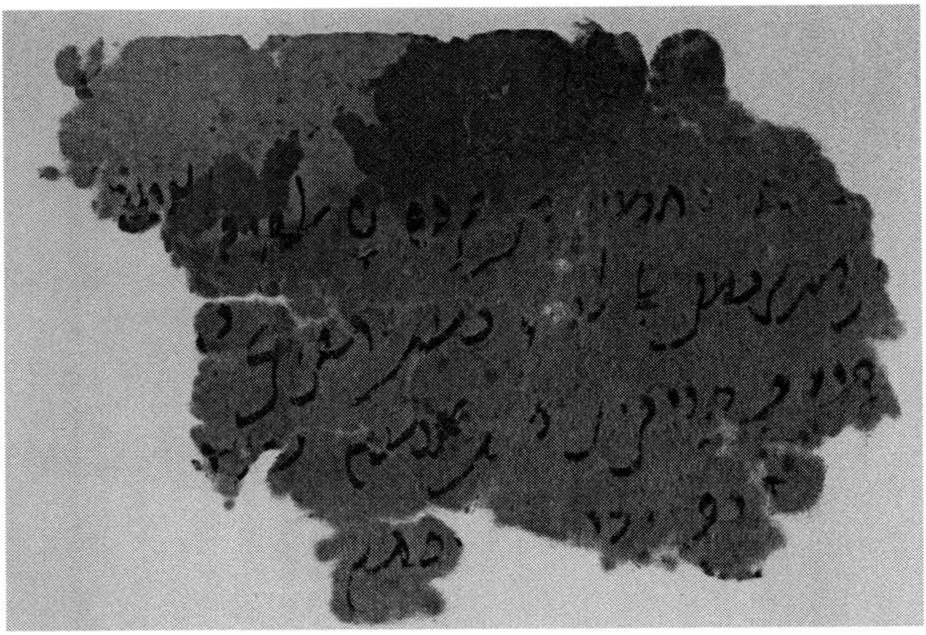

Plate 5: B 3078-2, Judaeo-Arabic text, possibly in the handwriting of Maimonides. Catalogue 22b. (Reproduced by courtesy of the University Librarian and Director, The John Rylands Library, The University of Manchester)

Plate 6: L 106-2, Targum Onqelos and Saadya's Tafsīr, Num. 4:1-16. Catalogue 46d and edition III above. (Reproduced by courtesy of the University Librarian and Director, The John Rylands Library, The University of Manchester)

A New Genizah Fragment of the *Aramaic Levi Document*

Gideon Bohak
Tel Aviv University

The text currently known as *Aramaic Levi* or as the *Aramaic Levi Document* was first discovered in the Cambridge Genizah collection at the very end of the nineteenth century.[1] The publication of the Cambridge fragment was soon followed by the identification of a second fragment, from the Bodleian Genizah collection, of the same work and of the very same manuscript (Pass and Arendzen 1900, Charles and Cowley 1907).[2] This was followed by the discovery, half a century later, that among the many fragments of non-biblical texts found at Qumran seven fragmentary copies of the same Levi text can be identified, thus proving beyond any doubt its great antiquity and its Jewish origins.[3] And in recent years, several important studies were devoted to the *Aramaic Levi Document* (=ALD), in an attempt to reconstruct its contents (based on the Genizah and Qumran fragments, and on identified Greek and Syriac excerpts from this work), and to elucidate its historical context within the Second Temple period, its relations with the Greek *Testament of Levi*, and its overall historical significance (Kugler 1996; Drawnel 2004; Greenfield, Stone and Eshel 2004).[4] In the present paper, I wish to contribute to these ongoing efforts by publishing one more Genizah fragment of this text, clearly deriving from the same manuscript as the Bodleian and Cambridge fragments and even from the same bifolium as the Cambridge one. I came across this new fragment while looking for magical texts among the Gaster Genizah fragments which are now part of the John

1 The present study is based on the results of a short research visit to Manchester in May 2008. I am grateful to Philip Alexander and Renate Smithuis for organizing this visit and making it so enjoyable. Renate Smithuis also checked my readings against the original fragment, and offered many important corrections and suggestions. I am furthermore grateful to Matthew Morgenstern, for his comments on an earlier draft of this paper. A Hebrew version of this paper was published in Bohak 2011.

2 Both fragments were re-edited by Puech 2002.

3 The Qumran fragments are 1Q21 (1QLevi) (edited by Milik 1955); 4Q213 (4QLevi[a]); 4Q213a (4QLevi[b]); 4Q213b (4QLevi[c]); 4Q214 (4QLevi[d]); 4Q214a (4QLevi[e]); 4Q214b (4Q Levi[f]) (all edited by Stone and Greenfield 1996).

4 For Milik's unpublished monograph on the Aramaic Levi materials, see Schattner-Rieser 2007.

Rylands Library's manuscript collections, and while the *Aramaic Levi Document* is unrelated to my current work on the Genizah magical texts, I felt that the fragment was too important to remain neglected.

P 1185

The fragment in question (P 1185, see Plates) is a small piece of parchment, 12.8 cm high and 11.4 cm wide, preserving the side margin, and a small part of the top margin, of the original bifolium. The manuscript was written by an experienced hand, and clearly belongs in the earliest layer of the Genizah fragments, before 1000 CE. The hand, the scribal habits (including the wide margins, the pricking used to draw the lines on the parchment, the absence of a justification to the left, and the use of // as line fillers and to mark the ends of some sections), and the contents (the story of Simeon and Levi's revenge against the people of Shechem) prove beyond any doubt that this is yet another fragment of the Genizah manuscript whose two other currently known fragments are Cambridge, University Library, T-S 16.94 and Oxford, Bodleian Heb. c. 27.56.

This fact is of great importance in reconstructing the size of the original bifolium (the Bodleian folio is 23.7 cm high and 22.5 cm wide; the Cambridge bifolium is 25.1 cm high and 36.8 cm wide, but is missing a column and a half of text), its structure (with two columns per folio, each with 23 lines, and our fragment clearly preserving the 'outer' column of its folio), the size of the top margin (which in the Bodleian fragment is 3 cm, in the Cambridge one 2.4–2.6 cm), and the width of the original lines (with some 18–27 letters per line in the Bodleian and Cambridge fragments).[5] Moreover, the broken column a of the Cambridge fragment clearly preserves a part of ALD's detailed account of the events surrounding Simeon and Levi's destruction of the city of Shechem and murder of its inhabitants in revenge for the rape of their sister Dinah by Shechem, the son of Hamor (see Genesis 34). Both sides of the new fragment clearly deal with the subsequent development of the same story, and so there is little doubt that the Manchester fragment came from the same folio as the broken columns a and b of the Cambridge fragment. This also helps settle the question of which side of the new fragment is recto and which is verso, since the fragment itself must be placed at the top left corner of the Cambridge bifolium. With the fragment's location ascertained, it may now be transcribed and translated.

5 The data about the Cambridge fragment are based on my own examination. I am grateful to Piet van Boxel for the data regarding the Oxford fragment.

Recto

[ ]ב?ו?
[ ]י?דע ד?י?טמאו? [ב?ב]נ?יהון
[ ]ה?ן ולא ישבקון יתהון עד
[די? כולהון?] יאבדו //
[אד]י?ן?[ח]מור ומלילו במילי
[א]ינש קריתהון //
[ה]ון למגזר ולמעבדה
[ ]למהוי להון חתנין
[ ]ר?ו?תהון ולאשליותן
[ ]י?ו עורלת
[בישרהון]ן? וחשבת

Notes

Lines 1–3: Given the space between the first preserved line and the top margin (*c.* 4.8 cm, when the margin itself should have been 2.4–2.6 cm), it seems that three lines of text are missing. At the end of line 3, one or two letters are partly preserved, but the reading is extremely doubtful.

Line 4: The reading of the first *yôd* is quite certain. The letter after the sequence דע seems to be a *dālet*, then perhaps a *yôd*, and then טמא, after which the bottom part of a *wāw* may perhaps be seen. This is followed by two or three letters of which nothing remains, but the rest of the line is clear.

Line 7: In the large lacuna, the upper tip(s) of one or two letters are preserved, which may be a *ṭêt*, but is more likely to be a *yôd wāw*, a *yôd* with a final *nûn*, or some similar combination.

Line 8: For the use of א(י)נש as a collective singular see, for example, *Genesis Apocryphon* XX: 17, 18, 19: אנש ביתה.

Line 11: The first two letters are only partly preserved; the first might be a *dālet*, *rêš*, *bêt* or a *kap*, or even a *sāmek*. The second letter can be a *wāw* or a *gîmel* or a *nûn*. The reading ולאשליותן is certain, although one would expect ולאשליותה(ו)ן.[6]

Line 12: The reading of the *yôd* is quite certain, but it is not clear whether the *waw* is the last letter of the first word, or the first letter of the second word.

Line 13: The first partly preserved letter can be a final *nûn*, a *yôd*, or even a *gîmel* or a *šîn*.

6 Note also the form מדיתון for *מדינתהון in Gen. Apoc. XX:4, with Fitzmyer 2004: 241.

Translation

1

2

3 [ ]

4 [ ] know that they [ ] polluted by their sons

5 [ ]them? and will not leave them until

6 they [all] perish.

7 Then? [they went to H]amor, and they spoke in words of

8 [ ] the men of their city,

9 [ ] them? to circumcise (themselves) and to make it

10 [ ] to become their bride-grooms,

11 [ ] them and to deceive them

12 [ ] the foreskin of

13 [their flesh] and I thought

Verso

1

2 מ?..[ ]

3 ואנה [ ]

4 ברז ונעול [ו]נקטול? לכל ב[ני]

5 שכם ארום יומא הדין יהב אל?[ ]

6 ועידנא דין סגר כולה?ו?ן? אל ביד[נא?]

7 למקטל אינון ולמעבד[דין]ז?[ר]ע?

8 דקשוט אדין ענה [שמעון]

9 אחי מקנא סגי מן [ ]

10 קום עול בחוכמת[ך]

11 וסב חרבי ודילך [ ]

12 ונעבד די[ן]

13 שכם ואל[ ]

14 [ ]ב?[ ]

Notes

Lines 1–2: Given the space between the first partly preserved line and the top margin (ca. 4.2 cm, when the margin itself should have been 2.4–2.6 cm), it seems that only two lines of text are missing. At the beginning of line 2, the letter *mēm* is almost fully preserved, but the subsequent letter is almost entirely effaced. It is followed by a letter which could be an *ʿayin* or a *šîn*, but other letters are also possible.

Line 4: After נעול, a word of three or four letters is missing, but a reconstruction such as לשכם seems a bit too long. The rest of the line poses no difficulties, except for the *lāmed* of נקטול, of which only the central tip is preserved.

Line 5: The *lāmed* of אל is doubtful, as only its central tip seems to be preserved.

Line 6: The letters after כול are doubtful; one alternative reading would be סגר כולם האל ביד[נו, with a sudden shift from Aramaic to Hebrew. The use of סגר, 'handed over' may itself be a Hebraism, and is paralleled in *Genesis Apocryphon* XXII: 17, די סגר שנאיך בידך (see Fitzmyer 2004: 250).[7]

Line 7: The last word is extremely doubtful; the only visible elements are the upper tips of two letters, which are consistent with the reading ז[ר]ע, but allow for other readings as well.

Line 10: For the pleonastic use of קום, compare the examples adduced by Sokoloff 1974: 144 and Fitzmyer 2004: 207.

Line 14: The only visible letter is the top part of a *bêt*, *dālet*, *kap* or a *rêš* (though other letters are also possible).

Translation

1

2 [ ]

3 and I [ ]

4 in secret, and we shall enter [ ] and kill all the so[ns of]

5 Shechem, for (on) this day God gave [ ],

6 and (on) this time God handed all of them into [our] hands,

7 to kill them and do [justice…] the seed?

8 of truth. Then answered [Simeon]

9 my brother, being greatly zealous about [ ]

10 Rise, enter in your wisdom [ ]

11 and take my sword and yours [ ]

12 and we shall do justice [ ]

13 Shechem, and God? [ ]

14 [ ]

7 The Hebraisms found in ALD (both in the Genizah and in the Qumran fragments) have often been noted. See Greenfield and Stone 1979: 228; Stadel 2008: 42–7.

The Fragment in Relation to T-S 16.94

The new fragment is quite small and seems to be unparalleled by any of the non-Genizah fragments of ALD, which therefore cannot help us in reconstructing its lacunae. And yet, the Manchester fragment does help fill some of the gaps between the badly broken columns a and b of the Cambridge fragment. To facilitate locating the new fragment on the Cambridge bifolium, we may offer the following reconstruction of the left half of the bifolium (its right half consists of the well preserved columns c-f of the Cambridge fragment):

Recto

Manchester recto		Cambridge a
	1	--------------------------- 1
	2	--------------------------- 2
]ב?ו?]	3	--------------------------- 3
]י?דע ד?י?טמאו? [ב?ב]נ?יהון]	4	--------------------------- 4
]ה?ן ולא ישבקון יתהון עד]	5	--------------------------- 5
[די? כולהון?] יאבדו //	6	--------------------------- 6
[אד]י?ן?[ח]מור ומלילו במילי	7	--------------------------- 7
] א]ינש קריתהון //	8	--------------------------- 8
] ה]ון למגזר ולמעבדה	9	--------------------------- 9
]]למהוי להון חתנין	10	--------------------------- 10
]]ר?ו?תהון ולאשליותן	11	--------------------------- 11
]]י?ו עורלת	12	--------------------------- 12
[בישרהון]ן? וחשבת	13	--------------------------- 13
---------------------------	14	--------------------------- 14
---------------------------	15	15 דטמאת לבנ?[ ]
---------------------------	16	16 דברת די כל אנ[ ]
---------------------------	17	17 למעבד כדין בכל?[ ]
---------------------------	18	18 יעקב אבי ורא[ובן אחי]
---------------------------	19	19 ואמרנן להון ב[ ]נה די ה[וו]
---------------------------	20	20 צביין אינון בברתן ונהוי כולן א[חין]
---------------------------	21	21 וחברין גז?ורו עורלת בי?שרכון
---------------------------	22	22 והתחמיון כו[אתן] ותהון חתימין
---------------------------	23	23 כואתן במילת [קשו]ט ונהוי לכ[ון]

א

Plate 1: P 1185-1. (Reproduced by courtesy of the University Librarian and Director, The John Rylands Library, The University of Manchester)

Verso

Cambridge b		Manchester verso	
---------------------------	1		1
---------------------------	2	מ?..[ ]	2
---------------------------	3	ואנה [ ]	3
---------------------------	4	ברז ונעול [ו]נקטול? לכל ב[ני]	4
---------------------------	5	שכם ארום יומא הדין יהב אל?[ ]	5
---------------------------	6	ועידנא דין סגר כולה?ו?ן? אל ביד[נא?]	6
---------------------------	7	למקטל אינון ולמעבד[דין]ז?[ר]ע?	7
---------------------------	8	דקשוט אדין ענה [שמעון]	8
---------------------------	9	אחי מקנא סגי מן [ ]	9
---------------------------	10	קום עול בחוכמת[ך]	10
---------------------------	11	וסב חרבי ודילך [ ]	11
---------------------------	12	ונעבד די[ן]	12
---------------------------	13	שכם ואל[ ]	13
---------------------------	14	[ ]ב?[ ]	14
[ ] אחי בכל עדן	15	---------------------------	15
[ ]א די הוו בשכם	16	---------------------------	16
[ ]אחי ואחוי דן	17	---------------------------	17
[ ]בשכם ומה	18	---------------------------	18
מי[ן עב]די חמסא ואחוי	19	---------------------------	19
אינ?ו?ן יהודה די אנה ושמעון	20	---------------------------	20
אחי אזלנא לה[ ]דה לראובן	21	---------------------------	21
אחונן די למדנ?[ח א]שר ושור	22	---------------------------	22
יהודה קדמא[ל]מ?שבק עאנא	23	---------------------------	23

As this reconstruction shows, there is a gap of only 3 lines between the preserved section of column a and the beginning of the recto of the Manchester fragment. After the preserved parts of the recto, 11 lines are missing before the verso, while all three sections clearly deal with the Shechem episode. But after the verso of the new fragment, some 23 lines are missing before we reach column b of the Cambridge fragment, and in this large gap the Shechem episode ends and new episodes begin.

Plate 2: P 1185-2. (Reproduced by courtesy of the University Librarian and Director, The John Rylands Library, The University of Manchester)

The Shechem Episode

In reconstructing the preserved sections of the Shechem episode in the ALD, we may now go further than had previously been possible.[8] As is now clear, column a of the Cambridge fragment does not describe the dialogue between Jacob's sons and the Shechemites, only their deliberations about how they should approach the Shechemites, with Jacob and Reuben apparently suggesting to demand circumcision of the Shechemites as a condition for their partnership with Jacob's clan. But at the beginning of the recto of the new fragment we seem to be told by Levi that he knew that this was not offered in earnest, since they (presumably, Jacob and Reuben) were intent upon killing all the Shechemites. Then, in a new paragraph, we hear how they went to speak to Hamor and the Shechemites, and told them to circumcise themselves if they wish to be married into them, but they did so only to deceive them, and in line 13 Levi expresses his own thoughts on the matter, which are not preserved.

Taking our cue from the *Testament of Levi* 6.3, as reconstructed by Charles on the basis of MS Vatican Graec. 731, we may suggest that Levi had advised Jacob and Reuben to tell Hamor and his people *not* to circumcise themselves (Charles 1908: 39, n. 13).[9] He objected to this move because he wanted to kill the Shechemites (in line with the angelic instructions he had received earlier in the narrative), and apparently thought that it was not right to kill circumcised persons and unnecessary to employ such a ruse when he had already been told by an angel that God was on his side. Therefore, his thoughts at this stage of the plot probably were that his relatives behaved badly when they deceived the Shechemites in this ugly manner.

But the Shechemites did circumcise themselves, and we next join the plot when someone suggests that they should seize the opportunity, go to Shechem in secret, and kill all its inhabitants. In response, one of the brothers, presumably Simeon, is urging Levi to take both their swords and bring justice upon the Shechemites. The reference to Levi's sword probably was intended to echo an earlier scene, where the angel had given a sword to Levi and instructed him to wreak his vengeance upon the people of Shechem (see *Testament of Levi* 5.3). The next paragraph probably told of the actual

8 For previous reconstructions see Baarda 1992; Kugel 1992; Drawnel 2004: 105–7, 228–30; Greenfield, Stone and Eshel 2004: 56–7, 110–16; see also Feldman 2004.

9 Compare de Jonge 1978: 31, who follows the majority reading.

slaughter which ensued, eventually reaching the scene narrated in column b of the Cambridge fragment, which seems to refer back to the Shechem incident as an event which had already transpired or to describe a totally different event which took place in the same geographic region.

While this reconstruction is far from complete, and leaves many gaps in our knowledge of ALD's version of the Shechem incident, it does provide some interesting insights on this text's relations to other texts which used it, or were used by its author and served as its sources. On the one hand, it shows once again how heavily abridged is the version of this story found in the Greek *Testament of Levi*, whose use of ALD, or a later version thereof, is hardly in doubt.

On the other hand, it opens once again the complex question of whether *Jubilees* used ALD (as assumed by most scholars) or the other way around (as argued by Kugel 2007). Although there is no doubt that ALD and *Jubilees* tell very different stories (with ALD providing a far more detailed account of the Shechem episode), there are some interesting points of contact between the new fragment and the account found in *Jubilees*. Perhaps the most striking example is the statement in Jub. 30.6: 'And the Lord handed them over into the hand of the sons of Jacob so that they might destroy them with the sword and execute judgement against them (...)' (Wintemute 1985: 112), which sounds like a direct echo of the statement found on lines 5-8 of the verso of the Manchester fragment.[10] This similarity is especially significant precisely because it is extra-biblical, and serves, *inter alia*, to turn Genesis 34's story of the duplicity and treachery of Jacob's sons into a story of the execution by Jacob's sons of a preordained plan of divine vengeance. And when we examine both passages in their own narrative contexts, *Jubilees*' use of the *Aramaic Levi Document*, abridging the story and turning a statement uttered by one of the brothers into a statement uttered by the narrator at a slightly later point in the story, seems much more plausible than the opposite scenario. This, however, is an issue which requires a more thorough analysis than is possible here.

Conclusion

To end this paper, let us return to the single Genizah manuscript of ALD, of which we now have one fragment in Cambridge, one in Oxford, and one in Manchester, all of

10 See also the translation and notes in VanderKam 1989, II: 192–3.

which add up to less than one half of the original manuscript.[11] The very fact that this Second Temple period text has reached the Cairo Genizah is quite remarkable, since it belongs in an extremely small group of Genizah copies of non-canonical texts from the Second Temple.[12] As such, it is an exception to the rule that ancient Jewish texts which did not interest the rabbis of late antiquity, or were deliberately ignored by them, did not reach the Jews of medieval Cairo. Moreover, the fact that the Genizah contains no other manuscripts of this work in Aramaic, Hebrew, or Judaeo-Arabic clearly shows that the Jews of medieval Cairo were not interested in such texts. At a relatively early date, someone still took it seriously enough to produce a carefully copied manuscript, written in the rather unusual format of two columns per page, but even though at least one copy of this work was still available in the tenth and perhaps also the eleventh century, it clearly did not enjoy a wide circulation in the medieval Jewish community. In Cairo, at least, the Jews had many other texts, which they apparently found much more interesting.

If the entire Genizah, with its 200,000 fragments of parchment and paper, apparently contains only a single copy of the *Aramaic Levi Document*, and if the Qumran fragments of this work are in a sad state of preservation, then our chances of ever reconstructing the text in its entirety are extremely small, unless it turns up elsewhere, in copies of whose very existence we are currently unaware. But the single Genizah copy of this text was written on parchment of good quality, and even when it crumbled it did not entirely vanish. Thus, the identification of a third fragment of this manuscript, more than a century after the first two were identified, leaves us some room for optimism. The new fragment may be quite small, but it does help us reconstruct more of this ancient text, and it opens the possibility that more fragments of the same manuscript still lie hidden in the nooks and crannies of all the libraries and collections where materials from the Cairo Genizah are to be found, and where some of them had been unduly neglected for far too long.

---

11 This calculation is based on the assumption that the original Genizah manuscript had three bifolia (see Kugler 1996: 232–3 and Greenfield, Stone and Eshel 2004: xiv), of which we now have ca. 70 per cent of the first bifolium, none of the second, and half of the third. Of course, the original manuscript may have been much longer, and may have contained many other works as well.

12 For useful surveys of this topic, see Schiffman 1997–2001: 137–61; Stone 2002: 307–18. See also Bohak 2012.

References

Baarda, Tjitze. 1992. 'The Shechem Episode in the Testament of Levi: A Comparison with Other Traditions', in J.N. Bremmer and F. García Martínez (eds), *Sacred History and Sacred Texts in Early Judaism: A Symposium in Honour of A.S. van der Woude* (Contributions to Biblical Exegesis and Theology 5, Kampen). 11–73

Bohak, Gideon. 2011. 'A New Genizah Fragment of the Aramaic Levi Document', *Tarbiz* 79, 373–83 (in Hebrew)

—— 2012. 'From Qumran to Cairo: The Lives and Times of a Jewish Exorcistic Formula (with an appendix by Shaul Shaked)', in Ildikó Csepregi and Charles Burnett (eds), *Ritual Healing: Magic, Ritual and Medical Therapy from Antiquity until the Early Modern Period* (Florence). 31–52

Charles, Robert H. 1908. *The Greek Versions of the Testaments of the Twelve Patriarchs*. (Oxford)

Charles, Robert H. and A. Cowley. 1907. 'An Early Source of the Testaments of the Twelve Patriarchs', *Jewish Quarterly Review* 19, 566–83

Drawnel, Henryk. 2004. *An Aramaic Wisdom Text from Qumran: A New Interpretation of the Levi Document* (Supplements to the Journal for the Study of Judaism 86. Leiden)

Feldman, Louis H. 2004. 'Philo, Pseudo-Philo, Josephus, and Theodotus on the Rape of Dinah', *Jewish Quarterly Review* 94, 253–77

Fitzmyer, Joseph A. 2004. *The Genesis Apocryphon of Qumran Cave 1 (1Q20): A Commentary*[3]. (Rome)

Greenfield, Jonas C. and Michael E. Stone. 1979. 'Remarks on the Aramaic Testament of Levi from the Geniza', *Revue biblique* 86, 214–30

Greenfield, Jonas C., Michael E. Stone and Esther Eshel. 2004. *The Aramaic Levi Document: Edition, Translation, Commentary*. (Studia in Veteris Testamenti Pseudepigrapha 19. Leiden)

Jonge, Marinus de. 1978. *The Testaments of the Twelve Patriarchs: A Critical Edition of the Greek Text*. (Pseudepigrapha Veteris Testamenti Graece I/II. Leiden)

Kugel, James L. 1992. 'The Story of Dinah in the *Testament of Levi*', *Harvard Theological Review* 85, 1–34

—— 2007. 'How Old is the *Aramaic Levi Document*?', *Dead Sea Discoveries* 14, 291–312

Kugler, Robert A. 1996. *From Patriarch to Priest: The Levi-Priestly Tradition from Aramaic Levi to Testament of Levi*. (SBL Early Judaism and Its Literature 9. Atlanta)

Milik, J.T. 1955. 'Aramaic Levi', in D. Barthélémy, J.T. Milik et al., *Discoveries in the Judaean Desert, I: Qumran Cave 1* (Oxford). 87–91

Pass, H.L. and J. Arendzen. 1900. 'Fragment of an Aramaic Text of the Testament of Levi', *Jewish Quarterly Review* 12, 651–61

Puech, Émile. 2002. 'Le Testament de Lévi en araméen de la Geniza du Caire', *Revue de Qumran* 20, 511–56

Schattner-Rieser, Ursula. 2007. 'J. T. Milik's Monograph on the Testament of Levi and the Reconstructed Aramaic text of the Prayer of Levi and the Vision of Levi's Ascent to Heaven from Qumran Caves 4 and 1', *Qumran Chronicle* 15, 139–54

Schiffman, Lawrence H. 1997–2001. 'Second Temple Literature and the Cairo Genizah', *Proceedings of the American Academy for Jewish Research* 63, 137–61

Sokoloff, Michael. 1974. *The Targum to Job from Qumran Cave XI*. (Ramat-Gan)

Stadel, Christian. 2008. *Hebraismen in den aramäischen Texten vom Toten Meer*. (Heidelberg)

Stone, Michael E. 2002. 'Aramaic Levi in its Contexts', *Jewish Studies Quarterly* 9, 307–26

Stone, Michael E. and Jonas C. Greenfield. 1996. 'Aramaic Levi Document', in G. Brooke et al., *Discoveries in the Judaean Desert, XXII: Qumran Cave 4 XVII Parabiblical Texts, Part 3* (Oxford). 1–72

VanderKam, James C. 1989. *The Book of Jubilees*. 2 vols, (Corpus Scriptorum Christianorum Orientalium, Scriptores Aethiopici 87–8. Leuven)

Wintemute, O.S. 1985. 'Jubilees', in James H. Charlesworth (ed.), *The Old Testament Pseudepigrapha*, vol. 2 (Garden City, NY). 35–142

Between Cambridge and Manchester: Reuniting a Leaf of Maimonides' *Guide for the Perplexed* from the Cairo Genizah

Ben Outhwaite and Friedrich Niessen[1]

Taylor-Schechter Genizah Research Unit, University of Cambridge

It is gratifying that even after a century of scholarly interest the Cairo Genizah can still produce exciting discoveries relating to the literary activity of Moses Maimonides (1138–1204), the towering figure of medieval Jewish Egypt. It is particularly fitting that the fragment described below, an autograph of Maimonides' greatest philosophical work, *Dalālat al-Ḥā'irīn* ('Guide for the Perplexed'), was discovered in 2004, the eight-hundredth anniversary of his death. Although the Genizah has provided a great number of Maimonidean works in autograph, this fragment represents only the sixth discovery of an autograph of the *Guide*.[2]

Since 2004, a number of further autographs by Maimonides have been discovered in the Taylor-Schechter Collection at Cambridge University Library, both of documents and of his literary works. These include three new responsa, another piece of his 'unpublished' halakhic work *Hilkôt ha-Yᵉrûšalmî*, and part of a letter apparently containing a medical recipe.[3] It is quite reasonable to assume that Maimonides' own personal archive was deposited in full into the Genizah of the Ben Ezra Synagogue in

1 Sadly, the co-author of this article, my gifted and much valued colleague, Friedrich Niessen, died in January 2009. This is a revised version of the article that originally appeared as Outhwaite and Niessen 2006: 287–97.

2 A large number of autographs are reproduced in Sassoon 1956–66, I: plates XX–LXI. A list of further autographs may be found in Hopkins 1983: 273–96. More recently Hopkins (2001) has published a considerable number of fragments of Maimonides' Mishnah commentary.

3 All those mentioned have been published online as the Genizah Research Unit of Cambridge University Library's 'Fragment of the Month', as follows (all URLs accessed August 2012): Ben Outhwaite, *Two New Responsa of Moses Maimonides* (http://www.lib.cam.ac.uk/Taylor-Schechter/fotm/april-2007.html); Mordechai A. Friedman and Amir Ashur, *A Newly-Discovered Autograph Responsum of Maimonides, Lower Script of a Pseudo-Palimpsest Colophon: T-S AS 221.306–307* (http://www.lib.cam.ac.uk/Taylor-Schechter/fotm/may-2012/index.html); Zvi Stampfer, *A New Autograph of Hilkhot ha-Yerushalmi by Maimonides, T-S NS 284.120* (http://www.lib.cam.ac.uk/Taylor-Schechter/fotm/september-2011/index.html); and Esther-Miriam Wagner, *A Newly-Discovered Fragment of a Letter Written by Maimonides: T-S AS 152.86* (http://www.lib.cam.ac.uk/Taylor-Schechter/fotm/october-2007/index.html).

Fustat, given the regularity with which fragments in his handwriting are being discovered, and we should certainly expect further discoveries to be made.[4]

The first autograph fragment of the *Guide* to be discovered consisted of two leaves from the Taylor-Schechter Collection and was published by Hirschfeld (1903: 677–81). These leaves, separate but grouped under the same classmark, T-S 10Ka4.1, represent Part 1, Chapters 64–5 and Part 2, Chapters 32–3 of the *Guide*. Yellin (1929/1930) subsequently published two leaves from the Mosseri Collection (Mosseri VIII.35), containing Part 1, Chapters 17–21. More recently Hopkins (1987) published ENA 3198.5 from the Jewish Theological Seminary, a fragment originally discovered in the 1940s (but not published) by M. Lutzki. This leaf represents Part 1, Chapters 2–3 of the *Guide*. In 1982 Hopkins discovered two small pieces from the Gaster Collection of the John Rylands University Library in Manchester, B 2597 and B 4094 (Hopkins 1985). These form the lower part of a single leaf from Part 2, Chapter 30 of the *Guide* and are of particular significance to the current discovery. The fifth autograph is a single torn leaf in the Mosseri Collection (Mosseri VIII.24.1) from Part 1, Chapter 60 (JNUL 1990: 212).

The newly-discovered autograph is Or.1081.2.44 in Cambridge University Library's Genizah Collection. The binder Or.1081.2 is composed of fragments from the Cairo Genizah that were obtained by the Library prior to Solomon Schechter's famous visit to Egypt in 1897.[5] It was probably bought from the bookseller S. Raffalovich, but there are few library records for these early Genizah acquisitions, and so its modern history is sketchy. Or.1081.2.44 is a damaged paper fragment, measuring 15.7 cm high by 15.8 cm wide and containing 17 lines on recto and 16 lines on verso; the lower third of the leaf has been torn away. It is heavily stained and rubbed, particularly on the verso, which may explain why, despite being in the unmistakeable hand used by Maimonides for his draft works, it has been overlooked for the last hundred years. The size of paper is the same as that used for the other known autographs of the *Guide*. The fact that they are all written in the same style and on similarly-sized pieces of paper, strongly suggests that all known autographs of the *Guide* derive from the same draft copy of the work. Hopkins (1987: 466) has similarly expressed this view, contrary to the earlier opinion of Chapira (1935: 11) who believed that the Mosseri and Cambridge fragments represent

4 It is possible that Maimonides' archive wasn't deposited immediately after his death but was retained by his descendants and only consigned to the Genizah later on, possibly in the fourteenth century; see Sirat and Di Donato 2011: 21.

5 For the full story of the discovery of the Cairo Genizah see Glickman 2011, Hoffman and Cole 2011, and Reif 2000.

different stages of the text's development and therefore derive from two originally separate drafts of the work.[6]

It can be confidently asserted that Or.1081.2.44 and other leaves from the draft *Guide* are in Maimonides' own hand thanks to a number of important discoveries from the Cairo Genizah of Maimonidean literary works, responsa and letters. Comparison of the present manuscript with other examples of Maimonides' handwriting, such as a draft of the opening of *Hilkôt Nizqê Māmôn* from his *Mishneh Torah* (T-S 10K8.1), a Judaeo-Arabic draft of his treatise *On Sexual Intercourse* (T-S Ar.44.79), and a responsum, signed, as was his practice, וכתב משה, 'Moses wrote this' (T-S 8K13.8), shows that the handwriting is identical. Maimonides, in fact, employed different styles of hand depending on the text being written, a neat hand — known as his 'slow cursive' — for formal letters and a far less legible hand — his 'quick cursive' — for draft literary works and responsa; the two hands are clearly related, however.[7] Ultimately the attribution of all Maimonidean autographs is securely rooted in S. Assaf's unearthing in 1943 of T-S 12.192, a letter not only written but also signed in full by the man himself, משה בר׳ מימון זצ״ל, 'Moses son of the scholar Maymûn of blessed memory' (Assaf 1943: 1–3, 7).

There can be no doubt that the current fragment of the *Guide* is related to at least one of the previous discoveries, since the two small fragments from the John Rylands Library in Manchester, B 2597 and B 4094, which together make up the lower third of a leaf are clearly the missing portion of Or.1081.2.44: the torn parts match very closely and only a tiny amount of text has been lost in-between. When the new Cambridge and two Manchester fragments are placed together, the text of the *Guide* preserved in them, Part 2, Chapter 30, corresponds to 249:9–250:25 in Munk's standard printed edition (1931).

Below we give the complete text of the new fragment, Or.1081.2.44, with notes detailing the differences from the printed edition and providing other relevant comments. Since B 2597 and B 4094 belong with the Cambridge fragment, we have provided a new transcription of their contents too. In his original publication of the Rylands fragments, Hopkins stated that 'The manuscripts are not well preserved (...). It is very likely that after appropriate treatment (...) more words and letters could be

6 For the most recent and thorough examination of the status of the Maimonidean drafts, see Sirat and Di Donato 2011: 49–52; they discuss the current leaf on 165–75, where they also give a French translation of the text preserved in it.

7 See the thorough discussion of the handwriting employed in different Maimonidean autographs in Sassoon 1956–66, I: 19–28.

extracted from the fragments than are visible on the photographs (...)' (1985: 713). To prepare the new edition, we obtained from the John Rylands Library a high-quality digital image of those fragments, which enabled us in many cases to add to or improve upon Hopkins' readings.[8] Since areas of the Cambridge fragment are similarly poorly preserved, we supplemented our examination of the manuscript itself with the use of a digital image, the manipulation of which elucidated some of the more illegible parts of the text.[9]

In the following transcription we have noted in every case where the manuscripts deviate from Munk's published edition. We have also drawn occasional comparisons with the important Arabic-script edition by Atay (1974), since this has, in a number of cases, preserved similar readings to our leaf. The differences between the draft and the Munk edition are mainly of two types, either reflecting the substitution of one word with a synonym — presumably for stylistic reasons — or the correction of typical Judaeo-Arabic features toward a more Classical Arabic idiom.

Transcription of Cambridge University Library Or.1081.2.44; Rylands Gaster Collection B 2597 and B 4094

Remarks on the Transcription

The following symbols are used: [ ] encloses restoration of text lost or illegible; [...] indicates where an unknown amount of text is lost; < > encloses minor additions to the text in the margin (major marginal additions are dealt with separately); // indicates the tear between Cambridge University Library Or.1081.2.44 and the two John Rylands fragments, B 2597 and B 4094. Maimonides' own signs of deletion (supralinear lines and the striking through of words) have been preserved as he wrote them.

As is common in Maimonides' autographs, he is inconsistent in his use of diacritics, sometimes including the diacritics for letters such as Arabic ث, represented by ת with two dots above it, or ج, represented by ג with a single dot above, and sometimes not.[10] For typographic reasons, we have noted where they appear in the

8 The authors would like to express their thanks to the staff of The John Rylands University Library, The University of Manchester, in particular Carol Burrows, Stella Butler, Dorothy Clayton and the photography department, for their superb efficiency in providing the images so quickly.

9 Thanks are due to Scott Maloney and Ellis Weinberger for their assistance in obtaining and manipulating the images.

10 For similar inconsistency in Maimonides' autographs of his Mishnah Commentary, see Hopkins 2001: xxviii.

autograph by the use of a Hebrew *gērēš* sign: Arabic j (ج) is represented by ג׳, ḏ (ذ) by ד׳, ẓ (ظ) by ט׳, ḍ (ض) by צ׳, ḫ (خ) by כ׳, t (ت) by ת״, ṯ (ث) by ת״׳.

Recto

אל[אנסא]ן [וכדל]ך [גא] אלנץ   עלי [ה]דא אלתר[תיב]
סוא ל[ם] יגאדר פיה שיא   מן הד[א]
וממא יג׳ב אן תעלמה   קולה[ם] כל [   ]
לקומתן נב[רא]ו ל[ד]עתן נבראו ל[צביונ]ם נבר[או] יק[ול]
אן כל מא כלק אנמא כ[ל]ק עלי כמאל כמיתה ועל[י]
צורת״ה ובאחסן אעראצ׳ה והו קולה לצביונם מן צ[בי]
היא לכל הארצות פאעלם הד׳א איצ׳א פהו אצל
כביר קד בֿצח ובאן   וממא יג׳ב אן ת״עת״ברה
ג[דא כונה] ד׳כר כ׳לק אדם פי ששת ימי בראשית וקאל זכר
ונקבה בראם ~~תם אפתתח~~ וכו׳ וכתם אלכל וקאל ויכלו וכו׳
תם אפתתח אפתתאח אכ׳ר לכ׳לק חוה מן אדם ודכר עץ
החיים ועץ הדעת וחדית אלנחש ות״לך אלקצה
וג׳על הד׳א כלה בעד אן חט אדם ~~בגן עדן~~ [וכ]ל
אלחכמים מג׳מעין אן הד׳א כלה כא[ן // יום אל]גמעה ואדא
חמלת אלנצוץ עלי טאהרהא ואנ[ה] // לם [י]תגיר אמר בוג׳ה
בעד ששת ימי // בראשית פלד׳[לך] לא יסתשנע שי מן
[ת]ל//ך אלאמור כמא קלנא אנה אלי אלאן לם תחצל טביעה
// מסתקרה ומע הדא קד דכרוא אשיא סאסמעהא
// לך מלתקטה מן [א]מאכנהא [וא]נבהך איצ׳א על[י] אשיא
//כמת״׳ל מא נבהונא הם [עליהם אלסלאם] ואעלם אן הד׳ה
// אלאשיא אלת״׳י אדכרהא לך מן [כלאם] אלחכמים אנמא הי אקאו[י]ל
// פי גאיה אלכמאל בינה אלתאו[יל] ל[לד״י ד׳כ]רוהא לה מחכמה
// ג׳דא פלד׳לך לא אבאלג פי שרחהא [ולא א]בסטהא לאן לא

Right-hand Margin

[...] טביעה וג׳וד אלעאלם אלספלי כלה ואלצ[ו] טארי עליה חסבך אן בעדם אלצו ת[בקי] // אלחאלה אלמסתקרה

Plate 1: Composite image of Cambridge University Library Or.1081.2.44 (recto) and John Rylands Library B 2597-1 and B 4094-1. (Reproduced by courtesy of the University Librarian and Director, The John Rylands Library, The University of Manchester and by kind permission of the Syndics of Cambridge University Library)

Plate 2: Composite image of Cambridge University Library Or.1081.2.44 (verso) and John Rylands Library B 2597-2 and B 4094-2. (Reproduced by courtesy of the University Librarian and Director, The John Rylands Library, The University of Manchester and by kind permission of the Syndics of Cambridge University Library)

Notes on the Transcription

Munk's edition (1931) is hereafter referred to as M, and Atay's Arabic edition (1974) as A. Principally for reasons of brevity, we have noted only the more significant differences between the current transcription and that of Hopkins' edition (1985) of the Rylands fragments (hereafter H). Subsequent references to M, A and H follow the form M (page:line).

Recto (including the margin) contains the text of M (249:9–250:1).

Recto:

1. אלנץ: M (249:11) אלנץ פי מעשה בראשית.

   וכדל[ך]: M (249:11) has the synonymous וכד׳א. See also verso line 6.

1–3. Maimonides left a space of about 1.5 cm in the middle of these lines, due to a vertical tear in the paper. As noted by Hirschfeld (1903: 677), it appears that Maimonides wrote his draft on whatever paper he had to hand, including pieces that evidently had some minor damage.

2. יגאדר פיה שיא: M (249:12) יגאדר שיא.

3. כל [...]: we would expect כל מעשה בראשית as in M (249:12–13), but the traces of text do not seem to support this assumption. The draft appears to have been phrased slightly differently at this point.

5–6. ועל[י] צורת״ה: M (249:14) ועלי כמאל צרותה.

8. בצה: there is a line of erasure above the ב; Maimonides probably began to write באן and then changed it to the hendiadys צח ובאן, the reading preserved in M (249:16).

9–10. זכר ונקבה בראם is a quotation from Gen. 5:2, whereas M (249:18) reads ברא אותם, which is from Gen. 1:27. Other manuscripts attest Gen. 5:2 at this point; see A (386: n. 1054).

10. אלכל: M (249:18) אלכ׳לק כלה.

11. אפתתאח: as is normal in Judaeo-Arabic, Maimonides omits the *'ālep* of accusative *tanwīn* on the undefined triptote אפתתאח (see Blau 1961a: 148). *'Ālep* was appended in later versions, אפתתאחא (M 249:19), in accordance with Classical Arabic grammar. For another occurrence of the omission of *'ālep* see the note to ט׳הר, verso l. 3.

13. כלה: M (249:21) כלה אנה כאן; A (386:10) كله انه.

   חט: M (249:21) has the synonymous ג׳על.

   ~~בגן עדן~~: this phrase has been deleted in the draft, but appears in M (249:21) as פי גן עדן.

14. אלחכמים: M (249:21) אלחכמים ז״ל.

   מג׳מעין: in place of the generalized Judaeo-Arabic oblique masculine plural ־ין, M (249:21) has the classicizing nominative form מג׳מעון.[11]

   הד׳א כלה כא[ן]: M (249:22) הד׳ה אלקצה כלהא כאנת.

---

11 For the use of the generalized plural ־ין in Judaeo-Arabic, see Blau 1961b: 31.

14–15. ואדא חמלת אלנצוץ עלי טאהרהא, ‘and if the verses are taken literally’, is a phrase lacking in M; a similar formulation occurs in the introduction to the *Guide*, פאד׳א חמלת עלי ט׳ואהרהא (M 11:16). Perhaps Maimonides deleted it at this point in his text to tone down what might otherwise have been understood as overt criticism of the rabbinical opinion he had just cited.

15. אנה: M (249:22) ואנה.

17. [ת]ל//ך : the word is split across both the Cambridge and John Rylands fragments, with the latter preserving only the tail of the *kap*.

20. [עליהם]: M (249:21) has the Hebrew blessing ז״ל.

23. ג׳דא: as noted by H (714: n. 11) the diacritic dot belonging above the ג (for Arabic ج) appears over the ד.

[... א]בסטהא : H (714:11) mistakenly read this as [... א]בטסהא and noted that it seemed to have been miswritten.

לאן לא : H (714:11) has לילא, which occurs in A (387:1), لئلا ; but the draft clearly reads לאן לא, as in M (249:28–250:1).

The margin contains the text of M (249:9–11).

1. טארי: in place of the usual Judaeo-Arabic spelling, M (249:10) has a more classicizing form, טארִ.[12]

Verso

אכון מגלה סוד　　　בל ד׳כר[י ל]הא [בתרתיב]
מא [ו]בתנביה יסיר　　　יכפי פי פהמהא [למ]תלך
ק[א]לוא אן אדם [ו]חוה　　　כלקא מעא מתחדין ט׳הר
[ל]ט׳הר ואנה קסם פאכ׳ד׳　　　נצפה והו חוה וקולה אחת
מצלעות[יו] קאל א[חד שקי]ה ואסת[ד]ל[וא] מן צלע המשכן
[אלדי ת]רגמתה סטר משכנה וכדלך קאלוא מן סטרוי
ואפ[הם] כיף כאן אלתב[יין] אנהמא [את]נין בגהה מא והמא
[וא]חד כמא קאל עצם מעצמי ובשר מ[בשרי וזאד ד׳לך] תא[כידא] <ב[קו]לה>
אן א[לא]סמי[ה] עליהמא ג׳מיעא ואחדה אש[ה כי] מאיש לוקחה
זאת ואכסד אתחאדהמא וקאל ודבק באש[תו והיו] ל[בשר אחד פמא]
[אשד ג׳ה]ל מן [לא יפ]הם אן הד׳א כלה למעני צרורה פקד
[באן הדא וממ]א יגב אן תעלמה ותתנבה עליה כון אלנחש
[לם יבאשר] אדם בוגה ולא כלמה ואנמא כאנת מחאור[ת]ה

12 Nouns that in Classical Arabic take the ending *-īn* (shortened from *-iyūn* and written with the *tanwīn kasra* sign) are usually written in Judaeo-Arabic with *-ī*, i.e., י-. See Blau 1961b: 107. The inclusion of טארי, a verbal noun from a root with final *hamza*, is due to the merging of final-*hamza* verbs with those of final-*ya* in Judaeo-Arabic. See Blau 1961a: 84.

14 [ומבאשרתה לחוה] ובתוסט חוה תאדי אדם והל[ך] מן אלנחש

15 [ומממ]א יג׳ב אן תעלמה מא בינוה פ[י]

16 // [אל]מ[דרש וד׳]לך א[נהם] // אעל//מוא א[ן // אלנ]חש מרכוב והו קדר

17 // גמל וראכבה הו אלד׳י [אג]וא חוה ואן אלראכ[ב כאן סמאל]

18 // והדה אלאסמיה יטלק[ו]נהא עלי אלס[טן תג׳ד]הם [י]ק[ולו]ן [פי]

19 // עדה מואצ׳ע ואלסטן אר[א]ד אן [י]עת״ר [אבר]הם חתי לא יג׳יב

20 // אלי תקריב יצחק וכדלך א[ראד אן יעת״ר יצ]חק חת[י] לא יטיע

21 // אבאה ודכרוא איצ׳א פי ה[ד׳ה אל]ק[צה אעני פ]י אלעקידה קאלוא

22 // בא סמאל אצל א[בינו אבר]הם [אמר] לו מה סבא [הוב]דת לבך וכו׳

23 // [פ]קד באן לך אן סמאל הו אל[ס]טן והד׳ה אלא[סמיה איצ׳א] למעני

24 // כמא אן אסמיה [אל]נחש למעני וקאלוא פי מגיה ל[כ׳ד]ע

25 // [ח]וה ה[י]ה [סמאל רוכ]ב עלי[ה] והקבה סוחק על גמל ורוכבו

Right-hand Margin

1 // [ואנ]מא מכנת [ ] בין אלנחש [וחוה] ובין זרעו וז[רע]ה

2 // [ולא שך אן זרעה] הו זרע [א]דם ואגרב מן הד׳א ארתבאט אל[נח]ש בחוה [אעני]

3 // [זרעו בזרעה רא]ש ועקב וכונהא גאלבה לה ברא[ש ו]הו גאל[ב להא ב]עקב

Notes on the Transcription

Verso contains the text of M (250:1–25).

1. בל: M (250:1) has the synonymous לכן.
2. בתנביה: A (387:2) shares the draft's reading, بتنبيه, but M (250:1) has ובתנביה.
3. [קא]לוא: M (250:2) פמן דלך קולהם.

   ט׳הר: M (250:3) has ט׳הרכא, with the *'ālep* denoting accusative *tanwīn*. The draft, as is usual in Judaeo-Arabic, doesn't indicate the case-ending.[13] See recto l. 11 for another occurrence.
4. חוה: M (250:3) חוה וקובל בה.
5. קאל: M (250:4) יעני.
6. משכנה: M (250:5) משכנא.

   וכדלך: M (250:5) has the synonymous וכד׳א. See recto l. 1 for a similar substitution.

   סטרוי: M (250:5) סטרוהי.
7. ואפהם: M (250:5) פאפהם.

   אתנין: M (250:6) has the Classical Arabic nominative form of the dual, אתנאן, in place of the draft's use of the oblique.[14]

13 The manuscript is faded and rubbed at this point, but no *'ālep* appears to have been written. For the loss of case-endings in Judaeo-Arabic, see Blau 1961b: 78–9, 167–9.

8. ב[קו]לה: the last word of the line is written in the left-hand margin

9. לוקחה: the draft writes לֻקֳחָה in the quotation from Gen. 2:23 with the vowel-letter *wāw*, as is common in post-biblical Hebrew orthography. M 250:8 follows the Masoretic Text's orthography with לקחה.

12. וממא: this section, from וממא to והל[ך] מן אלנחש (l. 12–14), occurs later in the text of the published editions (M 250:19–21). For והל[ך] מן אלנחש, 'he was killed by the serpent', M (250:21) reads the more classicizing ואהלכה אלנחש, 'the serpent killed him'.[15]

16. אעל//מוא: the word is split between the Cambridge and Rylands fragments. H (715:2) reads only the final *'ālep* in the Rylands fragment and reconstructs it wrongly as [דכ׳רו]א, the reading found in M (250:11).

19. ואלסטן: H (715:5) reads this as אן אלסטן, like אן אלשטן in M (250:13), after stating that he initially read it as ואלסטן (H 716: n. 5). In fact, his initial reading is preferable and the dot of ink that he took for the bottom of a final *nûn* is perhaps a slightly wayward diacritic from the *dālet* of וכד׳לך in the line below. Note that Maimonides writes *sāmek* for etymological *sîn* here and in line 18 above.

25. ה[י]ה [סמאל רוכ]ב עליה: H (716:11) has ה]יה סמאל רו[כב עליו. Hopkins notes that the reading עליה, found in A (388:4), may be possible. The traces of ink remaining in the fragment indicate that it should indeed be read עליה and not עליו.

Margin (verso)

1. Hopkins found the entire first line illegible, but enhancement of the digital image provided by the John Rylands University Library has elucidated parts of it.

   ואנ]מא מכנת ...]: this is a tentative reading of the almost illegible text. The draft differs considerably from the published editions at this point.

Conclusion

The newly-discovered autograph, Cambridge University Library Or.1081.2.44, when combined with Rylands Gaster Collection B 2597 and B 4094, forms a complete leaf of Maimonides' draft copy of the *Guide for the Perplexed*, Part 2, Chapter 30, and adds to our knowledge of the early history of that work. Autographs such as this provide valuable insight into Maimonides' techniques of composition and the evolution of his ideas, and it is to be hoped that continued scholarly investigation of the Cairo Genizah will bring forth yet more works from the great man's hand.

---

14 In Judaeo-Arabic the oblique form of the dual (like the oblique form of the masculine plural) became generalized. See Blau 1961b:, 78–9 1961a: 103–4.

15 מן can be used to denote the agent of a passive verb in Judaeo-Arabic, see Blau 1961a: 180.

References

Assaf, Simha. 1943. ‘מגנזי ה״גניזה״’, *Sinai* 13, 1–8

Atay, Hüseyin. 1974. *Delâletü'l-Hâirîn, Filozof Mûsâ ibn Meymûn el-Kurtubî 1135–1205.* (Ankara)

Blau, Joshua. 1961a. *A Grammar of Mediaeval Judaeo-Arabic.* (Jerusalem)

—— 1961b. *The Emergence and Linguistic Background of Judaeo-Arabic.* (Jerusalem)

Chapira, Bernard. 1935. ‘Un autographe de Maïmonide, fragment d’un commentaire arabe inédit sur le Michné Tora’, *Revue des études juives* 99, 8–13

Glickman, Mark. 2011. *Sacred Treasure – the Cairo Genizah: The Amazing Discoveries of Forgotten Jewish History in an Egyptian Synagogue Attic.* (Woodstock, Vermont)

Hirschfeld, Hartwig. 1903. ‘The Arabic Portion of the Cairo Genizah at Cambridge’, *Jewish Quarterly Review* 15:4, 677–97

Hoffman, Adina and Peter Cole. 2011. *Sacred Trash: the Lost and Found World of the Cairo Geniza.* (New York)

Hopkins, Simon. 1983. ‘A New Autograph Fragment of Maimonides’ *Hilkhot ha-Yerushalmi*’, *JSS* 28, 273–96

—— 1985. ‘Two New Maimonidean Autographs in the John Rylands University Library’, *Bulletin of the John Rylands University Library of Manchester* 67, 710–17

—— 1987. ‘An Unpublished Autograph Fragment of Maimonides’s “*Guide of the Perplexed*”’, *Bulletin of the School of Oriental and African Studies* 50:3, 465–9

—— 2001. *Maimonides’s Commentary on Tractate Shabbat: The Draft Commentary according to Autograph Fragments from the Cairo Genizah.* (Jerusalem)

JNUL (Jewish National and University Library). 1990. *Catalogue of the Jack Mosseri Collection, Edited by the Institute of Microfilmed Hebrew Manuscripts with the Collaboration of Numerous Specialists.* (Jerusalem) (in Hebrew)

Munk, Salomon. 1931. *المקור הערבי לפי הוצאת, دلالة الحائرين דלאלה אלחאירין (ספר מורה נבוכים) לרבנו משה בן מימון. בצרוף חלופי נוסחאות, מפתחות וקטעים מכתב ידו של הרמב״ם*. (Jerusalem)

Outhwaite, Ben and Friedrich Niessen. 2006. ‘A Newly-Discovered Autograph Fragment of Maimonides’ Guide for the Perplexed from the Cairo Genizah’, *JJS* 57:2, 287–97

Reif, Stefan C. 2000. *A Jewish Archive from Old Cairo: The History of Cambridge University’s Genizah Collection.* (Richmond, Surrey)

Sassoon, Solomon D. 1956–66. *Maimonidis Commentarius in Mischnam.* 3 vols, (Copenhagen)

Sirat, Colette and Silvia Di Donato. 2011. *Maïmonide et les brouillons autographes du* Dalâlat al-hâ’irîn (Guide des égarés). (Paris)

Yellin, David. 1929/1930. ‘Two leaves in Maimonides’ Autograph’, *Tarbiz* 1, 93–106

The Qillirian Q^{e}*rôbâ* והיה אויב מתגבר in the Rylands Genizah

Michael Rand
Academy of the Hebrew Language

Among the liturgical and poetic fragments found in the Rylands Genizah collection is a leaf containing a q^{e}*rôbâ* for the Seventeenth of Tammuz by the Classical Palestinian *payy*^{e}*ṭān* ’El‘azar b^{e}-rabbî Qillîr (fl. early seventh century). In the following I would like to present this item, together with related material, with a view to elucidating what it can contribute to our understanding of Qillirian compositional technique.

In the Palestinian liturgical rite for which Qillîr composed his *piyyûṭîm*, the *'amîdâ* of fast days (which does not include the recitation of the q^{e}*dûššâ*) may be accompanied by a q^{e}*rôbâ*. The basic classical q^{e}*rôbâ* is a poetic composition built up out of equivalent strophic units, one for each of the eighteen benedictions of the Palestinian *'amîdâ* (see Fleischer 2007: 199–202). In the case of q^{e}*rôbôt* for fast days, the sequence of these strophic units is interrupted in the sixth benediction (i.e., the one concluding with the formula המרבה לסלוח; for the text of the Palestinian *'amîdâ* see Ehrlich 2006 and Ehrlich 2007) by means of the insertion of penitential poems called s^{e}*lîḥôt* (see Fleischer 2007: 203–4). Originally, the sequence of strophic units making up the q^{e}*rôbâ* was meant to resume after the recitation of the s^{e}*lîḥôt*. However, in the observed practice of Genizah manuscripts (which presumably reflects the liturgical practice of the communities for which they were produced) it may happen that the sequence of the q^{e}*rôbâ*'s strophic units is truncated as a result of the insertion of the s^{e}*lîḥôt*, so that an incomplete q^{e}*rôbâ* containing only six strophic units remains. Such is the case with the Qillirian q^{e}*rôbâ* והיה אויב מתגבר.

The q^{e}*rôbâ* והיה אויב מתגבר was originally published by Fleischer as part of his investigation of the use of the list of twenty-four priestly courses in *piyyûṭ* (see Fleischer 1968b: 155–8; for the twenty-four priestly courses in *piyyûṭ*, see also Fleischer 2007: 152–3). Fleischer's publication was based on one manuscript witness: Cambridge, Westminster College, Liturgica II 84. This manuscript is a contiguous bifolium. The q^{e}*rôbâ* begins at the top of the recto of the first leaf, and continues to the bottom of the verso. At the top of the recto of the second leaf is copied the s^{e}*lîḥâ* אל תליני יחידתי מפחד מגורות (signed אברהם in the last strophe), which ends in the middle of the verso. The bottom portion of the verso is left blank (i.e., no *s*^{e}*lîḥôt* are copied after אל תליני יחידתי, nor is the strophic sequence of the *q*^{e}*rôbâ* resumed). It is now clear that the *q*^{e}*rôbâ* in question is attested in the Genizah in two recensions. The recension published by Fleischer — recension A — is attested in an additional manuscript: Cambridge, T-S NS 202.61. Unfortunately, this manuscript is severely damaged, and in its present state it contains the *q*^{e}*rôbâ* only up to the fourth benediction, so that no additional textual material can be gleaned from it. However, it provides at least two textual variants that allow for the improvement of the text published by Fleischer (see below). The main witness for recension B of the *q*^{e}*rôbâ* is MS Manchester, Rylands B 3045-1/2. With the help of this witness it is now possible to establish that MS Cincinnati, HUC Acc. 965 contains the text of recension B. Below are provided critical editions of both recensions, to a comparison of which I now turn.

Discussion of Recensions A and B

Recension A of the *q*^{e}*rôbâ* is built up out of strophic groups each of which contains a primary and a secondary strophe. The major strophes contain seven lines each. The first line of each strophe opens with a word from the framing verse והיה כי יאמרו אליך וגו' (Ezek. 21:12). The first five lines of each strophe are subject to a א"ב acrostic order, one letter per strophe. In the case of the second and sixth primary strophes, the sixth line begins with the expected acrostic letter as well (lines 17, 61). In the fifth primary strophe, the sixth line was apparently omitted by the copyist (line 50), so that it is impossible to know whether or not it was subject to the acrostic requirement. The last line of every primary strophe consists of a quote from Ezekiel,[1] no attempt being made to bring it in line with the acrostic structure of the first five (or six) lines.

In the case of all but the second primary strophe, the seventh line is entirely taken up by material quoted from Ezekiel (with the possible addition of a transition word in order to facilitate the incorporation of the quoted material into the new poetic context). In the text of the second primary strophe according to MS Westminster College, Liturgica II 84, the seventh line (line 18) is broken up by means of internal rhyme into two hemistichs, such that the second hemistich contains the expected

1 The seventh line of the third major strophe (line 29) reads: וגם במשפטי מאסו. These words appear to most closely correspond to the text במשפטי מאסו (Lev. 26:43). However, given the fact that all of the other major strophes quote from Ezekiel in their seventh lines, it is likely that the *payy*^{e}*ṭān* is alluding to ואת משפטי מאסו (Ezek. 20:13); cf. also the corresponding line in recension B, where it is clear that the latter source is quoted.

quote from Ezekiel, while the first contains additional literary material. However, the text in MS T-S NS 202.61 lacks the first hemistich, so that it seems safe to conclude that it is extraneous. This conclusion is confirmed by comparison to recension B, which quotes the same verse from Ezekiel in the corresponding position, and does not contain any additional material beyond the quote. In addition to this textual aberration, we find that the seventh line of the fourth primary strophe (line 40) is entirely taken up by a quote from Ezekiel as expected, without employing any additional material. However, a rhyming word is inserted into the middle of the line, such that it is broken up into two hemistichs. Thus, the scriptural material ואל כל פנים בושה ובכל ראשיהם קרחה (Ezek. 7:18) becomes an internally rhyming line: לכן כל פנים בושה הונחה / וכל פנים קרחה. This phenomenon is not paralleled in recension B, in which the corresponding line quotes the same scriptural material without assimilating it to an internal rhyme.

Each of the primary strophes is followed by a four-line secondary strophe. The two are connected by means of anadiplosis (שרשור). The secondary strophes contain the acrostic signature of the *payy^e^ṭān*: אלעזר ב[...].[2] The letters of the acrostic signature appear either in the odd lines of the secondary strophes — in the case of the second, fourth and fifth strophes — or in the first lines only — in the case of the first, third and sixth strophes.[3] In the third line of every secondary strophe appears a pair consisting of the name of one of the twenty-four priestly courses together with one of the twelve tribes. The fourth line of every secondary strophe is a scriptural quote. In all but the second secondary strophe, the quote occupies the entire line. In the second secondary strophe (line 22), the line begins with three words supplied by the *payy^e^ṭān*, and terminates in a quote.[4]

---

2 The full signature was presumably אלעזר בירבי קיליר חזק. This is the basic signature expected in a Qillirian *q^e^rôbâ* for 18 benedictions: see, for example, ויאהב אומן for Purim (Elizur 1995: 409–521; the signature is found in the major strophes); בהעצר אוצר for drought (Habermann 1944: 59–65); וספדה ארקה for mourning (Marcus 1933: 49–51).

3 In MS Westminster College, Liturgica II 84 both of the odd lines of the first secondary strophe begin with *'ayin*. This circumstance led Fleischer to conclude that the *q^e^rôbâ* contained an unusual spelling of the *payy^e^ṭān*'s name: 'לפי הנוסח שלפנינו חתום הפיוט "עלעזר ב..." והוא כנראה במקום "אלעזר ב[ירבי קליר]"... וקשה לומר שהנוסח משובש לפי שהע' שבראש החתימה, העולה מטור 8 להלן מחוזקת מכוח הע' שבטור 10' (see Fleischer 1968b: 155). This problem is resolved by MS T-S NS 202.61, which supplies a word beginning with the expected *'alep* in the beginning of the first line of the first secondary strophe. In light of this variant reading it seems that the fact that the third line of this strophe begins with *'ayin* is purely accidental and unrelated to the acrostic signature.

4 In general, the scriptural quotes in the last lines of the secondary strophes contain a (lexical) foreshadowing of the benediction formula that follows: עזרתי (line 11), referring to מגן אברהם; דעת (line 44), referring to חונן הדעת; שובינו (line 55), referring to הרוצה בתשובה; ועל כל פשעים תכסה אהבה (line 66),

From this description, it is clear that recension A of the *qᵉrôbâ* contains structural inconsistencies—namely, with regard to the acrostic structure of the primary and secondary strophes, with regard to the rhyme structure of the last lines of the primary strophes, as well as with regard to the textual contents of the last lines of the secondary strophes. To the extent that the available data allow us to evaluate the situation, all of these inconsistencies are resolved in recension B. This recension of the *qᵉrôbâ* retains unchanged the basic structural features seen in recension A: strophe size in both primary and secondary strophes, א"ב acrostic in the primary strophes and name acrostic in the secondary strophes. It furthermore retains the same framing verse at the beginnings of the primary strophes, and the same anadiplotic words connecting them to the secondary strophes. Unlike recension A, however, the acrostic structure in recension B is carried to its logical conclusion, such that all seven lines of the primary strophes are now subject to the א"ב acrostic (the quotes from Ezekiel in the seventh lines of these strophes are adjusted accordingly), and all four lines of the secondary strophes are subject to the name acrostic. The rhymes of the primary strophes in recension B are retained unchanged, as follows naturally from the retention of the anadiplotic words, which determine the rhymes of their respective strophes. In the secondary strophes, on the other hand, the rhyme in the first secondary strophe is retained, while in the other cases it is altered. This follows from the fact that in the secondary strophes, the scriptural quotes that constitute the last lines must now be selected in order to satisfy the newly imposed acrostic requirement. In the first secondary strophe in recension A, the quote in the last line begins with *'ālep* — איילותי לעזרתי חושה (line 11) — so that it may be retained.[5]

From the structural perspective, the result of the changes described here is a more tightly organized composition. All of the lines of recension B without exception are subject to some form of acrostic, and the internal rhyme observed in two cases in the

---

referring to המרבה לסלוח. This foreshadowing is lacking in the case of the second and third secondary strophes. In the former case, the lack is made good by means of the addition of the words supplied by the *payyᵉṭān*: למחיה בטל (line 22) referring both to the concluding formula מחיה המתים as well as to the dew whose mention in the second benediction is appropriate for the season.

5 Unfortunately, the last line of the second secondary strophe is missing in recension B, so we cannot know how the *payyᵉṭān* solved the problem of referring to the formula מחיה המתים together with dew (cf. the previous note). On the other hand, the last line of the third secondary strophe, which in recension A lacks any lexical reference to the following formula, האל הקדוש (cf. the previous note), now has such a reference: עליון על כל הארץ (line 33). In this case, the epithet עליון is apparently thought of as sufficient foreshadowing of the epithet קדוש. In the last line of the fourth secondary strophe, the reference to תורת משה עבדי (line 44) is likewise apparently considered a sufficient foreshadowing of חונן הדעת.

last lines of the primary strophes of recension A is done away with.[6] Because of this, it seems reasonable to surmise that recension A is the basis from which recension B was created: i.e., that the evolution of the text is from a less organized to a more organized form, one that is subject to more formal restrictions.[7] Support for this conclusion may be obtained by examining the textual changes involved in the transition from one recension to another. In some cases, the corresponding lines in recensions A and B are simply identical (allowing for minute variants resulting from the transmission of the text; e.g., lines 1, 5, 12). In others, the observed changes are trivial, involving addition, deletion or substitution, which do not alter the basic semantic character of the line. Thus, material may be added in order to satisfy the acrostic requirement, as in the case of line 6: מס כל לב בתהפוכות (recension A) → אבלי כבד ולבי מס בתהפוכות (recension B), as a result of the need to begin the line with *ʼalep*. A case of addition independent of the acrostic requirement may be observed in line 17: בכיה הילילו במרוצות (recension A) → בכיה ונהי יילילו במרוצות (recension B). For a case of deletion, see line 15: בכן אב ואם ובנים רוטשו בחוצות (recension A) → בנים ואבות רוטשנו בחוצות (recension B). A case of substitution may be observed in line 2: אותי כגהר ושימחותי הפוכות (recension A) → אותי כגהר במהומות כרוכות. In some cases, the lines are entirely unrelated, semantically or lexically (e.g., lines 8–9, 16). Thus far, we have seen changes performed on lines in which the rhyme has remained the same. On principle, the situation is the same in those cases where the rhyme changes. Thus, the change in line 30 involves deletion and addition: מאסו עשרת ולכן נהממו (recension A) → מאסו עשרת ונהממו בחרץ (recension B). In other cases, the lines are unrelated (e.g., lines 31–2).

In the cases that we have seen, the direction of the change is indifferent, and we have simply assumed that it proceeds from recension A to recension B. However, in one instance, it seems that the text in recension B is an improvement on that of recension A, lending support to the conclusion at which we arrived above on the basis

---

6 It cannot be determined with certainty whether the irregularly employed internal rhymes in recension A are the original intention of the *payyᵉṭān* or result from the development of the text in the course of copying. On the basis of the considerations given above, however, it seems reasonable to think that the internal rhyme in line 40 reflects the intention of the *payyᵉṭān* (since the line in question is based exclusively on a quote from Ezekiel), while the internal rhyme in line 18 is the product of textual accretion in the course of copying.

7 This conclusion rests on one of the most important methodological assumptions in the study of *piyyûṭ* literature, namely that the tendency in the evolution of *piyyûṭ* composition (both over time as well as within the *oeuvre* of a single *payyᵉṭān*) is from lesser to greater degrees of formal organization. For a discussion of this assumption, see Rand 2011.

of formal considerations. In lines 2–3, recension B reads: / אלי כבתולה היללתי בניבוכות אובכתי ורובכתי לסידור מערכות. Of interest are the two verbs with which line 3 opens. According to my interpretation, the root אבך is a secondary form of the hollow root בוך, and means something like 'to discomfit' in Qillirian *piyyûṭ* (see in the commentary, *ad loc.*). The root רבך is derived from the scriptural *terminus technicus* מֻרְבֶּכֶת 'mixed with oil', and means roughly 'to destroy'. Both roots are rather esoteric, even in *piyyûṭ* language, and are characteristic of Qillîr. It is clear that their juxtaposition in a binomial in the present case is quite successful, as the identity of their second and third root consonants for purposes of assonance is thereby exploited. In this regard, the text in recension A is less effective: אלי חגרתי ברביכות / אובכתי ונבוכותי על סידור מערכות. In this case, the binomial אובכתי ונבוכותי (which, from the etymological point of view, is a binomial of synonyms) does not have the same force of assonance, mostly on account of the difference in conjugation between the weak and the strong root. The root רבך, moreover, appears here in the rhyme position of the preceding line. This position, by necessarily stressing the *sound* element -כות, obscures the *etymological* significance of the root from which the sound element is derived. In short, from the compositional point of view, the text of recension B is an improvement upon that of recension A, and the improvement seems to be the result of intentional manipulation on the part of the *payy^{e}ṭān*.

We have thus established the relationship between the two recensions, together with the fact that the differences between them are best accounted for on the assumption of deliberate manipulation (rather than scribal changes entailed in textual transmission). The fact that the acrostic signature remains unchanged in the transition from recension to recension makes it most likely that the changes were made by Qillîr himself (rather than a later adapter). Adaptations by Qillîr of his own *piyyûṭîm* are known elsewhere, but the case under investigation here is the first of its kind. Thus, the Qillirian Purim *q^{e}rôbâ* ויאהב אומן is attested in two versions, one built up out of a sequence of one strophe per benediction (i.e., primary strophes only), and another built up out of strophic units containing a primary and a secondary strophe, the primary strophes being identical to those in the first version. As demonstrated by Elizur, the long version is an adaptation of the short one created by the *payy^{e}ṭān* himself (Elizur 1995: 514–21). In a second case, the Qillirian *q^{e}rôbâ* יעיב בדיאת עיט... for the Ninth of Av employs a series of eighteen strophic units consisting of a primary and a secondary strophe as opposed to the expected fourteen.[8] The last four secondary strophes show obvious structural deviations from the preceding fourteen, and Fleischer has shown that they constitute a re-worked version of the secondary strophes found in Qillîr's *piyyûṭ* אתה אלי אתה, an independent composition designed to 'fill out' the last four benedictions of an *'amîdâ* for the Ninth of Av in which Qillirian *qᵉrôbôt* for fourteen benedictions (only) were recited.[9] Unlike these two cases, however, the two recensions of the *qᵉrôbâ* והיה אויב מתגבר involve a re-working of literary material within the context of one and the same composition, which retains its basic structural properties in both.[10] With the addition of the present case, therefore, we are able to further appreciate the types of internal variation with regard to liturgical function contained within the Qillirian corpus: (1) multiple compositions for the same liturgical occasion (a commonplace phenomenon), (2) longer and shorter recensions of one composition for the same liturgical occasion, (3) structurally similar recensions of one composition for the same liturgical occasion, and (4) textual material belonging to one genre incorporated into a more extensive genre in which it serves a parallel function.

Recension A

Manuscripts:
Cambridge, Westminster College, Liturgica II 84 (א): lines 1–67
Cambridge, T-S NS 202.61 (ב): lines 1–38

Text:
Westminster College, Liturgica II 84

Notes:

8 The *qᵉrôbâ* is published in Fleischer 1968c: 37–49. The other four attested Qillirian *qᵉrôbôt* for the Ninth of Av employ a sequence of fourteen strophic units only, i.e., up till the benediction אלהי דויד ובונה ירושלים, at which point the *qînôt* are inserted.

9 The *piyyûṭ* אתה אלי אתה is published in Fleischer 1968a: 38–9. For the relationship between the secondary strophes of אתה אלי אתה and the secondary strophes of the last four benedictions of ...יעיב בדיאת עיט, see Fleischer 1968a: 35–6.

10 A similar case is known in the corpus of the late Classical *payyᵉṭān* Pinḥās, which contains two recensions of the *qᵉdûštā* וארץ אשר מארצות מוכשרת for Šᵉmînî ʿAṣeret. In both recensions, the first two *piyyûṭim* of the *qᵉdûštā* (i.e., the *māgēn* and the *mᵉḥayyeh*) show a basic similarity of structure — see Elizur 2004: 46–54, 439–94.

The commentary covers only those parts of the q^{e}*rôbâ* that are not paralleled in recension B. For those parts that are common to both recensions, see the commentary to the latter.

Sigla:

[..] = less than one word missing

[…] = one word or more missing

<> = abbreviation in the manuscript

+<>+ = material omitted by the scribe

בשמ<ך> רחמ<נא>

וְהָ[יָ]ה אוֹיֵב מִתְגַּבֵּר וְחוֹלֵשׁ דְּרוּכוֹת
אוֹתִי כְּגָהַר וְשִׂימְחוֹתַי הֲפוּכוֹת
אֱלַי חָגַרְתִּי בִּרְבִיכוֹת
אֲוּבַּכְתִּי וּנְבוּכוֹתִי עַל סִידּוּר מַעֲרָכוֹת
אָנַחְתִּי כְּנִשְׁתַּבְּרוּ לוּחוֹת נֶעֱרָכוֹת
מָס כָּל לֵב בְּתַהְפּוּכוֹת
וְהִנֵּה הַנָּשִׁים יֹשְׁבוֹת מְבַכּוֹת

מְ<בַכּוֹת> עת בָּא שׁוֹדֵד לְחָוֹרְשָׁהּ
וּבִמְצוֹדָה רָעָה הִכְפִּישָׁה
עָן יְהוֹיָרִיב וּבְנֵ[י] שֵׁבֶט רְאוּבֵן לְדָוֹרְשָׁה
אֱיָילוּתִי לְעֶזְרָתִי חוּשָׁה
ב<רוך מגן>

כִּי יֹאמְרוּ בְּהִיפָּרְצָם בִּפְרָצוֹת
בַּעֲווֹן פצעינו קָצַף גְּדוֹל דעות
בַּחֲרוֹן אַף הוּחַרְנוּ בִּנְפִיצוֹת
בְּכֵן אָב וָאֵם וּבָנִים רֻוטְּשׁוּ בְּחוּצוֹת
בֻּ[ו]לְעוּ הֲמוֹנִים וְהָתְעוּ כְּצֹאן מְנֻוּפָּצוֹת
בְּכִיָּה הֵילִילוּ בְּמְרוּצוֹת
כבטל נר נוצוצות / חָגְרוּ שַׂקִּים וְכִסְּתָה אוֹתָם פַּלָּצוּת

פַּ<לָּצוּת> לְעֵת ביעתם נָהוּ
וּלְכָל רְחוֹבוֹת מִסְפֵּד הִנְהוּ
לָכֵן יְדַעְיָה עִם שֵׁבֶט שִׁמְעוֹן חִיכּוּהוּ
לִמְחַיֶּה בְּטַל וְנָם אֲנִי אֲנִי הוּא
ב<רוך מחיה>

אֵלֶיךָ גָּעוּ כְּשֻׁוסוּ

גַּם זֶה בְּמָאֳסָם בְּלֵב הוּמַסּוּ
גּוֹעֲלוּ בְּכַעַס כְּמוֹ הִכְעִיסוּ
גַּם שִׁינּוּן אַרְבָּעִים שָׁכְחוּ וַיִּמְאֲסוּ
גְּזֵירָה כגזרה תָּעוּ וְנָסוּ
נדמה לחליל באהב נשו ובו שָׁשׂוּ
וְגַם בְּמִשְׁפָּטַי מָאָסוּ

מָ<אָסוּ> עֲשֶׂרֶת וְלָכֵן נֶהֱמְמוּ
מִמִּצְוֹת טָעוּ וּבְיַד צַר הוּשְׁמוּ
מִשְׁמַר חָרִים עִם שֵׁבֶט לֵוִי לוּלֵי נָמוּ
וְאַתָּה הוּא וּשְׁנוֹתֶיךָ לֹא יִתָּמּוּ
ב<רוך האל>

עַל מָה דְּחָפוּנִי אַחַר גֵּיו לְזָונְחָה
דּוֹעֲכוּ בְּהַבְלֵיהֶם וּשְׁכִינָה מֵהֶם בָּרְחָה
דָּצוּ וְשָׂשׂוּ אַחַר עַיִן אוֹתִי לְשָׁכְחָה
דִּיבְּרוּ קָלוֹן וְהָשְׁלְכוּ כַּסּוּחָה
דָּמְמוּ מִפִּיקּוּד לֵב מְשַׂמְּחָה
וְאֶל רָעָתָם מִיהֲרוּ בָּהּ לְבָוטְחָה
לָכֵן כָּל פָּנִים בּוּשָׁה הֻונְחָה / וְכָל רָאשֵׁיהֶם קָרְחָה

קָ<רְחָה> זָדוּ וְהֵיעֵיזוּ מֵצַח לְגַלּוֹת
סָרוּ מִדֶּרֶךְ לָשִׂים עֲלִילוֹת
זָמַם שְׁעוֹרִים עִם שֵׁבֶט יְהוּדָה חִין לְעַלּוֹת
וְדַעַת אֱלֹהִים מֵעוּלוֹת
ב<רוך חונן>

אַתָּה נֶאֱנָח הֵיהִרוּ בְּזָדוֹן
הֵימִרוּ כְּבוֹדָם וְהִשִּׁיאָם לֵב זָדוֹן
הָמוּ וְסָרְרוּ כְּפָרָה וּבוֹ הֻובְגְּדוּן
הֵיזִדוּ בְּעוֹרֶף וּפְנֵיהֶם הֵחֵידוּן
הֲלֹא עֲוֹנוֹתָם רָבוּ וְלָכֵן הֻונְדְּדוּן
+<>+
וְצָץ הַמַּטֶּה וּפָרַח הַזָּדוֹן

הַ<זָּדוֹן> רִיקְּפָנוּ מֵרוֹב רִשְׁעָתֵינוּ
בְּהַטּוֹתֵינוּ מֵאוֹרַח הֻוגְבַּר פִּשְׁעֵינוּ
רִנֵּן מַלְכִּיָּה עִם שֵׁבֶט יִשָּׂשכָר לְמוֹשִׁיעֵנוּ
שׁוּבֵינוּ אֱלֹהֵי יִשְׁעֵינוּ
ב<רוך הרוצה בתשובה>

וְאָמַרְתָּה אֶל שְׁמוּעָה   וִיכַחְנוּ מֵחֶזְיוֹנִים
וְגָעַלְנוּ וּמָאַסְנוּ וְנֶותַּנְנוּ בְּיַד מְעַנִּים
וּמָתְנֵינוּ חַלְחָלָה נִתְמַלְּאוּ כְּנִיתְלַהֲמְנוּ כְּרוֹגְנִים
וְנִיאַצְנוּ בְּכַחַשׁ וּבְרוֹעַ לִישׁוֹנִים
וּלְרַע טוֹב הָיִנוּ עוֹנִים
וְעֵת גָּבְרוּ עֲווֹנִים
גָּרַמְנוּ לַאֲבֹד תּוֹרָה מִכֹּהֵן וְעֵיצָה מִזְּקֵינִים

מִזְּקֵ<ינִים>   בְּיַד מְחַבְּלִים זוֹעַמְנוּ בְּאֵיבָה
זִילְזְלוּ וְנִיאֲצוּ בִּרְחוֹבוֹת רַבָּה
זָעַק מִיָּמִין עִם שֵׁבֶט זְבוּלוּן לְדוֹבְבָה
וְעַל כָּל פְּשָׁעִים תְּכַסֶּה אַהֲבָה
ב<רוך המרבה לסלוח>

חילופי נוסח:

כותרת: [...] י"ז בתמוז דר' א[..] *ב* 5 לוחות] ה[..]חו[..] *ב* 6 כל] ליתא *ב* 8 עת] איך *ב* 10 לדורשה] לדרשה *ב* 11 איילותי] אילותי *ב* 18 נוצוצות] הצ' השנייה תוקנה מו' *א* כבטל נר נוצוצות] ליתא *ב* 28 לחליל] לחלל (ל' ראשונה בספק) *ב* נשו] עשו *ב* 37 והשלכו] והושלכו *ב* 48 היזדו] מתוקן מן "היזוד" *א* 59 בכחש] הכ' תוקנה מאות לא ברורה *א*

קיצורים ביבליוגרפיים:

"אביך" = קרובה קילירית לט' באב; Goldschmidt 2002: 154–60
"אז בהלוך" = קינה קילירית לט' באב; Goldschmidt 2002: 98–100
"אז במלאת ספק" = קינה קילירית לט' באב; Goldschmidt 2002: 101–2
"אפסי חוג" = קדושתא קילירית לשבועות; Elizur 2000: 143–205
בית המדרש = Jellinek 1938
"בניין נופעל" = Moreshet 1980
גזניוס = Kautzsch 1910
"ליל אשר לאב הוחץ" = שבעתא קילירית לפסח; Elizur 2009: 28–41
"נשכחות" = Zulay 1995a
סוקולוף = Sokoloff 2002
"עיוני לשון" = Zulay 1995b
רנד = Rand 2006

פירוש הפיוט:

3. **אלי חגרתי**: מקביל ל"אלי... היללתי" בנוסח ב'. ללשון מטונימית דומה השווה "וגיל גבעות תחגֹרנה" (תה' סה, יג). וראה גם רנד §30*d*. **ברביכות**: השווה "ורובכתי" בנוסח ב' (טור 4), ובפירוש על אתר. 8. **עת**: יש לגרוס "אֵיךְ" ככתב יד *ב*. **לחורשה**: לחרוש את כנסת ישראל ולהשמידה; השווה "על גבי חרשו

חֹרשים" (תה' קכט, ג). 9. **ובמצודה רעה**: על פי "כדגים שנאחזים במצודה רעה" (קהלת ט, יב). **הכפישה**: על פי "הכפישני באפר" (איכה ג, טז). 10. **ען**: כמו: ענה. **לדורשה**: מקביל ל"אל לדרשה" בנוסח ב'. 13. **פצעינו**: צ"ל "בְּצָעֵינוּ". **בעוון פצעינו קצף**: על פי "בעון בצעו קצפתי" (יש' נז, יז). **גדול דעות**: צ"ל "גדול עֵצוֹת"; השווה בנוסח ב'. (המעתיק ניקד "דעֵות", ושמא כיוון לתיקון הנדרש). 14. **הוחרנו**: קריאת הח' בספק. פירושו כנראה: נשרפנו; והנטיה על דרך פעלי ע"ו. 16. **והתעו כצאן מנופצות**: על פי "צאן אֹבדות היה [קר' היו] עמי רֹעיהם התעום" (יר' נ, ו). **מנופצות**: מפוזרות. 18. **כבטל נר נוצוצות**: הצלעית כולה חסרה בכת יד ב, ויש כנראה להוציאה. והשווה גם נוסח ב', שאין בו מקבילה לצלעית הזאת. 19. **ביעתם**: יש לתקן ולקרוא "בִּיְעָתָם" (השווה נוסח ב'). 20. **ולכל רחובות מספד הנהו**: גרמו לכל הרחובות לנהות ולקונן. על פי "בכל רחובות מספד" עמוס ה, טז. 21. **חיכוהו**: כמו: חיכו לו (יורד לטור הבא). 22. **למחיה**: השווה "אני אמית ואחיה" (דב' לב, לט). **אני אני הוא**: שם. 23. **געו**: צעקו. **כשוסו**: כאשר היו משיסה לאויב. 24. **גם זה במאסם**: על פי "יען מאסכם בדבר הזה" (יש' ל, יב). פליישר מציע לפרש "זה" ככינוי לה' (על פי שמ' טו, ב), וגם זה נראה. **בלב הומסו**: נמס לבם (והשווה בטור 6). ללשון ראה "המסו את לבבנו" (דב' א, כח). 25. **גועלו**: השווה "וגעלה נפשי אתכם" (ויק' כו, ל). 26 **שינון ארבעים**: תלמוד תורה. שינון: על פי דב' ו, ז. **ארבעים**: ראה בפירוש לנוסח ב', טור 28. 27. **כגזרה**: נראית הצעת פליישר לתקן ולקרוא "כְּנִגְזָרָה". **תעו ונסו**: גלו מאדמתם. 28. **נדמה לחליל באהב נשו**: הנוסח נראה משובש ואין בידי לתקנו. כתב יד ב גורס "[..]ה ולחליל ב[..] עשו". 29. **במשפטי מאסו**: ויק' כו, מג; אך השווה במקום המקביל בנוסח ב'. 31. **הושמו**: שמא יש לנקד "הוּשַׁמּוּ". 33. **ואתה הוא וכו'**: תה' קב, כח. הציטוט אינו מביא לשון מעין החתימה. 35. **דועכו**: כלו. 36. **דצו וששו אחר עין**: השווה "ואחר עינַי הלך לבי" (איוב לא, ז). 37. **דיברו קלון וכו'**: מקביל לטור 36 בנוסח ב'. 39. **ואל רעתם מיהרו**: השווה "רגלים ממהרות לרוץ לרעה" (משלי ו, יח). 40. **לכן כל פנים**: הטור פוצל לשתי צלעיות על ידי הוספת המילה "הונחה" אל המקרא המצוטט; השווה בנוסח ב'. 41. **והיעיזו מצח לגלות**: השווה את הביטויים "עזות מצח" ו"גילוי פנים". 42. **סרו מדרך**: השווה "סורו מני דרך הטו מני ארח" (יש' ל, יא). **לשים עלילות**: לעשות מעשי חטא. 43. **זמם**: לשון כוונה ורצון. **חין לעלות**: לכוון את תפילתם כלפי מעלה. **חין**: לשון תפילה, על פי איוב מא, ד. 44. **ודעת אלהים וכו'**: הושע ו, ו. 45. **היהרו**: הפועל גזור-שם מן "יהיר". לכתיב החסר השווה "הימרו" בטור הבא ו"היזדו" בטור 48. **היהרו בזדון**: לצירוף הלשונות ראה "זד יהיר" (משלי כא, כד). 46. **הימרו**: השווה בנוסח ב'. 46. **והשיאם לב זדון**: על פי עב' ג. 47. **וסררו כפרה**: על פי הושע ד, טז. **ובו הובגדון**: פירושו כנראה שישראל נגררו אחרי הבגידה בה'. הובגדון: לסופית "-ן" בצורות עבר נסתרים, ראה גזניוס §44*l*. 48. **היזדו בעורף**: הקשו עורפם. הביטוי נראה מקוצר מן "הזידו ויקשו את ערפם" (נח' ט, טז). 48. **ופניהם החידון**: העזו פניהם. השימוש בלשון חידוד בביטוי הזה הוא כנראה מחידושי הפייטן (השווה משלי כז, יז). 49. **עונותם רבו**: על פי עזרא ט, ו. **הונדדון**: טולטלו ממקומם. 51. **וצץ המטה וכו'**: על פי יח' ז, י. 52. **מרוב**: קריאת הב' בספק. 53. **בהטותינו מאורח**: ראה בפירוש לטור 42. **הוגבר פשעינו**: לצירוף הלשונות ראה איוב לו, ט. 54. **רנן**: התפלל. 55. **שובינו** וכו׳: תה' פה, ה. 56. **ויכחנו מחזיונים**: מרדנו מחוסר נבואת אמת; לעניין דומה ראה גם בטור 62. 57. **וגעלנו ומאסנו**: צירף הלשונות על פי ויק' כו, מג (השווה טור 29). **ונותננו**: יש לראות כאן בניין נופעל; ראה "בניין נופעל", עמ' 137–8. 58. **ומתבינו חלחלה נתמלאו**: על פי יש' כא, ג. **כניתלהמנו כרוגנים**: על פי "דברי נרגן כמתלהמים" (משלי יח, ח; כו,

כב). 59 **וברוע לישונים**: ובלשון הרע. 60. **ולרע טוב וכו'**: על פי יש' ה, כ. 61. **גברו עוונים**: השווה תה' סה, ד. 62. **לאבד תורה מכהן ועיצה מזקינים**: על פי יח' ז, כו. 63. **מזקינים**: מפני חוסר הזקנים ועצתם הטובה. 64. **זילזלו וניאצו**: המחבלים. **רבה**: כינוי לירושלים על פי איכה א, א. 65. **לדובבה**: בניין הפולל משמש כפועל עומד בלשון הקילירי; "דובבו בקול תחנונים" ("אז בהלוך", טור 5). 66. **ועל כל פשעים וכו'**: משלי י, יב.

Recension B

Manuscripts:
Manchester, Rylands B 3045-1/2 (א): lines 1–50
Cincinnati, HUC Acc. 965 (ב): lines 1–7, 14–20

Text:
Rylands B 3045-1/2: lines 1–16, 18–19, 21–50
HUC Acc. 965: lines 17, 20

[..]ה לשבעה עשר בת[מוז]

[וְהָיָ]ה אוֹיֵב מִתְגַּבֵּר וְחוֹלֵשׁ דְּרוּכוֹת
אוֹתִי כְּגָ[הַר] בִּמְהוּמוֹת עֲרוּכוֹת
אֱלִי כִּבְתוּלָה הֵילַלְתִּי בניבות
אֱ[ו]בַּכְתִּי וְרֵובַּכְתִּי לְסִ[י]דּוּר מַעֲרָכוֹת
אָנַחְתִּי כְּנִשְׁתַּבְּרוּ הַלּוּחוֹת הַנֶּעֱרָכוֹת
אֶבְלִי כָּבֵד וְ[לִבִּי] מָס בְּתַהְפּוּכוֹת
אֲשֶׁר הַנָּשִׁים יוֹשְׁבוֹת הַתַּמּ[וּז] מְבַכּוֹת

מְבַ<כּוֹת> אֶת יוֹם זָנַח בּוֹ אִשָּׁה
אֲשֶׁר הָיְתָה כְּאַלְמָנָה וּגְרוּשָׁה
אָתָא יְהוֹיָרִיב וּרְאוּבֵן בּוֹ אֵל לְדָרְשָׁה
אֱיָלוּתִי לְעֶזְרָתִי חוּשָׁה
ב<רוך> מגן

כִּי יֹאמְרוּ בְּהִיפָּרְצָ[ם] פְּרָצוֹת
ב[.. ..]ם קָצַף [גְּ]דוֹל הָעֵיצוֹת
בַּחֲרוֹן אַף הִיזָּרְנוּ [בִּנְ]פִיצוֹת
בָּנִים וְאָבוֹת רֻוטַּשְׁנ[וּ בְּחוּצוֹת]
[בְּכֵן בְּבֶצַע] שֶׁהָלְכוּ בְּמוֹעֵצוֹת
בְּכִיָּה וָנֶהִי יְיֵלִ[ילוּ] בִּמְרוּצוֹת

בְּחָגְרָם שַׂקִּים וְכִסְּ[תָה אותם פַּלָּצוּת]

[פַּלָּצוּת] לְ[עֵת בְּ]עֲתָתַם נה[..]
לוּחוֹת [..]שתברו [...]
לָכֵן [...]
[...]
[ברוך מחיה]

[אֵלֶיךָ] [...]
[...]
[...]
[...]
[...] נִדְמֶה לְחִלּוּל עֵשָׂו וְשָׂשׂוּ
[גְּ]לוּפִי[ם] אַרְבָּעִים הֵיפִיסוּ
גַּם בְּחֻוקוֹתַי לֹא הָלָכוּ וְ[אֶת] מִשְׁפָּטַי מָאָסוּ

מָ<אָסוּ> עֲשֶׂרֶת וְנֶהְמְמוּ בְּחֶ[רֶ]ץ
עַל שִׁכְמָם טָעֲנוּ דוֹמֶה לְשֶׁרֶץ
עַל כֵּן חָרִים [עִ]ם לֵוִי יֵידְעוּ פּוֹעַל אֵל בְּמֶרֶץ
עֶלְיוֹן עַל כָּל הָאָרֶץ
ב<רוך> האל הקדוש

עַל מָה דָּת דָּחוּ אַחַר גֵּיו לְזָנְחָה
דָּצוּ בְּהַבְלֵיהֶם וּשְׁכִינָה מֵהֶם בָּרְחָה
דִּיבְּרוּ נְבָלָה וְהִשְׁלִכוּ כַּסּוּחָה
דִּיבָּה הוֹצִיאוּ עַל יוֹשְׁבֵי טְפוּחָה
דָּמְמוּ מִפִּיקוּדֵי לֵב מְשַׂמְּחָה
ד[..] בְּרָעָתָם בְּיָגוֹן וַאֲנָחָה
[דִּ]בֵּר לָכֵן בְּכָל פָּנִים בּ[וּ]שָׁה וּבְכָל רֹאשׁ קָרְחָה

[קָרְחָה] זִימַּנְתִּי לְנַצְּלָם מ[..]די
זֹאת לָהֶם [...]
[..]ם שְׁעוּרִים עִם יְהוּדָה [...]
[זִכְרוּ תּוֹרַת מֹ]שֶׁה עַבְדִּי
ב<רוך> חונן

[אַתָּה נֶאֱנָח] [... ..]דוּן
הֱמִירוּ כְּבוֹדָם לְאוֹכֵל [...]
[... ..]ה בְּמִירְדּוֹן
[...]
[...] חטאות[.. ...]

50 ידון [...]

חילופי נוסח:

3 בניבות] בניבוכות ב   18 וכס..] וכיסתה ב

פירוש הפיוט:

1. **והיה:** פסוק המסגרת יח' כא, יב. **וחולש:** לשון ניצחון והשמדה; השווה "ויחלֹש יהושע את עמלק... לפי חרב" (שמ' יז, יג). **דרוכות:** כנראה כמו: בקשתות דרוכות (ראה יש' ה, כח). 2. **אותי כגהר:** כאשר גער בי (ושאג עלי כאריה); ל"גהר" לשון גערה ומתן קול ראה "נשכחות", עמ' 447–446 ו"עיוני לשון", עמ' 467–466. **במהומות ערוכות:** במהומות שערך כנגדי. 3. **אלי כבתולה:** יואל א, ח. במקור המקראי המילה "אלי" היא פועל (ציווי לנוכחת) אך היא נתפסת על ידי הפייטן כצורה שמנית שמשמעה בכי ויללה; השווה "אלי כתנים בהעצימני" ("אאביך", טור 67). **בניבות:** יש לגרוס ככתב יד ב: בְּנִיבּוּכוֹת, ולפרש: ממעמקים. המילה גזורה כנראה מן "נבכי ים" (איוב לח, טז). אך שמא יש לתקן ולקרוא: בִּמְבוּכוֹת. 4. **אובכתי:** נבוכותי. השורש "אבך" הוא שורש תנייני הנגזר מן "בוך"; השווה "אאביך ביום מבך" ("אאביך", טור 1; וראה רנד, 12*r*§ והערה 268). **ורובכתי:** לשון בלילה וחליטה (ראה ויק' ו, יד ועוד) המשמשת כאן כמטפורה להשמדה ושוממות; השווה "ליל אשר רִיבֵּךְ פוטים [היינו איבד את המצרים]" ("ליל אשר לאב הוחץ", טור 119). **לסידור מערכות:** בזוכרי את התמיד, שבטל בי"ז בתמוז (ראה משנה תענית ד, ו), ואת סדר מערכות העצים על המזבח בכלל. לצירוף הלשונות ראה "דתניא מי שזכה בתרומת הדשן יזכה בסידור מערכה" (בבלי יומא כב ע"א; והשווה גם משנה תמיד ב, ג). 5. **אנחתי:** נאנחתי. הלשון על פי פסוק המסגרת ("על מה אתה נאנח"). **כנשתברו הלוחות:** ראה "בשבעה עשר בתמוז נשתברו הלוחות" (משנה תענית ד, ו). **הנערכות:** הלשון תמוהה במקצת, ומשמעה כנראה: הכתובות והניתנות (על ידי ה'). 6. **אבלי כבד:** הצירוף על פי בר' נ, יא; והשווה גם "כי אבל כבד" ("אאביך", טור 19). **ולבי מס:** הלשון על פי פסוק המסגרת ("ונמס כל לב"). **מס:** נמס. **בתהפוכות:** השימוש הנוכחי נגזר כנראה מן "נהפך לבי" (איכה א, כ). 7. **אשר:** כנראה כמו: כאשר. **הנשים וכו':** על פי יח ח, יד (ההשלמה על פי המקור). 8. **אשה:** סמל לכנסת ישראל; השווה "אשה יפת תואר מנוולת מצא" ("אז במלאת ספק", טור 2). 9. **היתה כאלמנה:** איכה א, א. **אלמנה וגרושה:** הצירוף על פי ויק' כא, יד ועוד. 10. **אתא וכו':** ביום הזה (היינו בי"ז בתמוז) באו יהויריב וראובן (המסמלים כאן את כלל ישראל) לדרוש את ה' ולשפוך את תפילתם לפניו. 11. **אילותי וכו':** תה' כב, כ. 12. **בהיפרצם פרצות:** כאשר האויב פרץ בם פרצות. להשלמה השווה את הטור המקביל בנוסח א'. ונראה שהוא רומז לאירוע נוסף של י"ז בתמוז: "הובקעה העיר" (משנה תענית ד, ו). 13. **קצף:** השווה יש' נז, יז, המובא בפירוש לטור 16. **גדול העיצות:** כינוי לה', על פי יר' לב, יט. להשלמה השווה את הטור המקביל בנוסח א'. 14. **היזרנו:** כמו: זֵרנו, היינו הפיצנו (בגוים). אך קריאת האותיות ז' ור' בספק. **בנפיצות:** לשון הפצה; השווה "ונפֻצות יהודה יקבץ" (יש' יא, יב) ועוד. 15. **בנים ואבות רוטשנו:** על פי "אם על בנים רֻטשה" (הושע י, יד). **רוטשנו בחוצות:** על פי "יְרֻטשו בראש כל חוצות" (נחום ג, י). 16. **בבצע שהלכו במועצות:** מפני שרדפו בצע במזימתם הרעה (המשפט יורד לטור הבא). הטור מצרף שני מקראות: "בעון בצעו קצפתי... וילך שובב בדרך לבו" (יש' נז, יז), "וילכו במֹעצות בשררות לבם" (יר' ז, כד). 17. **בכיה ונהי:**

הצמד על פי "בכי ונהי" (יר' ט, ט). **ונהי**: הניקוד כצורת הפסק על פי המקור. **יילילו**: ההשלמה מדעתי. **במרוצות**: על פי ההקשר יש לפרשו: ביגון נמרץ; לשורש "מרץ" בלשון הקילירי, ראה רנד, 8e§, הערה 98. אומנם צורת "פְּעוּלוֹת" קשה לאור פירוש זה, אך לדעתי קשה יותר לראות כאן את צורת הרבים של המילה המקראית "מְרוּצָה" שעניינה ריצה. 18. **בחגרם שקים וכו'**: על פי יח' ז, יח. 19. **פלצות לעת בעתתם**: על פי יש' כא, ד. **נה[..]**: המילה המקבילה בנוסח א' היא "נֶהִי", אך בכתב יד *ב* הטור מסתיים במילה לקויה שסופה "[..]ה". מכאן אולי יש להשלים "נֶהְ[תָה]" (שרידי ת' נראים בכתב יד א). 20. **לוחות [..]שתברו**: השווה טור 5. 21. **לכן [...]**: בטור זה נזכרו משמרת ידעיה ושבט שמעון (השווה בטור המקביל בנוסח א'). 27. **[...] נדמה לחלול עשו וששו**: על פי ההקשר (ראה טור 29) הטור עוסק בחילול המקדש (או שם ה' או כדומה) על ידי ישראל. **[...] נדמה**: יש לראות כאן כינוי לדבר שחיללוהו ישראל. 28. **גלופים ארבעים היפיסו**: ישראל הפרו ("היפיסו") את עשרת הדיברות שנחרתו ("גלופים") על הלוחות בעת שהותו של משה על הר סיני, ארבעים יום וארבעים לילה. ואפשר שיש להסב "ארבעים" על משקל הלוחות: "הלוחות היו משאוי ארבעים סאה" (ירושלמי תענית ד, ו [סח ע"ג]). **גלופים**: הקריאה קשה, אך ההשלמה נראית. לשורש "גלף" בהקשר לוחות הברית ראה "ימינך כחרטה גליפת כלולות" ("אפסי חוג", טור 10 [עמ' 144]). **היפיסו**: על פי הארמית הגלילית, שבה השורש "פסס", בניין אפעל, משמש לשון הפרה וחילול (ראה סוקולוף, עמ' 441–440) 29. **בחוקותי וכו'**: יח' כ, יג. ההשלמה והניקוד על פי המקור. 30. **עשרת**: עשרת הדיברות (ראה בטור 28). **בחרץ**: מלשון "כלה ונחרצה" (יש' י, כג) ועוד. 31. **על שכמם טענו דומה לשרץ**: נראה שיש לפרשו כמטפורה שמשמעה: נשאו ("על שכמם טענו") את עוונם ("דומה לשרץ"); השווה "אם יהיה השרץ בידו שלאדם אפי' טובל במי שילוח או במי בראשית אין לו טהרה עולמית. השליכו מידו מיד טהר" (ירושלמי תענית ב, א [סה ע"א]). 32. **יידעו פועל אל**: כמו: הודיעו; השווה "וַיַּגִּידוּ פֹּעַל אלהים" (תה' סד, י). ושמא יש לנקד "יֵדְעוּ" ולהשוות "למען אשר ידעו אשר אני יי'" (יח' כ,כו). **במרץ**: בזריזות (ראה במקור המצוטט בפירוש לטור 17). 33. **עליון וכו'**: תה' פג, יט; צז, ט. 34. **דת דחו וכו'**: השווה "וישלִכו את תורתך אחרי גַוּם" (נחמ' ט, כו) ועוד. 35. **דצו**: שמחו. 36. **דיברו נבלה**: השווה יש' ט, טז; לב, ו. **והשלכו כסוחה**: השווה יש' ה, כה. 37. **דיבה הוציאו וכו'**: השווה יר' כ, י; תה' לא, יד. **טפוחה**: כנראה כינוי לארץ, על פי "ידי יסדה ארץ וימיני טפחה שמים" (יש' מח, יג). לשימוש דומה בשורש "טפח" בכינוי לארץ ראה "טפח יסודות שקט" ("אפסי חוג", טור 9 [עמ' 144]). 38. **מפיקודי לב משמחה**: ממצוות התורה, על פי "פקודי יי' ישרים משמחי לב" (תה' יט, ט). 39. **ביגון ואנחה**: הצמד על פי יש' לה, י; נא יא. 40. **דבר**: הנושא כנראה ה'. **בכל פנים וכו'**: על פי יח' ז, יח. 41. **זימנתי**: נראה שה' הוא המדבר. **לנצלם**: כנראה לשון הסרה, אך קשה לדייק מפני ההקשר הלקוי. 44. **זכרו וכו'**: מל' ג, כב. 46. **המירו כבודם לאוכל [...]**: על פי "וימירו את כבודם בתבנית שור אֹכל עשב" (תה' קו, כ). 47. **במירדון**: כנראה כמו: במרד.

References

Ehrlich, Uri. 2007. 'קטעים נוספים מתפילת שמונה עשרה על פי מנהג ארץ ישראל', *קבץ על יד* 19 (29), 1–22

—— 2006. 'תפילת שמונה עשרה שלמה על פי מנהג ארץ ישראל', *קבץ על יד* 18 (28), 1–22

Elizur, Shulamit. 1995. '"ויאהב אומן" – קרובה קלירית לפורים בעיצוב מורחב', *Tarbiz* 64, 499–521

— 2000. *רבי אלעזר בירבי קליר – קדושתאות ליום מתן תורה*. (Jerusalem)

— 2004. *פיוטי רבי פינחס הכהן*. (Jerusalem)

— 2009. ‘סדרי פסוקים בפיוטים ובתפילות ישראל’, *Ginzei Qedem* 5, 9–63

Fleischer, Ezra. 1968a. ‘לעניין המשמרות בפיוטים’, *Sinai* 62, 13–40

— 1968b. ‘לעניין המשמרות בפיוטים’, *Sinai* 62, 142–62

— 1968c. ‘קרובה חמישית לתשעה באב מאת ר' אלעזר בירבי קליר’, *Sinai* 63, 32–49

— 2007. *שירת-הקודש העברית בימי-הביניים*^{2}. (Jerusalem)

Goldschmidt, Daniel. 2002. *סדר הקינות לתשעה באב*^{2}. (Jerusalem)

Habermann, Abraham Meir. 1944. ‘פיוטים עתיקים’, *Tarbiz* 14, 53–69

Jellinek, Adolph. 1938. *בית המדרש, מדרשים קטנים*^{2}. (Jerusalem)

Kautzsch, Emil (ed.). 1910. *Gesenius' Hebrew Grammar*^{2}. (Oxford)

Marcus, Joseph. 1933. *גנזי שירה ופיוט*. (New York)

Moreshet, Menahem. 1980. ‘על בניין נופעל בעברית הבתר-מקראית’, in Gad B. Sarfatti et al. (eds), *מחקרים בעברית ובלשונות שמיות מוקדשים לזכרו של פרופ' יחזקאל קוטשר* (Ramat Gan). 126–39

Rand, Michael. 2006. *Introduction to the Grammar of Hebrew Poetry in Byzantine Palestine*. (New Jersey)

— 2011. ‘Compositional Technique in Qillirian Piyyutim for Rain and Dew’, in B. Outhwaite and S. Bhayro (eds), *From a Sacred Source: Genizah Studies in Honour of Stefan C. Reif* (Études sur le Judaïsme Médiéval XLII, Cambridge Genizah Studies Series 1, Leiden/Boston). 249–87

Sokoloff, Michael. 2002. *A Dictionary of Jewish Palestinian Aramaic*. (Ramat Gan/Baltimore/London)

Zulay, Menahem. 1995a. ‘נשכחות בלשון הפיטנים’, in Ephraim Hazan (ed.), *ארץ ישראל ופיוטיה* (Jerusalem). 440–9

— 1995b. ‘עיוני לשון בפיוטי ינאי’, in Ephraim Hazan (ed.), *ארץ ישראל ופיוטיה* (Jerusalem). 451–527

A Genizah Leaf from the *Dīwān* of Š^{e}mû'ēl ha-Nāgîd

Michael Rand and Jonathan Vardi
Academy of the Hebrew Language   Hebrew University

The *Dīwān* of Š^{e}mû'ēl ha-Nāgîd

Among the remains of the Cairo Genizah is scattered a not insignificant number of leaves in which are copied poems by the first of the great Andalusian poets of the Golden Age — Š^{e}mû'ēl ha-Nāgîd (993–1056). From the point of view of provenance, i.e., the type of literary works from which they derive, these leaves may be grouped into a number of distinct categories. Of interest to us at the present moment are those leaves that stem from copies of the Nāgîd's *dīwān*.

Dīwān is a word of Persian origin, which entered into Arabic and was thence borrowed into Hebrew. In the latter, it was employed exclusively in a literary sense, to refer to a monographic collection of the poems of an individual poet. The appearance of the *dīwān* in Hebrew literary culture is basically simultaneous with the rise of Hebrew poetry in Muslim Andalusia, the first three such collections to have reached us being that of the poems of M^{e}naḥēm ben Sārûq (in the first generation of Andalusian poets), followed by that of the Nāgîd, together with that of his older contemporary Yiṣḥaq ibn Khalfun (in the second generation).[1] The *Dīwān* of the Nāgîd is apparently one of three distinct collections containing his poems, the other two bearing specific titles that were given to them at the time of their compilation: *Ben Mišlê* and *Ben Qohelet*.[2] It differs from the two latter in a number of important respects. First, it does not bear a specific title, being known by the generic term *dīwān*.[3] Second, as opposed to the *Dīwān*, the two named collections are organized

1 For Ibn Khalfun see Mirsky 1961. A photo of a leaf from his *dīwān* (Oxford Heb. d.36 fol. 10b = 2776.3) may be seen in Schirmann 1954, I: opposite p. 64. For the *dīwān* of M^{e}naḥēm ben Sārûq, see Fleischer 2010, I: 24–5.

2 Both of these collections have been edited twice: Abramson 1949, and Abramson 1954; Jarden 1982, and Jarden 1992.

3 On the authority of Mošeh ibn ʿEzraʾ (*Sēfer ha-ʾIyyûnîm w^{e}-ha-Diyyûnîm*), as well as that of Yiṣḥāq ben Yaʿaqôv (a fourteenth-century commentator on Ibn ʿEzra's *Sēfer ha-ʿAnaq*), the *Dīwān* is sometimes identified with an otherwise unknown collection of the Nagîd's poems called *Ben T^{e}hillîm*.

thematically as well as formally in a manner that is consistent and unified. With regard to thematic content, *Ben Mišlê* contains (short) poems the theme of which is subsumed under the category of 'wisdom', i.e., maxims aimed at inculcating proper conduct and worldly success. *Ben Qohelet*, on the other hand, contains poems mostly devoted to the 'philosophical' themes of the passage of time, and the inevitability of death. As to formal organization, both collections are preceded by short epigrams each containing twenty-two words (i.e., the number of letters of the Hebrew alphabet). The poems in each collection are organized into twenty-two alphabetically arranged sections, all of the poems of a given section opening with the same letter. In addition to this alphabetic organizational principle, the first few poems opening each of the sections are arranged in accordance with their rhyming syllables, such that the consonants opening the rhyming syllables of the poems of a given section spell out the corresponding word in the epigram opening the entire collection (e.g., the consonants opening the rhyming syllables of the poems appearing at the beginning of the first section spell out the first word of the epigram, and so forth). Finally, the poems of each section are arranged in accordance with the metrical patterns that they employ.

As opposed to *Ben Mišlê* and *Ben Qohelet*, the *Dīwān* has no single, consistent unifying principle, either thematic or formal.[4] It simply contains those poems that the Nāgîd composed in varying contexts and on varying themes over the course of his career. Many of the poems are historical/biographical in nature, describing the battles in which the Nāgîd took part as the *vizier* and military commander of the forces of Granada, together with the political machinations that brought them on. Others are amatory poems, in the style of Classical Arabic erotic poetry. Closely allied to these in terms of social context are poems devoted to the theme of wine drinking, as undertaken at the feasts held at the courts of Andalusian nobles, to whose class the Nāgîd belonged. Related to these are poetic descriptions of items belonging to the physical setting of such feasts (e.g., a fountain), or epigrams meant to be recited in their course. Yet other poems of the Nāgîd are personal in nature, such as a cycle devoted to the death of his brother Yiṣḥāq, or poems addressed to his son Y^{e}hôsēf.

The question of the status of *Ben T^{e}hillîm* is a vexed one, and cannot be satisfactorily resolved on the basis of the information currently available; for a review of the relevant data see Vardi and Rand forthcoming. For the present purposes, it is sufficient to refer to the collection that is of interest to us as the *Dīwān* (with a capital letter to distinguish the specific from the generic usage of the word).

4 The *Dīwān* has been edited twice: Habermann 1948 and Jarden 1966. Both editors re-arrange the poems contained within it in accordance with a thematic principle, each after his own fashion. Neither of these editions, therefore, presents the original order of poems within the *Dīwān*.

Still others are derived from poetic correspondences that the Nāgîd conducted with a number of individuals. Within the *Dīwān*, the poems are organized in accordance with several different principles: the chronological principle (i.e., ordering in accordance with the time of composition),[5] the thematic principle (i.e., poems on the same theme, or belonging to the same genre, being clustered together), and the length principle (longer poems coming first and shorter poems clustering at the end of the *Dīwān*). These principles sometimes reinforce one another (e.g., the historical/biographical poems are usually longer than the courtly poems), and sometimes interfere with one another. None is applied consistently. The result is that the *Dīwān* presents the reader with an eclectic collection within which tendencies towards internal organization are easily apparent and yet never fully realized.

Genizah Fragments of the *Dīwān*

The *Dīwān* was compiled in the Nāgîd's lifetime by his firstborn son Y^ehôsef, who describes his procedure in an Arabic introduction.[6] It was apparently disseminated rather quickly, as is witnessed by the fact that fragments of several copies of it are attested in the 'Classical' Genizah (i.e., among the documents stemming from the main period of deposit into the Genizah, roughly from the eleventh to the fourteenth centuries). As witnesses to the *Dīwān*, as well as to the poems contained within it, these fragments lay hidden away from the world until their discovery in the nineteenth century. Outside of the Genizah, only a single complete copy of the *Dīwān* is known to exist. This copy was identified and purchased by David Sassoon, who published the manuscript (Sassoon 1934). This manuscript, known as Sassoon 589, was copied in 1584, and contains the text of all three of the Nāgîd's poetic collections. Its importance for scholarship pertaining to the poetry of the Nāgîd is immense, as it not only provides the text of many poems that are not known from other sources, but also serves as evidence of the order of the poems within the compilation as it was

5 In his introduction to the *Dīwān*, the compiler/editor Y^ehôsēf ha-Nāgîd writes as follows: 'And I took no care in that which I gathered of this [material] with regard to chronological order, but rather wrote according to the order that came to hand' (translation ours). And yet despite Y^ehôsēf's disclaimer, the Arabic headers that precede the historical/biographical poems and indicate their dates make it clear that a basic chronological order is observed.

6 For the text of the introduction see Jarden 1966: 1. Y^ehôsēf composed his introduction during his father's lifetime. It is reasonable to suppose that he added to the collection over the course of the Nāgîd's life (as new poems were composed, or as older ones were 'found'), and also perhaps after his death. In any case, the text of the introduction as it now stands specifically refers to the Nāgîd as being alive.

produced by Yᵉhôsēf.[7] Comparison with the Genizah fragments of the *Dīwān* shows conclusively that this order was more or less canonical.[8]

The first manuscripts of the *Dīwān* to be discovered belong to the Firkovitch collection: Firkovitch II A 333.1 and 333.2. Of these, the former is by far the more extensive, containing 45 leaves belonging to a single *Dīwān* codex. Firkovitch II A 333.2 stems from the Genizah, as may be ascertained on the basis of the fact that other leaves from the same codex have been identified in 'official' Genizah collections (see note 11). The provenance of Firkovitch II A 333.1, on the other hand, cannot be established with certainty — it may derive from the Genizah or some other eastern source. These materials were studied by Harkavy, who published an annotated text (Harkavy 1879). With regard to Firkovitch II A 333.1, as may now be ascertained by means of comparison to the text of the *Dīwān* as it appears in Sassoon 589, Harkavy was able to correctly reconstruct the surviving individual quires of the *Dīwān* codex at his disposal, but owing to his ignorance of order of the composition as a whole, he was unable to put the quires in proper order. With the publication of Sassoon 589, leaves from Genizah codices of the *Dīwān* may now be ordered in accordance with the order of the poems as attested there.[9] In the case of those *Dīwān* codices of which a relatively large number of leaves have survived, the ability to reconstruct the order of poems within the original collection in effect means the ability to reconstruct a medieval book, quire by quire. This is true of two codices: the one published by Harkavy, as well as a second codex forty-seven of whose leaves

7 In addition to the poems of the Nāgîd, the *Dīwān* also contains a number of poems by Yiṣḥāq ibn Khalfun, included in it as part of the correspondence between the two. It is therefore also a source of paramount importance for the study of the *oeuvre* of Ibn Khalfūn.

8 The major apparent exception to this rule is constituted by the section of short poems at the end of the *Dīwān*. To the extent that it is possible to judge on the basis of the partial evidence, there exist two different sequences of short poems. However, the discrepancy between the two may well be the result of a local error in the course of the transmission of the *Dīwān*, whereas the original sequence was canonical in this case as well. The case of the short poems aside, the order of poems attested in the Genizah manuscripts of the *Dīwān* differs from the order in Sassoon 589 in minor details only. For an example of such a minor discrepancy, see Vardi 2010: 355–6, n. 9.

9 Poems that are found in the *Dīwān* may be attested in the Genizah outside of copies of *Dīwān* codices proper. We define as a *Dīwān* fragment any leaf showing evidence of the following two features: (1) the sequence of poems that is attested in the *Dīwān* copied in Sassoon 589, and (2) the presence of Arabic headers at the beginning of every poem, as attested (in Hebrew translation) in Sassoon 589. Only leaves meeting these two criteria (or leaves stemming from *Dīwān* codices other leaves belonging to which meet them) may be considered as representing copies of the *Dīwān*.

have been identified in the Genizah.[10] Other *Diwan* codices are represented in the Genizah by a much more limited number of leaves.[11] The purpose of the present article is to describe one such codex.

The *Dīwān* Codex in Question

The codex in question is represented by four leaves:

T-S NS 275.32a

Frankfurt 158 + Adler 3302.5 + Rylands B 8056 + Rylands AF 10

ENA 3685.11

Mosseri II.201

In the following, we describe the text of the *Dīwān* as it is attested in this codex, and provide a reconstructed composite image of leaf 2,[12] which is now composed of four separate fragments, together with a transcription. The poems in the codex are numbered in accordance with the sequence of poems attested in Sassoon 589, as established in ed. Sassoon. The numbering of the lines within each poem is also given in accordance with ed. Sassoon.

T-S NS 275.32a recto

הנה יחידתי (poem 3): stichs 15–31 (end of poem). Among all the poems that are copied in the surviving fragments, this is the only one that is *not* written colometrically. It is copied as a running text, with no regard for its division into stichs (בית) and hemi-stichs (דלת, סוגר).

מצולה את (poem 4): header + stichs 1–6 (end of poem). The text of the poem is copied two stichs per line.

לבבי קץ (poem 5): header + stichs 1–5 (end of poem).

הכימים בחרתם (poem 6): header + stichs 1–4. Stichs 3–4 are copied in the left margin of the page.

---

10 This codex is to be published by the present authors in a facsimile edition: Vardi and Rand forthcoming. A photo of a leaf from this codex (Cambridge T-S 13K5.7) may be seen in Schirmann 1954, I: opposite p. 80. This codex contains the only complete copy of the Arabic text of Yᵉhôsēf's introduction to the *Dīwān*. A photo of the leaf that opens with this introduction (Oxford Heb. e.45 fol. 91b = 2787.24) is published in Jarden 1966: 2.

11 A fragment of one such codex, Firkovitch II A 333.2, was published by Harkavy (see above). Other fragments stemming from this *Dīwān* codex are Firkovitch II A 192.4 (published in Elizur 1989/90) and ENA 1731.5-13 (published in Marcus 1930). Besides the two codices mentioned above, this one is the most extensive to have survived, containing twenty-two leaves. The others are represented by a much smaller number of leaves — six and less. A list of all known Genizah fragments of the various copies of the *Dīwān* is given in Vardi and Rand forthcoming.

12 The composite image was created with the help of Sergey Minov and Avi Shmidman, to both of whom we would like to record our gratitude.

Verso

הכימים בחרתם (continued from recto): stichs 5–23 (end of poem).

לשר רבי נסים (poem 7): stichs 1–8. Stichs 4–8 are copied in the left margin of the page.

Frankfurt 158 + Adler 3302.5 + Rylands B 8056 + Rylands AF 10 recto

אלוה עוז (poem 10): stichs 30–54. Stichs 34 and 36 are missing from this copy.

Verso

אלוה עוז (continued from recto): stichs 55–77. Stich 56 is missing from this copy.

ENA 3685.11 recto (only a fragment of the leaf is preserved)

אלוה עוז: stichs 78–91

Verso

אלוה עוז (continued from recto): stichs 101–13

Mosseri II.201 recto

אלוה עוז: stichs 123–49 (end of poem). Stichs 147–9 are copied in the left margin of the page.

Verso

בפיהו מור (poem 13): header + stichs 1–4 (end of poem).

יחידתי לבבך (poem 14): header + stichs 1–18.

It is evident from this catalogue that the *Dīwān* codex in question does not entirely reflect the text of the *Dīwān* as given in Sassoon 589 (together with Firkovitch II A 333.1 and the codex to be published by us [Vardi and Rand forthcoming]), in that it skips the poems הבמות פליליה (poem 11) and עלי כל איש (poem 12). This omission aside, the order of the poems in the present *Dīwān* codex exactly parallels the order given in Sassoon 589.[13]

The copying of the codex is not uniform. The number of lines per page ranges from 22 to 24. As noted above, not all of the poems are copied colometrically (see הנה יחידתי). Also, stichs are occasionally copied in the left margins of the pages, not always at the ends of the poems (see הכימים בחרתם and לשר רבי נסים). In a number of cases, the ends of lines that fall short of the average length are provided with filler marks (see in the facsimile, verso lines 1–2), whereas in other cases in the same poem, the last letter of the stich is elongated in order to fill out the line (see in the facsimile, verso lines 6–7, 9).

13 It should be noted that the suviving leaves of the *Dīwān* in question all stem from the beginning of the codex. We might speculate, therefore, that only the first few (two?) quires of the book were deposited into the Genizah to begin with.

Transcription of the Composite Leaf

The leaf whose composite image is provided in the present article is composed of four separate fragments. Three of these fragments are now housed in two separate collections, whereas the fourth, Frankfurt 158, is no longer extant, having been lost along with the rest of the Frankfurt Genizah collection during World War II. A photograph of this fragment is preserved among a series of photographs that was taken before the War on behalf of the Schocken Institute. The importance of the leaf to scholarship is twofold. First, it is an important witness to the text of the Nāgîd's poem אלוה עוז, as well as being an integral part of the Genizah codex fragments of which are described above. The other leaves of this codex are available relatively easily to scholars. On the other hand, the data supplied by the composite leaf can much more easily be appreciated on the basis of the composite image, rather than on the basis of each individual fragment. For this reason, we have thought it important to publish the image. Secondly, the existence of the composite serves to illustrate the advances made by Genizah scholarship in recent years, mostly as a result of the ongoing digitization of the various Genizah collections and their becoming easily available for study online. The leading role in this process has been played by the Friedberg Genizah Project. Alongside this Project we must cite the Genizah digitization project of the University of Manchester, the results of which are available on the website of the John Rylands University Library. In the field of Genizah poetry research, the single most important role is played by the data of the Ezra Fleischer Institute for the Research of Hebrew Poetry in the Genizah. The Institute has created a database in which the vast majority of Genizah poetry fragments have been catalogued. With the help of online digital images, therefore, researchers can now establish relatively easily and quickly which fragments of a particular text (be it a poem, or as in our case, a collection of poems) belong to the same copy/codex. This development has, in turn, helped Genizah poetry researchers to supplement their ability to reconstruct texts with an ability to reconstruct discreet copies/codices. As a result, Genizah poetry scholarship is now increasingly in a position to document not only a particular text but also the ways in which that text was copied in the materials that were deposited in the Genizah. The result is always a more nuanced understanding of the ways in which poetic texts were transmitted. The leaf that is published here in facsimile is an excellent illustration of the new possibilities now open to the field, both on account of the relatively large number of fragments of which it is composed, as well as their geographical dispersal. In sum, advances in

Genizah research are now making it increasingly possible to piece back together items that were presumably deposited into the Genizah as wholes, and only became fragmented in the course of the physical dispersal of the Genizah at the hands of European and American scholars, collectors, and tourists.

In the transcription that accompanies the composite image, lacunae in the text are filled in from Sassoon 589. The following symbols are employed:

Hollow letters (א)= lacunae

Letters with overdots (א̇) = doubtful reading

It is worth noting that in a number of significant cases, the readings of our codex (C^1) agree with those of Firkovitch II A 333.1 (F) against those of Sassoon 589 (S) and those of the codex to be published by us (Vardi and Rand forthcoming), where these are extant (C^2). The following are those cases that are attested in the composite leaf:

Recto, line 3: בפיד C^1 F *versus* כפיר S

Recto, line 9: והוקש C^1 F *versus* והרע S C^2 (Ox. Heb. e.45 fol. 92[ii]b = 2787.24)

These are the variants that are attested in the other leaves of the codex:

לבבי קץ, stich 2: ואיך יריב אשר המס לבבו / יקוד פירוד וכחסון אכלו C^1 (T-S NS 275.32a recto) F *versus* ואיך יריב אשר חמס לבבו / יקוד פירוד ובחרון אכלו S

אלוה עוז, stich 87: [ו]אם היום היום (!) לעבדך לא תקנא C^1 (ENA 3685.11 recto) and ואם היום לעבדך לא תקנא F *versus* ואם היום בזאת לי לא תקנא S

אלוה עוז, stich 91: [פתח דלתות ישוע]ת̇ך לעבדך̇ / [במקום צר וכל דלת סגורה] C^1 and פתח דלתות ישועתך לעבדך / במקום צר וכל דלת סגורה F *versus* פתח דלת במקום צר והושע / לעבדך וכל דלת סגורה S and [פ]ת̇ח דלת במקום צר והושע / לעב̇[ד]ך̇ [וכ]ל דלת ס̇[גור]ה̇ C^2 (T-S NS 300.46)

יחידתי לבבך, stich 10: עדי בקר שקידה C^1 (Mosseri II.201 verso) F *versus* עדי בקר יעודה S

These variants indicate that the text copied in the codex under investigation here is closely allied to the text of Firkovitch II A 333.1 as against the text of Sassoon 589. The fact that in the two cases where data are available the readings of the codex to be published by us agree with Sassoon 589 precludes the inference that the codex under investigation here along with Firkovitch II A 333.1 reflect a ‘Genizah version’, as against the version of Sassoon 589.

References

Abramson, Shraga. 1949. *בן משלי*. (Tel Aviv)

—— 1954. *בן קהלת*. (Tel Aviv)

Elizur, Shulamit. 1989/90. 'שירים חדשים לר' שמואל הנגיד', *Tarbiz* 59, 95–107

Fleischer, Ezra. 2010. 'לקדמוניות שירתנו בספרד: עיון בשירים ופיוטים של רבי מנחם בן סרוק', in Shulamit Elizur and Tovah Be'eri (eds), *השירה העברית בספרד ובשלוחותיה*, 3 vols (Jerusalem). 3–46

Habermann, Abraham Meir. 1948. *ר' שמואל הנגיד – דיואן*. (Tel Aviv)

Harkavy, A.A. 1879. *זכרון לראשונים וגם אחרונים – זכרון של רב שמואל הנגיד בן יוסף הלוי*. (St Petersburg)

Jarden, Dov. 1966. *דיואן שמואל הנגיד – בן תהלים*. (Jerusalem)

—— 1982. *דיואן שמואל הנגיד – בן משלי*. (Jerusalem)

—— 1992. *דיואן שמואל הנגיד – בן קהלת*. (Jerusalem)

Marcus, Joseph. 1930. 'משירי ר' שמואל הנגיד', *Mizrāḥ u-Ma'arāv* 4, 305–18

Mirsky, Aharon. 1961. *שירי ר' יצחק אבן כ'לפון*. (Jerusalem)

Sassoon, David Solomon. 1934. *Diwan of Shemuel Hannaghid*. (Oxford and London)

Schirmann, Hayyim. 1954–6. *השירה העברית בספרד ובפרובאנס*. 2 vols, (Jerusalem and Tel Aviv)

Vardi, Jonathan. 2010. 'שניים שהם אחד: שיר "חדש" לשמואל הנגיד', *Lešônenû* 72, 353–7

Vardi, Jonathan and Michael Rand. Forthcoming. *דיואן שמואל הנגיד – קודקס הגניזה*. (Jerusalem)

Frankfurt 158 + Adler 3302.5 + Rylands B 8056 + Rylands AF 10 recto

וְאָבַד בְּאֲבוֹד מַלְכּוֹ שְׁמוּאֵל / וְתוֹחַלְתּוֹ כְּבָר אָזְלָה וְסָרָה
וְחָרָה לִי וְחָרָה לֵאלֹהִים / וְאַפּוֹ בוֹ כְּאֵשׁ נִסַּק וְחָרָה
אֲזַי עָמַד בְּפִיד עַמִּים וְעָצַר / בְּעַמּוֹ אַחֲרֵי אָבִיו עֲצָרָה
וְכָתַב צוֹרְרֵי אֵלָיו בְּנַחַץ / כְּתָב חָזָק וְרָם מֵאֵין פְּצִירָה
וְאֵין שָׁלוֹם וְאֵין הַשְׁקֵט וְנֶפֶשׁ / יְהוּדִי זֶה בְּתוֹךְ גּוּפוֹ נְצוּרָה
וְאִם אַיִן דֵּעָה כִּי הַמְּלָכִים / עֲלֵי מִלְחַמְתְּךְ קָשְׁרוּ קְשִׁירָה
וְכֹה אשׁיב בְּסִפְרוֹ אִם אֲמַלֵּא / שְׁאֵילָתְךְ תְּבוֹאֵנִי מְאֵירָה
וְאִם אֶמְסוֹר בְּיַד צָרָיו מְשָׁרְתִי / תְּהִי נַפְשִׁי בְּיַד צָרַי מְסוּרָה
לְזֹאת קָצַף מְשַׂנְאִי זֶה וְאָחַז / בְּשִׂטְנָתוֹ וְהוּקַשׁ לוֹ וְחָרָה
וְלֹא נָח עַד אֲשֶׁר אָסַף חֲיָלָיו / עֲמָלֵק וֶאֱדוֹם וּבְנֵי קְטוּרָה
וְאֵל שָׁת מִן יְמֵי רֵאשִׁית לְנָפְלָם / בְּקִרְיַת מַעְיָן שׁוּחָה חֲפוּרָה
וְכָפַל אֶת נְסִיעוֹתָיו וּמִהֵר / כְּעוֹף יִרְכַּב כְּנַף רוּחַ וְיֵרָא
וְיָעַץ הוּא וְיָעַץ אֵל וְקָמָה / עֲצַת הָאֵל אֲשֶׁר אֵין לָהּ הֲפָרָה
וְיָצָא אָב בְּרָצָה הַקְּדוּמָה / וּבָא אֱלוּל בְּטוֹבָה לֹא אֲחוּרָה
וְתָקַע אָהֳלֹה בָּהָר בְּעֵבֶר / וְתִשְׁקְטֵנוּ בְּדֶרֶךְ הָעֲבָרָה
וְלֹא שַׁתְנוּ לְבָבֵינוּ לְחֵילוֹ / חֲשַׁבְנוּהוּ כְּאִלּוּ הוּא שְׁיָרָה
וְהִרְבָּה כַּאֲשֶׁר בָּא הַדְּבָרִים / וְשָׂפָה בִּי אֲנָשֵׁינוּ וְגָרָה
וּבְרָאוֹת צוֹרְרִי כִּי עַל לְשׁוֹנִי / בְּפֶה אֶחָד תְּדַבֵּר הַחֲבוּרָה
אֲזַי הֵרִיק חֲנִית רוֹמַח וְחֶרֶב / וְגַם סָגַר לְהִלָּחֵם סְגִירָה
וְקָם הַצַּר וְקָם הַצּוּר לְנֶגְדּוֹ / וְאֵיךְ תָּקוּם בְּקוּם צוּרִי הַיְצִירָה
וְעָמְדוּ הַחֲיָילוֹת מַעֲרָכָה / לְצוּמַּת מַעֲרֶכֶת צַר בְּשׁוּרָה
אֲנָשִׁים יַחְשְׁבוּ יוֹם אַף וְחֵימָה / וְקִנְאָה אֶת בְּכוֹר מָוֶת בְּכוּרָה
וְכָל אֶחָד מְבַקֵּשׁ לוֹ קְנוֹת שֵׁם / וְנַפְשׁוֹ כַּאֲשֶׁר יִקְנֶה מְכוּרָה

3 בפיד] Thus also in Firk. II A 333.1. Sassoon 589 reads: כְּפִיר, and this is to be preferred. 4 פצירה] After this stich, the following stich is missing: וְשָׁלַח לוֹ הֲתֵדַע כִּי שְׁמוּאֵל / לְחַיּוֹתוֹ בְּדָתֵנוּ עֲבֵירָה (Sassoon 589). 5 נצורה] After this stich, the following stich is missing: שְׁלַח אוֹתוֹ וְיָסוּרוּ מְדָנִים / וּמִדְיָנִים וְקַח עָלָיו פְּשָׁרָה (Sassoon 589). 7 אשיב] The proper reading is: הֲשִׁיב (Sassoon 589). It is possible that in the MS ה is corrected to א. 9 וחרה] Vocalized in the MS: וְחָרָה. 15 אהלה] Vocalized in the MS: אהלֹה. 17 והרבה] Vocalized in the MS: והִרְבָּה. 20 צורי] The proper reading is: צור (Sassoon 589).

Plate 1: Composite image of Frankfurt 158 (top), ENA 3302.5 (left), Rylands AF B 8056-1 (right), Rylands AF 10-1 (bottom). (Reproduced by courtesy of the University Librarian and Director, The John Rylands Library, The University of Manchester, by courtesy of the library of the Jewish Theological Seminary and by courtesy of the Schocken Institute for Jewish Research of the Jewish Theological Seminary of America, Jerusalem)

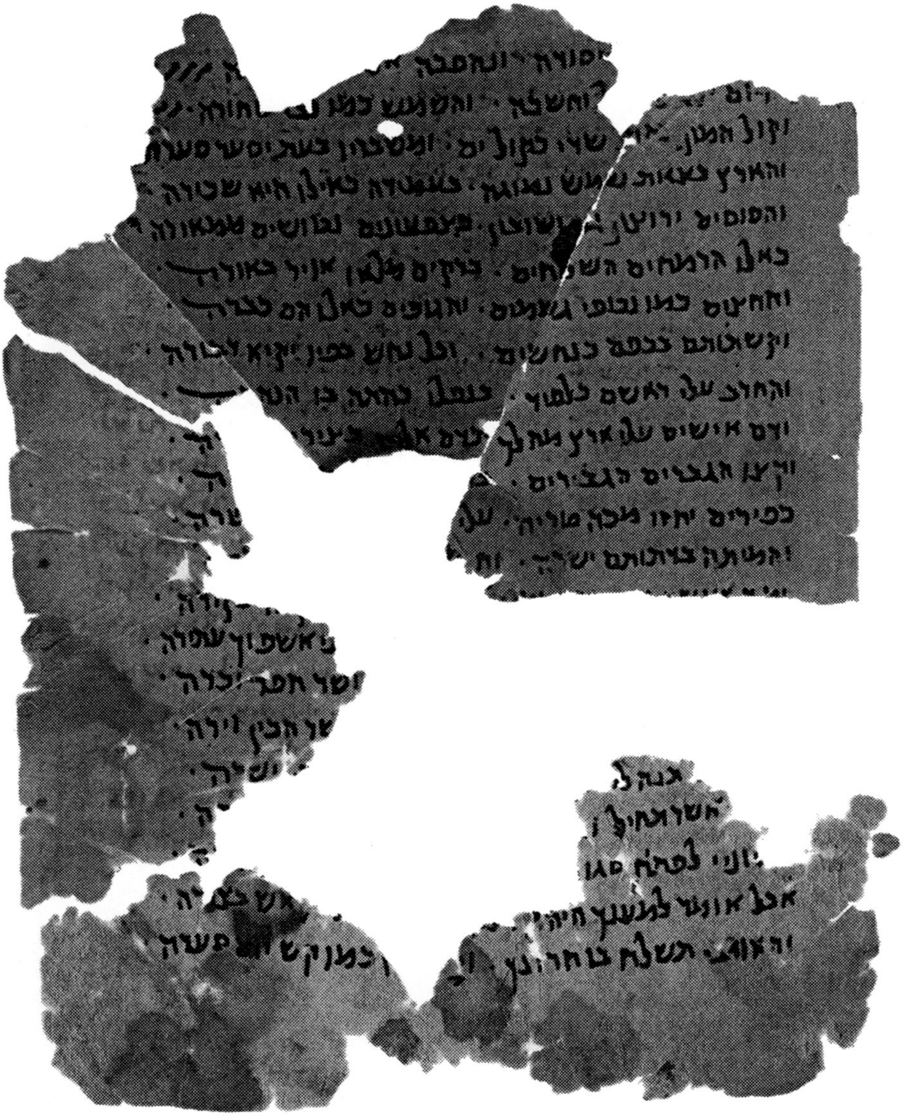

Plate 2: Composite image of Frankfurt 158 (top), Rylands B 8056-2 (left), ENA 3302.5 (right), Rylands AF 10-2 (bottom). (Reproduced by courtesy of the University Librarian and Director, The John Rylands Library, The University of Manchester, by courtesy of the library of the Jewish Theological Seminary and by courtesy of the Schocken Institute for Jewish Research of the Jewish Theological Seminary of America, Jerusalem)

Frankfurt 158 + Adler 3302.5 + Rylands B 8056 + Rylands AF 10 verso

וְנָעָה הָאֲדָמָה מִיְּסוֹדָהּ / וְנֶהֶפְכָה אֹ[.. ..]ה ///
וְהַיּוֹם יוֹם עֲרָפֶל וַחֲשֵׁכָה / וְהַשֶּׁמֶשׁ כְּמוֹ לִבִּי שְׁחוֹרָה //
וְקוֹל הָמוֹן כְּקוֹל שַׁדַּי כְּקוֹל יָם / וּמִשְׁבָּרָיו בְּעֵת יִסְעַר סערה
וְהָאָרֶץ בְּצֵאת שֶׁמֶשׁ נְמוֹגָה / בעמידה כְּאִילּוּ הִיא שְׁכוּרָה
וְהַסּוּסִים יְרוּצוּן גַּם יְשׁוּבוּן / כְּצִפְעוֹנִים נְטוּשִׁים מִמְּאוּרָה
כְּאִלּוּ הָרְמָחִים הַשְּׁלוּחִים / בְּרָקִים מִלְּאוּ אֲוִיר בְּאוֹרָה
וְהַחִצִּים כְּמוֹ נִטְפֵי גְשָׁמִים / וְהַגּוּפִים כְּאִלּוּ הֵם כְּבָרָה
וְקַשְּׁתוֹתָם בְּכַפָּם כַּנְּחָשִׁים / וְכָל נָחָשׁ בְּפִיו יָקִיא דְבוֹרָה
וְהַחֶרֶב עֲלֵי רֹאשָׁם כְּלַפִּיד / בְּנָפְלוֹ כַּהֲתָה בוֹ הַנְּהָרָה
וְדַם אִישִׁים עֲלֵי אֶרֶץ מְהַלֵּךְ / כְּדַם אֵלִים בצירי הַבָּצְרָה
וְקָצוּ הַגְּבָרִים הַגְּבִירִים / בְּחַיֵּיהֶם וְהַמִּיתָה בְּחוּרָה
כְּפִירִים יֶחֱזוּ מַכָּה טְרִיָּה / עֲלֵי רֹאשָׁם כְּאִלּוּ הִיא עֲטָרָה
וְהַמִּיתָה בְּדָתוֹתָם יְשָׁרָה / וְהַחַיִּים בְּעֵינֵיהֶם אֲסוּרָה
וּמָה אֶעֱשֶׂה וְאֵין מָנוֹס וּמִשְׁעָן / וּמִשְׁעָנָה וְהַתִּקְוָה עֲקוּרָה
מְשַׂנְאִים יִשְׁפְּכוּ דָמִים כְּמַיִם / בְּיוֹם צַר וַאֲנִי אֶשְׁפּוֹךְ עֲתִירָה
לְאֵל מַשְׁפִּיל וּמַפִּיל כָּל מְעַוֵּל / בְּגוּמָּצוֹ אֲשֶׁר חָפַר וְכָרָה
וּמֵשִׁיב יוֹם קְרָב חֶרֶב וְחִצִּים / בְּלֵב אוֹיֵב אֲשֶׁר הֵכִין וְיָרָה
וְלֹא אוֹמַר תְּנָה לִי אֵל תְּשׁוּעָה / לְמַעַן כִּי הֲלִיכָתִי יְשָׁרָה
וְתוֹרָתִי אֲשֶׁר תָּחִיל וְתֵלֵד / בְּעֵת תּוֹרַת בְּנֵי תוֹרָה עֲקָרָה
וְהֶגְיוֹנַיי לְפַתֵּיחַ סְגוּרוֹת / בְּלֵילוֹת קִדְּמוּ עֵינַי שְׁמוּרָה
אֲבָל אוֹמַר לְמַעַנְךָ הֱיֵה לִי / לְצוּר מָעוֹן וְחוֹמַת אֵשׁ בְּצוּרָה
וְהָאוֹיֵב תְּשַׁלַּח בּוֹ חֲרוֹנְךָ / וְיֹאכְלֵמוֹ כְּמוֹ קַשׁ יוֹם סְעָרָה

1 ה.. ..א] Sassoon 589 and Firk. II A 333.1 read: כְּמַהְפֵּכַת עֲמוֹרָה. There are no other known parallels to this stich. After this stich the following stich is missing: וּפָנִים קִבְּצוּ פָארוּר וְהָדָר / וְנֶהֶפְכוּ אֱלֵי שׁוּלֵי קְדֵרָה (Sassoon 589). 3 סערה] The proper reading is: סְעִירָה (Sassoon 589), as the word סְעָרָה is attested at the end of stich 77 (= line 22 of this page), whereas rhyme words are usually not repeated within the same poem. 4 בעמידה] The proper reading is בְּעָמְדֶיהָ (Sassoon 589). 10 בצירי] The proper reading is: בְּצִידֵי (Sassoon 589). 20 לפתיח] In the MS: לפת׳ח.

A Preliminary Catalogue of the Medical and Para-Medical Manuscripts in the Rylands Genizah Collection Together with the Partial Edition of Two Medical Fragments (A 589 and B 3239)

Efraim Lev and Renate Smithuis

University of Haifa University of Manchester

Preliminary Catalogue of Medical and Para-Medical Documents in the Rylands Genizah Collection

In this article we offer an overview of the medical and para-medical fragments identified to date in the Rylands Genizah collection, followed by the transcription, translation and analysis of two short medical texts found among them. The catalogue provides new information for the attention of researchers in the history of medicine and pharmacology. Even though the fragments are mostly small, they enable us to expand our knowledge regarding the medical learning and practices of the Jews in Cairo and of medieval medicine in general. The catalogue is limited to the medical pieces found in A 1-A 1921, B 1922-B 6000 and the Arabic series (Ar. 1-Ar. 840), which counts for the majority of the fragments. In addition, we have identified six fragments from the L series and described B 6210, which is an autograph by Maimonides. We will identify the other medical fragments in the Rylands Genizah collection at a later stage.

The catalogue describes each side of the fragment in accordance with the online database (http://enriqueta.man.ac.uk/luna/servlet/). Our description of the fragments basically follows the method established by the editors of the catalogues of the Cambridge Genizah collections. The entries are arranged as follows: (1) classmark; (2) main heading; (3) languages contained in the manuscript; (4) complementary information about the contents; (5) physical description, i.e. material, number of leaves, measurements in height by width and number of columns and/or lines.

We have distinguished between books and notebooks on the one hand, and prescriptions, lists of *materia medica*, letters, magical texts and amulets on the other (Lev 2004). This distinction is important for researchers: whereas the latter are clear evidence for the practical use of medical techniques and *materia medica* and the existence of certain diseases and their treatment among the Jewish community in Old Cairo, books have a more 'international' character. Books could have been written in one part of the Arab world, copied elsewhere and used in Egypt according to the medical needs and drugs available. Notebooks were usually copied from books for practical or personal use and can therefore be regarded as being between 'theory' and 'practice' (Lev and Amar 2007 and 2008).

Description of the Manuscripts

1a. A 103-1 (together with A 103-2; A 739-1,2; A 767-1,2) – Medical book, written in Judaeo-Arabic, dealing with medical theory. Paper; 1 leaf; 9.6 x 9; 11 lines.

1b. A 103-2 (together with A 103-1; A 739-1,2; A 767-1,2) – Medical book, written in Judaeo-Arabic, dealing with medical theory. Paper; 1 leaf; 9.6 x 9; 11 lines.

1c. A 739-1 (together with A 103-1,2; A 739-2; A 767-1,2) – Medical book, written in Judaeo-Arabic, dealing with medical theory. Paper; 1 leaf; 9.8 x 8.9; 11 lines.

1d. A 739-2 (together with A 103-1,2; A 739-1; A 767-1,2) – Medical book, written in Judaeo-Arabic, dealing with medical theory. Paper; 1 leaf; 9.8 x 8.9; 11 lines.

1e. A 767-1 (together with A 103-1,2; A 739-1,2; A 767-2) – Medical book, written in Judaeo-Arabic, dealing with medical theory. Paper; 1 leaf; 10.4 x 13.5; 11 lines.

1f. A 767-2 (together with A 103-1,2; A 739-1,2; A 767-1) – Medical book, written in Judaeo-Arabic, dealing with medical theory. Paper; 1 leaf; 10.4 x 13.5; 11 lines.

2a. A 195-1 (together with A 195-2) – Medical book, written in Judaeo-Arabic, mentioning a.o. saffron (זעפראן). Paper, 1 leaf; 11.6 x 10; 8 lines.[1]

2b. A 195-2 (together with A 195-1) – Medical book, written in Judaeo-Arabic, mentioning a.o. saffron (זעפראן) and the phlegmatic (אלבלגמי). Paper, 1 leaf; 11.6 x 10; 8 lines.

3a. A 455-1 (together with A 455-2) – Medical book, written in Hebrew, dealing with sleep, paralysis and the senses. Paper; 1 leaf; 15.2 x 13.5; 7 lines.

3b. A 455-2 (together with A 455-1) – Medical book, written in Hebrew, dealing with sleep, paralysis and the senses. Includes marginal note. Paper; 1 leaf; 15.2 x 13.5; 6 lines.

1 We thank Dr Butbul for this identification.

4a. A 504-1 (together with A 504-2) – Medical book with materia medica (book on simple drugs), consists of an alphabetical list of healing plants (the letter ב), violet (בנסג'), chamomile (באבונש), bezoar stone (באדורד) written in Judaeo-Spanish. Paper; 1 leaf; 16.8 x 13.4; 26 lines.

4b. A 504-2 (together with A 504-1) – Medical book with materia medica (book on simple drugs), consists of an alphabetical list of healing plants (the letter ב), sea lavender/white behen (בהמן), borax (בורק), written in Judaeo-Spanish. Paper; 1 leaf; 16.8 x 13.4; 27 lines.

5a. A 539-1 (together with A 539-2,3,4,5,6,7,8,9,10,11,12; B 3361-1; B 3362-1,2) – Medical book with materia medica (book on simple drugs), written in Hebrew. Belongs to the medical genre of the *Kutub al-Mufradāt* (see Ullmann 1970: ch. 14). Consists of an alphabetical list of healing plants and mineral substances. Entries are transcriptions of Arabic words (Judaeo-Arabic) which, in turn, are sometimes of Greek or Persian origin. Mentions for example: cinnamon (דרציני). Paper; 1 leaf; 12.6 x 12.6; 16 lines.

5b. A 539-2 (together with A 539-1,3,4,5,6,7,8,9,10,11,12; B 3361-1; B 3362-1,2) – Medical book with materia medica (book on simple drugs), written in Hebrew. Belongs to the medical genre of the *Kutub al-Mufradāt* (see Ullmann 1970: ch. 14). Consists of an alphabetical list of healing plants and mineral substances. Entries are transcriptions of Arabic words (Judaeo-Arabic) which, in turn, are sometimes of Greek or Persian origin. Mentions for example: dung (וסך), sea shell (ודע), hyssop (זופא), mercury (זיבק). Paper; 1 leaf; 12.6 x 12.6; 16 lines.

5c. A 539-3 (together with A 539-1,2,4,5,6,7,8,9,10,11,12; B 3361-1; B 3362-1,2) – Medical book with materia medica (book on simple drugs), written in Hebrew. Belongs to the medical genre of the *Kutub al-Mufradāt* (see Ullmann 1970: ch. 14). Consists of an alphabetical list of healing plants and mineral substances. Entries are transcriptions of Arabic words (Judaeo-Arabic) which, in turn, are sometimes of Greek or Persian origin. Mentions for example: dung (זבל). Paper; 1 leaf; 11.2 x 12.6; 14 lines.

5d. A 539-4 (together with A 539-1,2,3,5,6,7,8,9,10,11,12; B 3361-1; B 3362-1,2) – Medical book with materia medica (book on simple drugs), written in Hebrew. Belongs to the medical genre of the *Kutub al-Mufradāt* (see Ullmann 1970: ch. 14). Consists of an alphabetical list of healing plants and mineral substances. Entries are transcriptions of Arabic words (Judaeo-Arabic) which, in turn, are sometimes of Greek or Persian origin. Mentions for example: henna (חנא). Paper; 1 leaf; 11.2 x 12.6; 14 lines.

5e. A 539-5 (together with A 539-1,2,3,4,6,7,8,9,10,11,12; B 3361-1; B 3362-1,2) – Medical book with materia medica (book on simple drugs), written in Hebrew. Belongs to the medical genre of the *Kutub al-Mufradāt* (see Ullmann 1970: ch. 14). Consists of an alphabetical list of healing plants and mineral substances. Entries are transcriptions of Arabic words (Judaeo-Arabic) which, in turn, are sometimes of Greek or Persian origin. Mentions for example: glass (זג'אג), chick-pea (חמץ), tamarisk (טרפא). Paper; 1 leaf; 13.6 x 12.7; 17 lines.

5f. A 539-6 (together with A 539-1,2,3,4,5,7,8,9,10,11,12; B 3361-1; B 3362-1,2) – Medical book with materia medica (book on simple drugs), written in Hebrew. Belongs to the medical genre of the *Kutub al-Mufradāt* (see Ullmann 1970: ch. 14). Consists of an alphabetical list of healing plants and mineral substances. Entries are transcriptions of Arabic words (Judaeo-Arabic) which, in turn, are sometimes of Greek or Persian origin. Mentions for example: frankincense (כנדר), ground pine (כמפיטוס), sulfur (כברית), parsley (כרפס). Paper; 1 leaf; 13.6 x 12.7; 17 lines.

5g. A 539-7 (together with A 539-1,2,3,4,5,6,8,9,10,11,12; B 3361-1; B 3362-1,2) – Medical book with materia medica (book on simple drugs), written in Hebrew. Belongs to the medical genre of the *Kutub al-Mufradāt* (see Ullmann 1970: ch. 14). Consists of an alphabetical list of healing plants and mineral substances. Entries are transcriptions of Arabic words (Judaeo-Arabic) which, in turn, are sometimes of Greek or Persian origin. Paper; 1 leaf; 13.5 x 11.1; 18 lines.

5h. A 539-8 (together with A 539-1,2,3,4,5,6,7,9,10,11,12; B 3361-1; B 3362-1,2) – Medical book with materia medica (book on simple drugs), written in Hebrew. Belongs to the medical genre of the *Kutub al-Mufradāt* (see Ullmann 1970: ch. 14). Consists of an alphabetical list of healing plants and mineral substances. Entries are transcriptions of Arabic words (Judaeo-Arabic) which, in turn, are sometimes of Greek or Persian origin. Mentions for example: storax (לבני), flea wort (לשאן אלחמל), almonds (לוז חלו), bdellium (מקל). Paper; 1 leaf; 13.5 x 11.1; 17 lines.

5i. A 539-9 (together with A 539-1,2,3,4,5,6,7,8,10,11,12; B 3361-1; B 3362-1,2) – Medical book with materia medica (book on simple drugs), written in Hebrew. Belongs to the medical genre of the *Kutub al-Mufradāt* (see Ullmann 1970: ch. 14). Consists of an alphabetical list of healing plants and mineral substances. Entries are transcriptions of Arabic words (Judaeo-Arabic) which, in turn, are sometimes of Greek or Persian origin. Mentions for example: garum (מרי), mint (נענע), starch (נשאתג). Paper; 1 leaf; 11.3 x 11.4; 17 lines.

5j. A 539-10 (together with A 539-1,2,3,4,5,6,7,8,9,11,12; B 3361-1; B 3362-1,2) – Medical book with materia medica (book on simple drugs), written in Hebrew. Belongs to the medical genre of the *Kutub al-Mufradāt* (see Ullmann 1970: ch. 14). Consists of an alphabetical list of healing plants and mineral substances. Entries are transcriptions of Arabic words (Judaeo-Arabic) which, in turn, are sometimes of Greek or Persian origin. Mentions for example: crayfish (סרטן), meadow saffron (סרנג'א), hyssop (סעתר). Paper; 1 leaf; 11.3 x 11.4; 17 lines.

5k. A 539-11 (together with A 539-1,2,3,4,5,6,7,8,9,10,12; B 3361-1; B 3362-1,2) – Medical book with materia medica (book on simple drugs), written in Hebrew. Belongs to the medical genre of the *Kutub al-Mufradāt* (see Ullmann 1970: ch. 14). Consists of an alphabetical list of healing plants and mineral substances. Entries are transcriptions of Arabic words (Judaeo-Arabic) which, in turn, are sometimes of

Greek or Persian origin. Mentions for example: black nightshade (ענב אלתעלב), lion's leaf (ערטניתא). Paper; 1 leaf; 11 x 11.5; 16 lines.

5l. A 539-12 (together with A 539-1,2,3,4,5,6,7,8,9,10,11; B 3361-1; B 3362-1,2) – Medical book with materia medica (book on simple drugs), written in Hebrew. Belongs to the medical genre of the *Kutub al-Mufradāt* (see Ullmann 1970: ch. 14). Consists of an alphabetical list of healing plants and mineral substances. Entries are transcriptions of Arabic words (Judaeo-Arabic) which, in turn, are sometimes of Greek or Persian origin. Mentions for example: grey calamint (פודנג'), radish (פג'ל), stone pine (צנובר), aloe (צבר). Paper; 1 leaf; 11 x 11.5; 16 lines.

5m. B 3361-1 (verso B 3361-2 blank; together with A 539-1,2,3,4,5,6,7,8,9,10,11,12; B 3362-1,2) – Medical book with materia medica (book on simple drugs), written in Hebrew. Belongs to the medical genre of the *Kutub al-Mufradāt* (see Ullmann 1970: ch. 14). Consists of an alphabetical list of healing plants and mineral substances. Entries are transcriptions of Arabic words (Judaeo-Arabic). Paper; 1 leaf; 8.6 x 9.2; 11 lines.

5n. B 3362-1 (might be together with A 539-1,2,3,4,5,6,7,8,9,10,11,12; B 3361-1; B 3362-2) – Medical book with materia medica (book on simple drugs), written in Hebrew. Belongs to the medical genre of the *Kutub al-Mufradāt* (see Ullmann 1970: ch. 14). Consists of an alphabetical list of healing plants and mineral substances. Entries are transcriptions of Arabic words (Judaeo-Arabic). Mentions for example: cadmia (קלימיא) and alecost (קסט). Paper; 1 leaf; 7.9 x 8.6; 11 lines.

5o. B 3362-2 (might be together with A 539-1,2,3,4,5,6,7,8,9,10,11,12; B 3361-1; B 3362-1) – Medical book with materia medica (book on simple drugs), written in Hebrew. Belongs to the medical genre of the Kutub al-Mufradāt (see Ullmann 1970: ch. 14). Consists of an alphabetical list of healing plants and mineral substances. Entries are transcriptions of Arabic words (Judaeo-Arabic) which, in turn, are sometimes of Greek or Persian origin. Mentions for example: hematite (שאדנג'). Paper; 1 leaf; 7.9 x 8.6; 12 lines.

6a. A 552-1 (verso A 552-2 contains booklist) – Ethical (medical?) text on the left page (right page contains verses from Ecclesiastes). The ethical piece, which starts with משקה לרפואת הנפש, consists of a partially rhymed parody on a medical recipe. Paper; 2 leaves conjoined; 20.1 x 15.5; 28 lines.

7a. A 576-1 (together with A 576-2,3,4) – Medical book, written in Hebrew, end of chapter 1 and beginning of chapter 2. Galen quoted on line 22. Paper; 1 leaf; 21 x 14.8; 25 lines.

7b. A 576-2 (together with A 576-1,3,4) – Medical book, written in Hebrew, chapter 2 and beginning of chapter 3. Paper; 1 leaf; 21 x 14.8; 25 lines.

7c. A 576-3 (together with A 576-1,2,4) – Medical book, written in Hebrew. A certain Isaac quoted on line 6 and 'בס on line 25 (= Ibn Sīnā?). Paper; 1 leaf; 21.4 x 14.7; 25 lines.

7d. A 576-4 (together with A 576-1,2,3) – Medical book, written in Hebrew. Paper; 1 leaf; 21.4 x 14.7; 25 lines.

8a. A 589-1 – (together with A 589-2) A page with several recipes, one written in Judaeo-Arabic (on the left) for the treatment of leprosy. Another written in Hebrew (on the right) called 'black bandage'. Also mentions substances and their medical uses, such as pine and sandalwood. Paper; 1 leaf; 23.1 x 17.3; 22 lines.

8b. A 589-2 – (together with A 589-1) A page with two Hebrew prescriptions, the first one concerns black bile and mentions substances such as cassia, colocynth, lesser dodder and grey calamint and their quantities. The second one is the prescription of a purgative, mentioning medicinal substances such as lesser dodder and oxymel (syrup made of honey and vinegar) and their quantities. The other medical texts are in Judaeo-Arabic. Paper; 1 leaf; 23.1 x 17.3; 31 lines.

9a. A 666-1 (together with A 666-2) – Medical notebook (recipes), written in Judaeo-Arabic, mentioning ingredients and instructions (e.g. to gargle). Use of black and red ink. Paper; 1 leaf; 11.1 x 15.6; 7 lines.[2]

9b. A 666-2 (together with A 666-1) – Medical notebook (recipes), written in Judaeo-Arabic, mentioning ingredients and instructions. Use of black and red ink. Paper; 1 leaf; 11.1 x 15.6; 7 lines.

10a. A 678-1 (together with A 678-2) – Medical notebook (recipes), written in Judaeo-Arabic. Paper; 1 leaf; 12.8 x 7.8; 17 lines.

10b. A 678-2 (together with A 678-1) – Medical notebook (recipes), written in Judaeo-Arabic. Paper; 1 leaf; 12.8 x 7.8; 17 lines.

11a. A 692-1 (verso A 692-2 blank) – Medical book, written in Judaeo-Arabic. Opening page. The text begins with the basmallah and praises to the Lord, focusing on the physical qualities of the human body. The name אלמתטבב (line 15, medical practitioner without philosophical education; see Dols and Gamal 1984: 28, nt. 139) is mentioned as well as גאלינוס (Galen, line 16). Paper; 15.7 x 11.9; 18 lines.

12a. A 744-1 (together with A 744-2; A 992-1,2) – Medical book (or notebook), written in Judaeo-Arabic. On the qualities, benefits and effects of herbs and vegetables as a medicine. Paper; 1 leaf; 11.1 x 8.5; 9 lines.[3]

12b. A 744-2 (together with A 744-1; A 992-1,2) – Medical book (or notebook), written in Judaeo-Arabic. On the qualities, benefits and effects of herbs and vegetables as a medicine. Paper; 1 leaf; 11.1 x 8.5; 10 lines.

---

2 From here up to A 692-1 the fragments were identified by Dr Butbul.

3 We thank Dr Butbul for this identification.

12c. A 992-1 (together with A 992-2; A 744-1,2) – Medical book (or notebook), written in Judaeo-Arabic. On the qualities, benefits and effects of herbs and vegetables as a medicine. Paper; 1 leaf; 8.6 x 9.5; 8 lines.[4]

12d. A 992-2 (together with A 992-1; A 744-1,2) – Medical book (or notebook), written in Judaeo-Arabic. On the qualities, benefits and effects of herbs and vegetables as a medicine. Mentioned a.o. watermelon (בטיך) and cucumber (כיאר). Paper; 1 leaf; 8.6 x 9.5; 9 lines.

13a. A 955-1 (together with A 955-2). Medical text written in Hebrew. Text partially faded. Paper; 1 leaf; 12.3 x 13; 17 lines.

13b. A 955-2 (together with A 955-1). Medical text written in Hebrew. Most of the text faded. Paper; 1 leaf; 12.3 x 13; 17 lines.

14a. A 1015-1 (together with A 1015-2,3,4) – Medical book, written in Hebrew (with occasional Judaeo-Arabic words), on how to treat milt disorders. Drawing of a hand in the margin. Paper; 1 leaf; 9.2 x 16.4; 8 lines.

14b. A 1015-2 (together with A 1015-1,3,4) – Medical book, written in Hebrew, on how to treat milt disorders. Paper; 1 leaf; 9.2 x 16.4; 8 lines.

14c. A 1015-3 (together with A 1015-1,2,4) – Medical book, written in Hebrew, on how to treat milt disorders. Paper; 1 leaf; 13.3 x 15.5; 9 lines.

14d. A 1015-4 (together with A 1015-1,2,3) – Medical book, written in Hebrew, on how to treat milt disorders. Includes marginal notes in which Ibn Sīnā is cited. Paper; 1 leaf; 13.3 x 15.5; 9 lines.

15a. A 1019-1 (together with A 1019-2) – Epitomes (Mukhtaṣarāt) of Galen. Maimonides autograph. Part of an abbreviation of one of Galen's pathological treatises 'On the affected parts'. In total, Maimonides is thought to have abbreviated twenty-one works of Galen, about ten of which have been preserved. A 1019 and the 2 x 2 conjoined fragments of Cambridge, University Library, T-S Ar. 21.112 are from the same manuscript, with a join between A 1019 and Cambridge fragment four. Hopkins 1994 provides a facsimile edition, transcription and commentary. Paper; 1 leaf; 13.1 x 6; 22 lines.

15b. A 1019-2 (together with A 1019-1) – Epitomes (Mukhtaṣarāt) of Galen. Maimonides autograph. Part of an abbreviation of one of Galen's pathological treatises 'On the affected parts'. In total, Maimonides is thought to have abbreviated twenty-one works of Galen, about ten of which have been preserved. A 1019 and the 2 x 2 conjoined fragments of Cambridge, University Library, T-S Ar. 21.112 are from the same manuscript, with a join between A 1019 and Cambridge fragment four. Hopkins 1994 provides a facsimile edition, transcription and commentary. Paper; 1 leaf; 13.1 x 6; 18 lines.

---

4 We thank Dr Butbul for this identification.

16a. A 1382-1 (together with A 1382-2,3,4,5,6,7,8) – Medical book, written in Hebrew, deals with urine. Paper; 1 leaf; 8.2 x 11.1; 4 lines.

16b. A 1382-2 (together with A 1382-1,3,4,5,6,7,8) – Medical book, written in Hebrew, deals with urine. Paper; 1 leaf; 8.2 x 11.1; 4 lines.

16c. A 1382-3 (together with A 1382-1,2,4,5,6,7,8) – Medical book, written in Hebrew, deals with urine. Paper; 1 leaf; 8.2 x 8.5; 2 lines.

16d. A 1382-4 (together with A 1382-1,2,3,5,6,7,8) – Medical book, written in Hebrew, deals with urine. Paper; 1 leaf; 8.2 x 8.5; 2 lines.

16e. A 1382-5 (together with A 1382-1,2,3,4,6,7,8) – Medical book, written in Hebrew, deals with urine. Paper; 1 leaf; 5 x 6.5; 6 lines.

16f. A 1382-6 (together with A 1382-1,2,3,4,5,7,8) – Medical book, written in Hebrew, deals with urine. Paper; 1 leaf; 5 x 6.5; 0 lines.

16g. A 1382-7 (together with A 1382-1,2,3,4,5,6,8) – Medical book, written in Hebrew, deals with urine. Paper; 1 leaf; 2.3 x 5.5; 3 lines.

16h. A 1382-8 (together with A 1382-1,2,3,4,5,6,7) – Medical book, written in Hebrew, deals with urine. Paper; 1 leaf; 2.3 x 5.5; 4 lines.

17a. B 1991-1 (together with B 1991-2; B 2259-1,2; B 2585-1,2; B 2901-1,2; B 2914-1,2; B 5400-1,2) – Medical book, written in Hebrew, on hair problems and their treatments. End of chapter two and beginning of chapter three. Includes marginal note. Paper; 1 leaf; 10.6 x 15.5; 10 lines.

17b. B 1991-2 (together with B 1991-1; B 2259-1,2; B 2585-1,2; B 2901-1,2; B 2914-1,2; B 5400-1,2) – Medical book, written in Hebrew, on hair problems and their treatments. End of chapter three and beginning of chapter four. Galen mentioned on line 10. Paper; 1 leaf; 10.6 x 15.5; 12 lines.

17c. B 2259-1 (together with B 1991-1,2; B 2259-2; B 2585-1,2; B 2901-1,2; B 2914-1,2; B 5400-1,2) – Medical book, written in Hebrew, on hair and scalp problems and their treatments. End of chapter seven and beginning of chapter eight. Chapter eight on porrigo. Paper; 1 leaf; 12.6 x 15.6; 11 lines.

17d. B 2259-2 (together with B 1991-1,2; B 2259-1; B 2585-1,2; B 2901-1,2; B 2914-1,2; B 5400-1,2) – Medical book, written in Hebrew, on hair and scalp problems and their treatments. Paper; 1 leaf; 12.6 x 15.6; 12 lines.

17e. B 2585-1 (together with B 1991-1,2; B 2259-1,2; B 2585-2; B 2901-1,2; B 2914-1,2; B 5400-1,2) – Medical book, written in Hebrew, on skin diseases and their treatments. Includes marginal note. Paper; 2 leaves conjoined; 14.5 x 30.9; 15 lines.

17f. B 2585-2 (together with B 1991-1,2; B 2259-1,2; B 2585-1; B 2901-1,2; B 2914-1,2; B 5400-1,2) – Medical book, written in Hebrew, on skin diseases and their treatments. Includes beginning of chapter seven and marginal notes. Paper; 2 leaves conjoined; 14.5 x 30.9; 14 lines.

17g. B 2901-1 (together with B 1991-1,2; B 2259-1,2; B 2585-1,2; B 2901-2; B 2914-1,2; B 5400-1,2) – Medical book, written in Hebrew, on skin diseases and their treatments. Paper; 1 leaf; 12.5 x 16.1; 11 lines.

17h. B 2901-2 (together with B 1991-1,2; B 2259-1,2; B 2585-1,2; B 2901-1; B 2914-1,2; B 5400-1,2) – Medical book, written in Hebrew, on headache. Beginning of chapter ten. Paper; 1 leaf; 12.5 x 16.1; 11 lines.

17i. B 2914-1 (together with B 1991-1,2; B 2259-1,2; B 2585-1,2; B 2901-1,2; B 2914-2; B 5400-1,2) – Medical book, written in Hebrew, on skin diseases and their treatments. Includes beginning of chapter nine and marginal note. Paper; 2 leaves conjoined; 14.8 x 21; 15 lines.

17j. B 2914-2 (together with B 1991-1,2; B 2259-1,2; B 2585-1,2; B 2901-1,2; B 2914-1; B 5400-1,2) – Medical book, written in Hebrew, on headache. Galen quoted on lines 5 and 13 (on the right). Paper; 2 leaves conjoined; 14.8 x 21; 15 lines.

17k. B 5400-1 (together with B 1991-1,2; B 2259-1,2; B 2585-1,2; B 2901-1,2; B 2914-1,2; B 5400-2) – Medical book, written in Hebrew, on hair problems and their treatments. End of chapter four and beginning of chapter five. Paper; 1 leaf; 10.1 x 8.3; 11 lines.

17l. B 5400-2 (together with B 1991-1,2; B 2259-1,2; B 2585-1,2; B 2901-1,2; B 2914-1,2; B 5400-1) – Medical book, written in Hebrew, on hair problems and their treatments. End of chapter five and beginning of chapter six. Paper; 1 leaf; 10.1 x 8.3; 11 lines.

18a. B 2286-1 (together with B 2286-2) – Medical book, written in Judaeo-Arabic. Paper; 1 leaf; 11.7 x 12.6; 11 lines.

18b. B 2286-2 (together with B 2286-1) – Medical book, written in Judaeo-Arabic. Paper; 1 leaf; 11.7 x 12.6; 10 lines.

19a. B 2642-1 (together with B 2642-2) – Medical book with materia medica (book on simple drugs) written in Judaeo-Arabic, probably an abridged version of Ibn al-Bayṭār's *Kitāb al-Jāmi' li-mufradāt al-'adwiya wa'l-aġḏiya* (Cairo, 1874). Consists mainly of an alphabetical list of healing plants (letter כ'), such as lyceum (כולאן). Use of black and red ink. Paper; 1 leaf; 12.5 x 13.2; 11 lines.

19b. B 2642-2 (together with B 2642-1) – Medical book with materia medica (book on simple drugs) written in Judaeo-Arabic, probably an abridged version of Ibn al-Bayṭār's *Kitāb al-Jāmi' li-mufradāt al-adwiya wa'l-aġḏiya* (Cairo, 1874). Consists mainly of an alphabetical list of healing plants (letter

כ'). Here are mentioned scarabees (כ'נפיסא) and pig (כ'נזיר). Use of black and red ink. Paper; 1 leaf; 12.5 x 13.2; 11 lines.

20a. B 2683-2 (together with B 2683-1, which contains a few non-medical lines in Arabic) – Prescription, written in Judaeo-Arabic, which includes medicinal substances and their measurements. Mentioned are among others: berberry (ברבאריס), tamarisk (אלטרפא), sandalwood (סנדל מקציר), oxymel (סכנג'בין רומיני). Paper; 1 leaf; 10.4 x 6.4; 7 lines.

21a. B 2828-1 (verso B 2828-2 blank) – Prescription, written in Judaeo-Arabic, which includes medicinal substances and their measurements. Eye collyrium (*šiyaf*). Mentioned are among others: haematite (אלשאדנה), zinc (אלתותיא), Meccan lycium (אלכולאן אלמכי), cuttle-fish (זבד אלבחר). Paper; 1 leaf; 10.5 x 11.3; 8 lines.

22a. B 2836-1 (together with B 2836-2, which contains an unrelated text) – Some kind of Hebrew list (table of contents?) in which toothache is mentioned, among other things. Paper; 1 leaf; 11.6 x 11.1; 17 lines.

23a. B 2913-1 (verso B 2913-2 blank) – List of simples (medicinal substances) and their quantities written in Judaeo-Arabic. Including substances of organic origin (e.g. storax, tamarind, berberry, myrobalan [yellow and black], cloves, coriander) and in-organics (e.g. arsenic [2 kinds], mercury, lead, kohl). Paper; 1 leaf; 32.1 x 11.3; 30 lines.

24a. B 2929-1 (together with B 2929-2) – Medical book. Pharmacopoeia written in Judaeo-Arabic. On fevers. Includes a detailed description of recipes, names of medicinal substances, as well as preparatory and dietary instructions. Paper; 1 leaf; 8.8 x 6.6; 12 lines.

24b. B 2929-2 (together with B 2929-1) – Medical book. Pharmacopoeia written in Judaeo-Arabic. On fevers. Includes a detailed description of recipes, names of medicinal substances, as well as preparatory and dietary instructions. Mentioned among others are: honey (אלעסל), galingale (אלכולנג'אן), amomum (אלקאלקה). Paper; 1 leaf; 8.8 x 6.6; 14 lines.

25a. B 3147-1 (together with B 3147-2) – Medical book, contain recipes, written in Judaeo-Arabic. Paper; 1 leaf; 10.6 x 10.9; 16 lines.[5]

25b. B 3147-2 (together with B 3147-1) – Medical book, contain recipes, written in Judaeo-Arabic, mentioned are e.g. a cure for throat ache on lines 4-6: cinnamon (קרפה), pepper (פלפל) and garlic (תום). Paper; 1 leaf; 10.6 x 10.9; 16 lines.

5 With thanks to Dr Butbul.

26a. B 3238-1 (together with B 3238-2) – Medical notebook, written in Judaeo-Arabic, mentions sugar and sea shell among other medicinal substances. Text partially faded. Paper; 1 leaf; 14.4 x 12.5; 20 lines.

26b. B 3238-2 (together with B 3238-1) – Medical notebook, written in Judaeo-Arabic, mentions a few recipes for unknown uses and medicinal substances. Text partially faded. Paper; 1 leaf; 14.4 x 12.5; 19 lines.

27a. B 3239-1 (together with B 3239-2) – Medical notebook, including a few recipes for eye diseases, written in Judaeo-Arabic: (1) eye collyrium (*šiyāf*) – mentioned among other medicinal substances are saffron, frankincense, myrrah, two kinds of arsenic (realgar and orpiment); (2) eye collyrium for the treatment of a dermatological disorder (of the eye). Paper; 1 leaf; 9.4 x 7.4; 10 lines.

27b. B 3239-2 (together with B 3239-1) – Medical notebook, including a few recipes for eye diseases, written in Judaeo-Arabic: eye collyrium for the treatment of wet eye using zinc, musk oil and rose. Paper; 1 leaf; 9.4 x 7.4; 9 lines.

28a. B 3267-2 (together with B 3267-1, which only contains a few words) – Medical text, written in Hebrew. Verso also includes the mirror-wise imprint of the text of another fragment. Paper; 1 leaf; 17 x 13.4; 12 lines.

29a. B 3287-1 (verso B 3287-2 blank) – Divination or an instruction for a divination to know whether a person is ill or not (גורל החולה), written in Hebrew. Includes drawing of a circular diagram. Paper; 1 leaf; 13.6 x 12.1; 8 lines.

30a. B 3591-1 (together with B 3591-2) – Notebook or part of a private book (copied by the owner), written in Hebrew. Chapter on eye diseases, section one on the inflammation of the eyes (i.e. conjunctivitis, *ramad* in Arabic). Non-alphabetical list of drugs and medical remedies to treat conjunctivitis. Mentioned among other medicinal substances (with their Arabic names) are: roots of anemone (שורש שקאיק אלנעמאן), sweet clover (אכליל אלמלך), chamomile (בבונג'), big and small raisins (זבובים). Page numbered one (א). Paper; 1 leaf; 11.5 x 16; 28 lines.

30b. B 3591-2 (together with B 3591-1) – Notebook or part of a private book (copied by the owner), written in Hebrew. Non-alphabetical list of drugs and medical remedies to treat conjunctivitis. Mentioned among other medicinal substances (with their Arabic names) are: flea-wort (בזר קטונה), all kinds of milk (החלבים), fringed rue (סדב), quail (שליו), frankincense (כנדר), cock (חלמון ביצה), raisins (זבובים). Paper; 1 leaf; 11.5 x 16; 29 lines.

31a. B 4303-1 (together with B 4303-2) – Medical book written in Judaeo-Arabic. Possibly quasi-medicine. Includes beginning of a chapter and doodle. Paper; 1 leaf; 11.8 x 5.8; 15 lines.

31b. B 4303-2 (together with B 4303-1) – Medical book written in Judaeo-Arabic. Possibly quasi-medicine. Mentions the spleen and twice (Ibn) Sina. Paper; 1 leaf; 11.8 x 5.8; 17 lines.

32a. B 4769-1 (together with B 4769-2) – Medical text written in Hebrew. Paper; 1 leaf; 5.8 x 6.1; 7 lines.

32b. B 4769-2 (together with B 4769-1) – Medical text written in Hebrew. Paper; 1 leaf; 5.8 x 6.1; 7 lines.

33a. B 4806-1 (together with B 4806-2) – Medical text written in Hebrew. Paper; 1 leaf; 7.4 x 10.7; 5 lines.

33b. B 4806-2 (together with B 4806-1) – Medical text written in Hebrew. The spleen mentioned. Paper; 1 leaf; 7.4 x 10.7; 5 lines.

34a. B 5625-1 (together with B 5625-2) – Medical book (recipes), written in Hebrew. Paper; 1 leaf; 11.1 x 10.7; 18 lines.

34b. B 5625-2 (together with B 5625-1) – Medical book (recipes), written in Hebrew. Catchword. Paper; 1 leaf; 11.1 x 10.7; 22 lines.

35a. B 5664-1 (together with B 5664-2) – Prescription, written in Judaeo-Arabic. Includes medicinal substances and their measurements. Mentioned are e.g.: kohl (כחל אסוד), black cumin (חבה אלקצה), vinegar (כל כמר), dried cane (אלקצב אליאבס). Paper; 1 leaf; 6.7 x 7.7; 8 lines.[6]

35b. B 5664-2 (together with B 5664-1) – Prescription, written in Judaeo-Arabic. Includes medicinal substances and their measurements. Mentioned are e.g.: burnt goat horn (קרן מאעז מחרוק), eggplant (באדנגאן), wine (כמר). Paper; 1 leaf; 6.7 x 7.7; 3 lines.

36a. B 6210-1 (together with B 6210-2) – Medical notebook, written in Judaeo-Arabic. Maimonides autograph. On the brain. Original fragment seems lost, but photograph of printout from microfilm available in the online database. Paper; 1 leaf; *c.* 12 x 8.5; 13 lines.

36b. B 6210-2 (together with B 6210-1) – Medical notebook, written in Judaeo-Arabic. Maimonides autograph. On the brain. Original fragment seems lost, but photograph of printout from microfilm available in the online database. Paper; 1 leaf; *c.* 12 x 8.5; 10 lines.

37a. L 92-1 (together with L 92-2,3,4,5,6; L 136-3,4,5,6) – Medical book, pharmacopoeia, written in Judaeo-Arabic. This is a copy of the Arabic translation of the Salernitan dispensary, Antidotarium Nicolai, on compound drugs (see Ullmann 1970: 311). Including title-page and paragraphs 1, 2, 3. Each paragraph consists of the name of the remedy, description of its medical uses and benefits, and detailed description of the recipe, including names of medicinal substances used as well as preparation instructions. Paper; 1 leaf; 27.3 x 8.8; 31 lines.

---

6 The transcription of the text on this fragment can be found at http://gravitas.princeton.edu/tg/tt/.

37b. L 92-2 (together with L 92-1,3,4,5,6; L 136-3,4,5,6) – Medical book, pharmacopoeia, written in Judaeo-Arabic. This is a copy of the Arabic translation of the Salernitan dispensary, Antidotarium Nicolai, on compound drugs (see Ullmann 1970: 311). Each paragraph consists of the name of the remedy, description of its medical uses and benefits, and detailed description of the recipe, including names of medicinal substances used as well as preparation instructions. Paper; 1 leaf; 27.3 x 8.8; 33 lines.

37c. L 92-3 (together with L 92-1,2,4,5,6; L 136-3,4,5,6) – Medical book, pharmacopoeia, written in Judaeo-Arabic. This is a copy of the Arabic translation of the Salernitan dispensary, *Antidotarium Nicolai*, on compound drugs (see Ullmann 1970: 311). Including paragraphs 3, 4, 5. Each paragraph consists of the name of the remedy, description of its medical uses and benefits, and detailed description of the recipe, including names of medicinal substances used as well as preparation instructions. Paper; 1 leaf; 27.5 x 8.8; 33 lines.

37d. L 92-4 (together with L 92-1,2,3,5,6; L 136-3,4,5,6) – Medical book, pharmacopoeia, written in Judaeo-Arabic. This is a copy of the Arabic translation of the Salernitan dispensary, Antidotarium Nicolai, on compound drugs (see Ullmann 1970: 311). Each paragraph consists of the name of the remedy, description of its medical uses and benefits, and detailed description of the recipe, including names of medicinal substances used as well as preparation instructions. Paper; 1 leaf; 27.5 x 8.8; 30 lines.

37e. L 92-5 (together with L 92-1,2,3,4,6; L 136-3,4,5,6) – Medical book, pharmacopoeia, written in Judaeo-Arabic. This is a copy of the Arabic translation of the Salernitan dispensary, *Antidotarium Nicolai*, on compound drugs (see Ullmann 1970: 311). Including paragraphs 35, 36, 37, 38, 39. Each paragraph consists of the name of the remedy, description of its medical uses and benefits, and detailed description of the recipe, including names of medicinal substances used as well as preparation instructions. Paper; 1 leaf; 27.5 x 17.4; 33 lines.

37f. L 92-6 (together with L 92-1,2,3,4,5; L 136-3,4,5,6) – Medical book, pharmacopoeia, written in Judaeo-Arabic. This is a copy of the Arabic translation of the Salernitan dispensary, *Antidotarium Nicolai*, on compound drugs (see Ullmann 1970: 311). Each paragraph consists of the name of the remedy, description of its medical uses and benefits, and detailed description of the recipe, including names of medicinal substances used as well as preparation instructions. Paper; 1 leaf; 27.5 x 17.4; 34 lines.

37g. L 136-3 (together with L 92-1,2,3,4,5,6; L 136-4,5,6) – Medical book, pharmacopoeia, written in Judaeo-Arabic. This is a copy of the Arabic translation of the Salernitan dispensary, *Antidotarium Nicolai*, on compound drugs (see Ullmann 1970: 311). Each paragraph consists of the name of the remedy, description of its medical uses and benefits, and detailed description of the recipe, including names of medicinal substances used as well as preparation instructions. Paper; 1 leaf; 27.4 x 9.1; 33 lines.

37h. L 136-4 (together with L 92-1,2,3,4,5,6; L 136-3,5,6) – Medical book, pharmacopoeia, written in Judaeo-Arabic. This is a copy of the Arabic translation of the Salernitan dispensary, *Antidotarium Nicolai*, on compound drugs (see Ullmann 1970: 311). Includes paragraphs 68-73. Each paragraph consists of the name of the remedy, description of its medical uses and benefits, and detailed description of the recipe, including names of medicinal substances used as well as preparation instructions. Paper; 1 leaf; 27.4 x 9.1; 32 lines.

37i. L 136-5 (together with L 92-1,2,3,4,5,6; L 136-3,4,6) – Medical book, pharmacopoeia, written in Judaeo-Arabic. This is a copy of the Arabic translation of the Salernitan dispensary, Antidotarium Nicolai, on compound drugs (see Ullmann 1970: 311). Each paragraph consists of the name of the remedy, description of its medical uses and benefits, and detailed description of the recipe, including names of medicinal substances used as well as preparation instructions. Paper; 1 leaf; 27 x 8.4; 33 lines.

37j. L 136-6 (together with L 92-1,2,3,4,5,6; L 136-3,4,5) – Medical book, pharmacopoeia, written in Judaeo-Arabic. This is a copy of the Arabic translation of the Salernitan dispensary, *Antidotarium Nicolai*, on compound drugs (see Ullmann 1970: 311). Includes paragraphs 73-76. Each paragraph consists of the name of the remedy, description of its medical uses and benefits, and detailed description of the recipe, including names of medicinal substances used as well as preparation instructions. Text virtually faded. Paper; 1 leaf; 27 x 8.4; *c.* 18 lines.

38a. L 136-1 (together with L 136-2) – Commentary on section 5.24-34 of the *Aphorisms* of Hippocrates, written in Hebrew. The *Aphorisms* are quoted in full. On menstruation and pregnancy. Paper; 1 leaf; 27.6 x 17.3; 21 lines.

38b. L 136-2 (together with L 136-1) – Commentary on section 5.35-9 of the *Aphorisms* of Hippocrates, written in Hebrew. The *Aphorisms* are quoted in full. On menstruation and pregnancy. Includes a drawing (possibly of a medical instrument) and a note in pencil possibly written by Moses Gaster, which reads among other things 'En Ya'akov'. Paper; 1 leaf; 27.6 x 17.3; 21 lines.

39a. Ar. 83-1 (together with Ar. 83-2) – Medical book, written in Arabic. Text discusses cases such as shivering caused by drinking cold water. A title written in bold letters reads 'treatment of these diseases and similar cases'. Paper; 1 leaf; 17.8 x 13.5; 15 lines.

39b. Ar. 83-2 (together with Ar. 83-1) – Medical book, written in Arabic. Text discusses the treatment of certain cases. Includes marginal note. Paper; 1 leaf; 17.8 x 13.5; 15 lines.

40a. Ar. 103-1 (together with Ar. 103-2; Ar. 123-1,2 and probably Ar. 467-1,2) – Medical book, Muḥammad Ibn Ibrāhīm Ibn al-Akfānī (*c.* 1286–1348 or 9)'s *Kitāb Ġunyat al-labīb 'inda ġaybat al-ṭabīb* (A Sufficient Book for the Intelligent Person to use in the Absence of a Physician), written in Arabic. Medical self-help book. Text advises on the natural treatment of several conditions: what should a barren woman eat and do in order to have children; how to speed up a delivery of a baby. Use of brown ink. Text partially faded. Paper; 1 leaf; 18.4 x 13.8; 14 lines.

40b. Ar. 103-2 (together with Ar. 103-1; Ar. 123-1,2 and probably Ar. 467-1,2) – Medical book, Muḥammad Ibn Ibrāhīm Ibn al-Akfānī (*c.* 1286–1348 or 9)'s *Kitāb Ġunyat al-labīb 'inda ġaybat al-ṭabīb* (A Sufficient Book for the Intelligent Person to use in the Absence of a Physician), written in Arabic. Medical self-help book. Text advises on the natural treatment of several conditions: how to speed up a delivery of a baby and aching joints. Use of brown and red ink. Paper; 1 leaf; 18.4 x 13.8; 13 lines.

40c. Ar. 123-1 (together with Ar. 123-2; Ar. 103-1,2 and probably Ar. 467-1,2) – Medical book, Muḥammad Ibn Ibrahim Ibn al-Akfānī (*c.* 1286–1348 or 9)'s *Kitāb Ġunyat al-labīb 'inda ġaybat al-ṭabīb* (A Sufficient Book for the Intelligent Person to use in the Absence of a Physician), written in Arabic. Medical self-help book. Title-page with underneath a text in another hand and ink. On the right part of Chapter One on nutrition. Use of vocalisation signs and black, brown and red ink. Text partially faded. Marginal notes. Paper; 2 leaves conjoined; 18.5 x 26.4; 16 lines.

40d. Ar. 123-2 (together with Ar. 123-1; Ar. 103-1,2 and probably Ar. 467-1,2) – Medical book, Muḥammad Ibn Ibrahim Ibn al-Akfānī (*c.* 1286–1348 or 9)'s *Kitāb Ġunyat al-labīb 'inda ġaybat al-ṭabīb* (A Sufficient Book for the Intelligent Person to use in the Absence of a Physician), written in Arabic. Medical self-help book. According to the Introduction, this treatise indicates how to keep one's health and to keep away from diseases, as well as how to treat diseases in the absence of a physician. Mention of categories of food. Start of Chapter One on nutrition. Use of vocalisation signs and black, brown and red ink. Paper; 2 leaves conjoined; 18.5 x 26.4; 14 lines.

40e. Ar. 467-1 (together with Ar. 467-2 and probably Ar. 103-1,2 and Ar. 123-1,2) – Medical book, Muḥammad Ibn Ibrāhīm Ibn al-Akfānī (*c.* 1286–1348 or 9)'s *Ġunyat al-labīb 'inda ġaybat al-ṭabīb* (A Sufficient Book for the Intelligent Person to use in the Absence of a Physician), medical self-help book. Most of the text faded. Written in Arabic. Paper; 1 leaf; 12.2 x 8.2; 5 lines.

40f. Ar. 467-2 (together with Ar. 467-1 and probably Ar. 103-1,2 and Ar. 123-1,2) – Medical book, Muḥammad Ibn Ibrāhīm Ibn al-Akfānī (*c.* 1286–1348 or 9)'s *Ġunyat al-labīb 'inda ġaybat al-ṭabīb* (A Sufficient Book for the Intelligent Person to use in the Absence of a Physician), medical self-help book. Most of the text faded. Written in Arabic. Paper; 1 leaf; 12.2 x 8.2; 5 lines.

41a. Ar. 122-1 (together with Ar. 122-2) – Medical book, written in Arabic. Use of black and red ink. Most of the text faded. Paper; 1 leaf; 10.4 x 10.8; 11 lines.

41b. Ar. 122-2 (together with Ar. 122-1) – Medical book, written in Arabic. Use of black and red ink. Most of the text faded. Paper; 1 leaf; 10.4 x 10.8; 10 lines.

42a. Ar. 152-1 (together with Ar. 152-2) – Medical book (probably), written in Arabic. Discusses the roots, flowers, leaves and seeds of a tree. Paper; 1 leaf; 12.5 x 7.2; 8 lines.

42b. Ar. 152-2 (together with Ar. 152-1) – Medical book (probably), written in Arabic. Disease (*dā'*) mentioned. Paper; 1 leaf; 12.5 x 7.2; 8 lines.

43a. Ar. 188-1 (together with Ar. 188-2) – Medical book, The Canon of Medicine of Ibn Sīnā, written in Arabic. Book III, Section 16, end of Maqala 4 and Book III, Section 17, Maqāla 1 (Baghdad 1970, II: 472.25-473.9 and 480.14-30). Paper; 2 leaves conjoined; 24.2 x 33; 20 lines.

43b. Ar. 188-2 (together with Ar. 188-1) – Medical book, The Canon of Medicine of Ibn Sīnā, written in Arabic. Book III, Section 16, Maqalat 4-5 and Book III, Section 17, Maqāla 1 (see Baghdad 1970, II: 473.9-25 and 479.29-480.14). Paper; 2 leaves conjoined; 24.2 x 33; 21 lines.

44a. Ar. 252-1 (together with Ar. 252-2) – Medical book, on the Kinds of Fever (*Kitāb Aṣnāf al-ḥumayyāt*) of Galen in the translation of Ḥunayn ibn Isḥāq al-'Ibādī (809?–873), written in Arabic. Second maqāla (towards the very end of the book (Wernhard 2004: 334.6–335.2). Use of black and probably red ink. Paper; 1 leaf; 17.7 x 12.7; 19 lines.

44b. Ar. 252-2 (together with Ar. 252-1) – Medical book, on the Kinds of Fever (*Kitāb Aṣnāf al-ḥumayyāt*) of Galen in the translation of Ḥunayn ibn Isḥāq al-'Ibādī (809?–873), written in Arabic. Second maqāla (towards the very end of the book (Wernhard 2004: 335.2–13. Use of black and probably red ink. Paper; 1 leaf; 17.7 x 12.7; 15 lines.

45a. Ar. 311-1 (together with Ar. 311-2) – Medical book, *Aphorisms* of Hippocrates (5.48–53?), written in Arabic. On menstruation and pregnancy. Use of black and red ink. Marginal note. Paper; 1 leaf; 17.8 x 13; 11 lines.

45b. Ar. 311-2 (together with Ar. 311-1) – Medical book, *Aphorisms* of Hippocrates (5.53–58?), written in Arabic. On menstruation and pregnancy. Use of black and red ink. Marginal notes. Paper; 1 leaf; 17.8 x 13; 11 lines.

46a. Ar. 320-1 (together with Ar. 320-2; Ar. 321-1,2; Ar. 613-1,2,3,4; Ar. 615-1,2?) – Medical book, written in Arabic. Hippocrates mentioned several times. Paper; 1 leaf; 24 x 11; 21 lines.

46b. Ar. 320-2 (together with Ar. 320-1; Ar. 321-1,2; Ar. 613-1,2,3,4; Ar. 615-1,2?) – Medical book, written in Arabic. Use of black and red ink. Text partially faded. Paper; 1 leaf; 24 x 11; 20 lines.

46c. Ar. 321-1 (together with Ar. 321-2; Ar. 320-1,2; Ar. 613-1,2,3,4; Ar. 615-1,2?) – Medical book, written in Arabic. Hippocrates mentioned several times. Text partially faded. Paper; 1 leaf; 24.1 x 13.1; 21 lines.

46d. Ar. 321-2 (together with Ar. 321-1; Ar. 320-1,2; Ar. 613-1,2,3,4; Ar. 615-1,2?) – Medical book, written in Arabic. Hippocrates mentioned. Use of black and red ink. Paper; 1 leaf; 24.1 x 13.1; 21 lines.

46e. Ar. 613-1 (together with Ar. 613-2,3,4; Ar. 320-1,2; Ar. 321-1,2; Ar. 615-1,2?) – Medical book, written in Arabic. Use of black and red ink. Text partially faded. Paper; 2 leaves; 7.5 x 6.4; 6 lines.

46f. Ar. 613-2 (together with Ar. 613-1,3,4; Ar. 320-1,2; Ar. 321-1,2; Ar. 615-1,2?) – Medical book, written in Arabic. Hippocrates mentioned. Paper; 2 leaves; 7.5 x 6.4; 7 lines.

46g. Ar. 613-3 (together with Ar. 613-1,2,4; Ar. 320-1,2; Ar. 321-1,2; Ar. 615-1,2?) – Medical book, written in Arabic. Hippocrates mentioned. Use of black and red ink. Paper; 2 leaves; 7.8 x 5; 7 lines.

46h. Ar. 613-4 (together with Ar. 613-1,2,3; Ar. 320-1,2; Ar. 321-1,2; Ar. 615-1,2?) – Medical book, written in Arabic. Use of black and red ink. Paper; 2 leaves; 7.8 x 5; 9 lines.

46i. Ar. 615-1 (together with Ar. 615-2 and possibly Ar. 320-1,2; Ar. 321-1,2; Ar. 613-1,2,3,4) – Medical book, written in Arabic. Text partially faded. Paper; 1 leaf; 11.3 x 4.1; 8 lines.

46j. Ar. 615-2 (together with Ar. 615-1 and possibly Ar. 320-1,2; Ar. 321-1,2; Ar. 613-1,2,3,4) – Medical book, written in Arabic. Most of the text faded. Paper; 1 leaf; 11.3 x 4.1; ca. 8 lines.

47a. Ar. 341-1 (together with Ar. 341-2) – Medical book, written in Arabic. List of chapters, e.g. on the nerves and ligaments and their benefits. Paper; 1 leaf; 7 x 11.7; 4 lines.

47b. Ar. 341-2 (together with Ar. 341-1) – Medical book, written in Arabic. Basmallah followed by the title 'Everything that should be said about the organs'. Paper; 1 leaf; 7 x 11.7; 6 lines.

48a. Ar. 435-1 (together with Ar. 435-2) – Medical text, written in Arabic. Organs (stomach, tongue) and musk mentioned. Paper; 1 leaf; 5.7 x 6.7; 4 lines.

48b. Ar. 435-2 (together with Ar. 435-1) – Medical text (recipe?), written in Arabic. Rhubarb (*rawwand*) and seeds (*bizr*) mentioned. Paper; 1 leaf; 5.7 x 6.7; 4 lines.

49a. Ar. 475-1 (together with Ar. 475-2) – Probably a medical book, written in Arabic. Apparently mentions 'beneficial for dropsy'. Paper; 1 leaf; 5 x 5.3; 6 lines.

49b. Ar. 475-2 (together with Ar. 475-1) – Probably a medical book, written in Arabic. Paper; 1 leaf; 5 x 5.3; 6 lines.

50a. Ar. 479-1 (together with Ar. 479-2; Ar. 481-1,2) – Medical book, *The Canon of Medicine* of Ibn Sīnā, written in Arabic. Book III, Section 6 (compare Baghdad 1970, II: pp. 180.21-2 for lines 1-2, 181.7 line 3). Apparently, a few quotes from the sixth section on the mouth and tongue in the third book on particular diseases. Use of black and red ink. Paper; 1 leaf; 10 x 10.6; 6 lines.

50b. Ar. 479-2 (together with Ar. 479-1; Ar. 481-1,2) – Medical book, *The Canon of Medicine* of Ibn Sīnā, written in Arabic. Book III, Section 6, final Chapter (Baghdad 1970, II: 183.33). Title of the last Chapter 'on [leaving] the mouth open' of the sixth section on the mouth and tongue in the third book on particular diseases legible only. Use of black and red ink. Most of the text faded. Paper; 1 leaf; 10 x 10.6; *c.* 2 lines.

50c. Ar. 481-1 (together with Ar. 481-2; Ar. 479-1,2) – Medical book, *The Canon of Medicine* of Ibn Sīnā, written in Arabic. Book III, end of Section 5, Maqāla 2 (Baghdad 1970, II: 173.30 (line 2) and 174.32 (line 5) for the titles of the chapters only. Legible in red are the titles of two chapters, but the intermediate texts cannot be properly traced in the edition. Part of the fifth section on the nose in the third book on particular diseases. Use of black and red ink. Text partially faded. Paper; 1 leaf; 10 x 10.7; 6 lines.

50d. Ar. 481-2 (together with Ar. 481-1; Ar. 479-1,2) – Medical book, *The Canon of Medicine* of Ibn Sīnā, written in Arabic. Book III, Section 6 (Baghdad 1970, II: 176.32 for line 2 and 177.33 line 4 for the titles of the chapters only). Legible in red are the titles of two chapters, but the intermediate texts cannot be properly traced in the edition. Part of the sixth section on the mouth and tongue nose in the third book on particular diseases. Use of black and red ink. Text partially faded. Paper; 1 leaf; 10 x 10.7; 6 lines.

51a. Ar. 497-1 (together with Ar. 497-2,3,4) – Medical book, *Aphorisms* of Hippocrates, written in Arabic. Use of black and red ink. Text partially faded. Paper; 1 leaf; 15.7 x 14.1; 11 lines.

51b. Ar. 497-2 (together with Ar. 497-1,3,4) – Medical book, *Aphorisms* of Hippocrates, written in Arabic. Use of black and red ink. Text partially faded. Paper; 1 leaf; 15.7 x 14.1; 11 lines.

51c. Ar. 497-3 (together with Ar. 497-1,2,4) – Medical book, *Aphorisms* of Hippocrates, written in Arabic. Text partially faded. Paper; 1 leaf; 7.5 x 6; 5 lines.

51d. Ar. 497-4 (together with Ar. 497-1,2,3) – Medical book, *Aphorisms* of Hippocrates, written in Arabic. Text partially faded. Paper; 1 leaf; 7.5 x 6; 5 lines.

52a. Ar. 543-1 (together with Ar. 543-2) – Medical book, ʿAlī ibn ʿĪsā's *Taḏkirat al-Kaḥḥālīn* (*Memorandum for Oculists*), written in Arabic. Title-page. Use of black and brown ink. Paper; 1 leaf; 9 x 9.7; 4 lines.

52b. Ar. 543-2 (together with Ar. 543-1) – Medical book, ʿAlī ibn ʿĪsā's *Taḏkirat al-Kaḥḥālīn* (*Memorandum for Oculists*), written in Arabic. Beginning of Preface in which Galen is mentioned. Instead of a reference to ʿAlī ibn ʿĪsā a reference to al-mutaṭabbib is found. Use of black and brown ink. Paper; 1 leaf; 9 x 9.7; 4 lines.

53a. Ar. 711-1 (together with Ar. 711-2) – Medical book, written in Arabic. Ophthalmological text. Discussion on the sclera (*ṣulbat al-'ayn*). Text partially faded. Paper; 1 leaf; 9.5 x 8.7; 6 lines.

53b. Ar. 711-2 (together with Ar. 711-1) – Medical book, written in Arabic. Ophthalmological text. Most of the text faded. Paper; 1 leaf; 9.5 x 8.7; 6 lines.

54a. Ar. 720-1 (together with Ar. 720-2) – Medical book, written in Arabic. On spots and freckles. Use of black and red ink. Text partially faded. Paper; 1 leaf; 9.8 x 11.2; 6 lines.

54b. Ar. 720-2 (together with Ar. 720-1) – Medical book, written in Arabic. Use of black and red ink. Most of the text faded. Paper; 1 leaf; 9.8 x 11.2; 6 lines.

55a. Ar. 826-1 (together with Ar. 826-2) – Medical book, written in Arabic. On fever (see verso). Text partially faded. Paper; 1 leaf; 4.6 x 7; 5 lines.

55b. Ar. 826-2 (together with Ar. 826-1) – Medical book, written in Arabic. On fever. Text partially faded. Paper; 1 leaf; 4.6 x 7; 4 lines.

Besides the above described fragments we have identified a few more fragments which in all likelihood are medical — in general these were small, damaged and hard to read:

56a. A 1062-1 (together with A 1062-2) – Judaeo-Arabic text. Medical? Sparsely vocalised. Text partially faded. Paper; 1 leaf; 21.2 x 15.4; 13 lines.

56b. A 1062-2 (together with A 1062-1) – Judaeo-Arabic text. Medical? Al-Rāzī quoted on line 6 ff. Use of black and red ink. Sparsely vocalized (Tiberian). Paper; 1 leaf; 21.2 x 15.4; 14 lines.

57a. A 1718-1 (together with A 1718-2, A 1750-1,2) – Medical book written in Hebrew? Paper; 1 leaf; 7.8 x 4.7; 4 lines.

57b. A 1718-2 (together with A 1718-1, A 1750-1,2) – Medical book written in Hebrew? Paper; 1 leaf; 7.8 x 4.7; 6 lines.

57c. A 1750-1 (together with A 1750-2, A 1718-1,2) – Medical book written in Hebrew? Paper; 1 leaf; 5.8 x 5.6; 11 lines.

57d. A 1750-2 (together with A 1750-1, A 1718-1,2) – Medical book written in Hebrew? Paper; 1 leaf; 5.8 x 5.6; 11 lines.

58a. Ar. 493-1 (verso Ar. 493-2 blank) – Medical prescriptions? Written in Arabic. The word 'šurb' (drinking or drink) is repeated. Paper; 1 leaf; 9.3 x 7.2; 4 lines.

Findings

Eighty-seven fragments (seventy-one classmarks) were clearly identified as related to medicine out of mainly the first 6,840 classmarks in the John Rylands Genizah collection. Three further fragments might be part of medical books or other medical texts as well, while one fragment from the Arabic series might contain medical prescriptions – these are presented above separately.

In the field of theoretical medicine, seventy-one fragments are part of medical books (a total of twenty-three books in the A and B series and seventeen in the Arabic series), about more than one-third of which (i.e. twenty-five) are found, importantly, in the relatively small Arabic series. Four of the books involve *materia medica* (A 504-1,2; A 539-1-12+B 3361-1,2+B 3362-1,2; A 744+A 992; B 2642-1,2). One pharmacopoeia (L 92 and L 136-3,4,5,6) has been identified as a Judaeo-Arabic copy of the Arabic translation of the Salernitan dispensary *Antidotarium Nicolai*. A second pharmacopoeia is probably an abridged version of Ibn al-Bayṭār's *Kitāb al-Jāmiʿ li-mufradāt al-adwiya wa'l-aġḏiya* (B 2929-1,2). The Rylands Library also preserves an autograph of Maimonides belonging to his Epitomes (Mukhtaṣarāt) of Galen's 'On the affected parts' (A 1019-1,2). We furthermore identified a Hebrew commentary on the *Aphorisms* of Hippocrates (L 136-1,2) and two Arabic versions of the same *Aphorisms* (Ar. 311, Ar. 497). The Arabic series comprises several fragments of Ibn Sīnā's *Canon of Medicine* (Ar. 188, Ar. 479, Ar. 481), one fragment from Galen's *Book on the Kinds of Fever* (Ar. 252) and ʿAlī ibn ʿĪsā's *Memorandum for Oculists* (Ar. 543), and two or three fragments from Muḥammad Ibn Ibrāhīm ibn al-Akfānī's entertaining thirteenth-century medical self-help book *Ġunyat al-labīb* (Ar. 103, Ar. 123, Ar. 467[?]). The rest of the books are mainly dealing with medical theory and general medicine.

Nine of the fragments are notebooks. One of these is an autograph of Maimonides (B 6210-1,2). We also found a number of prescriptions on two fragments (A 589-1-2, see below for their partial edition; B 2828-1). Two fragments containing medical recipes (B 2683-2; B 3147) and a fragment with a list of materia medica and their measurements (B 2913-1) represent additional fragments of practical medicine. Two medical pieces (A 552-1; B 3287-1) can be described as belonging to pseudo-medicine. Thus the vast majority of medical fragments in the Rylands Genizah collection consist of theoretical fragments. Perhaps unsurprisingly, all medical fragments identified in the Arabic series are of a theoretical nature, with the possible exception of one fragment (Ar. 493-1). This matches the situation found in the Taylor-Schechter and Mosseri collections.

We know that one fragment (A 1019) of the Rylands Genizah collection comes from the same autograph manuscript written by Maimonides as Cambridge, University Library, T-S Ar. 21.112 (Hopkins 1994). It is to be expected that more links between the Genizah collection of the Rylands and those of other libraries will be discovered in due course. The hand of B 3239 is similar to Mosseri VI.38.1 (medical book, maybe quasi-medical, possibly alchemy). Regarding the languages of the medical documents, apart from one Judaeo-Spanish fragment, the fragments were written in Hebrew (31 fragments), Judaeo-Arabic (21 items) and Arabic (25 fragments). One fragment shows a combination of Hebrew and Judaeo-Arabic recipes (A 589).

Two Medical Documents

We have chosen two small fragments, which are parts of notebooks, for publication to give an idea of the variety of medical documents found in the Rylands Genizah collection. A transcription of the more substantial fragments, such as those belonging to the same medical work, will have to be reserved for later publications. A 589 is an intriguing fragment which seems to contain the personal notes of one and the same medical doctor. He probably jotted down prescriptions and treatment methods at different times, using different types of ink and writing in varying sizes of script. Thus he wrote most of the verso in an ink which has almost completely faded over time. Remarkably, he used Hebrew and Judaeo-Arabic interchangeably. Here we transcribe and translate two of the texts preserved on the fragment, which all deal with the purging of black bile. It should be noted, however, that A 589 contains another rather interesting Judaeo-Arabic text on the left side of the recto dealing with the treatment of leprosy. The other fragment which is transcribed below (B 3239) is a small fragment with only a few partial lines preserved on it with advice how to make eye collyria.

Sigla in the transcriptions:

[ ] Hypothetical reconstruction of the text

... Faded letters or letters which are difficult to decipher

A 589-1 – A Bandage for Black Bile[7]

Transcription

6 לתחבושת יקח ?חופנה ט[א]מוס[8] ויט[ח]ון אותה
7 השחורה ?בקרים ויקלוף קליפתו וישימהו
8 בכלי נחושת וישים עליו חלב
9 ?שעור (= שעיר?) ולא שיכסהו ויבשלהו בא[ש]
10 רכה עד שיכלה החלב ואז יוסיף עליו שומן
11 בקר או חלאבו ויבשלהו עד שיתעבה ויעשה
12 ממנו תחבושת וישים אותה על בגד[ו] ויחבוש
13 הבטן ישלשל הש[ח]ורה ואם יחבוש בו בירכים
14 ישלשל הליחות הפעם ואם יחבשו בו השחי
15 ישלשל האדומה וכשתרצה להפסיק שלשולו
16 תסיר התחבושת ותרחץ המקום במים קרים
17 וזה יעשו לזקנים או לנערים אשר טבעם
18 חלש ואינם יכולים לסבול ?שתייתהם משלשל

Translation

6 One should take a ?handful of Tamus and grind it
7 in ?cold ?water. One should peel it, put it
8 in a copper receptacle, pour ?goat's milk over it,
9 and, without covering it, cook it on a gentle heat
10 until the milk evaporates. Then one should add cow's fat
11 or [cow's] milk to it, cook it until it thickens, make
12 a bandage of it, put it on his clothing and apply it to
13 [his] belly. It will purge the black bile. If one applies it to the knees,
14 it will purge the [superfluous] humors. If they apply it to his arm-pit,
15 it will purge the yellow bile. When you want to stop purging him,
16 you should remove the bandage and wash the area with cold water.
17 They should do this to elderly people or youngsters who are
18 weak by nature and cannot bear to be administered purgatives.

---

7 We would like to thank Gerrit Bos for his useful comments on the transcriptions and translations in this article. Any errors remain our own.

8 The *'ālep* is very insecure. Since the whole prescription is written in Hebrew, we — very tentatively — read it as טאמוס and identify it as Tamus (*Tamus communis*) or common black bryony (English common name). It is a vine that is used until the present day in the Middle East as a purgative (compare Lev and Amar 2008: 366–7). Gerrit Bos suggested to us the alternative reading: טום וין identified as *Adiantum capillus-veneris* (maidenhair fern).

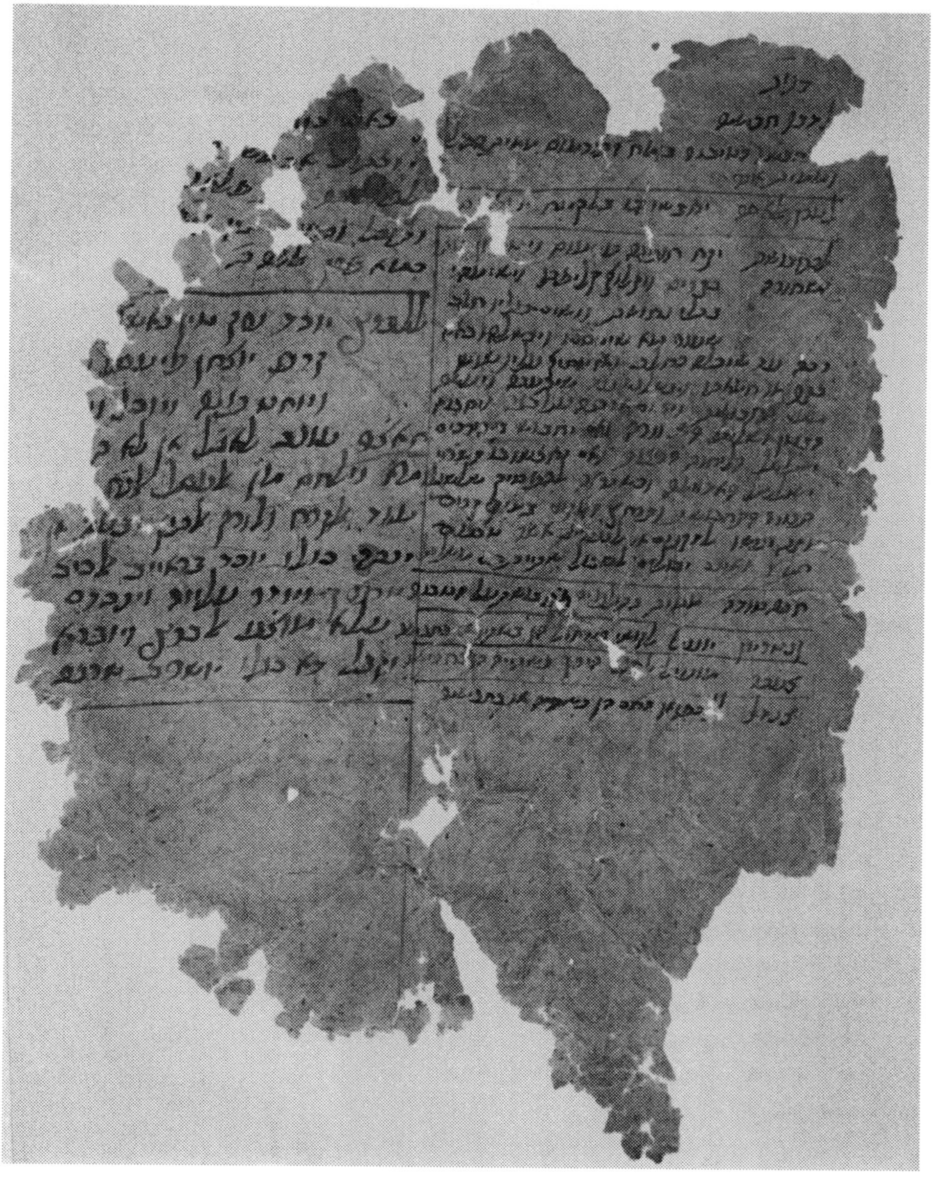

Plate 1: A 589-1. (Reproduced by courtesy of the University Librarian and Director, The John Rylands Library, The University of Manchester)

A 589-2 – Black bile

Transcription

1 למרה שחורה
2 סנה - ?תנביל[9] - אפתימון – אשתיואן - חנטל – קורט[ם] הנדי - פותנאג'
3 א[10] א ב א[11] ד א
4 מי שי[ר]צה להסיר שחורה רבה יתיך ו' מתקל אפתימון
5 בתוך שני אוקיות סכנג'בין ויאכל אותו והאפתימון
6 עם סכנג'בין משלשל שחורה ?נקייה אבל הוא
7 לא כתב כי אם ב' דרהם לבד עם וקייה א'
8 סכננג'בין וב' אוקיות מים קרים וכתבו רוב
9 האחרונים שאם ילקח עם מי הגבינה משלשל
10 השחורה שלשול גדול ובפרט לבעלי
11 הסרטאן ולצמחים ?המעינושים ואם ישתו
12 אותו עם בשול הבנפסג' משלשל שחורה
13 צפראויות

Translation

1 Black bile
2 Cassia Betel-pepper Lesser dodder Black spleenwort Colocynth Nile ipomoea Peppermint
3 1 1 2 1 4 1
4 Anyone who wants to remove a lot of black bile should dissolve six mit̲qāl[12] of lesser dodder
5 in two ounces[13] of Oxymel and eat it. The lesser dodder
6 with oxymel purges black bile…, but he
7 did not write except for only two dirhams[14] with one ounce of
8 oxymel and two ounces of cold water. Most
9 later [authors] wrote that if one takes [it] with whey, it purges
10 black bile very well, especially for
11 those suffering from cancer and abscesses... And if they drink
12 that with sweet violet, it purges black and
13 yellow bile.

---

9 Admittedly, the *taw* looks much more like a *ṭēt*.
10 The letter looks like something in between an *'ālep* and a *bēt*.
11 Same remark.
12 *Mit̲qāl* = 4.68 grams (4.46 grams according to Levey 1966: 25).
13 *Uqiya* = 37.44 grams (33.8 grams according to Levey 1966: 25).
14 *Dirham* = 3.125 grams. Goitein 1967-1993, I: 360.

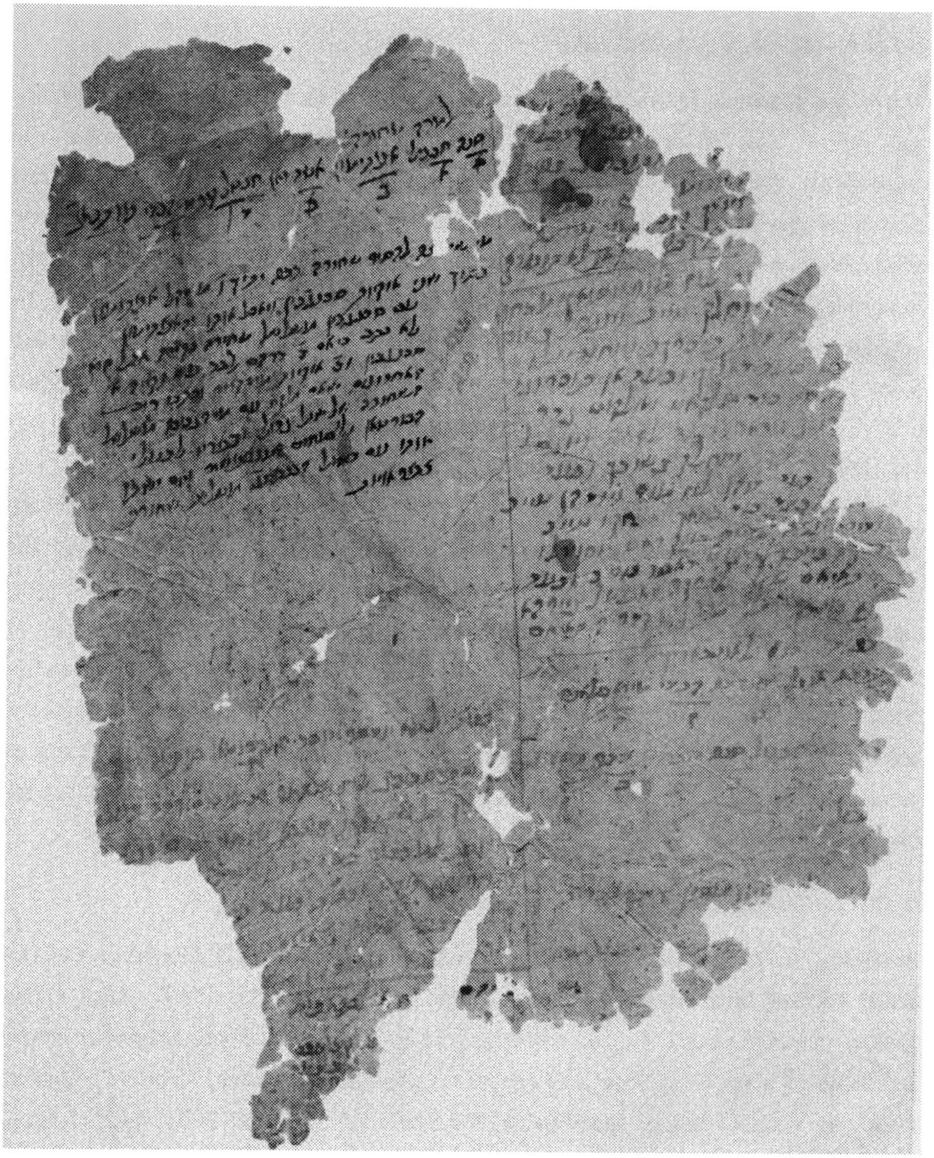

Plate 2: A 589-2. (Reproduced by courtesy of the University Librarian and Director, The John Rylands Library, The University of Manchester)

Commentary

A 589-1 – Bandage for black bile

The recipe presented in this fragment is a poultice used as a plaster to draw out black and yellow bile. In humoral theory black and yellow bile are associated with respectively the spleen and the gallbladder. The recipe is made up of a few substances, such as ground Tamus, milk and cow's fat boiled together in a copper pot. When thick enough, the poultice was smeared on a cloth and applied to the body. According to the writer, using it on different body parts will give different results: 'If applied to the stomach, it will purge the black bile', 'If applied to the knees, it will purge the superfluous humors' and 'If applied to the arm-pit, it will purge the yellow bile.' To end the treatment and stop purging the patient, one should, according to our practitioner, 'remove the bandage and wash the area with cold water'.

The external use of a purgative is quite unique. The practitioner meant to insert the active material through the skin and not as was usually done — internally through the stomach. This healing method should probably be explained by the age restrictions mentioned at the end of the recipe: 'They should do this to elderly people or youngsters who are weak by nature and cannot bear to be administered purgatives.' In other words, this bandage was probably meant as a substitute treatment for patients who could not bare the regular treatment, i.e. the internal use of a purging drug as mentioned on the other side of the fragment (A 589-2), due to their age and poor physical condition.

A 589-2 – Purging black bile

According to the classical authorities, an excess of black bile is dangerous and can cause various fatal diseases (Flashar 1966, Timken-Zinkann 1968). Thus Galen (second century) stated: '(…) he will be seized by one of the afflictions of people who are prone to black bile. Such are: cancer, elephantiasis, the itch, "leprosy", quartan fever and what is called, specifically, "melancholia"' (Powell 2003: 115). Islamic medieval sources, similarly to classical medicine, determined that black bile 'nourishes malignant diseases like cancer, elephantiasis (*juḏām*), malignant tumours etc.' (Ullmann 1978: 59).

The best way to prevent these diseases, according to medieval medical authorities, was to purge the black bile. A case in point is Sābūr ibn Sahl (d. 869), who mentions in his dispensatory several substances known for their purgative qualities in recipes for the treatment of black bile and leprosy, such as colocynth, Cretan dodder, cassia and mountain mint (Kahl 2009: 176–84). Maimonides, in his *Medical Aphorisms*, emphasises the thickness of black bile in comparison to the other humours. He also points out its connection to leprosy and the need to use relatively powerful drugs in order to eliminate it. Among other purging substances Maimonides mentions the colocynth (Rosner and Muntner 1971: 250–1, nos. 11, 13, 15 and 192, no. 98). Ibn Tilmīḏ (eleventh-twelfth century) lists in his dispensatory a few remedies to expel or purge black bile. He considers various kinds of dodder an important ingredient similar to the lesser dodder mentioned in our fragment (Kahl 2007: 205–6, 218).

We can learn about the connection between black bile and leprosy from a legal-medical document found in the Genizah. The fragment (Cambridge, University Library, T-S NS 327.51), dated 23 February 1262, deals with the restriction of the Jewish leper Ibrāhīm al-Yahūdī to mix freely among Muslims. In this fragment, published by Isaacs, the two certifying witnesses, probably physicians or medical officers, wrote that the patient 'has been affected by such black bile as has caused him to develop leprosy' (Isaacs 1991). Leprosy (*baraṣ*) is indeed the subject of a Judaeo-Arabic prescription written on the left side of A 589-1.

Here follows a short review of the main substances mentioned in the two recipes. The descriptions summarize the information found in Lev and Amar 2008 without repeating the bibliographical references found there.

1. **Betel-pepper,** *tanbūl* in Arabic, is identified as *Piper betel* (Piperaceae). It is a slender climbing vine with heart-shaped leaves and small spherical fruits. In various tropical lands and islands the seeds are chewed to expel stomach worms and as sedative and astringent. It figures in a Genizah list of *materia medica* and in a few medical books in a recipe for palpitation, as a purgative, an emmenagogue and an abortifacient. Ibn Sina (980–1037) recommends betel pepper for various medicinal uses, including helping digestion. Leaves of betel-pepper were traded within the Genizah society, as was the fruit, which is mentioned in merchants' letters regarding its trade in Alexandria and Cairo in the eleventh century (Lev and Amar, 2008: 357–8).

2. **Black Spleenwort,** *aštuwan* in Arabic, is identified as *Asplenium onoperis* (Aspleniaceae). It is a short perennial fern that was believed effective against black bile in both East and West. Black spleenwort figures in six lists of *materia medica* and in a prescription found in the Cambridge Genizah collection. The physician Assaf (ca. fifth-seventh century?) describes 'Asplinion' and calls it 'the deer tongue'. According to him the plant is recommended to treat haemorrhoids and ailments of the intestines, and for urine flow. In European traditional medicine people used the plant to treat bile, spleen, melancholy, and hypochondria, whilst believing the medication should not be given to women for fear it would cause infertility (Lev and Amar, 2008: 116).

3. **Cassia** or Senna, *sanā* in Arabic, is a tropical or temperate perennial plant, shrub or tree of the genus *Cassia*. The main and most common species is *Cassia acutifolia* (Fabaceae). The dried leaves provide an extract used as a cathartic. Its uses as a medicinal plant began in the ninth or tenth century. Cassia figures in five lists of *materia medica* and in thirteen prescriptions found in the Cambridge Genizah collection. Among other things it is used to treat fever and as an aphrodisiac. It also appears in recipes for the treatment of stones in the bladder found in medical books. Al-Kindī (*c.* 801–873) states that Meccan senna is a component in a medicine from which an infusion is prepared. Maimonides lists many uses for cassia, mainly as a remedy for the intestines. The 'sini' is a hot and dry drug. Ibn al-Bayṭār (d. 1248), quoting other sources, says that cassia is a well-known medicine and is used among other things as a purgative. Cassia was brought to Europe by Muslim physicians and was used throughout the Middle East and Europe as a cathartic substance. Frederick Hasselquist (1722–52) reported that Egyptian farmers collected this plant and sold it to Jewish licensed dealers who exported it to Europe, mainly to Marseilles and Venice, for medicinal use. Cassia was imported from Cairo into Sicily and North Africa (Lev and Amar 2008: 128–30).
4. **Cheese water**, *mā' al-jibn* in Arabic, was used in medicine as one among several milk products, according to al-Kindī, for the treatment of leprosy, haemorrhoids and the eyes. The medical use of cheese water (whey) is described by Ibn Bayṭār. The Jews of Iraq made extensive use of milk, cheese, and cheese water, which served mainly to improve virility (Lev and Amar 2008: 133–4).
5. **Colocynth**, *ḥanẓal* in Arabic, is also known as bitter gourd, bitter apple and identified as *Citrullus colocynthis* (Cucurbitaceae). It is a perennial herbaceous plant of which the fruit is very bitter and has the size of an orange. It grows mainly in the Arabia-Sahara region. Dioscorides (first century) describes the use of the *kolokunthis* pulp as a purgative, an expectorant, an abortifacient, and to relieve toothache. Colocynth is found in one list of *materia medica* and three prescriptions found in the Cambridge Genizah collection, mainly as a purgative. One prescription was written by Maimonides (T-S Ar.30.286). Colocynth is also mentioned in a Genizah lexicon of *materia medica* and in medical books. Ibn al-Bayṭār mentions the medical applications of its fruit as useful for the treatment of constipation, headache, toothache, muscle pains and spasms, epilepsy, lung disease, depression and diseases of the kidney and the urinary tract (Lev and Amar 2008: 385–6).

    The leaves were used to treat leprosy. Al-Qazwīnī (1203–83) writes that its leaves cure haemorrhage, depression and epilepsy. He adds that boiled in milk, the fruit acts as a purgative. Colocynth was also used as a remedy for leprosy, arthritis and other diseases. Traditional Arab medicine includes the use of colocynth fruit and seeds to treat diabetes, paralysis, face spasms, haemorrhoids, and arthritis, and pains of the stomach and heart. The Sinai Bedouins used the plant as a purgative and to treat muscle pain and toothache. The pulp of the colocynth was widely used in Europe, India, the Middle East, and North Africa to treat various symptoms and diseases such as warts, and internal cancers (leukaemia and breast cancer). Jewish citizens of Gaza in the nineteenth century bought quantities of colocynth fruits from the local Bedouins and distributed them throughout Europe for medicinal uses (Lev and Amar, 2008: 386–7).

6. **Dodder of Thyme**, *afītīmūn* in Arabic, is also known as Lesser or Heath Dodder and identified as *Cuscuta epithymum* (Convolvulaceae). It is a parasitic vine of plants of the Mediterranean region, and is known throughout the Near East. It is mentioned in medical writings in Mesopotamia mainly as a remedy for stomach disorders. Dioscorides notes the use of *Epithumon* especially for treating mucus and black bile (Lev and Amar 2008: 161).

   Dodder of thyme figures in eight prescriptions found in the Cambridge Genizah collection, e.g. for treating hallucination. It is also mentioned in a few general medical books, in books on fevers, toxicology, palpitation and dermatology, and in pharmacopoeias. According to al-Kindī, *afītīmūn* was a component in a preparation for reducing fever. Al-Bīrūnī (973–1048) relates its use for treating influenza, spasms, epilepsy, and depression. Ibn al-Bayṭār lists the following medicinal uses of dodder of thyme according to classical and Arab physicians: treating various types of mucus (bile), nervous and mental disorders, muscular cramps, swellings, and intestinal worms. Maimonides, in a letter, does not recommend the use of dodder jam because it causes the 'purging of the intestines and their drying out'. From other references it seems that *afītīmūn*, being a hot and dry drug, was administered as a light purgative. The plant was in demand in Egypt mainly for its medicinal uses, and was imported from Crete (Lev and Amar, 2008: 161–2).

7. ***Fuḏanj*** is a collective name for various species of aromatic plants of the Lamiaceae family (Lev and Amar 2008: 30), mainly peppermint (*Mentha pulegium*). Many species of this family were used in the medieval period and a few were known as purgatives.

8. **Milk** – boiling milk with another purgative such as colocynth was a known procedure in the medieval period (Lev and Amar 2008: 386).

9. **Nile ipomoea**, *Qurṭum hindī* or *Ḥabb al-nīl* in Arabic (Issa Bey 1930: 99, 19), is identified as *Ipomoea hederacea* (Convolyulacea). The seeds of the plant that grows in India are brown or black and are exported to Egypt. The seeds are used as diuretic, purgative and vermifuge (Ducros 1930: 44–5).

10. **Oxymel,** *sikanjabīn* in Arabic, is a syrup made of honey and vinegar. Dioscorides used oxymel for arthritis and epilepsy. Oxymel figures in three prescriptions found in the Cambridge Genizah collection. It is also mentioned in medical books as a laxative, and deemed useful for the burning of black bile and phlegm according to one Genizah fragment. Goitein writes that according to the Genizah fragments oxymel was a very common and widely utilized medicinal liquid (Lev and Amar 2008: 460, 566–7).

11. **Sweet Violet**, *banafsaj* in Arabic, is identified as *Viola odorata* (Violaceae). It is a perennial with heart-shaped leaves and small, purple coloured and sweet scented flowers. Dioscorides reports the use of the plant *Ion* to treat epilepsy and throat inflammation. Products of sweet violet figure in two lists of *materia medica* and in thirteen prescriptions found in Cambridge Genizah collection for swelling, hallucination, treating the face and the eyes, as an aphrodisiac and for an alchemical astrological

preparation. It is also mentioned in many medical books found in the same collection in recipes for various uses, such as for the treatment of black and red bile (T-S AS 111.22). Sweet violet is also mentioned in a tabulated work on medicine concerning treatment of, among other things, elephantiasis (T-S Ar.41.137). According to Maimonides, violet was a cold and moist drug and a mild purgative. Ibn al-Bayṭār notes in his entry *banafsaj* that the substance was used among other uses as a medication for the stomach. Various types of violet, especially sweet violet, were used in Iran to reduce fever, relieve headache, as a mild purgative, as a medication for constipation, as a soothing drug and to induce perspiration (Lev and Amar, 2008: 299–301).

B 3239 – Eye collyrium

B 3239-1

Transcription	Translation
1 --גן ----	*1* …
2 אלצלא----	*2* …
3 אשיאף ----	*3* Collyria …
4 יוכד זעפראן וכנדר ומר ----	*4* One should take saffron, frankincense, myrrh …
5 דרהם זרניך אחמר זרניך ----	*5* … a *dirham* of realgar and orpiment.
6 ו... דרהם ?שמע מ----	*6* And … a *dirham* of ?wax
7 מעגונה במא ----	*7* kneaded with the juice of …
8 ויגפף נאפע ----	*8* and dried, it is beneficial…
9 אשיאף ----	*9* Collyria …
10 ינפע מן אלגרב ו----	*10* It is beneficial against trachoma and…

B 3239-2

Transcription	Translation
1 ---- [יס]תעמ[ל]	*1* One should use …
2 ---- [אנש]אללה	*2* … if God wills.
3 ---- [א]ש[י]אף -----	*3* Collyria …
4 [א]לעין ויביד אלרטובה ובקאיא	*4* the eye and it will remove the wetness and remnants…
5 [י]וכד תותיא כצרא ?י' ?א'	*5* Take zinc …
6 ---- ...אק... ... ד	*6* …
7 ---- מסך קיראטין	*7* … musk oil (two *qīrāṭs*[15])
8 ---- ורד ויעגן בה	*8* … rose. One should soak it with it
9 ---- ...חק ?ואלזבל וישיף	*9* … ?dung and one should apply the collyrium ...
10 ---- [ינ]פע אן שאללה	*10* Beneficial, if God wills.

[15] *Qīrāṭ* = 0.195 grams (0.223 grams according to Levey 1966: 25).

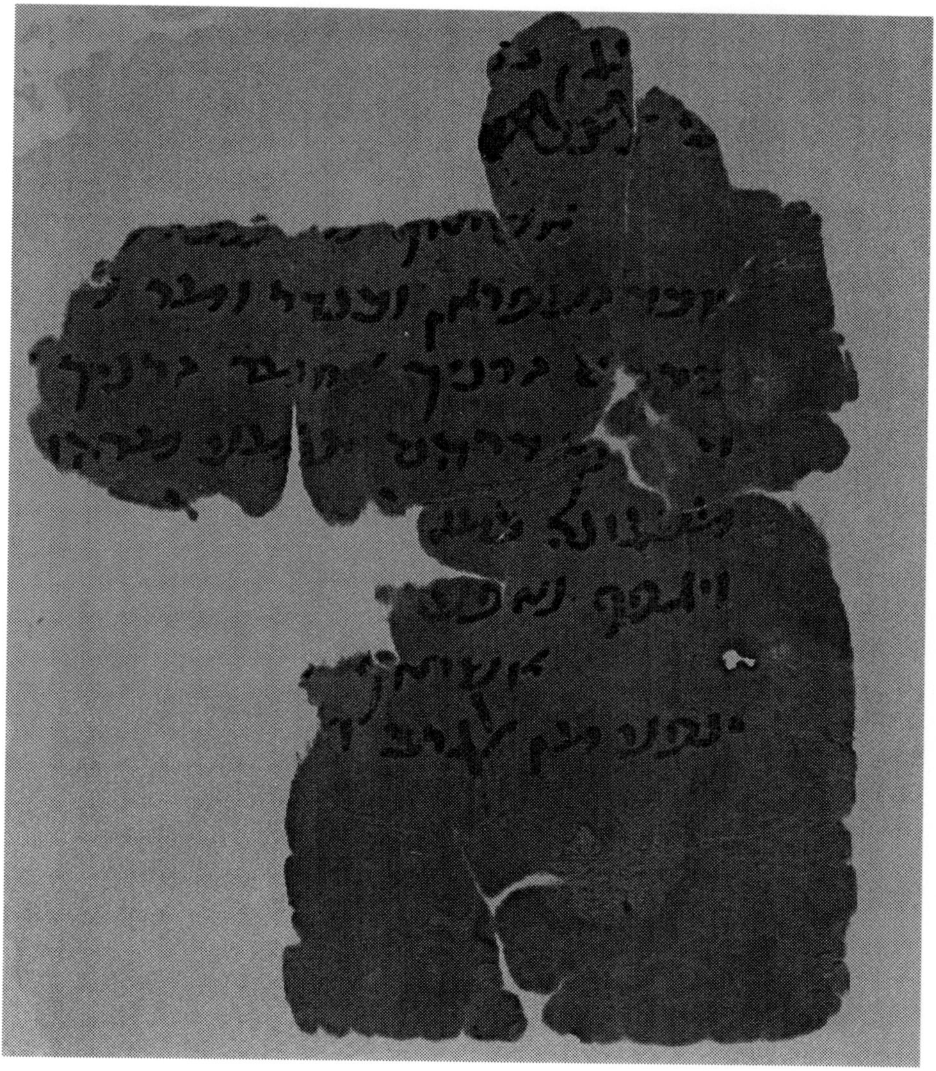

Plate 3: B 3239-1. (Reproduced by courtesy of the University Librarian and Director, The John Rylands Library, The University of Manchester)

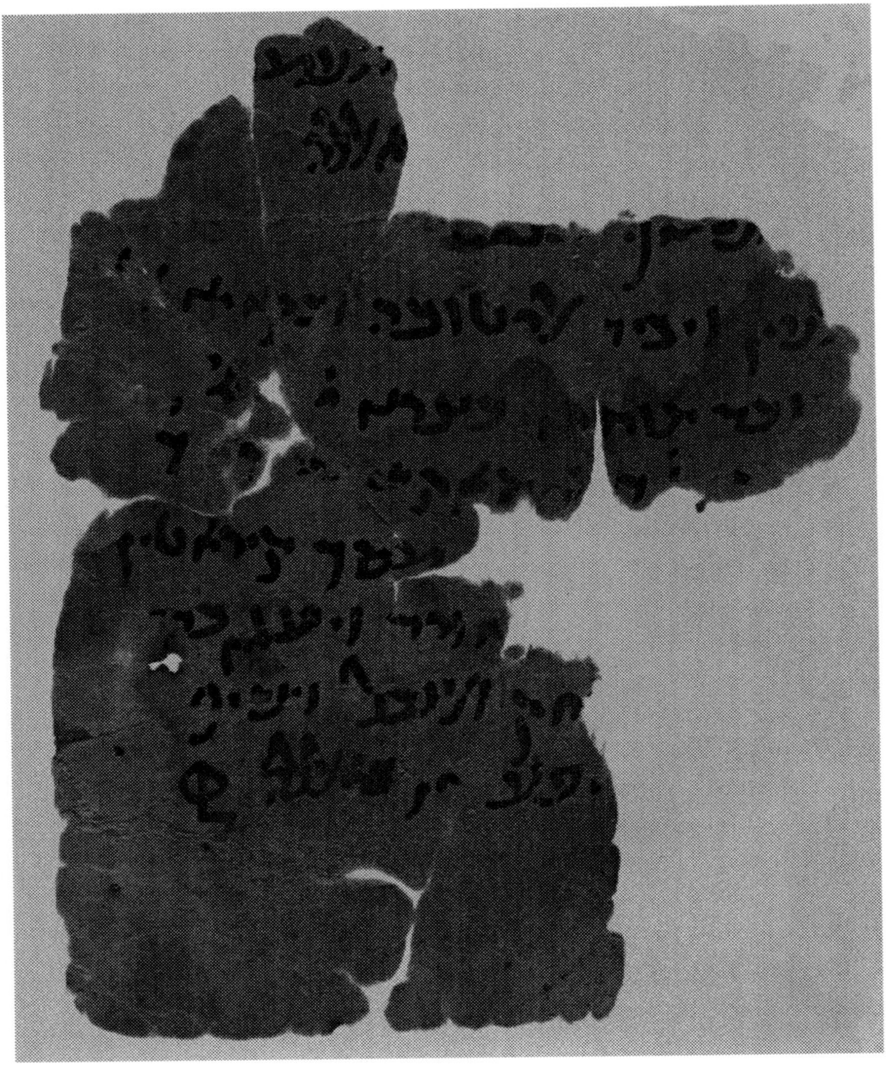

Plate 4: B 3239-2. (Reproduced by courtesy of the University Librarian and Director, The John Rylands Library, The University of Manchester)

Commentary

The study of ophthalmology has a long, distinguished history not least due to the fact that throughout the ages people in hot climates have been suffering from various serious eye diseases requiring treatment (Krause 1934, Nielsen 1974, Hirschberg 1982–94, Sandford-Smith 1997[3]). The Greek medical tradition, which lasted for more than a thousand years from Hippocrates (*c.* 460–*c.* 370 BCE) to Paul of Aegina (seventh century), produced, as far as we know, only five textbooks on ophthalmology, none of which has been preserved. In five hundred years, Arabs produced more than thirty such monographs, of which the majority was written by specialised oculists (Hirschberg 1982–94, II: 99). Savage-Smith stated about Arabic medieval medicine: 'The only area, other than pharmacology, that could truly be called a specialty was ophthalmology, and for this area there developed an extensive specialist literature' (1996: 948). However, it should be mentioned that Arab ophthalmologists, Muslims as well as Jews and Christians, 'maintained the values of Greek ophthalmology, while making some important original contributions' (Albert and Edwards 1996: 29).

Nearly every medical compendium has chapters concerning eye diseases. To mention a few examples: Al-Rāzī (865–925) (see 1955–71), Ibn Sīnā (980–1037) (see 1970), Ibn Abī al-Bayān (1161–1240), a Karaite court physician to one of Saladin's successors in Egypt (Sbath 1932–3), and the Jewish physician active in Egypt Kohēn Attār al-Isrā'īlī (thirteenth century) (see 1940). More precisely, Al-Kindī, in his *Medical Formulary* or *Aqrābaḏīn*, describes hundreds of medical prescriptions of his time out of which thirty are dedicated to the treatment of eye diseases (Levey 1966: 162–86, 196, 204–6). Sābūr ibn Sahl mentions in his short formulary, *Al-Aqrābaḏīn al-ṣaġīr*, over a dozen of recipes that deal, though often not exclusively, with eye diseases (Kahl 2003: nos. 4, 16, 154, 278, 358–9, 361, 364, 367, 369, 370, 372–3, 378).

As noted above, also a large number of monographs were devoted to ophthalmology. While Ḥunayn ibn Isḥāq (809–77) wrote the influential *Ten Treatises on the Eye* (Meyerhof 1928), his teacher Ibn Masawayh (777–857) produced the oldest specialized treatises extant in the field of Arabic ophthalmology. Their books were to a large extent based on Greek sources (Ullmann 1970: 204–6). About a century later, a practising oculist in Baghdad, ʿAlī ibn ʿĪsā (ninth-tenth century), wrote one of the most highly regarded ophthalmologic manuals of the Middle Ages, the *Taḏkirat al-Kaḥḥālīn* or *Memorandum for Oculists* (Wood 1936, Ullmann 1970:

208–9). Being the most copied (Judaeo-)Arabic medical work in the Cairo Genizah (Polliack 1998: 13), Isaacs (1994) identified sixty-three fragments of it in the T-S Genizah collection of the Cambridge University Library alone, half of them in Judaeo-Arabic and half in Arabic. Apart from these, he discovered at least seventy-six unidentified fragments of books dealing with eye diseases. About ten percent of the T-S medical fragments relate to ophthalmology. This situation seems not to be immediately mirrored in Manchester. So far we have only identified five clearly ophthalmologic fragments — B 3239, which we edited and translated above, B 2828-1 and B 3591, the latter of which is a very interesting fragment with recipes to treat conjunctivitus (*ramad*), Ar. 711 and just one fragment of ʿAlī ibn ʿĪsā's *Taḏkirat al-Kaḥḥālīn* (Ar. 543).

The substances that are mentioned in the recipes of collyria in the above fragment B 3239 are well known and indeed used for the treatment of eye diseases. As a matter of fact, they all appear in the twenty-seventh chapter at the end of the *Taḏkirat al-Kaḥḥālīn*, where ʿAlī ibn ʿĪsā lists the simple drugs and remedial agents for the eyes with their Galenic and therapeutic properties (Wood 1936: 47–82, Sharafi 1964: 345–86).

B 3239 mentions two eye diseases — *jarab* and *ruṭūba. Jarab* or trachoma is nowadays still a widespread disease which affects the eyelids and causes the conjunctiva, which lines the inside of the eyelids, to inflame. An infectious disease, it can cause a rather painful type of blindness, whereby the eyelids turn inward, causing the eyelashes, as well as the roughened conjunctiva, to scratch the eyeballs (compare Sandford-Smith 1997[3]: 105–20). ʿAlī ibn ʿĪsā describes four varieties of the disease and advises oculists to treat the patient with a combination of methods, such as applying several types of eye collyrium (red, green and white), bloodletting the temples and prescribing purgatives. Of the many active ingredients of the collyria ʿAlī ibn ʿĪsā mentions, only saffron and myrrh appear in our fragment B 3239 (Al-Sharafi 1964: 76–84, Wood 1936: 85–9). ʿAlī ibn ʿĪsā notes the drying and cleansing properties of saffron. Since trachoma is accompanied with lots of eye tearing, this substance was an obvious choice of ingredient for him (Wood 1936: 75). Myrrh also desiccates, according to ʿAlī ibn ʿĪsā, and prevents the eye from scarring. It was used in numerous medicines during the Middle Ages (Wood 1936: 65).

Ruṭūba, literally wetness of the eye, refers to an eye condition, where the cornea is covered in too much fluid (that might be slightly thicker than normal tears), which can cause, according to ʿAlī ibn ʿĪsā, solidification, thickening or swelling of the tissues. An abundance of fluid can also cause the cornea to inflame (Wood 1936: 165–6). The word *ruṭūba* is furthermore used in ophthalmology to describe the various fluids found on top and inside the eye, such as the crystalline humour (*ruṭūba jalīdīya*), vitreous humour (*ruṭūba zujājīya*) and aqueous humour (*ruṭūba bayḍīya*), but it is clear from the context that this term is not being alluded to (Al-Sharafi 1964: 16–20, 26–7; Wood 1936: 12–14, 17–18).

Here follows a short review of the main substances mentioned in the two recipes. The descriptions summarize the information found in Lev and Amar 2008 without repeating the bibliographical references found there.

1. Arsenic is a chemical element with the atomic number 33. There are two main kinds of arsenic sulphide minerals: **orpiment**, which is yellow in colour, *zirnīkh* or *zirnīkh aṣfar* in Arabic, and the red-coloured stone **realgar**, *zirnīkh aḥmar* in Arabic, popularly also known as rat powder (*rahj al-fār*, from which the word realgar derives). Despite the fact that both minerals are highly toxic, they were used in medieval medicine besides their application as poisons. Dioscorides mentions a few types of arsenic and notes that orpiment (*arsenikon*) and realgar (*sandarache*) are suitable for clearing the voice and for the treatment of asthma, ulcers in the mouth and nostrils, other pustules, and baldness. According to al-Kindi, realgar is an ingredient in a medication for stomach ulcers and in toothpaste for the treatment of rotten teeth. According to Maimonides, yellow and red *zirnīkh* were components in a solution for the removal of hair without causing harm or injury. Two types of arsenic are defined by him as medicines that are 'nearly as powerful as fire' and were used for the treatment of 'ugly boils that are putrid'.

Different kinds of arsenic figure in four lists of *materia medica*, three prescriptions and several fragments of medical books found in the Cambridge Genizah collection. Arsenic was a commodity which was traded in the Mediterranean and imported from Europe. In traditional medicine in Iran and Iraq arsenic sulphate is used as a general medicine to reinforce the nerves. Mixed with lime, it is used to remove hair (Lev and Amar 2008: 104–6).

2. Dung, *zibl* (among other things) in Arabic, of cows, chickens, pigeons, horses and other animals as well as humans was used in ancient and medieval medicine and is mentioned in numerous medieval remedies (Wood 1936: 55; Kahl 2003: 135; Kahl 2007: 278, 287; Kahl 2009: 208–11).

3. Frankincense, *lubbān* or *kundur* in Arabic, is also known as olibanum. It is a resin of the *Boswellia carteri* (Burseraceae), an evergreen tree. The resin has been used for medicinal purposes since early times. In the Bible frankincense is one of the four constituents of incense burnt in the Sanctuary (Exod. 30:47). Frankincense was extremely expensive (Isa. 43:23), because it was brought from a great distance – according to scripture from Ethiopia (Jer. 13:9). The Jewish sages held lengthy discussions about frankincense and its uses. Classical physicians describe its resin, the methods for its production, and its medical uses. Dioscorides for example, in his entry *Libanonthus*, notes that 'frankincense is grown in Arabia, while the colour of its resin is white, oily and burns nicely'. According to the same physician, frankincense and the soot that was created by burning it served as a cure for intestinal diseases. Myrrh and frankincense — the main sources of wealth of the Arabian desert — constituted the main components of the regional trade. These substances enriched the Nabateans and were the cause of bitter Nabatean-Roman wars over the control of their trade. Al-Kindī describes the use of the resin as a component in medical preparations. Benevenutus claimed that olibanum was a main component in the medication (an ointment) called 'Jerusalem electuary' to treat cataract. Maimonides lists many medical uses of frankincense, for instance as a component in the 'royal medicine' against melancholy, in a medication for rabid dog bite and stings of the scorpion and spider. According to him, frankincense was a hot and dry drug. Ibn al-Bayṭār emphasized its value for treating eye infections and diseases.

Frankincense figures in ten lists of *materia medica* and six prescriptions found in the Cambridge Genizah collection, mainly for cleaning the teeth and chewing gum. The substance is also mentioned in fragments of medical books. According to the Genizah, frankincense was an important and expensive commodity traded in the medieval Mediterranean world (Lev and Amar 2008: 168–70).

4. **Myrrh**, *murr* in Arabic, is a crystallized reddish-yellow aromatic resin that emerges from ducts found in the stem and branches of the *Commiphora myrrha* (Burseraceae), a small, deciduous tree or thorny shrub which grows in the deserts of Africa and Arabia. Myrrh resin is one of the most ancient medicinal substances and its constituents have been tested up to the present day. It is mentioned in the Ebers papyrus as a component in various medications and an ingredient in incense in other cultures. Dioscorides states that the pure variety causes heat, induces sleep, dries and constricts, and serves as an external and internal medication and as incense. Myrrh is listed among the valuable merchandise traded in the East, the Arabian Peninsula particularly, throughout history. According to al-Kindī, myrrh is a component in many medications to treat stomach ulcers, pus-infected sores, toothache, contaminated wounds, eye diseases and haemorrhages. According to Maimonides, myrrh was the main component in the 'great theriac' and in a medication against snakebite, as described by Galen. It was also an ingredient in a theriac intended for bites by stray dogs. Myrrh figures in six lists of *materia medica*, six prescriptions found in the Cambridge Genizah collection, mainly for eye diseases and cough, and in fragments of medical books in recipes for the treatment of stomach and liver complaints, coughs and colds (Lev and Amar 2008: 221–2).

5. **Musk**, *misk* in Arabic, is a substance used as a perfume and medicine. Its source is the anal glands of the musk deer *Moschus moschiferus* (Cervidae), which inhabits the mountains of Central Asia. In the Middle Ages musk was used as an important spice and was imported overland from Asia. Maimonides states that musk was a component in a medication against headache and eye ache and a medicine for treating diarrhoea. Tibetan musk was used as a component in a vendor's powder to cause instant sleep. Ibn al-Bayṭār in his entry musk described it as a hot and dry drug to counter the odour of sweat and bad breath, to strengthen the heart and brain, and to strengthen the male sexual organs. According to him,

musk also alleviates headache and cleanses the eyes. Musk figures in four lists of *materia medica,* two prescriptions and in medical books found in the Cambridge Genizah collection as one of the simples which were useful for treating various diseases including headaches and diseases of the brain. Musk is mentioned in many Genizah fragments as a commodity in various Mediterranean cities (Lev and Amar 2008: 215–17).

6. **Rose** [dog rose], *nasrīn* or *ward* in Arabic, identified as *Rosa canina* (Rosaceae). The wild dog rose is a large shrub, which grows in the Mediterranean mountains and groves. The medicinal use of the dog rose is described by physicians of the classical period. Dioscorides, for example, describes various medicinal uses of dog rose: to treat stomach disorders, headaches, gynaecological problems, skin diseases, wounds, and the eyes and gums. Benevenutus states that rose sugar is a component in a medication called the 'Jerusalem pill', which was used to cure cataract, while 'dried rose leaves' are an ingredient in a medication called 'Jerusalem collyrium'. Al-Qazwīnī (1203–83) cites contemporary physicians who recommend the plant for easing pain, treating eye inflammation, haemorrhages, and fainting fits. Different products of rose figure in fourteen lists of *materia medica* and in fifty-seven prescriptions found in the Cambridge Genizah collection: for treating liver ailments, lice, weak eyesight and migraine, eye diseases, cleaning the teeth, and as a purgative. It also appears in many fragments of medical books in recipes for chewing gum, the treatment of the eyes, children with umbilical hernia and incessant crying, quartan fever, burning black bile and phlegm. Rose is mentioned in a letter addressed to a higher authority, reporting special treatment of some eye complaints including inflammation, dimness of vision and widening of the pupils, while the use of certain lamellas, potions, and eye drops is recommended (T-S NS 327.93). Rose water is mentioned as an important commodity in several Genizah fragments concerning trade in the eleventh-century Mediterranean (Amar and Lev 2008: 261–6).

7. **Saffron**, *za'farān* in Arabic, consists of the orange floral stigmas of the *Crocus sativus* (Iridaceae). It was used in Assyria and Babylon to cure urinary problems, stomach disorders, and women's ailments, and also for disinfection during childbirth. Similar uses were made of it in ancient Egyptian medicine. Dioscorides describes saffron as a diuretic drug used for curing the eyes and for women's ailments, womb disorders, skin diseases, and ear inflammations. Al-Kindī reports that saffron is an important component in many medications, including for the eyes. Benevenutus mentions the use of saffron in a medication for cataract called the 'Jerusalem Electuary'. Ibn al-Bayṭār says that saffron is a drug to sharpen the senses, prompt the memory, slow the heartbeat, improve eyesight and relieve aches. Al-Qazwini also describes saffron, citing Ibn Sīnā, who stated that the seeds are soporific and improve the eyesight, while the plant itself is a sexual stimulant and a diuretic. Saffron figures in at least twenty-one lists of *materia medica* and in thirteen prescriptions found in the Cambridge Genizah collection, mainly for eye diseases. It is also mentioned in many Genizah fragments of medical books, such as in recipes for the treatment of a hot and burning sensation in the eye, weak and dim vision, drooping

eyelids, lippitude, inversion, and lice of the eyelids. It was also used in epiphoral drops to increase the flow of tears. According to many eleventh-century Genizah fragments saffron was an important commodity traded by land and sea (Lev and Amar 2008: 270–3).

8. *Šiyāf, ašyāf* is a general name for eye medicines and collyria. The word is mentioned in more than fifty Genizah fragments (Lev and Amar 2008: 568).

9. Wax, *šam'* in Arabic, is produced from the beeswax glands of young bees. It contains esters of fatty acids and sugars. The ancient Egyptians used melted wax with oil as a base for ointments. In ancient Babylonia, wax was used for various purposes, including the preservation of food and medicine. Classical physicians such as Hippocrates and Dioscorides describe the use of wax (*keros*) for various medical purposes. Ibn al-Bayṭār cites Ibn Sina describing the use of wax for medical purposes such as a component in poisons and to treat indigestion. Several kinds of wax figure in four lists of *materia medica* and eleven prescriptions found in the Cambridge Genizah collection, for eye diseases, as a depilatory for hairy women, and as an aphrodisiac. Wax is also mentioned in fragments of medical books in recipes for fever, skin application, sciatica, varicose veins, convulsion and tetany, fever, and colic. Wax is still sold in the markets and used in Middle Eastern traditional medicine. Yemenite Jews used wax to soften and heal wounds and as a component in ointments. The Jews of Iraq also used it as a component in various medicines (Lev and Amar 2008: 315–17).

10. Zinc is a hard, bluish-white metallic element that appears in nature as calamite and sulphide from which it is manufactured by smelting and refining. Modern scholars agree that the medieval *tūtyā* in its narrow sense means zinc at different stages of oxidation. Zinc has been medicinally used since early times in various ancient civilizations, including the Babylonian and the Roman. Dioscorides describes the medicinal uses of *diphruges* as a cure for skin diseases, wounds, and tumours. Those uses were due to its drying and cooling qualities. Al-Tamimi reports that *tūtyā* was collected on seashores along the coast of Lebanon and was used to treat eye diseases. Al-Kindī writes that zinc is used in many remedies for the treatment of eye diseases, mainly to reduce humidity, to clear cataracts, and to improve the eyesight. Al-Biruni was of the opinion that zinc should be used to cure external cancerous sores. Benevenutus describes a Jerusalemite remedy for the treatment of the eyes. Among the different substances he mentions white wine and *tūtyā*, and in a different remedy he mentions 'Alexandrine *tūtyā*, rose leaves and white wine as a cure for other eye diseases. Al-Qazwīnī relates about different kinds of zinc (white, yellow and green) and points out that their origin is the Indian Ocean and its shores (e.g. Yemen).

One of the practical medicinal uses of zinc was to eliminate bad smells such as sweat and urine. Zinc figures in eight lists of *materia medica*, seven prescriptions and two letters found in the Cambridge Genizah collection, mainly for the treatment of eye diseases. Zinc appears in many fragments of medical books, e.g. as a simple in a list of substances used for the treatment of eye diseases such as redness, itching, and excessive lachrymation. Several Genizah letters describe the trade in several kinds of zinc in Egypt, Sicily and other locations, mainly for medicinal uses such as treating eye diseases. In traditional medicine, Yemenite Jews used zinc to treat eye diseases, cancerous wounds, and wounds of the sexual organs. Babylonian Jews used zinc for external uses such as the treatment of eye diseases and swollen lips (Lev and Amar 2008: 322–4).

Acknowledgments

The authors would like to express their sincere thanks to Dr Sagit Butbul for allowing us to publish her identifications of medical fragments in especially the Arabic series, as well as to Professor Gerrit Bos, University of Cologne, Dr Leigh Chipman, Ben-Gurion University and Dr Yaron Serri, Zefad Academic College, Israel for their helpful remarks. We would like to thank the Syndics of Manchester University Library for permission to publish the Genizah fragments.

References

Albert Daniel M. and Diane D. Edwards. 1996. *The History of Ophthalmology*. (Cambridge, Massachusetts)

Dols, Michael W. and Adil S. Gamal. 1984. *Medieval Islamic Medicine: Ibn Riḍwān's Treatise "On the Prevention of Bodily Ills in Egypt"*. (Berkeley/Los Angeles/London)

Ducros, A.H. 1930. 'Essai sur le Droguier Populaire Arabe de l'Inspectorat des Pharmacies du Caire', *Mémoires Présentés à l'Institut d'Égypte* 15, 1–165

Flashar, Hellmut. 1966. *Melancholie und Melancholiker in den medizinischen Theorien der Antike*. (Berlin)

Goitein, Shlomo D. 1967-1993. *A Mediterranean Society: The Jewish Communities of the Arab World as Portrayed in the Documents of the Cairo Geniza*. 6 vols, (Berkeley)

Hirschberg, Julius. 1982–94. *The History of Ophthalmology*. 11 vols, (Bonn)

Hopkins, Simon. 1994. 'A New Autograph Fragment of Maimonides's *Epitomes* of Galen (*De Locis Affectis*)', *Bulletin of the School of Oriental and African Studies* 57, 126–32

Ibn al-Bayṭār. 1874. *Kitab al-jami' li-mufradat al-'adwiya wa'l-aghdhiya.* (Cairo)

Ibn Sīnā. 1970. *Qanun fi al-ṭibb.* 3 vols, (Baghdad)

Isaacs, Haskell D. 1991. 'A Medieval Arab Medical Certificate', *Medical History* 35:2, 250–7

—— (with the assistance of Colin F. Baker). 1994. *Medical and Para-Medical Manuscripts in the Cambridge Genizah Collection*. (Cambridge)

Issa Bey, A. 1930. *Dictionnaire des noms des plantes en latin, français, anglais et arabe.* (Cairo)

Kahl, Oliver. 2003. *Sābūr ibn Sahl / The Small Dispensatory*. (Leiden/Boston)

—— 2007. *The Dispensatory of Ibn at-Tilmīḏ: Arabic Text, English Translation, Study and Glossaries*. (Leiden/Boston)

—— 2009. *Sābūr ibn Sahl's Dispensatory in the Recension of the 'Aḍūdī Hospital.* (Leiden/Boston)

Kohēn al-Attār al-Isrā'īlī. 1940. *Minhag ad-Dukkan.* (Cairo)

Krause, Arlington C. 1934. 'Assyro-Babylonian Ophthalmology', *Annals of Medical History* (New Series) 6, 42–55

Lev, Efraim. 2004. 'Work in Progress: The Research of Medical Knowledge in the Cairo Genizah – Past, Present and Future', in S. Reif (ed.), *The Written Word Remains: The Archive and the Achievement* (Cambridge). 37–51

Lev, Efraim and Zohar Amar. 2007. 'Practice versus Theory: Medieval *Materia Medica* According to the Cairo Genizah', *Medical History* 51:4, 507–26

—— 2008. *Practical Materia Medica of the Medieval Eastern Mediterranean According to the Cairo Genizah*. (Leiden)

Levey, Martin. 1966. *The Medical Formulary or* Aqrābādhīn *of al-Kindī*. (Madison, Milwaukee/London)

Meyerhof, Max. 1928. *The Book of the Ten Treatises on the Eye Ascribed to Hunain ibn Ishâq (809–877 A.D.)*. (Cairo)

Nielsen, Harald. 1974. *Ancient Ophthalmological Agents: A Pharmaco-Historical Study of the Collyria and Seals for Collyria Used During Roman Antiquity, As Well As of the Most Frequent Components of the Collyria*. (Odense)

Polliack, Meira. 1998. *Genres in Judaeo-Arabic Literature*. (Tel Aviv)

Powell, Owen. 2003. *Galen / On the Properties of Foodstuffs (De Alimentorum Facultatibus)*. (Cambridge)

Rāzī, Abū Bakr Muḥammad ibn Zakariyā al-. 1955–71. *Kitāb al-Ḥāwī fī al-Ṭibb*. 23 vols, (Hyderabad)

Rosner, Fred and Suessman Muntner 1971. *The Medical Aphorisms of Moses Maimonides*. (New York)

Sandford-Smith, John. 1997. *Eye Diseases in Hot Climates*[3]. (Oxford)

Savage-Smith, Emilie. 1996. 'Medicine', in R. Rashed (ed.), *Encyclopedia of the History of Arabic Science*. 3 vols, (London/New-York), vol. 3, 903–62

Sbath, Paul. 1932–3. 'Al-Dustur al-bimaristani: le formulaire des hôpitaux d'Ibn Abil Bayan, médicin du Bimaristan Annacery au Caire au xiiie siècle', *Bulletin de l'Institut d'Égypte* 15, 13–78

Sharafi, G.M. al-. 1964. *Tadhkhiratu'l-Kahhālīn by 'Ali b. Īsa al-Kaḥḥāl*. (Hyderabad)

Timken-Zinkann, Reinhard F. 1968. 'Black Bile: A Review of Recent Attempts to Trace the Origin of the Teaching on Melancholia to Medical Observations', *Medical History* 12, 288–92

Ullmann, Manfred. 1970. *Die Medizin im Islam*. (Leiden/Köln)

—— 1978. *Islamic Medicine*. (Edinburgh)

Wernhard, M. 2004. 'Galen über die Arten der Fieber in der arabischen Version des Ḥunain ibn Isḥaq'. Unpublished PhD thesis, Ludwig Maximilian University of Munich

Wood, Casey A. 1936. *Memorandum Book of a Tenth-Century Oculist for the Use of Modern Oculists*. (Chicago)

A Medieval Judaeo-Arabic Glossary of Drugs' Names in the Taylor-Schechter Genizah Collection, Cambridge

Efraim Lev and Zohar Amar

University of Haifa Bar-Ilan University

Introduction

One of the many aspects of Jewish life and, more generally, of Mediterranean society, on which the Genizah documents throw a flood of light is medical practice. From them one can learn much about physicians and their status, medical institutions, diseases and ailments, treatment theories and methods, as well as the medicinal substances that were applied. Some of these matters were initially dealt with by scholars such as Goitein (1963; 1967–93, I: 267; II: 247–58) as a facet of other concerns, such as the diverse professional classes of the Jewish community in Old Cairo. Since then other scholars, such as Dietrich (1954), Baker (1996), Fenton (1980), Cohen (1993), Dvorjetski (1990) and Isaacs (1991), have studied and published relevant documents or have focused on specific medical issues. Medicine as a subject matter in its own right in the Genizah has been given due attention only in the last two decades, with Isaacs' publication of the catalogue of medical and para-medical manuscripts in the Cambridge Genizah collections (1994).

This article is one of the first fruits of a long-term interdisciplinary research project led by the authors to study and uncover the practical medical activity of Mediterranean society according to the Genizah fragments, as against earlier theoretical knowledge. The project deals with practical *vs.* theoretical *materia medica*, the identification of medical books and practitioners, the reconstruction of the medical library, and so on (Lev 2004, 2007; Lev and Amar 2006, 2007, 2008; Chipman and Lev 2006, 2008; Lev and Chipman 2007; Amar and Lev 2007; Lev, Chipman and Niessen 2008; Niessen and Lev 2008; Geva-Kleinberger and Lev 2009).

Medical Synonym Glossaries (Dictionaries of Drug Names)

Due to the progress of Arab science in general, and medicine and pharmacology in particular, in the tenth–thirteenth centuries, a rich mass of medical literature developed, including synonym glossaries of drug names (Ullmann 1978: 41–51). The medieval Arabic medical library consisted of works in various fields: general medical books, theoretical as well as practical, translated medical literature, interpretations of classical medical books,[1] original books on specific diseases, pharmacopoeias, *materia medica*, and more.

Gradually a literary genre evolved concentrating on explanations of drug names.[2] It came into being in a setting wherein medieval Arab physicians and pharmacists had to deal professionally every day with hundreds of medicinal substances from all over the Old World, that is, from India to Spain. These substances were mentioned in books that were original and indigenous as well as translated and imported; the relevant drugs were identified in different geographical locations and often had several nicknames. Each substance, regardless of origin — animal, plant, inorganic, or some kind of combination — had different names in different languages, according to its geographic origin or ethnic background. This was undoubtedly very impractical for merchants, traders, and medical practitioners, and potentially dangerous for patients. Maimonides himself testifies to this situation: 'For a single remedy may carry several names by the representative of the same language, as a consequence of a coincidence in naming or a difference in the origin of the terminology by the inhabitants of various regions' (Rosner 1995: 3).

Frequently practitioners studied at one place and practiced at another; in any case, they consulted medical books written or translated all over the Muslim world and wrote prescriptions that had to be understood, and the substances recognized, by the local pharmacists. The latter were obliged to order the materials from various merchants who acquired them from all over the Old World, east as well as west (Lev and Amar 2008: 74–80). To prevent confusion, traders as well as physicians and pharmacists had to use some kind of idiosyncratic lists of synonyms, dictionaries, and other kinds of aids, which were crucial for mutual understanding and ensuring that they obtained the correct substances. We know of dozens of such works. Thus Meyerhof mentions thirty in his introduction (1940; see also Muntner 1969: 7–9). The works list drug names in different dialects and languages: Syrian, Latin, Greek, Persian, standard Arabic, Berber, Spanish, Sanskrit, and so on. The authors of medical

1 Especially by Hippocrates and Galen; see, e.g., the abbreviated interpretations by Maimonides of Galen's work 'On Temperaments' (T-S Ar.21.112) and 'On the faculties of foods' (T-S Ar.44.51) as published by Stern (1956–66, III: 12–17) and Rosner and Muntner (1970–1).

2 The roots of this genre can already be found in ancient Greek literature, e.g. Dioscorides' book on *materia medica*. For a fine, early description of this issue see the introduction in Meyerhof (1940).

synonym glossaries include several members of the Andalusian school among whom Jonah Ibn Janāḥ (Amar and Serri 2000/01), Ibn Biklārish (Amar and Serri 2001), Maimonides (Meyerhof 1935: 23–4; Levey 1973: 154–5), and al-Idrīsī, who, exceptionally, included a lot of Hebrew words (Amar and Serri 2005).

In addition to the more professional works, plenty of unofficial ones existed which were put together as pamphlets or copied out in notebooks for personal use.[3] The copyists (e.g., merchants or physicians) wrote out brief lists of drug names, mainly the common ones of the period and geographical area in which they lived. A link between these lists and the professional literature is noticeable, but in most cases it is hard to identify the exact source or sources (Gigandet 2001: 383, 395).

Document T-S NS 224.146

Genizah fragment T-S NS 224.146, we believe, is a synonym glossary probably written in medieval Cairo by an anonymous Jew with the aim of overcoming the problem of identifying drug names. This fragment is cryptically described by Isaacs and Baker (1994: 64, no. 842) as a list of simples, actions and uses. Its technical description is 'Judaeo-Arabic, oriental semi-cursive script; paper; 1 leaf; mutilated and stained, 14.8 x 8.7, 16 lines (recto); 5 lines verso'. According to our knowledge, it is the only example of this specific type identified in the Cairo Genizah so far. While we don't know date and place of composition, from a palaeographic point of view it was apparently written in the twelfth or thirteenth century.

In what follows we present a transcription and translation of the recto and verso of the document, followed by a discussion of the medicinal substances cited. Medical prescriptions and lists of *materia medica* found in the Cairo Genizah and previous works on the medicinal substances of the medieval Levant and their uses contributed to the identification process. They also served to clarify the medical uses of the substances mentioned in our fragment in the middle ages and in Middle Eastern traditional medicine in the twentieth century.

Sigla in the transcriptions:

[ ] Hypothetical reconstruction of the text

---

3 According to Bos and Mensching (2005, 2001) dozens of such notebooks written in Hebrew, Judaeo-Arabic, Persian, Ladino, Yiddish and other languages have been catalogued by the Institute of Microfilmed Hebrew Manuscripts.

… Faded letter(s) or letter(s) which is / are difficult to decipher

? Preceding letter insecure

Text

(Recto)

1 [אל]באב אלאו[ל]

2 ... אל עטר

3 ... בל יונאני

4 [להלי]לג' אלאסוד הו אלכאבלי

5 [אלה]ל[י]לג' אלאצפר הו אלאצ[פר]

6 [אל]אשק הו אלכלך

7 [אל]ס[ו]רנג'אן הו אלכמירת אל...

8 אלעאקר קרחה הו אלעוד אלקרח

9 ערק אלדואד הו אלצפד[4]

10 אלמיויזג'[5] הו זביב אלגבל

11 אלמא קראח הו אלמא חלו

12 אלברשאושאן הו כספרת ביר

13 פהו רג'ל אלג'ראב והו סאק אלר[ציף]

14 אל איר?סה[6] הו ערק אל[טיב]

15 אלחצ'צ' הו אל[פילזהרג'][7]

16 אלסק...[8]

(Verso)

17 הו אל סל[ג'ם]

18 [דאר] ציני הו קרפה

19 ק?[רי]צ הו אלאנג'[רה]

20 ...אק אל....אסה הו אלג?...

21 אלנחס אלמחרק הו רס?[ח'תג'?]

---

4 The reading seems corrupt here, since it is likely that the scribe should rather have written ערק אל ג'דואר הו אלצפר.

5 This looks like a corruption of 'אלמיובזג. Perhaps the terms were copied from another text which read a smallish *bêt* which was then misread for a *yôd*.

6 There is a slight doubt over the *rêš*, because *lāmed* also seems a possibility here. Moreover, Dozy does mention إيرسا as an alternative for إيرس but, strictly speaking, one would in that case expect an *'ālep* rather than a *hēh* in the Hebrew orthography.

7 We make this suggestion because of the possible remnant of a *lāmed* at the very end of the line on the fragment.

8 Hypothesis: [אלסק[מוניא הו אלמחמודה.

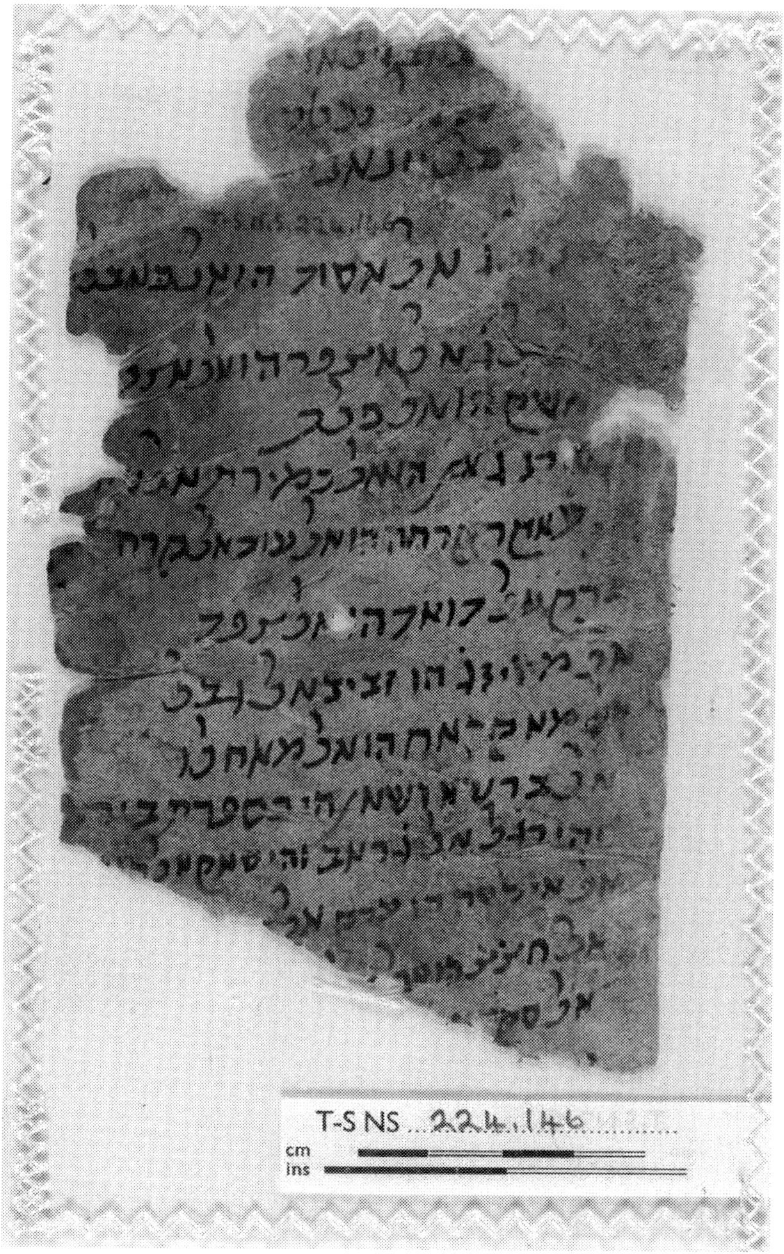

Plate 1: T-S NS 224.146 (recto). (Reproduced by kind permission of the Syndics of Cambridge University Library)

Plate 2: T-S NS 224.146 (verso). (Reproduced by kind permission of the Syndics of Cambridge University Library)

Translation

1 Chapter one

2 … perfume

3 … Greek

4 Black [myrobalan, *halīlaj*] is (myrobalan of) the Kabuli (type)

5 Yellow [myrobalan] is (myrobalan of) the yellow (type)

6 Ammoniacum (*uššaq*) is galbanum (*kalakh*)

7 Meadow saffron (*sūranjān*) is meadow saffron (*khamīra*) of …

8 Pellitory of Spain (*'āqir qariḥa*) is pellitory of Spain (*'ūd qariḥ*)

9 Zedoary's root (*'irq al-jadwar*) is turmeric (*al-ṣ-f-r*, literally 'yellow')

10 Stavesacre (*mayūbazaj*) is lice-bane (*zabīb al-jabal*)

11 Pure water (*mā' qaraḥ*) is sweet water (*mā' ḥulw*)

12 Venus hair fern (*barshāwushān*) is black maidenhair fern (*kuz*[*b*]*arat al-bi'r*)

13 and that is *rijl al-ġurāb* which is *sāq ra*[*ṣīf*]

14 Iris (*īrisā*) is [fragrant] root (*'irq* [*ṭayyib*])

15 Lycium (*ḥaḍaḍ*) is [boxthorn] ([*fīlzahraj*])

16 Sc[?ammony (?*sqamūniyā*) is Syrian bindweed (?*maḥmūda*)]

17 is [turnip]

18 Cinnamon ([*dār*] *ṣīnī*) is cinnamon (*qirfa*)

19 Nettle (*q*[*urray*]*ṣ*) is nettle (*anj*[*ura*])

20 ???

21 Burnt copper (*nuḥas muḥarraq*) is ?*rawsḥatj*

Commentary

Lines 4–5: The Arabic synonym for black myrobalan (*Terminalia chebula*) is abbreviated here as *al-kabūlī*,[9] while the Arabic synonym for yellow myrobalan (*Terminalia citrina*) is abbreviated here as *al-aṣfar*, literally 'yellow'. Both substances are fruits of tropical trees native to South-East Asia, which were used for the treatment of a wide variety of ailments, mainly haemorrhoids and intestinal problems (Ibn al-Bayṭar 1874, IV: 198). The various kinds of myrobalan were considered some of the most important drugs in medieval times; they are mentioned more than any other substance in prescriptions

9 The identification of black myrobalan with the Kabuli kind is problematic since they are apparently two different species (Muntner 1969: no. 112, n. 21). Ibn al-Bayṭār (1874: IV, 196) notes in his book that the two names are confusing, since the Kabuli kind is black as well.

and lists of *materia medica* in the Genizah, in merchants' letters, and in other commercial documents of the medieval Mediterranean (Lev and Amar 2008: 218–21). This kind of myrobalan and others are still in use in traditional medicine and can be found in the markets of Cairo and other Middle Eastern cities (Ducros 1930: 8–9, nos. 13–15; Meyerhof 1918: nos. 328–31; Lev and Amar 2000 and 2002a). The fruits of the black kind are today still called 'the king of the drugs' by consumers of traditional medicine in the area (Lev and Amar 2002b: 118).

Line 6: Galbanum (*al-kalakh*) and ammoniacum (*uššaq*) belong to the same family of plants (*Apiaceae*) and have similar properties. *Uššaq* refers to the Irano-Turanian plant Ammoniacum (*Dorema ammoniacum*). Its resin was used in medieval times for the treatment of pains, intestinal worms, putrescent wounds, eye diseases, and madness. It was considered a strong purgative, a hot and dry drug, and was used extensively for cooling the blood, draining liquid and phlegm, and as disinfectant (Lev and Amar 2008: 333–4). It is still sold in shops of traditional substances in Egypt (Meyerhof 1918: no. 486) and several Middle Eastern countries for similar uses (Lev and Amar 2002b: 192). It is mentioned frequently in prescriptions and lists of *materia medica* in the Genizah.

Line 7: These kinds of meadow saffron (*Colchicum sp.*) were used in the middle ages for the treatment of kidney stones, mental illnesses, haemorrhoids, and abscesses. Ibn al-Bayṭār notes how the women in Egypt use the plant together with orchid to prepare a medication for fattening without harmful side effects. He also quotes al-Rāzī who claimed that the plant contributes to sexual appetite, makes the face rosy, and gives it beauty (Lev and Amar 2008: 446–7). Meadow saffron bulbs are still in use in traditional medicine and can be found in the markets of Cairo (Ducros 1930: no. 131; Meyerhof 1918: no. 162). There seems to be a grammatical error here with *khamīra* having the definite article despite being in the *status constructus* (*khamīrat*).

Line 8: These are two names for pellitory of Spain (*Anacylus pyrethrum*) which is a perennial plant mainly growing in Spain and Morocco. Classical physicians such as Dioscorides describe the use of the roots for the treatment of paralysis, toothache, and excess phlegm. According to Arabic medieval literature it was used to cleanse spots, treat sore throat, insanity and pustules in the neck, for brushing the teeth, and to relieve head and stomach aches. Ibn al-Bayṭār quotes classical and Arab physicians describing the main uses of the roots to relieve toothache and to treat malaria, the shivers (chills), paralysis, swellings, and scorpion stings. Pellitory of Spain is mentioned in several prescriptions, lists of *materia medica*, and merchants' letters found in the Cairo Genizah (Lev and Amar 2008: 464–5). It is still in use in traditional medicine and can be found in the markets of Cairo and other Middle Eastern cities (Ducros 1930: no. 166; Lev and Amar 2002b: 202). There is a slight grammatical error here in that the definite article has been forgotten before the adjective *qariḥa*.

Line 9: This line is apparently corrupt. If we are correct in changing the reading to Zedoary root (*Curcuma zedoaria*), the synonym 'yellow' might suggest that the author in fact meant to refer to a different, albeit similar, substance also belonging to the Zingiberaceae family, namely turmeric (*Curcuma longa*, *kurkum* in Arabic). Turmeric was used by Arab practitioners, among other things, to strengthen the teeth (toothpaste) and to treat the throat, gums, mouth sores, and haemorrhoids (Lev and Amar 2008: 305–7). No evidence has been found so far for the use of Zedoary in prescriptions in medieval Cairo according to the Genizah documents. However, it must have been in use as it still is in traditional medicine (Meyerhof 1918: no. 172, Lev and Amar 2000 and 2002a).

Line 10: The two words are synonyms for *Delphinium staphisagria*, a native Mediterranean plant of the *Ranunculaceae* family which grows in much of Europe and Asia today. Since Antiquity the seeds were used to remove body-lice. In the medieval Muslim world *Delphinium staphisagria* was also used to treat epilepsy and neck pustules (Lev and Amar 2008: 489). In modern Egypt the drug is used in traditional medicine as an emetic, as well as against lice and itches (Ducros 1930: no. 113; Meyerhof 1918: no. 441).

Line 11: The medicinal uses of water are discussed widely in medieval medical literature (e.g. Ibn al-Bayṭār 1874, IV: 127–32), and different kinds of water were commonly used in Arab medicine and pharmacology (Bos 1992: 57). Pure water is mentioned in a Genizah document (T-S Ar.180.6). The definitive articles have been omitted before the two adjectives.

Line 12: It should be noted that the copyist writes כספרה instead of the usual כזברה (Judeo-Arabic) or כוסבר[ה] (already thus in the Mishnah for 'coriander'). These two words are synonyms to denote the fern *Adiantum capillus-veneris*. Dioscorides describes its medicinal uses such as curing asthma and dysentery, eliminating stones in the urinary tract, strengthening the stomach, curing bites and stings, accelerating menstruation, stopping haemorrhages, and strengthening the hair. According to medieval physicians the plant was good against snakebite and hair loss, for example (Lev and Amar 2008: 443–4). Maidenhair is mentioned in several prescriptions and lists of *materia medica* found in the Cairo Genizah. The plant is still in use in traditional medicine and can be found in the markets of Cairo and several Middle Eastern cities (Ducros 1930: no. 200; Meyerhof 1918: no. 211).

Line 13: Presumably this line gives two more synonyms for *Adiantum capillus-veneris*. To start with the latter, סאק ר[צי]ף (*sāq raṣīf*) is indeed mentioned by Ibn al-Bayṭār (1874, I: 86) and Ibn al-'Umar (Saqqa 1975: 19, though note the misspelling there) as a synonym for black maidenhair fern. However, we haven't been able to identify *rijl al-ġurāb* (literally, crow's foot) as a synonym for the same plant. Instead we found a variety of suggestions regarding its identification, such as: wart cress aka swine's cress or *Coronopus* (*Coronopus* meaning crow's foot; Issa 1930: 142, no. 13), chervil (Dozy 1927, I: 514[10]; see also Ducros 1930: 63, no. 110; Issa 1930: 40, no. 18), and Star-of-the-earth (*Plantago coronopus*; Issa 1930: 1942, no. 13). In the fragment the definite article is missing before *raṣīf*.

10 Dozy lists a number of plants of which the Arabic name consists of the foot or leg of a certain animal: *rijl al-asad* (pied-de-lion), *rijl al-baqara* (pied-de-veau), *rijl al-dajāja* (a type of chamomile), *rijl al-arnab* (pied-de-lièvre).

Line 14: We suggest the reading *'irq ṭayyib*, not least because Ducros (1930: 104, no. 182; yet compare Dozy 1881, II: 119, عرق; see also Issa 1930: 100, no. 12) mentions it as the popular Arabic name for iris. Since the roots of various types of irises are fragrant, they were not only popular for their medicinal properties but also used to make perfume (Lev and Amar 2008: 423–5). Again the definite article is missing here, this time before *'irq*.

Line 15: *Lycium* is an evergreen spiny tangled bush of the *Solanaceae* family. *Ḥaḍaḍ* (or *ḥuḍuḍ*) and *fīlzahraj* are two synonyms for this plant known in Arabic (Dozy 1881, II: 303, فيلزهرج; Issa 1930: 112, no. 15). *Lycium* or boxthorn was used by medieval physicians especially to treat eye problems but also to cure gum and skin diseases, and so forth. It is mentioned in several prescriptions, lists of *materia medica* and merchants' letters found in the Cairo Genizah (Lev and Amar 2008: 121). Boxthorn is still used in traditional medicine and can be found in the markets of Cairo (Ducros 1930: 96, no. 168 where the two terms are mentioned under عوسج; Meyerhof 1918: no. 223).

Line 16: Even though only two letters are properly legible here, we suggest the intended plant might have been scammony (*Convolvulus scammonia*), with a common name for it in Arabic being *al-maḥmūda* (Dozy 1881, I: 321). Scammony was imported from Syria and Palestine for extensive medicinal use, not least as a purgative. Scammony is mentioned in Genizah fragments as a commodity traded and sold throughout North Africa (Lev and Amar 2008: 280–2).

Line 17: One of two Arabic synonyms for bird rape, also named turnip (*Brassica campestris*) (Meyerhof 1940: no. 273). It is an ancient cultivated plant that was known in China, Egypt, Greece and Rome. Bird rape was seen by medieval physicians as an effective concoction for improved coitus and to sharpen the eyesight (Rosner and Muntner 1970–1: 22).

Line 18: Cinnamon is widely attested as an important simple in medieval medicine (Lev and Amar 2008: 143–6).

Line 19: Most likely, the original text showed two Arabic synonyms for nettle here (*Urtica*, of which *Urtica urens* and *Urtica pilulifera* are the most widespread in the Middle East) (Dozy 1881, II: 336; Muntner 1969: 19, no. 14; Issa 1930: 186, no. 6). The genus is characterized by its stinging hairs. Dioscorides lists its medical uses, including treating dog bite, gangrene, stomach ulcers and cancerous growths, stopping blood haemorrhages, and accelerating menstruation (Gunther 1959: IV.94). The medieval Arabic physicians used it, for example, for the treatment of asthma (Bos 2002: 70), as an antidote to poisons and against snakebites (e.g. Levey 1966: 59; Muntner 1942: 126). Nettle is still in use in traditional medicine and can be found in the markets of Cairo and various Middle Eastern cities (Ducros 1930: 10, no. 17; Meyerhof 1918: no. 391; Lev and Amar 2002b: 168).

Line 20: Unfortunately, this line is too hard to decipher.

Line 21: Both synonyms for burnt copper were known to Maimonides (Muntner 1969: 99, no. 357). It is an inorganic material, usually red in colour, which was mainly used in various eye treatments (Lev and

Amar 2008: 389–90). This material is still sold in Jordan and Syria as a medicinal substance (Lev and Amar 2002a: 136).

Discussion

T-S NS 224.146 consists of fifteen identified medicinal substances, which are all vegetal except for one inorganic substance. Each substance is listed in the form of two synonyms, apart from black maidenhair fern for which four synonyms are given. They are all mentioned with their Arabic names (some of which are of Persian provenance) in various dialects despite the apparent reference to Greek on line three, which initially raises the expectancy that Greek terms might also be included here. This is unlike the professional medical synonym glossaries, which give names in up to twenty languages and dialects (Amar and Serri 2005). It is therefore likely that the writer of this list meant to include only the most common drug names for his personal use in a certain time and place.

We get the impression that the writer of T-S NS 224.146 was most likely a non-medical professional, perhaps a merchant or a trader (if not his slightly more clueless assistant) rather than a pharmacist or physician, who merely copied some of the names from another source for his personal use (or indeed that of his boss). First of all, the list seems improvised as it is not in alphabetical order, contrary to contemporary books of this genre and also in spite of the promising 'Chapter One' on the first line, while the Judaeo-Arabic transcription is not always consistent. More importantly, the writer makes several mistakes. The most telling of these is found on line 9, where the first letter of the Arabic term for Zedoary (*jadwar* or *zadwar*) is missing, and the two letters 'r' were mistakenly changed to 'd', letters which are obviously very similar in Hebrew script, after which the same curiously happens to the word for 'yellow'. Interestingly, on line 13 the 'zb' in the first word of the Arabic term for black maidenhair fern *kuzbarat al-bi'r* is rather written with 'sp'. This mistake might reflect the dialect or origin of the writer of the list (or the source the writer might have copied from). As a matter of fact, in spoken Arabic the substitution of these two sounds is very common. In the commentary we already noted the several grammatical imprecisions.

When we compared the identified substances in our list with the lists of medicinal substances mentioned in the literature of the Levant (Lev 2003), and especially with the *materia medica* in actual use by medieval people in Cairo according to the hundreds of prescriptions and dozens of lists of *materia medica* discovered in the Genizah, we realized that nearly all the substances mentioned in T-S NS 224.146 are among the most commonly used and frequently mentioned there (Lev and Amar 2008: 71, 516–49). Indeed most of these are also found in Maimonides' book on drug names, which says it includes only the most useful ones (Muntner 1969: 15). We already showed in the commentary how most substances mentioned in our document share a rich pharmacological history which remains unbroken to present-day traditional medicine in various countries of the Arab world.

Conclusion

Due to the progress of Arab science, especially in the fields of medicine and pharmacology during the tenth to thirteenth centuries, a rich medical literature developed. One of its sub-genres was the explanation of drug names which evolved due to the fact that medieval Arab pharmacists and physicians had to deal with hundreds of medicinal substances that were traded from India to Spain. After all, these drugs were named differently in different geographical locations, and went by various nicknames and synonyms – a situation which could be confusing for merchants, traders, pharmacists and medical practitioners alike. We suggest that Genizah fragment T-S NS 224.146 might have had a very practical use because: (1) the list is short, (2) it is not in alphabetical order, contrary to contemporary books of this genre, (3) the Judeo-Arabic transcription is not always consistent, (4) the writer includes only the commonest and most useful drug names, and (5) the copyist made several clumsy mistakes, and his handwriting is quite sloppy.

Acknowledgments

This research would not have taken place without the generous grant of St John's College, Cambridge which hosted Prof. Efraim Lev as an Overseas Visiting Scholar (2003–4). The authors would like to express their thanks to Dr Yaron Serri and Dr Leigh Chipman for their helpful remarks. Special thanks to our colleagues at the Taylor-Schechter Genizah Research Unit at Cambridge University Library, who shared with us generously their knowledge and experience and supported us with helpful remarks: Dr Ben Outhwaite (head), Professor Stefan Reif (former head), the late Shulie Reif, Dr Avihai Shivtiel, the late Dr Friedrich Niessen, Dr Rebecca Jefferson, Ellis Weinberger and Sara Sykes. The authors would like to thank the Syndicate of Cambridge University Library for its permission to publish the Cairo Genizah fragments presented in this article.

References

Amar, Zohar and Efraim Lev. 2007. 'The Significance of the Genizah's Medical Documents for the Study of Medieval Mediterranean Trade', *Journal of the Economic and Social History of the Orient* 50/4, 524–41

Amar, Zohar and Yaron Serri. 2000/01. 'Compilation from Jonah Ibn Ğanāḥ's Dictionary of Medical Terms', *Lĕšonénu* 63, 279–91 (in Hebrew)

—— 2001. 'Ibn Biklārish: Legendary Spanish Physician', *קורות* 15, 79–81 (in Hebrew)

—— 2005. 'Traces of Hebrew Language Traditions in al-Idrīsī's Medical Dictionary', *Lĕšonénu* 67/2, 179–94 (in Hebrew)

Baker, Colin F. 1996. 'Islamic and Jewish Medicine in the Medieval Mediterranean World: The Genizah Evidence', *Journal of the Royal Society of Medicine* 89, 577–80

Bos, Gerrit. 1992. *Quṣtā ibn Lūqā's Medical Regime for the Pilgrims to Mecca.* (Leiden)

Bos, Gerrit and Guido Mensching. 2001. 'Shem Tov Ben Isaac, Glossary of Botanical Terms nrs 1–18', *Jewish Quarterly Review* 92, 21–40

—— 2002. *Maimonides on Asthma: a Parallel Arabic-English Text.* (Provo, Utah)

—— 2005. 'The Literature of Hebrew Medical Synonyms: Romance and Latin Terms and their Identification', *Aleph* 5, 169–211

Chipman, Leigh N. and Efraim Lev. 2006. 'Syrup from the Apothecary's Shop: A Genizah Fragment Containing one of the Earliest Manuscripts of *Minhāj al-Dukkān*', *Journal of Semitic Studies* 50/1, 137–67

—— 2008. 'Take a Lame and Decrepit Female Hyena...: A Genizah Study of Two Additional Fragments of Manuscripts of Sābūr Ibn Sahl's *al-Aqrābādhīn al-Ṣaghīr*', *Early Science and Medicine* 13/4, 361–83

Cohen, Mark R. 1993. 'The Burdensome Life of a Jewish Physician and Communal Leader: A Geniza Fragment from the Alliance Israélite Universelle Collection', *Jerusalem Studies in Arabic and Islam* 16, 125–36

Dietrich, Albert. 1954. *Zum Drogenhandel im Islamischen Ägypten.* (Heidelberg)

Dozy, Reinhart P.A. 1881. *Supplément aux dictionnaires arabes.* 2 vols, (Leiden)

Ducros, M.A.H. 1930. *Essai sur le droguier populaire arabe de l'inspectorat des pharmacies du Caire.* (Mémoires Présentés à l'Institut d'Égypte 15, Cairo)

Dvorjetski, Esti. 1990. 'The Contribution of the Geniza to the Study of the Medicinal Hot Springs in Eretz-Israel', in R. Margolin *et al.* (eds), *Proceedings of the Twelfth World Congress of Jewish Studies.* 2 vols, (Jerusalem), vol. 2, 85–93

Fenton, Paul. 1980. 'The Importance of the Cairo Genizah for the History of Medicine', *Medical History* 24, 347–8

Geva-Kleinberger, Aharon and Efraim Lev. 2009. 'Language Passivity in the Medical Arabic and Judaeo-Arabic Prescriptions of the Cairo Genizah', *Journal of Semitic Studies* 54/2, 435–58

Gigandet, Suzanne. 2001. *La Risāla al-Hārūniyya de Masīḥ B. Ḥakam Al-Dimašqī: Médecin.* (Damascus)

Goitein, Shlomo D. 1963. 'The Medical Profession in the Light of the Cairo Genizah Documents', *Hebrew Union College Annual* 34, 177–94

—— 1967–93. *A Mediterranean Society: The Jewish Communities of the Arab World as Portrayed in the Documents of the Cairo Geniza*. 6 vols, (Berkeley)

Gunther, Robert T., *The Greek Herbal of Dioscorides*. (New York)

Ibn al-Bayṭar. 1874. *Kitab al-Jami' li-mufradat al-adwiya wa'l-aghdhiya*. 4 vols, (Cairo)

Isaacs, Haskell D. 1979–80. 'The Impact of Western Medicine on Muslim Physicians and their Writing in the 17th Century', *Bulletin of the British Association of Orientalists* 11, 52–7

—— 1991. 'A Medieval Arab Medical Certificate', *Medical History* 35, 250–7

—— (with the assistance of C.F. Baker). 1994. *Medical and Para-Medical Manuscripts in the Cambridge Genizah Collections*. (Cambridge)

Issa Bey, Ahmed. 1930. *Dictionnaire des noms des plantes en latin, français,anglais et arabe*. (Cairo)

Lev, Efraim. 2003. *Medicinal Substances in Jerusalem from Early Times to the Present Day*. (Oxford)

—— 2004. 'Work in Progress – the Research of Medical Knowledge in the Cairo Genizah – Past, Present and Future', in S.C. Reif (ed.), *The Written Word Remains – The Archive and the Achievement: Taylor-Schechter Genizah Research Unit at Cambridge University Library* (Cambridge). 37–51

—— 2007. 'Drugs Held and Sold by Pharmacists of the Jewish Community of Medieval (11th–14th Centuries) Cairo According to Lists of *Materia Medica* Found at the Taylor-Schechter Genizah collection, Cambridge', *Journal of Ethnopharmacology* 110, 275–93

Lev, Efraim and Zohar Amar. 2000. 'Ethnopharmacological Survey of Traditional Drugs Sold in Israel at the End of the 20th Century', *Journal of Ethnopharmacology* 72, 191–205

—— 2002a. 'Ethnopharmacological Survey of Traditional Drugs Sold in the Kingdom of Jordan', *Journal of Ethnopharmacology* 82, 131–45

—— 2002b. *Ethnic Medicinal Substances of the Land of Israel*. (Jerusalem) (in Hebrew)

—— 2006. 'Reconstruction of the Inventory of *Materia Medica* Used by Members of the Jewish Community of Medieval Cairo According to Prescriptions Found in the Taylor-Schechter Genizah Collection, Cambridge', *Journal of Ethnopharmacology* 108, 428–44

—— 2007. 'Medieval *Materia Medica* – Practice vs. Theory – the Case of the Cairo Genizah', *Medical History* 51, 507–26

—— 2008. *Practical Materia Medica of the Medieval Eastern Mediterranean According to the Cairo Genizah*. (Leiden)

Lev, Efraim, Leigh Chipman and Friedrich Niessen. 2008. 'A Hospital Handbook for the Community: Evidence for the Extensive Use of Ibn Abī 'l-Bayān's *al-Dustūr al-bīmāristānī* by the Jewish practitioners of Medieval Cairo', *Journal of Semitic Studies* 53/1, 103–18

Lev, Efraim and Leigh N. Chipman. 2007. 'Fragments of Judeo-Arabic Manuscripts of Sābūr Ibn Sahl *al-Aqrābādhīn al-Ṣaghīr* Found in the Taylor-Schechter Cairo Genizah Collection', *Medieval Encounter* 13, 347–62

Levey, Martin. 1966. *Medieval Arabic Toxicology*. (Philadelphia)

—— 1973. *Early Arabic Pharmacology*. (Leiden)

Meyerhof, Max. 1918. 'Der Bazar der Drogen und Wohlgerüche in Kairo', *Archiv für Wirtschaftsforschung im Orient (Weimar)*, 1–40, 185–218

—— 1935. 'Esquisse d'histoire de la pharmacologie et botanique chez les musulmans d'Espagne', *al-Andalus* 3, 1–41

—— 1940. *Un glossaire de matière médicale de Maimonide*. (Mémoires Présentés à l'Institut d'Égypte 41, Cairo)

Muntner, Süssmann. 1942. *Moses Maimonides / Poisons and their Antidotes*. (Jerusalem) (in Hebrew)

—— 1969. *Moses Maimonides / Lexicography of Drugs*. (Jerusalem) (in Hebrew)

Niessen, Friedrich and Efraim Lev. 2008. 'Addenda to Isaacs' Catalogue 'Medical and Para-Medical Manuscripts in the Cambridge Genizah Collections Together with the Edition of Two Medical Documents T-S 12.33 and T-S NS 297.56', *Hebrew Union College Annual* 77, 131–65

Rosner, Fred. 1995. *Moses Maimonides' Glossary of Drug Names*. (Haifa)

Rosner, Fred and Süssmann Muntner. 1970–71. *The Medical Aphorisms of Moses Maimonides*. (New York)

Saqqa, Mustafa. 1975. *Malik al-Muzaffar Yusuf Ibn 'Umar / Al-Mu'tamad fi al-adwiya al-mufrada.* (Beirut)

Stern, Samuel M. 1956–66. *Maimonidis Commentarius in Mischnam*. 3 vols, (Copenhagen)

Ullmann, Manfred. 1978. *Islamic Medicine*. (Edinburgh)

Four Amulets and an Exorcism from the Rylands Genizah Collection

Gideon Bohak and Renate Smithuis

Tel-Aviv University University of Manchester

Like any other Genizah collection, the Rylands Genizah contains several types of magical texts, such as amulets, magical recipes and mystical texts with magical elements. The fragments tend to be rather small, but nevertheless we have been able to extract from them some very interesting historical material. In the present article we wish to demonstrate some of the diversity of the collection by editing and translating four medieval and early modern amulets and a remarkable early modern exorcism aimed at exorcizing from a widow who is about to re-marry the ghost of her late husband.

In transcribing and translating the fragments, we have used the following *sigla*:

[ ] Lacunae and hypothetical reconstruction of the text

? Reading of preceding letter uncertain

{ } Deletions from the original text

< > Interlinear glosses and other additions to the original text

An Amulet for Abū Saʿd ben Baladayn (B 6755 and B 6757)

It is clear that fragments B 6755 (which measures 142 x 89 mm) and B 6757 (103 x 41 mm) are from one and the same amulet. They are written in the same hand on the same type of paper with similar vertical fold lines, and their versos are both blank (see Plates 1–2). They also are very close in contents, for they are both parts of an amulet in which the same two names occur: Abū Saʿd and Abū Fatḥ. And the fact that their numbers are almost consecutive probably shows that they 'travelled' together to the Rylands collection, and may even have still been a single fragment a few decades or a century ago.

When one compares the right margins of the rectos of these two fragments, one notices that the right margin of B 6757 is considerably wider than that of B 6755, which probably shows that the original amulet was written on an irregular piece of paper, torn off a larger sheet, quite a common occurrence in this type of texts. Be that as it may, the join proposed here is corroborated both by the smooth flow of the text on the recto and by the creases and fold lines which are visible on the verso of the entire amulet. We can thus determine the original size of the fragment as approximately 144 x 115 mm. When joined together, B 6755 and B 6757 make up about 80 per cent of the original piece of paper, and will henceforth be treated as a single fragment. The text is relatively well preserved, but is not always easy to decipher, given the many lacunae, the irregularity and hurried nature of the script, and the presence of a few interlinear insertions and glosses, in a different ink.

The complete page consisted of a single amulet, the purpose of which was to give charm and grace to Abū Saʿd ben Baladayn (אבוסעד בן בלדין), and protect him against his enemy Abu'l-Fatḥ Naṣr Allah ibn Maʿrāḍ (אבו אלפתח נצר אללה אבן מעראץ). Another amulet for the same individual may be found in the Cambridge University Library — Or.1080 5.4, and was published by Peter Schäfer and Shaul Shaked (Schäfer and Shaked 1994, I: 151–9, with plates on 285–6).[1] The Cambridge amulet is, except for one Judaeo-Arabic formula, written in Hebrew and Aramaic, whereas our amulet is written mostly in Judaeo-Arabic, and there is little textual overlap between the two amulets, except for the Hebrew opening formula יהי רצון מלפניך ('May it be your will'), and the phrase מן אליום אלי אבד אלאבד אמן אמן סלה סלה ('from this day forever and ever Amen Amen Sela Sela'). Like our amulet, the Cambridge amulet seeks to protect אבוסעד בן בלדין against his enemies and to prevent them from thinking or speaking evil of him, but unlike our amulet it does not name any specific opponents. However, as far as we can tell the two amulets were written by the same person, as may be judged both from the shape of the individual letters and from the way in which the written text on both amulets tends to slope downwards towards the ends of the lines. If this observation is correct, we have here a client who went to the same amulet producer and obtained two different amulets, probably on two different occasions. And like many other amulets worn and used by the Jews of medieval Cairo, this one too ended up in the Cairo Genizah.[2]

The Cambridge amulet was dated by Schäfer and Shaked to the middle of the twelfth century, and Edna Engel dated both the Cambridge and Manchester amulets to the twelfth–thirteenth centuries. Unfortunately, all our attempts to identify Abū Saʿd ben Baladayn and his enemy, Abu'l-Fatḥ Naṣr Allah ibn Maʿrāḍ, in other Genizah

1 MTKG I, No. 11. For a detailed discussion of amulets for charm and grace see Saar 2008.

2 For other Genizah amulets, and a detailed introduction, see Schiffman and Swartz 1992.

documents (including Goitein's onomastic index cards, available on microfilm at Tel-Aviv University Library) have not met with any success.[3] However, this is not very surprising, since the Genizah amulets and magical texts often identify persons by their mothers' names, while all other Genizah documents use patronymics as the standard means of identification. Thus, it is not impossible that our Abū Saʿd is the same as one of the other people of that name who appear in the Genizah documents, and are identified there by their fathers' names, but we could find no evidence with which to support such an hypothesis.[4] And as for Abu'l-Fatḥ Naṣr Allah ibn Maʿrāḍ, we are again unable to adduce any other occurrence of the (female?) name Maʿrāḍ in other Genizah documents, and are not even sure whether Abū Saʿd's opponent was a Jew or a Muslim. Be this as it may, the significance of our amulet lies mainly in the fact that it joins the previously published Cambridge amulet and shows how two amulets could be written by a single amulet producer for a single client, perhaps on two different occasions.

Text

יהי רצ[ון מלפניך   י]ה?ו?ה[5] אלהי ואלהי אבותי
שתהא[6]]   אב]וסעד <בן בלדין>[7] פיקלב
<אבו אלפתח]   ]> אבן מער?[אץ   ]ל?ה? ענדה חן וחסד>
ורו?ח? ורחמ?[ים   י]ה יה יה יה יה
יה יה יה[אשב]ע?ת על[י]ך חסדיאל[8] המלאך
ועוז?יאל[בקוה ת] ש ר ק צ פ ע ס
נ מ ל כ [י ט ח ז ו ה ד ג ב] א? בקו?[ה] הדה {אלאסמ}[9]
אלאסמא א[א]בוסעד בעיניך

---

3 While the name בלדין is otherwise unattested in the Genizah documents known to us, we assume that it was pronounced Baladayn (as against Schäfer and Shaked's Baldīn), perhaps an apocopated form of Sitt al-Baladein, 'the mistress of the two villages', a common type of name in Genizah documents.

4 For a comprehensive prosopography of Genizah magical texts, including an attempt to identify some of the persons for or against whom magical texts were produced in the non-magical documents from the Cairo Genizah, see Bohak and Saar forthcoming.

5 It should be noted that the Cambridge amulet uses יוי instead of the Tetragrammaton. Relatively much text has been lost here between the two fragments, which suggests that the opening formula was longer than the standard יהי רצון מלפניך יהוה אלהי(נו) ואלהי אבותי(נו).

6 The word שתהא seems to be a correction added with the interlinear glosses.

7 Here and in line 16, it seems as if the scribe first left a blank after Abū Saʿd's name, and only later filled in his mother's name, when he also added the other names between the lines of the original amulet. Presumably, he was aware of his client's name, but not of that of his client's mother, and was aware of only a part of the victim's name, and added the full name only later. See also note 10 below.

8 חסדיאל is frequently found in amulets for charm and grace. See e.g. Schäfer and Shaked 1994, I: 65.

9 It seems as if the scribe began writing אלאסמא, saw that he ran out of space, and started again on the next line.

9 ובעיני כל[ו]אגעל מ?חבתה פי
10 קלבהם ופ[י? קלב?] <[א]בואלפתח נצר אללה> [א]בן מעראץ ותפול
11 עלי <[א]בואלפת[ח נצ]ר? אללה> בן מ?[ערא]ץ?[10]   ועלי כל מן יטלב
12 אן [י]כלם?[11] <אב[ו]סע[ד בן בלד]ין> בכלמ?[ה   ] אמתה ופחד[12] עוזי וזמרת יה?[13]
13 יה ש?מ?יה עליהם תיפול אמתה ופחד[14] בשם
14 יה וזמרת ע[ו]זי   ובקוה ת[15] ש ר ק צ ע
15 ס נ מ ל כ י ט ח ז ו ה ד[ג] ב א בקוה
16 הדה אלאסמא אכ?פי אבוסעד <בן בלדין>
17 [?]ר כל מן יטלב לה אדיה? בשם אהיה
18 אהיה אהיה ובשם אבאביב[16] יה ובשם
19 אדירירון[17] קדוש קדוש אמן אמן אמן
20 מן אליום אלי אבד אלאבד אמן אמן סלה סלה הללויה

Translation

1 May it be your wi[ll   ], the Lord, my God, and the God of my fathers

2 that [the   ] of [Ab]ū Saʿd <ben Baladayn> will be in the heart of

3 <Abu'l-Fatḥ [   ]> Ibn Maʿrāḍ [   ] with him charm and grace

4 and respite(?) and mer[cy   Y]H YH YH YH YH YH

5 YH YH YH [I adju]re you, the angel Ḥasdiel

6 and Uziel [by the power of T] Š R Q Z P ᶜ S

7 N M L K [Y Ṭ Ḥ Z W H D G B] ', by the power of these {name}

8 names [A]bū Saʿd in your eyes

9 and in the eyes of all [and] place love for him in

---

10 The large space after the name might indicate that when the amulet was produced, a space was left blank after בן מעראץ, but the scribe subsequently added the rest of the victim's name, אבו אלפתח נצר אללה between the lines. See also note 7 above.

11 The final *mēm* seems to be a correction to the original text, which may have read יכלמה.

12 Based on Exod. 15:16 (see also note 14 below).

13 Superscript ת. Divine name might also read עזי וזמרת יה ('My strength and song is YH...') found in Exod. 15:2, Isa. 12:2 and Ps. 118:14. This verse appears in other amulets as well. See e.g. Schäfer and Shaked 1994, I: 178, 1b, 2.

14 Exod. 15:16 reads תפל עליהם אימתה ופחד. 'Fear and dread shall fall upon them.' This verse also appears in the Cambridge amulet. See Schäfer and Shaked 1994, I: 222, 9.

15 A little stroke is placed on top of each letter of the alphabet (lines 17–18). Note that the scribe forgot the letter *pēh* in his alphabetical sequence.

16 This name is also known from other amulets. See e.g. Schäfer and Shaked 1994, I: 222, 16, and the following note.

17 This name is also known from other amulets. See e.g. Schäfer and Shaked 1994: I, 31, 1 and 222, 13. Both 'B'BYB and 'DYRYRON appear at the beginnings of two acrostic lists of divine names incorporated in a well-known list of the seventy names of God, and see further Rohrbacher-Sticker 1991/92.

10 their heart and i[n the heart of] <Abu'l-Fatḥ Naṣr Allah> Ibn Maʿrāḍ. And there *shall fall*

11 *upon* <Abu'l-Fatḥ Naṣr Allah> ben M[aʿrāḍ] (vac) and upon all those who wish

12 to [s]peak a [ ] word [against?] <Abū Saʿ[d ben Balad]ayn> *fear and dread. And my strength and song is YH*

13 YH is his name; *upon them shall fall fear and dread* in the name of

14 YH, and song, my strength.[18] And by the power of T Š R Q Ṣ ʿ

15 S N M L K Y Ṭ Ḥ Z W H D [G] B ', by the power of

16 these names, hide Abū Saʿd <ben Baladayn>

17 [from?] all those who wish for him harm(?).[19] By the name Ehyeh

18 Ehyeh Ehyeh and by the name 'B'BYB YH, and by the name

19 'DYRYRWN, Holy, Holy, Holy, amen, amen, amen

20 from this day forever and ever. Amen. Amen. Sela. Sela. Hallelujah.

Summary

While the present amulet is badly mutilated, it has the advantage of joining a previously published amulet prepared by the same person for the same client. Moreover, whereas the Cambridge amulet only seeks to give Abū Saʿd ben Baladayn charm and grace 'in the eyes of the ministers and judges and all who see him (בעיני השרים והשפטים ובעיני כל רואיו)', the Manchester amulet mentions one of these persons by name. In the future, it might even be possible to identify this Abu'l-Fatḥ Naṣr Allah ibn Maʿrāḍ, and thus learn more about the specific social circumstances which led to the production of this specific amulet. But even if the protagonists remain unidentified, the very need of a single person for more than one amulet for charm and grace is a remarkable demonstration of the centrality of such practices in the lives of Jews in medieval Cairo.

---

18 I.e., עזי וזמרת יה written backwards, a common occurrence in Jewish magical texts.

19 We hesitantly take אדיה as اذية, 'damages, troubles, harms'. Another reading, אדיר, Hebrew for 'great' (a common epithet of God) is possible, but does not seem to fit in syntactically. Alternatively, it might be a phonetic pronunciation of ألضير, 'harm, damage'.

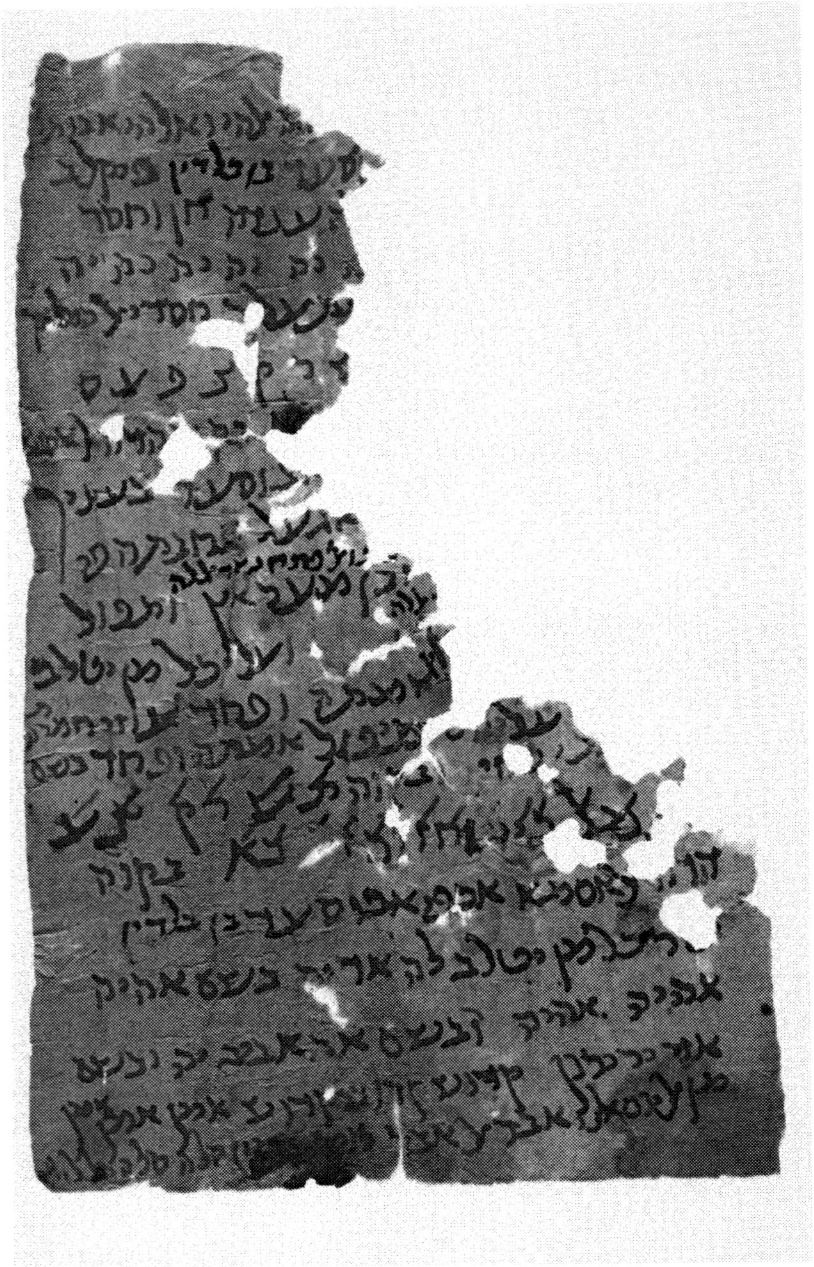

Plate 1: B 6755-1. (Reproduced by courtesy of the University Librarian and Director, The John Rylands Library, The University of Manchester)

Plate 2: B 6757-1. (Reproduced by courtesy of the University Librarian and Director, The John Rylands Library, The University of Manchester)

Three Scorpion Amulets (A 897, A 1252 and B 5682)

Given the pervasiveness and danger of venomous scorpions in much of the Middle East and North Africa, it is hardly surprising that amulets against them were in common use from Antiquity to Modern times.[20] In the Cairo Genizah, the scorpion amulets are extremely common, and they tend to be generic (that is, prepared in advance, and without reference to a specific client), small in size, and quite formulaic in their contents. In some cases, they were 'mass produced' in large quantities, when a scribe took a sheet of paper, wrote upon it numerous identical scorpion amulets side by side, and then tore off one amulet at a time when a client requested such an amulet (Bohak 2009: 35–49). In many others, they were hastily scribbled on small sheets of paper, and presumably worn by children and adults alike in little pouches around their necks or ankles. In more recent times, some scorpion amulets were intended to protect an entire household rather than a single person, and were prominently placed outside one's home or on one's door.[21]

The contents of the Genizah scorpion amulets tend to be quite repetitive, and to consist of the following elements:

1. Word-triangles: A prominent feature of the Genizah scorpion amulets is the use of 'word-triangles', i.e., triangular shapes created by writing a word, name, or meaningless magic word in such a way that in each consecutive line one letter is omitted either at the beginning or at the end of the word or on both sides. The commonest triangles used in scorpion amulets are based on the words אפדירטא (or אפרידיטא), whose origins lie in the Greek word Aphrodite,[22] אפיקורוס, clearly going back to the Greek name Epicurus, perhaps that of the famous philosopher, and אבליגמא, whose origins are still elusive.[23]
2. An adjuration of the scorpion: Another prominent feature of the Genizah scorpion amulets is the adjuration of the scorpion itself not to harm its potential victims. The commonest type of adjuration is 'in the name of Rabbi Judah son of Ezekiel', a Babylonian rabbi of the third century CE whose

---

20 For a useful survey of earlier (non-Jewish) evidence see Dalrymple 2007.

21 For this practice, as observed among the Jews of Morocco in the nineteenth century, see Leared 1876 (repr. 1985): 175–6 and the amulet printed on 177. Leared also explains that such amulets were all written by a rabbi on the first night of Sivan, which might also explain the tendency to 'mass produce' them.

22 For an Aphrodite-triangle on a Christian Greek scorpion amulet see PGM 2, translated in Meyer and Smith 1994: 48–9, no. 25.

23 Note how a nineteenth-century rabbi, Abraham Hamawy (1879: 34b), reports the use of these word-triangles (אפיקורוס אפילוגמא אפיריריטא) in Jewish scorpion amulets, and stresses that their origins or meaning are unknown to him. We owe this reference to Nissim Hamoi, who is writing his Ph.D. on Abraham Hamawy and his magical recipe books.

effective curses against those who offended him (b. Qid. 70a–b, Mo'ed Q. 17a) made him extremely popular in later Jewish curses and excommunications.

3 An image of a scorpion: To enhance their magical efficacy, most of the Genizah scorpion amulets contain an image — often a very crude image — of a scorpion. This sets them apart from all other types of Genizah amulets and magical texts, where iconography of this type is almost entirely unattested.[24] Moreover, this feature clearly was common to the scorpion amulets of 'pagans', Jews, Christians, and Muslims alike from Antiquity to modern times, and — together with their small size — makes the Genizah scorpion amulets look quite like the Greek or Arabic scorpion amulets found in many other manuscript collections.[25]

4. Biblical verses: As in almost all other types of Jewish amulets and magical texts, where the use of biblical verses is pervasive, the scorpion amulets too occasionally add some biblical verses with obvious apotropaic value, to enhance the amulet's efficacy.

In the Manchester Genizah collections, there are several scorpion amulets, and we edit here three typical specimens — two individual amulets and one for an entire household — which join the growing body of published and unpublished scorpion amulets from the Cairo Genizah.[26] We have asked Dr Edna Engel to date these fragments, and she suggested that A 1252 might be the earliest specimen, dating from the thirteenth or fourteenth century, although it might also be from a later date. B 5682 possibly comes next chronologically, probably dating from the beginning of the sixteenth century, or otherwise from the fifteenth century. A 897 clearly is a later fragment, which was written no earlier than the sixteenth century. In what follows, we have ordered the amulets in accordance with this chronological sequence.

A 1252

This paper fragment (93 x 64 mm) has numerous holes, which do not really disrupt the reading. The verso is blank. This is a very simple scorpion amulet with only two word-triangles — the אבליגמא–triangle in its standard form and a garbled and abridged version of the אפרידיטא–triangle — written in large semi-cursive script and a

24 In other types of Jewish magical texts one occasionally finds images of scorpions, but their functions there seem to be quite different. For a pertinent example see Levene 2002: 23, fig. 10.

25 For a Greek example (PGM CXIII), see Daniel and Maltomini 1990, I: 46, no. 17, which was translated by Kotansky in Betz 1992: 313. For Arabic examples, see Froschauer and Römer 2009: 120–2, nos 57–61 and colour plates 4 and 7.

26 To the three examples published by Bohak 2009 may now be added T–S NS 31.37; NS 172.75; NS 293.9; AS 143.287; AS 186.48; AS 202.255; Paris, AIU VI.C.11; VI.C.20. One more Manchester fragment, B 5404, seems like a scorpion amulet, but is too mutilated to be published here.

beautifully clear picture of a scorpion.[27] It probably comes from the same sheet of 'mass produced' amulets as T–S NS 293.9 (unpublished), which is *c.* 88 x 69 mm and displays exactly the same text and design and clearly was produced by the very same hand as the Manchester amulet.

1	'BLYGM'	'PRWDW
2	BL[Y]GM'	PRWDW
3	LY[G]M'	RWDW
4	YGM'	WDW
5	GM'	DW
6	M'	W
7	'	
	(A drawing of a scorpion)	

1	אבליגמא	אפרודו
2	בל[י]גמא	פרודו
3	לי[ג]מא	רודו
4	יגמא	ודו
5	גמא	דו
6	מא	ו
7	א	
	(ציור של עקרב)	

B 5682

The bottom left corner of this paper fragment (87 x 91mm) is missing, and there are a few tiny holes. The verso is blank. This amulet is written in a hasty, unsophisticated cursive hand. It contains the three word-triangles which commonly appear on the scorpion amulets (though in all three cases the producer did not bother to complete the triangles all the way to the bottom), as well as the most common formula of adjuration of the harmful scorpion. But unlike most scorpion amulets, it contains no image. It may have come from a 'mass produced' sheet of amulets, as its text is nearly identical with that of T–S NS 172.75 (unpublished), which measures *c.* 72 x 74 mm and is written by the same hand as this one.

1	'BLYGM'	'PRYDYṬ'	'PYQWRWS
2	BLYGM'	PRYDYṬ'	PYQWRWS
3	LYGM'	RYDYṬ'	YQWRWS
4	GM'	YDYṬ'	QWRWS
5	M'	YDṬ'	WRWS
6		DṬ'	RWS
7		Ṭ'	
8	You scorpion son of a scorpion shall be under the excommunication		

1	אבליגמא	אפרידיטא	אפיקורוס
2	בליגמא	פרידיטא	פיקורוס
3	ליגמא	רידיטא	יקורוס
4	גמא	ידיטא	קורוס
5	מא	ידטא	ורוס
6		דטא	רוס
7		טא	
8	עקרב בן עקרב תהא בשמתא		

27 For online images of the Rylands Genizah fragments see http://enriqueta.man.ac.uk /luna/servlet/ManchesterDev~95~2

9	of the rabbis, of Rav Judah son of Ezekiel, that you shall not	9 דרבנן דרב יהודה בר יחזקאל דלא
10	harm in this house and this town? ???? fr[om]	10 תזיק בביתא הדין ובמת?א דא? ב?נ?י?ר?[28] מ[ן]
11	this day and forever. [Amen Amen]	11 יומא דנן ולעלם [אמן אמן][29]

A 897

This is a well preserved paper fragment (101 x 112 mm) but for a few tiny holes and some effacement of the ink. The verso is blank. Being somewhat larger and displaying a more spacious layout than the other two fragments, this one is less likely to be a 'mass-produced' amulet. It is nicely executed in a cursive hand with the three traditional word-triangles (though two of the 'words' got slightly garbled), a drawing of two schematic scorpions at the bottom of the page, and the addition of two apotropaic verses from the book of Psalms. An unusual feature of this specific amulet is the adjuration of the scorpion not in the name of R. Judah son of Ezekiel, but of R. Judah the Prince (the famous editor of the Mishnah), as well as the spelling of his name as יאודה rather than יהודה.

1	===	===[30] 1
2	*The angel of the Lord encamps around those who fear him, and delivers them.*	2 חונה מלאך ה' סביב ליריאיו ויחלצם[31]
3	*For he shall give his angels charge over you, to guard you in all your ways.*	3 כי מלאכיו יצוה לך לשמרך בכל דרכיך[32]

4	'PRYGM'	'PYQWRWS	'PRYṬM'	אפריטמא	אפיקורוס	אפריגמא	4
5	PRYGM'	PYQWRWS	PRYṬM'	פריטמא	פיקורוס	פריגמא	5
6	RYGM'	YQWRWS	RYṬM'	ריטמא	יקורוס	ריגמא	6
7	YGM'	QWRWS	YṬM'	יטמא	קורוס	יגמא	7
8	GM'	WRWS	ṬM'	טמא	ורוס	גמא	8
9	M'	RWS	M'	מא	רוס	מא	9
10	'	WS	'	א	וס	א	10
11		S			ס		11

---

28 One would expect מתא דא קהיר or even מתא דקאהיר, but this is not what the text seems to say.

29 Only a tiny section of the top part of these words is preserved, but a comparison with T–S NS 172.75 makes this reconstruction certain.

30 Unfortunately, we cannot make out the meaning of this ligature or monogram.

31 Ps. 34:8.

32 Ps. 91:11.

12 Be banned and excommunicated from the mouth of Rabbi Judah the Prince, you scorpion daughter of a scorpion,	12 תהא בחרם ובשמתא מפומיה דרבי יאודה נשיאה עקרבת בת עקרבת]
13 that you shall not come out, and if you come out you shall not harm and if you harm, you shall not kill anyone of this house.	13 דלא תפוק ואי תפוק לא תזיק ואי תזיק לא תקטול לחד מן הדין בית[א]
(A schematic drawing of two scorpions)	(ציור סכמאטי של שני עקרבים)

Summary

While none of these amulets is of great historical or artistic value, their great frequency is a clear testimony not only of the fear of scorpions in the medieval and modern Near East, but also of the pervasive Jewish belief in the power of amulets. Moreover, these amulets furnish yet another example of how the Jewish magical tradition incorporated 'pagan' Greek or Greco-Egyptian magical technology (including the use of word-triangles, and especially with words like Aphrodite!), with Jewish materials (such as the ban in the name of R. Judah son of Ezekiel), and produced magical artefacts which were not that different from those produced by the Jews' neighbours at the very same time. Of course, since the scorpion amulets are always 'generic' and contain no mention of the client's name, we cannot tell who wore or used them, but it seems quite likely that Jews, Christians and Muslims all shared the production and use of these and similar amulets.

An Exorcism (A 643)

Of all the magic-related fragments in the collections of the Rylands Library, the present fragment is perhaps the most interesting, by virtue of its unique nature. However, to understand its uniqueness, we must first briefly survey Early-Modern Jewish exorcisms and the sources currently available for their academic study.

In a recent book, J.H. Chajes (2003) describes the fascinating world of Jewish men and women possessed by spirits, and the exorcists who tried to alleviate their afflictions, from the sixteenth century and onwards.[33] He notes that accounts of spirit possessions start to appear around the second half of the sixteenth century (from the 1540s), when, after a very long hiatus in which there are no reports of Jewish

33 For other recent studies of this theme, see the essays in Goldish 2003.

exorcisms, a remarkable surge in such narratives occurred which lasted until deep into the seventeenth century. Typical regions where cases of spirit possession were reported are Palestine/Syria, Italy and North Africa, with the Kabbalistic centre of Safed as one of the main places from which possession stories emanated. The accounts were often carefully written and sent in the form of broadsheets to the wider world by Kabbalistic rabbis, and their edifying and propagandistic aspects are readily apparent.[34] In these stories both men and women — but mostly women rather than men — began to suffer from a variety of mental and physical afflictions after the roaming soul of a deceased person has lodged itself temporarily in their body.[35] Thus, unlike earlier Jewish exorcisms, which usually consisted of the expulsion of a malevolent demon out of its hapless victim, in these later Jewish exorcisms it is a ghost — usually the ghost of a recently deceased person — which entered a victim and had to be expelled.[36] The belief system behind this practice was the Kabbalistic doctrine of the transmigration of souls (*gilgûl*), which already appears in *Sēfer ha-Bāhîr* (twelfth century) and which was further developed by the Safed kabbalists, and especially by Isaac Luria (the Ari) and his disciple Ḥayyîm Vital. According to this doctrine, the entry of the soul of a deceased person into a living person was a way for that soul to atone for its past sins, but also a source of great danger to the person into whom it entered, hence the need to expel it as swiftly as possible. To do so, the victims sometimes were brought before professional exorcists, including even Muslim or Christian experts, but more often they were brought before a Jewish holy man (a *Ba'al Shem*, a 'Master of [God's] Name') or a rabbi, or even a group of rabbis, who performed the exorcistic ritual as a kind of public spectacle, which often took place in the synagogue. It is these kinds of spectacles that generated the eye-witness accounts and stories collected by Nigal and analysed by Chajes and others, and that served as the inspiration for Ansky's famous play, *The Dibbûq*.

In addition to such reports, we also have a second source of information on the procedures involved in such exorcisms, namely, the exorcistic formulae used by the exorcists themselves, be they the reports of Ḥayyîm Vital of the ritual procedures he learned from Isaac Luria, the exorcistic formulae found in numerous manuscripts of so-called 'practical Kabbalah', or the information provided by those rabbis who

34 For a useful collection of such accounts see Nigal 1994, whose own introduction (pp. 11–60) provides an excellent survey of many aspects of these exorcism-stories.

35 For the gendered aspects of these *dibbûq*-stories, see Chajes 2003: 97–118 and Elior 2008.

36 For the Jewish exorcisms of earlier periods see Eshel 1999; Seidel 2003: 73–95; Bohak 2008: 88–114.

discussed the halakhic contexts or implications of such rituals.[37] The combination of these different types of sources enables a general reconstruction of the procedures involved. These included both the attempt to get in contact with the possessing spirit in order to find out who it had been in a former life and why it had entered its victim, and the attempt to scare it out with threats, adjurations, fumigations, and even physical violence, and/or to draw it out with promises of prayers on its behalf or other assistance in its attempts to be absolved of its sins and thus stop the process of transmigration.

The reports of successful exorcisms and the recommendations and magical recipes for exorcizing ghosts are extremely valuable sources of information, but a third type of sources, namely, the actual spells used in any specific case, has so far been lacking. Hence the importance of the following fragment, A 643 (Plate 3), which seems to contain just such a text. It is a well-preserved piece of light-coloured paper, measuring 149 x 115 mm, and is written on one side only, in a neat cursive Sephardic hand. According to Dr Edna Engel, the handwriting points to the second half of the sixteenth century or thereafter, which fits well with the general historical occurrence of possession, as outlined above. Unfortunately, it is difficult to deduce the place of origin of this piece, although the first possibility which one should consider — assuming that this is a Cairo Genizah fragment — is of course Cairo.[38] That it comes from somewhere in the Arabic-speaking world seems clear enough from the name of one of the main protagonists, Qamar (the Arabic word for 'Moon'), daughter of Raḥma (Arabic for 'Mercy'). Another protagonist, Nissîm son of בוניה, has a Hebrew name, but his mother's name seems to be Spanish, which would fit well within the context of the post-1492 Ottoman Empire. The third protagonist, Joseph Moses son of Sarah, has two Hebrew names, and his mother too had a Hebrew name. Thus, while we cannot tell where exactly this social drama took place, Egypt or Palestine would be the most likely candidates.

Unfortunately, no details are provided of the exact relations between the three protagonists who figure in our piece, but the most likely scenario would be that Nissîm ben Bôniyâ and Qamar bat Raḥma had once been married, and when he died, and she remarried, his ghost had to be kept away from her so that it would do no harm to her or to her new husband, Joseph Moses ben Sarah. The latter probably had been married at least once before, since the ghost is explicitly told not to harm his children.

37 For Vital's exorcistic practices, see Benayahu 1967: 290–306.

38 For the Genizah fragments of this 'post-classical' period and their significance for the study of Kabbalah see Benayahu 1980.

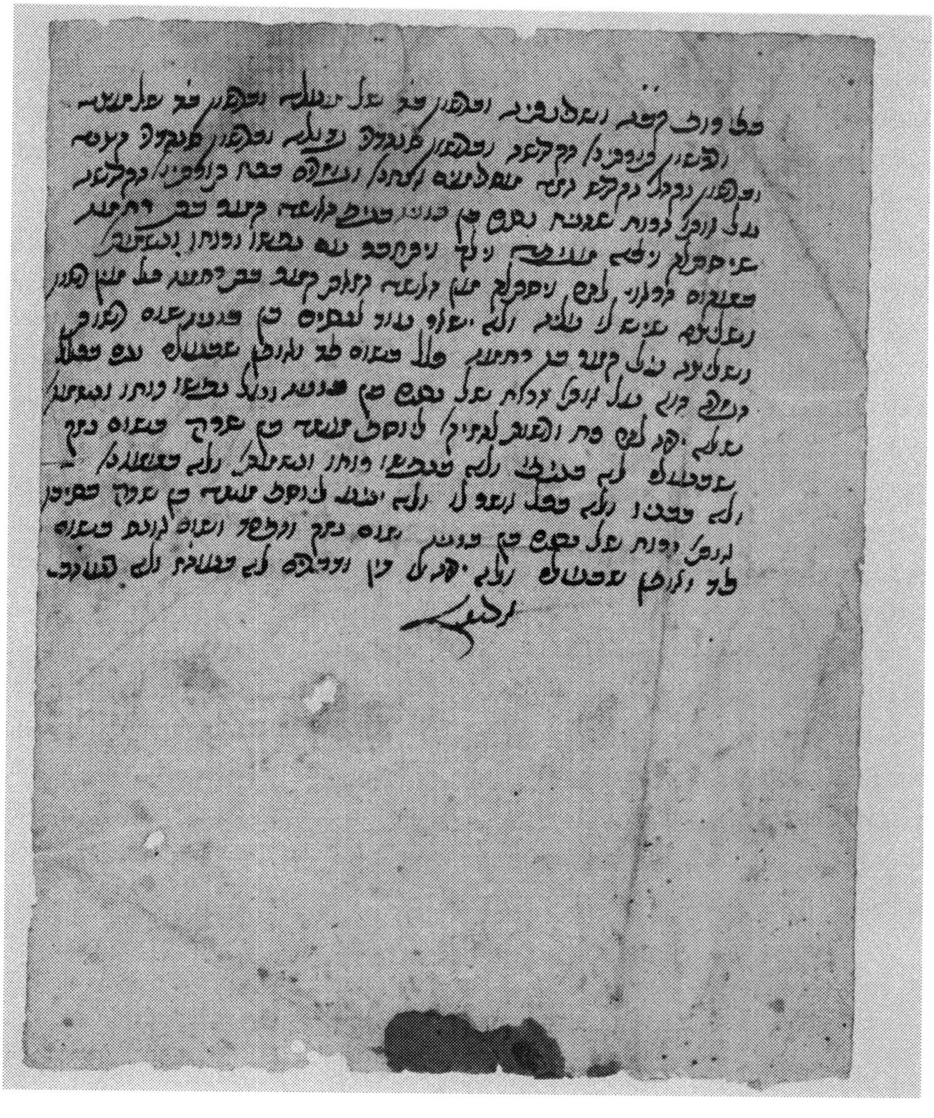

Plate 3: A 643-1. (Reproduced by courtesy of the University Librarian and Director, The John Rylands Library, The University of Manchester)

That this indeed is the likeliest scenario is made clear by an elaborate ritual described by R. Yaʿaqôv Š^{e}ʾaltîʾēl Nîniyô (first half of the nineteenth century) in 1843 (Nîniyô 1843: 112b–113a).[39] The ritual, attributed to the famous Kabbalist Rabbi Šālôm Šarʿabî (1720–77), was influenced by the idea expressed in the Zohar that a man's spirit enters his wife upon the first consummation of their marriage, not to leave her even after his death, and thus poses a great danger to anyone who marries a widow.[40] Thus, the ritual seeks to solve this problem by exorcizing the 'remains' of her later husband from a widow who is about to be re-married.[41] It involves a gathering of ten men (a *minyān*), before whom the husband explains the situation, and prays that God would protect him from the ghost of his wife's late husband. His hearers then respond, reciting a prayer which clearly is the same text as we find in our fragment, with only the slightest of differences, all of which are noted below. But, of course, where the formula adduced by Nîniyô only has *P(*^{e}*lônî) B(ar/Bat) P(*^{e}*lônît)* (so-and-so son/daughter of so-and-so), our fragment provides the names of the actual protagonists and of their mothers, as is the norm in non-Jewish and Jewish magical texts from antiquity to the present.[42]

If R. Šālôm Šarʿabî indeed composed the entire ritual *de novo*, then our fragment clearly cannot predate the middle of the eighteenth century. If, however, the fragment is older, it would prove that Šarʿabî did not compose this adjuration formula himself, but borrowed it from existing sources, or that the attribution itself is spurious, quite a common occurrence in this type of texts. Be that as it may, the Rylands exorcism seems to be a unicum, since we are not aware of any other examples of this kind of exorcism in any other Genizah collection.[43]

1 בצירוף קב"ה ושכינתיה וברשות ב"ד של מעלה וברשות ב"ד של מטה
2 וברשות תורתינו הקדושה וברשות סנהדרי גדולה וברשות סנהדרי קטנה
3 וברשות הקהל הקדוש הזה מסכימים אנחנו וגוזרים בכח תורתינו הקדושה
4 על אותו הרוח שהניח נסים בן בוניה[44] בגוף האשה[45] קמר בת רחמה

39 The ritual is also discussed by Margalioth 1931, who reprints the text on 16a–b. We are grateful to Boaz Huss for alerting us to this source and the ones mentioned in the next footnote.

40 See Zohar משפטים 2.101b–102b. This issue was much discussed by later kabbalists, including Ḥayyim Vital, *שער הפסוקים* to כי תצא and Isaiah Horowitz, *שני לוחות הברית* to the same Torah portion (in both cases, in a section titled סוד הייבום והחליצה).

41 For Šarʿabî and his successors see Giller 2008, who does not discuss our ritual.

42 For using the mother's name, see Bohak 2008: 286.

43 Gideon Bohak is presently working on a catalogue of the magical texts from the Cairo Genizah, based on a hand-list prepared by Shaul Shaked and on his own survey of the entire Cambridge Genizah collection, which includes *c.* 70 per cent of all Genizah fragments worldwide. And see Bohak 2010.

44 Nîniyô 1843: 113a adds נ"ע, 'May he rest in paradise'.

5 שיסתלק ויצא מגופה וילך ויתחבר עם נפשו ורוחו ונשמתו
6 במקום הראוי להם ויסתלק מן האשה הזאת קמר בת רחמה כל מין רשות
7 ושליטה שיש לו עליה ולא ישאר עוד לנסים בן בוניה[46] שום רשות
8 ושליטה על[47] קמר בת רחמה כלל בשום צד ואופן שבעולם וגם בכלל
9 הגזרה הוא[48] על אותו הרוח של נסים בן בוניה ועל נפשו רוחו ונשמתו
10 שלא יהיה להם כח ורשות להזיקו ליוסף משה בן שרה[49] בשום נזק
11 שבעולם לא בגופו ולא בנפשו רוחו ונשמתו ולא בממונו
12 ולא בבניו[50] ולא בכל אשר לו ולא יגיע ליוסף משה בן שרה בסיבת
13 אותו הרוח של נסים בן בוניה שום נזק והפסד ושום אונס[51] בשום
14 צד ואופן שבעולם ולא יהיה לו[52] דין ודברים לא בעוה"ז ולא בעוה"ב
15 אכי"ר[53]>

Translation

1 By the joining of the Holy One, blessed be He, and his Šᵉkînâh, and by the authority of the Heavenly Court and by the authority of the Earthly Court,

2 and by the authority of our Holy Torah, and by the authority of the Great Sanhedrin, and by the authority of the Small Sanhedrin,

3 and by the authority of this holy congregation, we agree and decree by the power of our Holy Torah

4 upon that spirit which Nissîm ben Bôniyâh has left inside the body of the woman Qamar bat Raḥma,

5 that it shall leave her body and shall go and reunite with his (vital) soul, his spirit and his (rational) soul

6 in the place which is appropriate for them, and that it shall leave this woman, Qamar bat Raḥma, (and forego) all authority

7 and control that it has over her; and Nissîm ben Bôniyâh shall have no more authority

8 and control whatsoever over Qamar bat Raḥma in any form or manner at all. And also included

9 in the decree upon that spirit of Nissîm ben Bôniyâh and upon his (vital) soul, his spirit and his (rational) soul

10 that they shall have no power or authority to harm Joseph Moses ben Sarah in any way

11 at all, neither his body, nor his (vital) soul, his spirit or his (rational) soul, nor his finances,

---

45 Nîniyô 1843 adds הזאת, 'this (woman)'.

46 Nîniyô 1843 adds הנז', 'the above-mentioned'.

47 Nîniyô 1843 adds האשה, 'the woman'.

48 Nîniyô 1843 has היא.

49 Nîniyô 1843 adds 'may the Lord protect and save him'.

50 Nîniyô 1843 reverses the order, ולא בבניו כשיהיה לו ולא בממונו, 'nor his sons (if he has any) nor his finances'.

51 Nîniyô 1843 has עונש, 'punishment'.

52 Nîniyô 1843 has עמו.

53 Nîniyô 1843 has a different ending formula, אמן נצח סלה ועד, 'Amen, (for) eternity, Selah, forever'.

12 nor his sons or all that he possesses, and no harm or loss shall come to Joseph Moses ben Sarah because of

13 this spirit of Nissîm ben Bôniyâh, and no compulsion in any

14 form or manner at all, and he shall have no legal cause (against him), neither in this world nor in the world to come.

15 Amen, may it be Thy will.

Summary

The exorcism on A 643 is a striking find in the Rylands Genizah. Neatly written on a small piece of paper, the Hebrew text of the exorcism is relatively easy to understand and contextualize, but is, as far as we know, a unique example of an exorcism written and used at an actual ceremony. In this case, the '*dibbûq*' is the ghost of a dead husband, which had to be expelled from the troubled widow in order to assure that neither she nor her future husband are damaged by it. Our fragment preserves the formulaic answer to the husband's prayer, as uttered and apparently also written by the other members of the *minyān* gathered for this occasion. It follows more or less exactly the wording of such a prayer ascribed to the famous Yemenite Kabbalist Rabbi Šālôm Šarʿabî, who attracted a large circle of followers in Jerusalem soon after his arrival there and became the pillar of the Kabbalistic *yᵉšibâ* of Beit El. Regardless of whether he indeed composed this prayer or not, our fragment provides important evidence for the spread and use of Kabbalistic *dibbûq*-exorcisms in Oriental Jewish society in the early modern and modern periods.

Conclusions

The five fragments published here are a very mixed bag — one amulet for charm and grace of the twelfth or thirteenth century, three scorpion-amulets of the thirteenth to sixteenth century or even later, and one exorcism from the second half of the sixteenth century or later. The relative lateness of these fragments fits well with the overall picture we have of the Rylands Genizah, consisting of parts of the personal acquisitions of Moses Gaster. Thus it is not unusual to find in his collection fragments dating even from the eighteenth and nineteenth centuries, but these fragments too are of great historical value. And as this paper illustrates, the earlier layers of the Cairo Genizah also are well represented in the Rylands collection, including one amulet for a person whose other amulet is found in the Cambridge Genizah collections, and two scorpion-amulets probably torn off the same 'mass produced' pages as two Cambridge amulets. In the future, more such links and joins between the Rylands magical texts and those of other Genizah collections are likely to emerge.

The five fragments published here are but a small sample of the magical texts from the Cairo Genizah, and — apart from the last fragment — are not very unusual. And yet, they too deserve their day in court, since more than any other documents these humble amulets show how pervasive was the recourse to amulets and magic in Genizah society, a fact which Genizah scholars of earlier generations often tended to ignore.

References

Benayahu, Meir. 1967. *ספר תולדות האר"י: גלגולי נוסחאותיו וערכו מבחינה היסטורית נוספו עליו הנהגות האר"י ואזכרות ראשונות* (Jerusalem)

—— 1980. 'The Significance of the Geniza Documents of the Sixteenth-Eighteenth Centuries', in M.A. Friedman (ed.), *Cairo Geniza Studies* (Tel Aviv). 161–8 (in Hebrew)

Betz, Hans Dieter (ed.). 1992 *The Greek Magical Papyri in Translation, Including the Demotic Spells*[2]. (Chicago)

Bohak, Gideon. 2008. *Ancient Jewish Magic: A History*. (Cambridge)

—— 2009. 'Some "Mass Produced" Scorpion-Amulets from the Cairo Genizah', in Zuleika Rodgers, Margaret Daly-Denton and Anne Fitzpatrick McKinley (eds), *A Wandering Galilean: Essays in Honor of Seán Freyne* (Supplements to the Journal for the Study of Judaism 132, Leiden). 35–49

—— 2010. 'Towards a Catalogue of the Magical, Astrological, Divinatory and Alchemical Fragments from the Cambridge Genizah Collections', in Ben Outhwaite and Siam Bhayro (eds), *'From a Sacred Source': Genizah Studies in Honour of Professor Stefan C. Reif* (Études sur le Judaïsme Médiéval 42; Cambridge Genizah Studies Series 1, Leiden). 53–79

Bohak, Gideon and Ortal-Paz Saar. Forthcoming. 'Genizah Magical Texts Prepared For or Against Named Individuals', *Revue des études juives*

Chajes, J.H. 2003. *Between Worlds: Dybbuks, Exorcists, and Early Modern Judaism*. (Philadelphia)

Dalrymple, Jon. 2007. 'Snakes and Scorpions in Late Antique Egypt: Remarks on Papyri Documenting Envenomation', in Jaakko Frösén, Tiina Purola and Erja Salmenkivi (eds), *Proceedings of the 24th International Congress of Papyrology (Helsinki, 1–7 August, 2004)*. 2 vols, (Commentationes Humanarum Litterarum 122, Helsinki). Vol. 1: 205–13

Daniel, Robert W. and Franco Maltomini. 1990–2. *Supplementum Magicum: Edited with Translations and Notes*. 2 vols, (Papyrologica Coloniensia 16, Opladen)

Elior, Rachel. 2008. *Dybbuks and Jewish Women in Social History, Mysticism and Folklore*, trans. Joel Linsider. (Jerusalem and New York)

Eshel, Esther. 1999. 'Demonology in Palestine during the Second Temple Period'. Unpublished Ph.D. dissertation, The Hebrew University (in Hebrew)

Froschauer, Harald and Cornelia Römer. 2009. *Zwischen Magie und Wisssenschaft: Ärzte und Heilkunst in den Papyri aus Ägypten*. (Nilus 13, Vienna)

Giller, Pinchas. 2008. *Shalom Shar'abi and the Kabbalists of Beit El*. (Oxford)

Goldish, Matt (ed.). 2003. *Spirit Possession in Judaism: Cases and Contexts from the Middle Ages to the Present*. (Detroit)

Hamawy, Abraham. 1879. *לדרוש אלהים*. (Livorno)

Leared, Arthur. 1876 (repr. 1985). *Morocco and the Moors: Being an Account of Travels, With a General Description of the Country and Its People.* (London)

Levene, Dan. 2002. *Curse or Blessing, What's in the Magic Bowl?* (Parkes Institute Pamphlet 2, Southampton)

Margalioth, Isaiah Asher Selig. 1931. *ישב רוחו*. (Jerusalem)

Meyer, Marvin and Richard Smith. 1994. *Ancient Christian Magic: Coptic Texts of Ritual Power.* (San Francisco)

Nigal, Gedalya. 1994. *"Dybbuk" Tales in Jewish Literature*[2]. (Jerusalem) (in Hebrew)

Nîniyô, Ya'aqôv Šĕ'altî'el. 1843. *שפת אמת* (printed as an appendix to *אמת ליעקוב*). (Livorno)

Rohrbacher-Sticker, Claudia. 1991/92. 'Die Namen Gottes und die Namen Metatrons: Zwei Geniza-Fragmente im *Hekhalot*-Literatur', *Frankfurter Judaistische Beiträge* 19, 95–168

Saar, Ortal-Paz. 2008. 'Jewish Love Magic from Late Antiquity to the Middle Ages'. Unpublished Ph.D. dissertation, Tel-Aviv University (in Hebrew)

Schäfer, Peter and Shaul Shaked. 1994–99. *Magische Texte aus der Kairoer Geniza*. 3 vols, (Tübingen)

Schiffman, Lawrence H. and Michael D. Swartz. 1992. *Hebrew and Aramaic Incantation Texts from the Cairo Genizah: Selected Texts from Taylor-Schechter Box K1*. (Sheffield)

Seidel, Jonathan, 2003. 'Possession and Exorcism in the Magical Texts of the Cairo Geniza', in M. Goldish (ed.), *Spirit Possession in Judaism: Cases and Contexts from the Middle Ages to the Present* (Detroit 2003). 73–95

A Judaeo-Arabic Document from Ottoman Egypt in the Rylands Genizah Collection

Geoffrey Khan
University of Cambridge

The majority of the manuscripts in the Genizah collections are datable to the Fatimid and Ayyubid periods (tenth–thirteenth centuries) in Egypt. Thereafter the material becomes sparser, no doubt due to the fact that the Jewish community of Fustat became reduced in size and importance, with an increasing number of Jews settling in al-Qāhira in the Mamluk period. After the influx of Sephardi Jews into Egypt in the sixteenth century the quantity of material that was deposited in the Genizah increased somewhat and over the subsequent three centuries in the Ottoman period until the discovery of the Genizah by scholars in the nineteenth century a considerable number of manuscripts and printed texts were added by the local Jewish community.

A large proportion of the material preserved from the Fatimid and Ayyubid periods is written in Judaeo-Arabic. The same applies to the fragments datable to the Mamluk period down to the period of the Sephardi expulsions. From the sixteenth century onwards most manuscripts, both documentary and literary, were written either in Hebrew or in Judaeo-Spanish. There are, nevertheless, a small number of Judaeo-Arabic fragments, which are, for the most part, popular stories and private letters.

Most of the Judaeo-Arabic letters that have been preserved from the Ottoman period were written at the end of the eighteenth or the beginning of the nineteenth centuries. A large proportion of these originate from the archives of two families of Jewish traders. Unlike the medieval Judaeo-Arabic letters from the Genizah, which have been extensively published and studied, these late Judaeo-Arabic letters have attracted relatively little attention. Not only are they an important source for the socio-economic history of Egypt of the period but they are also of considerable linguistic interest.[1] These late documents can be found in most Genizah collections, although their distribution across them is uneven. It is of interest to note that the Genizah collections of the Alliance Israélite Universelle in Paris and the John Rylands University Library in

1 I am currently preparing the corpus of Judaeo-Arabic letters for publication accompanied with a grammatical description and glossary.

Manchester contain a conspicuously large proportion of this late corpus relative to the overall size of these collections. The proportional size of the late documentary corpus in these libraries is far greater than that of the late documents in the Taylor-Schechter collection in Cambridge, which is the largest of the Genizah collections.

Most of the letters present considerable difficulties of interpretation due to the fact that the writers, who were clearly collaborating closely with one another, frequently allude to events and details of mercantile transactions with which the addressee would be expected to be familiar but which remain obscure to the modern reader.

In earlier papers I have described some of the significant features of the language of these documents and published the text of two of them (Khan 1991, 1992, 2006).[2] In this paper I present an edition of a further document from the corpus preserved in the Rylands Genizah collection with linguistic comments.

There are considerable differences between the Judaeo-Arabic of these late Genizah documents and that of the medieval documents. The Genizah documents from the Middle Ages are written in what is generally known as Classical Judaeo-Arabic. This exhibits a certain number of vernacular features and also some degree of variation across different texts. This variation correlates in general with factors such as the geographical origin of the writers, the register of the texts and the period in which they were written (Wagner 2010). Despite the occurrence of these occasional vernacular features and variation, the outward form of Judaeo-Arabic throughout the Middle Ages, as reflected by the orthography with which it has been transmitted to us, is close to that of the literary Classical Arabic language. An examination of vocalized Judaeo-Arabic Genizah texts from the Middle Ages, however, demonstrates that when the texts were read aloud the language had a phonological form that was much closer to that of vernacular Arabic than is reflected by the standardized orthography. There was, in fact, a considerable gap between orthography and pronunciation. In some cases the dialectal pronunciation conflicts with the orthography. This applies, for example, to the third masculine suffix, which was regularly vocalized with its dialectal form *–u* although it is normally spelt with *hēh* in imitation of Classical Arabic (henceforth CA), e.g.

וּבַעַד מַוּתֻה 'and after his death' (T-S Ar. 8.3, fol. 14v = CA *wa-ba'da mawtihi*)

מַעֻה 'with him' (T-S Ar. 8.3, fol. 15r = CA *ma'ahu*)

2 For a detailed study of literary Judaeo-Arabic texts written in post-medieval Egypt see Hary 1992, 2009.

In many cases the orthography of the medieval texts is ambiguous with regard to the phonological form and could in principle be read with that of CA or with a phonological form that is characteristic of modern Arabic dialects. The vocalization in such contexts generally reflects a vernacular reading. In most vocalized manuscripts, for example, the vowel signs indicate that the language was read without the final short vowels of CA, e.g.

מַא אַעְטַׂם וְאַכְבַּר וְאַגַל מִנְהַא 'what is mightier, greater and more majestic than them' (T-S Ar. 8.3, fol. 14r = CA *mā a'ẓamu wa-akbaru wa-ajallu minhā*)

The pronominal suffixes have dialectal forms, which are invariable for case. In addition to the third masculine suffix *–u*, which is discussed above, note also:

מִן מַדְּחַךְ 'of your praise' (T-S Ar. 8.3, fol. 12v = CA *min madḥika*)

מִן יַדְּהֻם 'from their hand' (T-S Ar. 8.3, fol. 12v = CA *min yadihim*)

There are numerous reflections of the raising of *a* vowels by the process of *imāla*, e.g.

עֲלֵי עִבֵּאדַּךְ 'on your servants' (T-S Ar. 8.3, fol. 16v = CA *'alā 'ibādika*)

Various other types of vocalism characteristic of dialects are found, such as that of the imperfect prefix, e.g.

יִרְגַע 'he returns' (T-S Ar. 8.3, fol. 14v = CA *yarji'u*)

חַתַּי יִפְתַח 'until he opens' (T-S Ar. 8.3, fol. 15v = CA *ḥattā yaftaḥa*)

It is significant, however, that most texts exhibit also pseudo-Classical features in the reading reflected by the vocalization. One such phenomenon, for example, is the occurrence of an */a/* vowel in a number of contexts where CA has an */i/* without there being any clear dialectal background for the */a/*. It appears that the scribe is aware that CA has */a/* in many situations where vernacular dialects have */i/* and in his attempt to give the language an appearance of CA substitutes */a/* for */i/* by hypercorrection even where */i/* is the norm in CA. Examples:

אַנְמַא 'only' (T-S Ar. 8.3, fol. 16v = CA *innamā*)

קַד אַנְכַּסַר קַלְבִּי 'my heart has been broken' (T-S Ar. 8.3, fol. 16v = CA *qad inkasara qalbī*)

אַסְתַּיקַטְֹת 'I woke up' (T-S Ar. 54.11, fol.1r = CA *istayqaẓtu*)

There is a major shift in the Judaeo-Arabic of the Genizah documents datable to the Ottoman period. The vernacular dialectal elements are far more conspicuous in these late documents. One reason for this is that in the Ottoman period the standardized orthography of the Middle Ages was adapted to correspond more closely to the way that the language was pronounced. The third masculine suffix, for example, is spelt with a final *wāw*, which corresponds to the reading of the medieval texts reflected by the vocalized manuscripts but not the medieval orthography: ביתו 'his house' (= Classic Judaeo-Arabic [henceforth CJA] בַּיְתֻהּ).

A few features of the medieval orthography, nevertheless, survived as isolated vestiges, which still disguise some features of the vernacular pronunciation. This is seen in some vocalized Judaeo-Arabic texts from the Ottoman period in cases such as the following:

קֻצוּר עַאלְיַא 'lofty palaces' (Ar. 54.63, fol. 2v = CA *quṣūr 'āliya*, Modern Egyptian Arabic [henceforth MEA] *quṣūr 'alya*)

Here an *a* vowel that in CA is long and occurs in an open syllable is written with the vowel letter *'ālep*, but the vocalization nevertheless reflects a pronunciation in which it occurs in a closed syllable and was presumably pronounced short, as in Modern Egyptian Arabic. This must be regarded as a case of conservative orthography, which is not adapted to pronunciation.

The existence of a number of hypercorrect features in the pronunciation reflected by the vocalization of the late Judaeo-Arabic manuscripts indicates that the writers were aiming at a type of pronunciation that was a higher register than that of the vernacular dialect. This phenomenon can be identified, for example, in the retention of *hamzatu'lwaṣl* after a word ending in a vowel:

וַאִסְמַע 'and listen' (Ar. 54.63, fol. 2r = CA *wa'sma'*)

הַדַא אַל כַּאפֵר 'this disbeliever' (Ar. 54.63, fol. 1v = CA *hāḏā'l-kāfir*)

Another case of hypercorrection is the occasional occurrence of short /*a*/ where /*i*/ is found in both Classical Arabic and Modern Egyptian Arabic, e.g.

אַנְסַאן 'person' (Ar. 54.63, fol. 2r = CA *insān*)

Moreover, even where there is no issue of orthographic representation, the grammatical structure of the language in certain cases is unlikely to correspond to what existed in the vernacular of the writer. Such cases can be regarded as literary features. What is significant is that these literary features do not correspond exactly to what one finds in Classical Arabic. Furthermore, some of them do not occur, or are found only very rarely, in medieval Judaeo-Arabic. One such example is the negative particle *lam*, which is used in the late Judaeo-Arabic Genizah documents as a general negator before all verb forms and even in verbless nominal clauses. Some of these features that are unlikely to correspond to the usage of the contemporary vernacular may have their roots in an earlier period of the development of the vernacular. In most cases, however, the immediate source for these features in the Judaeo-Arabic documents appears to be an Arabic dialectal literary language that was in general use in Ottoman Egypt.[3] Furthermore, in late Judaeo-Arabic vocalized manuscripts many constructions that appear from the orthography to have a CA phonological form have a vocalization that reflects a pronunciation deviating from that of CA, e.g.

אֶלְּדִי 'which' (Ar. 54.63, fol. 1v = CA *allaḏī*, MEA *illi*)

פְּצַאר מַאשִׁי 'and he came walking' (Ar. 54.63, fol. 4r = CA *fa-ṣāra*)

לַאֵנַהוּ 'because he …' (Ar. 54.63, fol. 1v = CA *li'annahu*)

גַאוְבַהוּ 'he answered him' (Ar. 54.63, fol. 1v = CA *jāwabahu*, MEA *jawbu*)

Finally, where the written language of the documents reflects the contemporary vernacular dialect of the writer, this dialect does not always correspond to what exists in Modern Cairene Arabic, although the writers were residents of the Cairo area. Such deviations from Modern Cairene Arabic reflect features of the Jewish dialect of Cairo, which differed in some details from the Muslim dialect, as is shown by the surviving remnants of the dialect that are still spoken today by Jews who were brought up in Cairo.[4]

3 For a more detailed discussion of these issues see Khan 1991.

4 Cf. Blanc 1974. A detailed study of the Jewish dialect is in preparation by Gabriel Rosenbaum.

Rylands Genizah Collection L 192

Text

בע"ה יום ג' ٢٥ חשון תקס"ט
אה' אלסניור קארו פראנסיס קומפנייא יצ"ו[5] סט
אדש"ו[6] סבב דיל כטין נערפכום באין סאבק תא' וצלנה
מורסלכום לגאיית נו' ٢ והיום ארסלנה לכום
מע סלאמת אללה תעאלא אמאנה נו' ١٣ צוח'
עומר שראדה וצ̇ענהא טאי ד̇אלך תטלעו עליה
ואנתו בכיר ונערפכום מן קבל נו' ٢٠ ונו' 1 ונו' ٢
אתצרפנא פיהום ערך ١٥٠ ביל אצעאר אלקדימה
ונקבצ̇ו ריאל ביל סער אלקדים וכ̇ד̇אלך באקי אל עומלה
וביל שוכוך מן קלית אל טאליב ולם פי טרפנה לא
ביע ולא שרה ואל באלד ואקפה ואין שא אללה יכון
וצלוכום מכאתיבנא ואל מכתוב אלדי פי אל בוואלץ̇
ואין כאן קבצ̇תהום ארסלו ערפונא כיף קבצ̇תו
אל מעמלה אין כאנת ראיגה פיל קבץ̇ ארסלו
ע[ר]פונא נקבצ̇ו בוואליץ̇ בתמן אל פצ̇ה ואמס תאריכו
[וצלנ]א מכתובכום מחרר ١٢ תא' וארסלתו תערפונא
[ ] תחריג עלא אל פצ̇ה אין לם ינזלוהא לאכן
[ ] לם יעיקו אין כאן אסערהא טרפכום מהאווד
[ ] אל אחריות לאין אחסבו חסאבכום פי אלד̇י
[ ]ף בסבעין פצ̇ה אל אלף ביל צאג לאין
[ ]צ̇ו̇ר טרפנא חאסן אבו אל פצ̇ל ופי טרפו
פ[ ]סאת במוגיב אכדהום מן גיר מיעיאר[7]
יכון מע[רוף]ו וקאל לנא אל מד̇כור לו כאן ביערף
אין פיל בובאת לם יפתשו כאן גאב בדאל אל צורה
כמסין וסאבק תא' ארסלנא לכום צוח' אחמד שלתות
חמטה[8] פרד ٦ ומוצליח פרד ٢ ומגויז פחם 1 ואוגרתהום
כ̇אלצה אל פרדין אל מוצליח ואל מגויז אל פחם
תעטיהום למ"ר חמי ותרסלו תטמנונא עלא אל
דורה אין כאן אתצרפתו פיהא לאין זוהור כאבר פי
טרפנא אין חוצ̇ור ארבע מראכיב פרנסאוי פי נא א[מון]
ופיהום מתגאר ואין שא אללה תכונו אכדתו אל [ ]
פצ̇ה מן סעור חכם ישראל הלוי וקאיידותהא[9] ל[ ]

---

5 ישמרהו צורו ויחיהו

6 אחרי דרישת שלום

7 The reading מיעיאר is clearly the one that is intended, but the writer omitted the lefthand stroke from the *'ayin*.

8 The meaning of this word is obscure. It is possibly related to حماطة *ḥamāṭa* 'wild fig tree'.

33 ותרסלו תטמנונא עלא כאמל אחואלכום ואמס תא׳
34 חוצ̇ור טרפנא סעד פינתו ואברהם הלוי סכנדרי
35 יבלגו לכום ד״ש ואין ראינה אל חאל כדה בארץ̆

Margin

1 אעלמו אין נתוגהו טרפכום סאעה עלא גאפלה [ ]אל לאין זעלנא קאוי ולם תכלונא מן גיר אל
2 שטר ואל לולי ואל שעיר בתוע אברהם מימון לאגל מא [ ] לו ואחנא פ̇אייתין ונקבצ̇ו אל פ̇ילוס וכאמל מא
3 לכום מן אל כדאם ואל מצאליח עלא אל ראס ואל עין ואל מחביב אלדי פי נו׳ ٢ באקייה טרפנא מן קלית אל ביע ואל שרה
4 אין שא אללה לם יכון אלא כ̇יר וש׳ ממני הצעיר
5 אברהם הלוי
נרבוע״א[10]
יצ״ו[11] ס״ט[12]

Plate 1: L 192-1. (Reproduced by courtesy of the University Librarian and Director, The John Rylands Library, The University of Manchester)

9 This is a mistake for קאיידתוהא.

10 Perhaps an abbreviation of נחה רוחו בגן ויגן עליו אלהים 'May his spirit rest in the Garden and may God protect him'.

11 ישמרהו צורו ויחיהו 'May his Rock guard him and preserve his life'.

12 סופו טוב 'May his end be good' or ספרדי טהור 'pure Sephardi'.

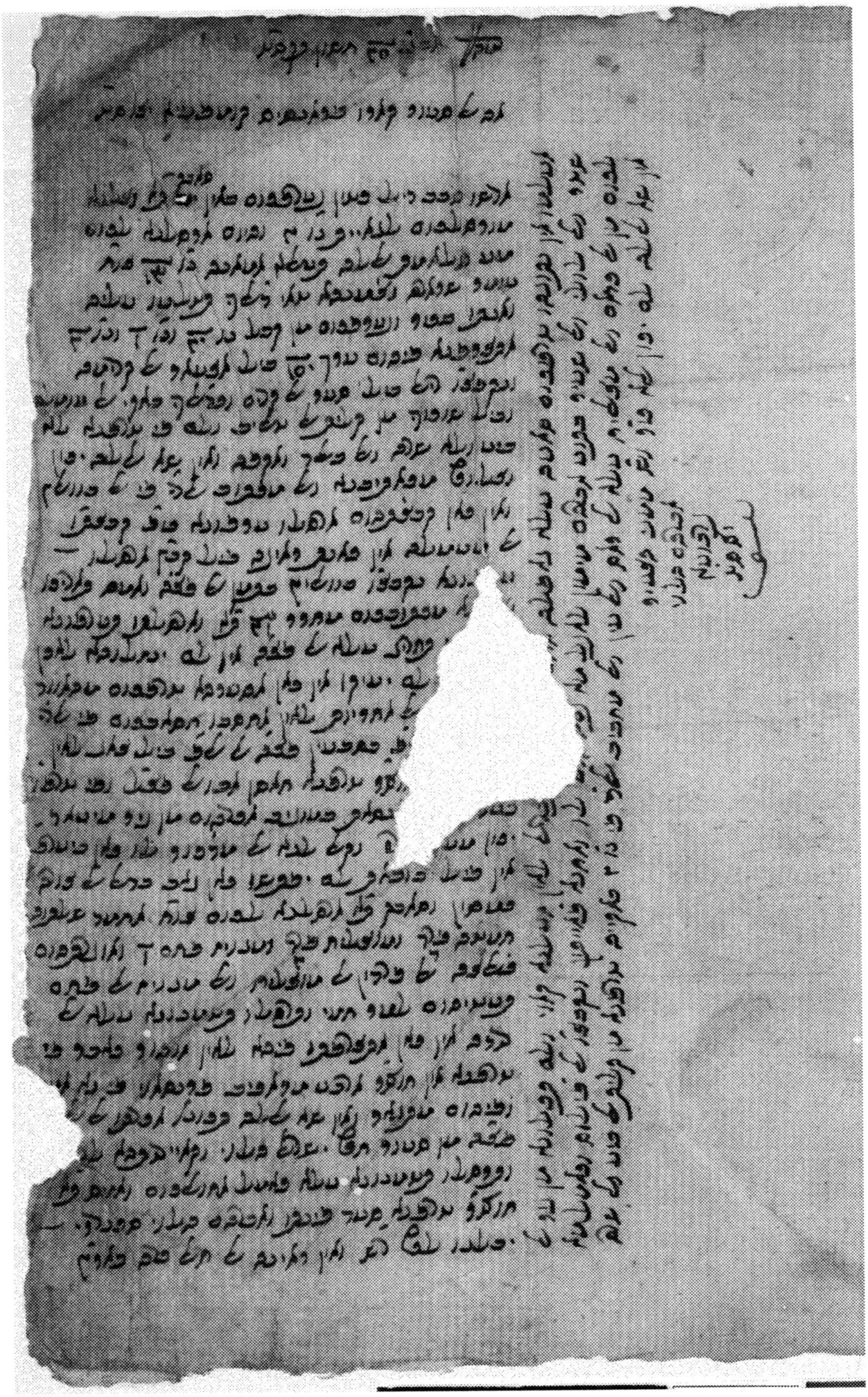

Plate 2: (Close-up) L 192-1. (Reproduced by courtesy of the University Librarian and Director, The John Rylands Library, The University of Manchester)

Translation

1 In the name of God. Tuesday 25th of Ḥešwan 569.[13]

2 Our friend Mr Karo Francis and Company, may his Lord guard him and preserve his life.

3 Greetings.[14] The reason I am writing[15] is to inform you that the previous day[16]

4 your dispatch arrived up to (consignment) number 2, and today we sent to you

5 with the safekeeping of God, may he be exalted, the consignment number 13 by the agency of

6 ʿUmar Serāda. We have placed it enclosed with this (letter) so that you can check it

7 at your leisure. We inform you with regard to number 20, number 1 and number 2

8 that we disposed of them at a value of 150 according to the old prices.

9 We receive *riyāl*s at the old price and likewise the remaining currencies

10 are uncertain on account of the lack of demand. In our place there is no

11 sale or purchase and the country has come to a standstill. God willing

12 our letters will have reached you together with the letter that is in the money orders.

13 If you have cashed them (the money orders), send and tell us what kind of

14 deal you have received. If trade is brisk send and

15 tell us and we shall acquire money orders for the price of the silver. Yesterday

16 your letter dated 21 of the month[17] arrived. You sent to inform us

17 [ ] the difficulty over the silver if they do not lower it. But

18 [ ] they will not be an obstacle if the prices in your place are moderate

19 [ ] the responsibility, because you should calculate your accounts with regard to what

20 [ ] at 70 silver pieces a thousand in high quality currency because

21 [ ] Ḥasan Abū'l-Faḍl came to us and in his place

22 [ ] on account of their taking without any standard.

23 Take note [ ]. The aforementioned said to us if he had known

24 that they are not inspecting at the doors (of the warehouses), he would have brought instead of one purse

25 fifty (purses). The previous day we sent to you with Aḥmad Shaltūt

26 wild figs (?) in 6 single items, salt in 2 single items and a double item of coal. Their hire

27 should be paid with two items of salt and a double item of coal.

28 Give them to my lord my father-in-law. Send and reassure me concerning the

29 maize as to whether you have disposed of it, because there is a report in

---

13 Tuesday 15 November, 1808.

14 Literally: After greetings.

15 Literally: The cause of these lines.

16 Literally: what precedes its (i.e. this letter's) date.

17 Literally: of its (i.e. the letter's) date.

30 our place that four French ships have arrived in Alexandria

31 containing merchandise. God willing you will have taken the [ ]

32 silver from Ṣaʿūr ha-Levi, the Jewish sage, and have recorded it [ ]

33 Write to reassure us regarding how everything is going with you. Yesterday

34 Saʿd Pinto and Abraham ha-Levi Skandari came to us.

35 They convey to you their greetings. If we see the situation (continues) to be so inactive,[18]

Margin

1 take note that we shall come to you some time without warning [ ] because we have become very angry. Do not leave us without

2 the half share, and the pearls and the barley of Abraham Maimon on account of [ ] as in passing we shall receive the cash and we would be happy to perform

3 any services you may request or deal with any matters of concern that you may have.[19] The *maḥbūb* coins[20] that are in (consignment) number 2 remain in our place, due to lack of selling and buying.

4 God willing all will be well. Greetings from me, the humble

5 Abraham ha-Levi

Grammatical notes[21]

1. Features Inherited from CJA Orthography

1.1 Ḍād

The letter *ḍād* is regularly represented by *ṣādê* with an upper diacritical dot. This type of orthography originated in CJA, which imitated the form of the *ḍād* in the Arabic alphabet (*ṣād* with an upper diacritic). Examples: וצׄענהא 'we have placed it' (6), ונקבצׄו 'we receive' (9), פצׄה 'silver' (15), אבו אל פצׄל 'Abū'l-Faḍl' (21), חוצׄור 'arrived' (30).

1.2 Mater Lectionis 'Ālep Representing a Historically Long Vowel

There are a few cases in which *mater lectionis 'ālep* is used where CA would have a long /*ā*/ vowel and where CJA orthography would in principle have *mater lectionis*, but where the vowel would be short in MCA. This applies to vowels in originally open syllables, which become closed in MCA, e.g. כׄאלצה (MCA *khalṣa* = CA

18 Literally: cold.

19 Literally: All you have with regard to services and matters of interest is on the head and the eye.

20 For the currencies that were circulating in Egypt at this period see Raymond 1973, I: 17–52.

21 In the ensuing notes the following abbreviations are used: CA = Classical Arabic, CJA = Classic Judaeo-Arabic, MCA = Modern (Muslim) Cairene Arabic.

khāliṣa) 'it (feminine singular) is sold' (27), ואקפה (MCA *wa'fa* = CA *wāqifa*) 'standing (feminine singular)' (11), באקייה (MCA *ba'ya* = CA *bāqiya*) 'remaining (feminine singular) (margin 3), ראיגה (MCA *rayga* = CA *rā'ija*) 'selling briskly' (14), פֿאייתין (MCA *faytīn* = CA *fā'itūna*) 'passing (masculine plural)' (margin 2), חסאבכום (MCA = *ḥisabkum* = CA *ḥisābukum*) (19), אחואלכום (MCA = *aḥwalkum* = CA *aḥwālikum*) 'your conditions' (33).

1.3 The Definite Article

The definite article is written אל in all contexts, including before 'sun letters' where the */l/* would have been assimilated in the spoken language, e.g. אל טאליב 'the one who demands' (10), אל צורה 'the purse' (24), אל שעיר 'the barley' (margin 2), אל ראס 'the head' (margin 3), אל שרה 'the sale' (margin 3). Note also that the article is regularly written as a separate word.

2. Elements of Orthography that Deviate from the Norm in Classic Judaeo-Arabic

2.1 Ẓā'

The emphatical letter *ẓā'* is represented by the Hebrew letter *zayin* in the word זוהור (CA *ẓahara*, MCA *ẓahar*) 'it appeared' (29) rather than *ṭēt* with an upper diacritic (ט̇), which is the normal CJA orthography.

2.2 Lack of Mater Lectionis 'Ālep for Historically Long /ā/

A *mater lectionis 'ālep* is omitted on some occasions in contexts where the long */ā/* is shortened in MCA. This is the case with historically long */ā/* in originally open syllables closed by the elision of the following vowel, e.g. אסערהא (*as'arhā* = CA *as'āruhā*) 'its prices' (18), and historically long */ā/* in unstressed open syllables, e.g. בובאת (*bawwabāt* = CA *bawwābāt*) 'doors' (24), ואל מחביב (*wa'l-maḥabīb* = CA *wa'l-maḥābīb*) 'and the *maḥbūb* coins' (margin 3). The omission of *mater lectionis 'ālep* in these contexts, therefore, may be interpreted as reflecting the shortness of the vowel in the spoken vernacular of the writer. In some cases the vowel is represented by an *'ālep* in these contexts due to orthographic conservatism, e.g. חסאבכום (= CA *ḥisābukum*) (19), מכאתיבנא (= CA *makātībunā*) 'our letters' (12). The omission of the *'ālep* in the first plural verbal suffix of וצ̇ענהא 'we have placed it' (6) appears to be a defective spelling since the vowel is long in both CA and MCA in this morphological context.

2.3 Scriptio Plena of Short /a/

In several cases *mater lectionis 'ālep* is used where both CA and MCA have a short vowel, e.g. באלד (*balad*) 'town' (11), כאבר (*khabar*) 'news' (29), חאסן (*Ḥasan*) 'Ḥasan' (21), טאי (*ṭayy*) 'within' (6). This is not a practice either of CJA orthography or of Rabbinic Hebrew orthography. It may have developed in the orthography of late Judaeo-Arabic by analogy with historical spellings with *mater lectionis 'ālep* such as those described in §1.2, where the vowel would have been pronounced as short */a/* in the spoken vernacular.

2.4 Scriptio Plena of long /ā/

In CA and CJA long */ā/* in a few words are written defectively. This applies to demonstrative pronouns. In our document the */ā/* is represented by a *mater lectionis* in such cases, e.g. ד̇אלך (CA ذلك, CJA ד̇לך) 'that' (6).

2.5 Scriptio Plena of Short /i/ and Short /u/

In many cases short */i/* is represented by *mater lectionis yod*, e.g. מראכיב (*marākib*) 'ships' (30), קלית (*qillit*) 'paucity of' (10), טאליב (*ṭālib*) 'one who demands' (10), במוגיב (*bimūjib*) 'on account of' (22).

Likewise short */u/* is frequently represented by *mater lectionis waw*, e.g. נערפכום (*na'arrafkum*) 'we inform you' (3), מורסלכום (*mursalkum*) 'your missive' (4), עומר (*'Umar*) ʿUmar (6), פיהום (*fīhum*) 'in them' (8), אל עומלה (*al-'umla*) 'the currency' (9), שוכוך (*šukūk*) 'doubts' (10), ואוגרתהום (*wi'ujrithum*) 'and their allowance' (26).

The use of *matres lectionis* to represent short */i/* and */u/* is not unknown in CJA texts, especially the use of *wāw* for short */u/* (Blau 1980: 21). Their occurrence in this text, however, is far more regular and corresponds closely to the practice of rabbinic Hebrew orthography.

2.6 Word Final Matres Lectionis

When a word ends in an */a/* vowel it is represented in the orthography either by *mater lectionis hēh* or *'ālep*, in accordance with rabbinic Hebrew and Aramaic spelling, e.g. ארסלנה 'we sent' (4), טרפנה 'our place' (10), שרה 'purchase' (11), אתצרפנא 'we have disposed of' (8), זעלנא 'we have become angry' (margin 1), וצ̇ענהא 'we have placed it' (6), לא 'not' (11). This includes cases where CA has an *alif maqṣūra* and CJA a *yôd*, e.g. עלא (28), עלא (17) (CA على, CJA עלי) 'upon', תעאלא (CA تعالى, CJA תעאלי) 'may he be exalted' (5)

2.7 Consonantal /y/ and /w/

Consonantal */y/* and */w/* in word-internal position are generally represented by double *wāw* and *yôd* respectively to distinguish them from *matres lectionis*, e.g. פֿאייתין (MCA *faytīn*) 'passing' (margin 2), באקייה (MCA *ba'ya*) 'remaining' (margin 3), בוואליץ (MCA *bawalīṣ*) 'money orders' (15).

3. Assimilation

The spelling of form אצעאר 'prices' (8) reflects the spread of pharyngalization from the pharyngal /'/ to the adjacent sibilant: *aṣ'ār* < *as'ār*. Contrast the form סער (*si'r*) 'price' (9), in which the sibilant is not in contact with the pharyngal.

4. The Demonstrative Pronoun

The attributive demonstrative pronoun has the form דיל. It is invariable and is placed before the noun it qualifies, written as a separate word: סבב דיל כטין 'the reason for these few lines (literally: couple of lines)' (3). In MCA the demonstrative pronoun is placed after the noun, except in a few fixed phrases such as *dilwa'ti* 'now'. Its placement after the noun is attested already in medieval Judaeo-Arabic texts of Egyptian origin (Blau 1958: 91). Also in the Egyptian dialectal passages of the seventeenth-century work *Hazz al-quḥūf fī šarḥ qaṣīd Abī Šādūf* ('The Confounding of Brains by the Exposition of the Ode of Abū Šādūf') by al-Širbīnī the demonstrative is generally placed after the noun (Doss 1979: 353–5). The source of the preposing of the demonstrative in the language of the late Judaeo-Arabic documents, therefore, appears not to be the spoken vernacular of the writer. Rather, it is likely to be a literary dialectal form of Egyptian Arabic that is attested in a variety of sources from the Mamluk period onwards.[22]

5. Relative Particle

The relative particle is the invariable form אלדי. This is a pseudo-literary form in that it resembles the masculine singular form of the CA relative pronoun, but is fossilized and is not inflected for gender or number, e.g. ואל מכתוב אלדי פי אל בוואליץ 'and the letter that is in the money orders' (12), ואל מחביב אלדי פי נו' ٢ באקייה טרפנא 'The *maḥbūb* coins that are in (consignment) number 2 remain in our place' (margin 3). Although this fossilized relative particle looks like CA from the orthography, late

22 For further discussion of this issue see Khan 1991: 231.

Egyptian Judaeo-Arabic texts with vocalization show, as remarked already, that its pronunciation deviated from that of CA, e.g. אֶלַדִי (Ar. 54.63, fol. 1v), has a vocalism that is a blend of CA *allaḏī* and vernacular *illi*.

6. Negation

The general negator before all verb forms and in nominal sentences is לם. Although the form *lam* exists marginally in MCA as an emphatic negator (Rosenbaum 2002: 588–94), the regular occurrence of the particle in the language of the late Judaeo-Arabic documents is likely to be a pseudo-literary feature. Examples: אין לם ינזלוהא 'if they do not lower it' (17), פיל בובאת לם יפתשו 'they do not check at the doors' (24), ולם תכלונא מן גיר אל שטר 'Do not leave us without the half share' (margin 1–2), אין שא אללה לם יכון אלא כ̇יר 'God willing all will be well' (margin 4).

Note, however, that the particle לא is used before nouns in the construction ולם פי טרפנה לא ביע ולא שרה 'In our place there is neither sale nor purchase' (10–11).

7. Differences from MCA

Some aspects of the language of the document differ both from CA and from MCA and are likely to be distinctive features of the Jewish Cairene dialect that was spoken by the writer.

7.1 First Plural Imperfect Forms

One of the most conspicuous of these features is the presence of the ending *-u* on first plural imperfect verbal forms, e.g. ונקבצ̇ו ריאל ביל סער אלקדים 'we receive *riyāl*s at the old price' (9), ונקבצ̇ו אל פ̇ילוס 'we shall receive the cash' (margin 2), נתוגהו טרפכום 'we shall come to your place' (margin 1). This form, however, is not consistently used for the first plural, as is shown by the form נערפכום (3), which is likely to be first plural ('we inform you') given the fact that the writer refers to himself with first plural reference elsewhere in the text.

The forms *niqtil* — *niqtilu* for the first singular and first plural of the imperfect are not found in the standard Muslim Cairene dialect, but are a feature of the Jewish dialect of Cairo. It is relevant to note that in the Jewish dialect the first plural form *niqtilu* is not used consistently, rather the first plural is expressed interchangeably by *niqtilu* and *niqtil* (Blanc 1974), exactly as in our document.

7.2 Vocalism of Verbal Forms

In a number of cases the vocalism of verbal forms differs from what is found in MCA or CA. This is the case in verbs that have the vocalic pattern *qaṭal* in MCA and CA but appear from their orthography to have the vocalic pattern *quṭul* in this document, e.g. זוהור (CA *ẓahara*, MCA *ẓahar*) 'it appeared' (29), חוצ̇ור (CA *ḥaḍara*, MCA *ḥaḍar*) 'he arrived' (34). This may be a reflection of a distinctive feature of the Jewish dialect of Cairo at that period. The use of the *quṭul* vocalism for verbs that in MCA have the *qaṭal* or *qiṭil* pattern is still found in the surviving spoken Jewish Cairene dialect.[23]

8. Hebrew Elements

A number of Hebrew elements are found in the document. Some are formulaic abbreviations, e.g. בע"ה (= בעזרת השם) 'God willing' (1), אה' (= אהובנו) 'our beloved (friend)', אדש"ו (= אחרי דרישת שלום) 'after offering greetings' (3). Some, however, are words used outside of formulaic phraseology, e.g. והיום 'today' (4), ערך 'value' (8), אל אחריות 'the responsibility' (19).

References

Blanc, Haim. 1974. 'The *Nekteb-Nektebu* Imperfect in a Variety of Cairene Arabic', *Israel Oriental Studies* 4, 206–26

Blau, Joshua. 1958. 'השתקפותם של להגים בטכסטים ערביים-יהודיים מימי הביניים', *Tarbiz* 27, 83–92

—— 1980. *A Grammar of Mediaeval Judaeo-Arabic*², (Jerusalem) (in Hebrew)

Doss, Madiha. 1979. 'The Position of the Demonstrative *da, di* in Egyptian Arabic: A Diachronic Inquiry', *Annales Islamologiques* 15, 349–57

Hary, Benjamin H. 1992. *Multiglossia in Judeo-Arabic: With an Edition, Translation, and Grammatical Study of the Cairene Purim Scroll.* (Leiden)

—— 2009. *Translating Religion: Linguistic Analysis of Judeo-Arabic Sacred Texts from Egypt.* (Leiden)

Khan, Geoffrey. 1991. 'A Linguistic Analysis of the Judaeo-Arabic of Late Genizah Documents and its Comparison with Classical Judaeo-Arabic', *Sefunot* 20, 223–34 (in Hebrew)

—— 1992. 'Notes on the Grammar of a Late Judaeo-Arabic Text', *Jerusalem Studies in Arabic and Islam* 15, 220–39

—— 2006. 'A Judaeo-Arabic Commercial Letter from Early Nineteenth Century Egypt', *Ginzei Qedem* 2, 37*–59*

Raymond, André. 1973–4. *Artisans et commerçants au Caire au XVIIIe siècle.* 2 vols, (Damascus)

23 Gabriel Rosenbaum (personal communication).

Rosenbaum, Gabriel. 2002. 'The Particles *ma* and *lam* and Emphatic Negation in Egyptian Arabic', in W. Arnold and H. Bobzin (eds), *"Sprich doch mit deinen Knechten aramäisch, wir verstehen es!": 60 Beiträge zur Semitistik, Festschrift für Otto Jastrow zum 60. Geburtstag* (Wiesbaden). 583–98

Wagner, Esther-Miriam. 2010. *Linguistic Variety of Judaeo-Arabic Letters from the Cairo Genizah.* (Leiden)

Rylands Gaster Heb. Ms. 1623/3 and the *Qiṣṣat Mujādalat al-Usquf*

Philip Alexander and Sagit Butbul

Manchester and Israel

Rylands Gaster Heb. ms. 1623/3: Physical Description

Rylands Gaster Heb. ms. 1623/3 is the remains of a small booklet now measuring 15.5 cm in height by 5.0–5.5 cm in width. Physically it is in very poor condition. The paper is brittle, and each page has been torn vertically from top to bottom more or less down the middle. The tears match so closely and the edges are so even that it looks as if someone deliberately ripped the booklet in half. The result is that every page has lost either the ends or the beginnings of its lines, which makes reconstructing the text frustrating. The long quotation of Ps. 115:5–9 on f. 8a (i.e. Gaster Heb. ms. 1623/3–15)[1] allows us to estimate that the length of the original lines was, at a maximum, no more than 30 letter-spaces per line, and often less. In other words there is not much writing missing, and this should be borne in mind when attempting to fill the lacunae. On the basis of this calculation of line length the undamaged booklet probably measured no more than 10 cm in width.

A number of pages have suffered severe damage at the bottom, affecting the last four or five lines of text. The fundamental cause of this was damp which made the pages stick together. When they were separated, sometimes fragments were torn off and subsequently lost; sometimes the writing more or less vanished, leaving apparently blank paper; sometimes the paper laminated, and the top layer either disappeared or remained stuck to the opposite page, occasionally with its writing showing through in reverse; sometimes writing from the opposite page imprinted itself in reverse, overprinting the original letters, and creating a confusing jumble of pen-strokes. In a few cases the imprinted letters puzzlingly appear to be upside down.

1 In the online catalogue the images are numbered as follows: f. 1a-b = 1623/3-1-2, f. 2a-b = 1623/3-3-4, and so forth, up to f. 12a-b = 1623/3-23-24.

The yield from trying to unscramble this mess is likely to be so small that we have not attempted it.

The handwriting is in a large, black, rather clumsy square script. Letter size is uneven, as is line length and line spacing, and the number of lines per page ranges from 19 (3a) to 16 (8b). The manuscript is written in a semi-phonetic spelling: the spelling employed is basically phonetic, while integrating features of standard Judaeo-Arabic orthography, as shown by the following characteristics: (1) representation of the definite article: the *lām* of the definite article is dropped in front of a 'sun letter', e.g.: אסמא (السماء; 3b.5,11); ארב (الرب; 6a.3; 7b.4; 10a.2); אתורה (التوراة; 8a.11); (2) the use of *matres lectionis* to mark short vowels, e.g.: כ'ומס (خُمس; 1a.3); ואגליק (وأغلِق; 2a.12); קולתום (قُلتُم; 7a.7); and the lack thereof for long vowels, e.g.: אנגר (النجار; 11a.5). Masoretic *niqqud* is occasionally used to mark /i/ and /u/ vowels instead of using *matres lectionis*, e.g.: קֻרבאן (قُربان; 9a.7); אלמִית (الميِّت; 9a.9); ואזֻבור (والزُّبور; 6a.1); (3) the suffix pronoun of the third person singular after consonants is written constantly - וה : ליאנוה (لأنه; 2a.7). The hallmark, however, of phonetic spelling is not found here: the consonant *ḍ* is represented in this manuscript by *ṣādê* with a dot above it (in our transcription 'צ), just as in the standard Judaeo-Arabic spelling, and not with a *dālet* (ד), e.g. ריצ'אהום (رِضاهُم; 6a.10); איצ'א (أيضا; 10b.4).[2] The consonant *ẓ* is represented by *ṣādê* as well, with the addition of a dot above it (in our transcription 'צ), or by *ṭēt* with a dot above it (in our transcription 'ט), both a common characteristic of standard Judaeo-Arabic spelling, e.g.: נצ'ר (نظر; 2a.5); ינט'ור (ينظر; 6a.6). This is not a professionally copied text, but a scholar's notebook, written for his own use.

The bifolia are still precariously held together by some stitching belonging to the original binding, which helps to determine the order of the pages. The stitching holds together the remains of three quires. In the case of two of these (A [1//2] and B [3//4]) only the outermost sheets survive, while the third (C [5,6,7,8//9,10,11,12]) preserves 8 sheets, with its middle opening at pages 8b + 9a. It is probable, but not certain, that this quire is complete. A – B – C is the order in which we have edited the text below, because it was the way we found the manuscript, and there does not seem to be any obviously better order, but the binding would allow two other arrangements, viz., C – A – B, or B – C – A. Page 4 is a blackened remnant with only a few traces of writing on it. It is slightly odd that a page, so disproportionately damaged, is now *inside* the manuscript. It is possible that at some time the manuscript was folded in such a way that page 4 was exposed on the outside.

2 Cf., however, ודעתני (5a.7) ودعتني, for which a *dāgēš* was added, perhaps with the verb وضع in mind.

Plate 1: Gaster Heb. ms. 1623/3, fols 3–5. (Reproduced by courtesy of the University Librarian and Director, The John Rylands Library, The University of Manchester)

If quires A and B originally had, like quire C, at least eight sheets each, the original booklet would have comprised at least 24 sheets = 48 pages = 96 sides. Given that the present manuscript opens and closes *in mediis rebus*, additional quires must be postulated containing the beginning and end of the work. The original booklet, then, had room for a considerable amount of text. The style and thematic content of the extant fragments (insofar as we can discern the latter), are sufficiently uniform and coherent throughout to suggest that we are dealing with a single work.

The text is preserved inside a brown A5 envelope, sent through the post and addressed to Dr Moses Gaster, 193 Maida Vale, London. Gaster has scrawled in pencil on the envelope: 'Geniza Cairo. Polemical treatise. Christian or Antichristian.' Also preserved in the envelope is the following note: 'Je reconnais avoir reçu de M^r^ le Dr Gaster une copie d'un manuscript judéo-arabe de onze feuillets contennant un traité judéo-chrétien. I. Broydé. Londres, ce 7 octobre 1895.' The most obvious way to understand this is that at some point Gaster loaned the manuscript to I. Broydé and got from him a memo to this effect. The memo, however, was kept after the manuscript was returned, presumably in the envelope in which it is now contained: the handwriting of the address is the same as the handwriting of the note. Broydé describes the text as a 'Judeo-Christian treatise'. Gaster himself describes it as a 'polemical treatise, Christian or Antichristian'. Though the text is written in Judeo-Arabic it clearly has Christian content. There are frequent references to Jesus and quotations from the Gospels, but it is obviously hostile to Christianity, and clearly part of a Jewish anti-Christian polemic.

The *Qiṣṣat Mujādalat al-Usquf*

Our text has affinities with the Jewish anti-Christian treatise known as the *Qiṣṣat mujādalat al-usquf*. The *Qiṣṣa* was a popular work in the Middle Ages, which circulated not only in Judaeo-Arabic, but in Hebrew as well, in an adaptation that went under the title of the *Book of Nestor the Priest*. Appendix 1 gives the manuscripts of the *Qiṣṣa* known to date. The fullest is Bibliothèque Nationale, ms héb. 755, though it is manifestly corrupt in places. The vast majority of the copies of the work (around twenty-nine in total, represented by thirty-six separate manuscripts and manuscript fragments: see Appendix 2) come from the Genizah. The prevalence of copies of the *Qiṣṣa* in the Genizah strengthens the claim that our manuscript is, as

Gaster stated, of the same provenance, but no other fragments of our precise text have been found elsewhere in the Genizah.

Daniel Lasker and Sarah Stroumsa published a full edition of the *Qiṣṣa* in 1996. They note that there are various recensions of the work, differing, at times, widely from each other (see Appendix 2). The *Qiṣṣa* was clearly an active text, readily adapted and changed, as it was copied and recopied. It is a classic example of a 'school text' or an 'open book', that is to say a work that never seems to have reached definitive closure – a point to which we will return in a moment. This transmission history is apparent on the face of the *Qiṣṣa*, for although it manifests a certain coherence in its topical arrangement and narrative frame, it contains numerous repetitions – the same point, with the same proof-texts, being made again and again in slightly different ways. These probably originated as alternative formulations of the same argument. Lasker and Stroumsa try to bring some order into the textual chaos by presenting a partially synoptic edition which takes as its base text (*nusaḥ 'iqqārî*) the Paris manuscript and its allies, and presents against this, where it is extant, any strongly differing parallel text (*nusaḥ maqbîl*) which cannot be accommodated within the *apparatus criticus* of the Paris manuscript. But even this layout cannot cope with all the textual diversity of the *Qiṣṣa*, and in an appendix to their edition they set out variants of certain pericopes that cannot be presented within the *apparatus criticus* of the *parallel* text. They remark: 'The existing body of identified fragments suggests the possibility that when such [new] fragments are found, the text they preserve may differ, even considerably, from the text of the fragments published here' (Lasker and Stroumsa 1996, I: 40).

The main similarities between the Rylands manuscript and the *Qiṣṣa* are as follows.

1. The Rylands text, like the *Qiṣṣa*, clearly quotes extensively from the New Testament (Matthew, Mark, Luke, John, and Paul) to refute Christianity, and many of the verses quoted are the same.

2. Its referencing system to the Gospels follows the same unusual system as the *Qiṣṣa*. See 1a.3, 'in the fifth [part] of the book of John', 1b.3, 'in the first [part of the book] of John', 5b.4, 'in the first fifth [from the beginning of the book of John]', with the notes *ad loca*.

3. The name of Jesus is spelt in different ways: יסוס, following the Greek, is the commonest form (e.g. 7a.9, 10b.5), but ישוע is also well attested (e.g. 2b.13, 3a.14), and even, possibly, יושוע (3b.9), which involves an acknowledgement of the Hebrew derivation of the name. It is interesting that we do not find the pejorative ישו, which is standard in the Talmud and the *Tôlᵉdôt Yēšû*. Even more noteworthy, given its greater size, is the general absence of ישו from the *Qiṣṣa*, though it very

occasionally turns up as a variant. This suggests a certain seriousness of polemical purpose – a desire to depend on rational argument, rather than denigration – a point to which we will return presently. This variation in the spelling of the name of Jesus is perplexing. In certain circumstances it would be taken as evidence for the source-critical history of a work, for its reliance on different sources, but the pattern of the variation appears too random for this explanation to work here.[3]

4. Like the *Qiṣṣa*, the Rylands text has a Christian addressee, frequently referred to in the second person singular. Occasionally second person plural forms are found, where this individual is identified with Christians in general.

5. Like the *Qiṣṣa*, the Rylands text strongly favours the rhetorical device of the dilemma: You must either say *x* or *y*: if you say *x* the following unpalatable consequence ensues, but if you say *y*, the following equally unpalatable consequence ensues. You are caught on the horns of a dilemma.

6. Certain sections of our text are close to the *Qiṣṣa*, either in terms of thematic content, or even, occasionally, of wording. Where verbal overlaps occur, the Rylands text agrees sometimes more closely with the *Qiṣṣa's* base text, but more frequently more closely with the parallel text, and it seems generally to have been shorter, certainly as against the Paris manuscript of the *Qiṣṣa*. It appears to have stripped the tradition down to its bare essentials, eliminating 'padding' such as honorifics (e.g. instead of 'Moses the prophet, peace be upon him' it will simply have 'Moses'). The prolixity and repetition of most versions of the *Qiṣṣa* certainly give ample scope for shortening, but in some cases the shortening in the Rylands text seems to have been extreme.

These similarities are sufficient to establish that the Rylands text is a Jewish anti-Christian polemic of the same genre as the *Qiṣṣa*, but it is a moot point whether it can meaningfully be seen as a *version* of the *Qiṣṣa*. Against the similarities we have to set the differences. The verbal overlaps, even when they occur, are seldom exact, and seldom allow us to restore much of the missing Rylands text, or materially reconstruct it. There is no way, as far as we can see, that the Rylands text can be slotted into *any* version of the *Qiṣṣa* published by Lasker and Stroumsa. And there is a significant quantity of material in the Rylands text which simply cannot be paralleled in *any* of the Lasker-Stroumsa versions of the *Qiṣṣa*. We express this opinion with due caution. It would be rash of us to claim to have identified every parallel or lack of parallel between our text and the *Qiṣṣa*. Others, without doubt, will spot parallels we have missed. But unless we are very much mistaken, we have done enough to establish

3 See further Lasker and Stroumsa 1996, I: 23–6.

that, with respect to both the order of topics and the content, the Rylands text differs substantially from *any* of the versions of the *Qiṣṣa* exemplified by the Lasker-Stroumsa edition. Indeed, we might possibly go further and say that the Lasker-Stroumsa versions are textually closer to each other than they are individually or collectively to the Rylands text. How we construe the relationship of the Rylands text to the *Qiṣṣa* depends on what sort of literary entity we conceive the *Qiṣṣa* to be. If, as we suggested earlier, we take the *Qiṣṣa* to be an example of an 'open book', that is to say, a text whose multifarious versions, though sharing a certain thematic unity and a certain narrative framework, were creatively copied and recopied, and never reached definitive closure, then Rylands 1623/3 can be seen as another creative reworking of this tradition. The shared narrative framework (the second person address to an individual Christian) is particularly important in bracketing the various versions together. If, however, we conceive of the *Qiṣṣa* in more static terms, as a single authored text, then the relationship of the Rylands manuscript to it becomes deeply problematic, and it is hard to see Rylands 1623/3 as a version of the *Qiṣṣa*.[4]

4 On the concept of the 'open book' see Alexander and Samely 1993. 'Open books' are common in the Jewish textual tradition. The *Tôlᵉdôt Yēšû* and the Heikhalot literature are cases in point. 'Open books' create acute problems for text-editing, which cannot be adequately handled within the conventions of classical text-criticism (diplomatic *v.* eclectic text + *apparatus criticus*). They require synoptic editions. Lasker and Stroumsa do offer a kind of synoptic edition, but, whether wittingly or unwittingly, they give the impression that the Paris manuscript is somehow the 'original' text and the parallel versions recensions of it. On internal source-critical analysis it would seem obvious, however, that P is a late manifestation of the tradition. On the theoretical issues involved here see Alexander 1993 and the articles by Peter Schäfer and Chaim Milikowsky in Goodman and Alexander 2010.

Edition of Rylands Heb. 1623/3 with Notes[5]

1a (Gaster Heb. ms. 1623/3-1)

1 א(כ')וה לם יעלמהא (ת)]
2 עלמהא וכיף יכון אל(.)]
3 פי כ'ומס כיתב יוח[נא
4 וחדי ואין ארדת אד[ין
5 מוציבה מן אגלאני (.)]
6 ואלה' אלדי ארסלני ו]
7 רגלין אתנין צאדִק(י)[ן
8 נפסי ואלה' אלדי ארס[לני
9 ישהד עלי שהד(ת)[יה
10 (ות)כון שהדתוה ש[הדה
11 קולתום הומא את(ו)]
12 באלה' (.)תוה קאל פי (.)]
13 (.....ו)ם מעי אל(.)]
14 (.....)ום (ה)[ ](ומ)[ ] ו(..)]
15 ( )]
16] [
17] [
18] [
19] [
20 [

Notes

Line 1: א(כ')וה: the second letter appears to have been corrected. The scribe first wrote ן, but then corrected to כ.

Lines 2–6: cf. *Qiṣṣa* 40 (base text):

וכיף יכון אלמסיח אלאה, והו מכתוב פי אלאנג'יל פי כ'מס כתב יוחנא: אני ליס אדין אלנאס וחדי ואן ארדת אדין פליס דיני במציב מע אני ליס וחדי אדין בל אנא ואלד'י ארסלני.

'And how can Christ be a God, when it is written in the Gospel, in the fifth [part] of the book of John: "I do not judge people by myself. If I had wanted to judge [by myself], then my judgement would not be valid. But I do not judge alone; rather, I judge together with the one who has sent me (cf. John 8:15–

5 We offer only an indicative photo of the manuscript (Plate 1 above). For a full set of images see the Genizah database on the Manchester University Library website http://enriqueta.man.ac.uk/luna/servlet/. Editorial conventions:] = left-hand edge of fragment; [= right-hand edge of fragment; [ ] = hole in the paper, or a line missing because the paper is missing; ( ) = paper now blank which once contained writing; (.) = traces of a letter but it is no longer identifiable; (א) = identification of the letter uncertain; /א/ = interlinear insertion; {א} = correction by the present editors.

16)"?'[6] The quotation from John is inexact and in fact says the opposite of the original: 'I judge no one. Yet even if I do judge, my judgment is valid; for it is not I alone who judges, but I and the father who sent me.' The alteration, however, is understandable since the original text of John is paradoxical, and appears to contradict itself. The text of John continues: 'In your law it is written that the testimony of two men is valid. I testify on my own behalf, and the Father who sent me testifies on my behalf' (John 8:17–18). Some of the wording here is reflected in the Rylands text, which seems to have continued the Gospel quotation and the discussion of it beyond what we find in the *Qiṣṣa*.

Line 3: פי כ'ומס כיתב יוח[נא, 'in the fifth [part] of the book of Jo[hn': see above on the biblical referencing system of our text. The system is found only in the *Qiṣṣa*. It may relate to collections of testimonies extracted by Jewish scholars for polemical purposes from the Gospels.[7]

Lines 7–14 appear to have contained text not in our versions of the *Qiṣṣa*.

Line 15: the paper has laminated, the top layer peeling off and taking the writing with it.

Lines 16–20: a piece is missing from the bottom of the page. It could have accommodated five lines of writing.

1b (Gaster Heb. ms. 1623/3-2)

1](.) אתנין פקד

2]ה לאנוה לא אילה

3]קאל איצ'א פי אוול

4 ו]חנא קד עלימו

5]לתני וקד ביינת

6](.) אכברני אסם

7]איסם אלה' או

8]פאן קולת ביין

9 אי](ס)ם נפסוה ומ(.)

10](.)ן ואן קול[תם](..)

11](.)[ ](.לת...)

12](..) (.....)

13] [

14] [

15] [

16] [

17] [

18] [

19] [

6 The English translations of the *Qiṣṣa* are based on Lasker and Stroumsa 1996, with small adjustments here and there.

7 See the discussion in Lasker and Stroumsa 1996, I: 17–18.

Notes

Lines 1–7: cf. *Qiṣṣa* 41–2 (base text):

(41) ואן קלתם: את'נין, פקד כפרתם באללה לאן מכתוב פי שריעה' מוסי ע'ה' ותוראתה: אנא אנא הו וליס אלאה סואיי, אנא אמית ואחיי אוהנת ואנא אשפי וליס מן עקאבי מכ'לץ.

(42) וקאל איצ'א פי אול ג'זו מן כתאב יוחנא: קד עלמוא אנך אנת אלד'י ארסלתני וקדביינת להם אסמך. פאכ'ברני, אסם מן ביין להם?

'(41) And if you say, "[they are] two", then you disbelieve in God, for it is written in the law of Moses, in his Torah: "I, I am he, there is no God beside me. I kill and I bring to life, I bring illness and heal, and there is none that can deliver [anyone] from my punishment" (Deuteronomy 32:39). (42) He also said in the first part of the book of John: "They know that you are the one who had sent me, and I have disclosed to them your name (cf. John 17:25–6)." Tell me then, whose name did he disclose to them?' The quotation from John 17:25–6 seems certain, but it is not from 'the first part of the book of John'! For the biblical referencing system of our text see 1a.3 *note*.

Lines 8–10: the discussion of the name that Jesus revealed appears to have continued with text not in our versions of the *Qiṣṣa*.

Lines 9–12: signs of imprinting from the opposite page (2a).

Lines 13–19: a piece is missing from the bottom of the page. It could have accommodated seven lines of text.

2a (Gaster Heb. ms. 1623/3-3)

1 אן ק(בצ)ה(ו) לם ירא[
2 וכאן מוסא אד'א ד[הב
3 אלה' כשף וגהוה ואד'[א
4 גטא וגהוה ואנת ת(ע)[לם
5 אלה' וקד נצ'ר אליה אלב[
6 פארא מוסא אכר[
7 ליאנוה נצר נפסוה[
8 וקאל אלה' למוסא קול [
9 אחד איאכום אן ת[
10 ותתרכוני ותעבוד[ון גירי
11 תסגדון לגירי פאמ[א
12 ואגליק אבואב אס(מ)[א
13 אלא אלארץ' ולא תו(.)[
14 איי כ'אף ואיי פא(..)[
15 (ל.ר..) ובאסמי א(.)[
16](ר.מ..)[
17] [
18] [
19] [

Notes

1a+1b and 2a+2b together form the outer bifolium of a quire. Assuming there were the same number of bifolia in this quire (quire A) as in quire C (= 5a-12b), then there are three bifolia = 12 sides missing between 1b and 2a.

Lines 2–3: cf. *Qiṣṣa* 184 (base text): אליס תעלם אן אללה כלם מוסי כ'מס מאיה וסבעין מרה אלי יום ופאתה, לאן אללה תע' אכרם מוסי, פכאן אד'א ד'הב אלי מכ'אטבה כשף וג'הה, ואד'א עאד אלי בני אסראיל גטא וג'הה ('Do you not know that until the day of Moses' death God spoke to him five hundred and seventy times, for God, the exalted, had honoured Moses. When Moses went to speak to God, he would uncover his face, but when he returned to the Israelites, he would cover his face with a veil'). The argument is that God honoured Moses more than Jesus with direct revelations.

Lines 8–11: the argument here presumably involved a condemnation of Christians for worshipping Jesus in defiance of the biblical prescriptions to worship God alone, but the biblical allusions appear to be a composite of several different biblical verses. We cannot find exact parallels in the *Qiṣṣa*, but cf. *Qiṣṣa* 66 (parallel text), [ת'ם] קאל אללה למוסי קל לבני אסראיל אללה אלאהך תכ'אף ואיאה תעבד ('God said to Moses, "Say to the Children of Israel, you shall fear the Lord your God, and him you shall serve"'). For the general argument see *Qiṣṣa* 168–9 (base text): '(168) I believe and testify before God, the exalted, that you have neither religion nor sense. You worship a human being like yourself. He was seen among the created beings. He was not [even] of the elite. You take him for a worshipped Lord, then you say that he was humiliated, tortured and crucified, and he was subjected to unseemly torments. It would be fitting for you to extinguish your lights and cover up your shame, and not to expose yourself any further. For since you stand before God, with your false law, you anger and irritate His angels, His prophets and apostles, and you do not think of the [awaiting] punishment. (169) Do you not know that God, the exalted, commanded in His holy Torah, saying, "Whoever worships anyone but Me (כל מן יעבד גירי), I will not spare him from violent punishment. Whoever makes sacrifices to idols rather than to God alone will be uprooted." He did not say: "To God and the Messiah His son".' The biblical text quoted in 169 is a paraphrastic composite of Exod. 22:19, Deut. 8:19 and Deut. 11:16–17.

Line 12: the restoration אס]מא (= السماء; cf. 3b.5 below) is tempting: 'I will shut the gates of heaven' – a divine punishment for worshipping other gods. There is surely an allusion to Deut. 11:16–17, 'Take heed to yourselves, lest your heart be deceived, and you turn aside and serve other gods and worship them; and the anger of the Lord be kindled against you, and he shut up the heavens, that there be no rain, and that the land yield not its fruit.'

Lines 15–16: part of the paper has laminated, the top layer peeling off and taking the writing with it.

Lines 17–19: a piece is missing from the bottom of the page. It could have accommodated three lines of text.

2b (Gaster Heb. ms. 1623/3–4)

1]פעלת פהאת (.)
2](.) אצבי כדאליך
3]יך ישר' כאפוה
4]אלאול והוא אלאכיר
5]אי פהאדא שהדת
6](.) ואחד ואנת
7](ת)לאתה כמא וגדנא
8]ארבעה זעם
9 ישו]ע אבן אלה' פתעלא
10 ש](ה)דה ושהיד לוקא
11 אס]מא אנפתחת וקאל
12 ישו]ע אבני וחביבי יום
13 וק]אל לישוע מן נצ'ר
14 אבי ואנא ואבי
15 א]חד אלכצלת[ין
16](.)ב/א/(.)[
17] [
18] [
19] [

Notes

Lines 2–16: cf. *Qiṣṣa* 67–9 (parallel text):

(67) וקאל דאוד פי אלזבור פי מזמור ע' (נ"א כ'מסין) לך וחדך כ'טית ואלסוא קדאמך עמלת פהד'א שהאדת דאוד עליה אלסלאם וכד'לך שהדת ג'מיע אלאנביא וכד'לך שהד ישעיה אלנבי עליה אלסלאם: קאל אלרב מלך אסראיל מכ'לצא רב אלג'יוש, אנא אלאול ואנא אלאכ'ר וליס מעי אלאה אכ'ר סואיי פהד'ה שהאדת ישעיה אלנבי עליה אלסלאם וג'מיע אלאנביא אן אללה ואחד ואנת תזעם ת'לאת'ה. תעאלי אללה ען ד'לך עלוא כבירא! וכד'לך וג'דנא פי אנג'ילכם זעם מרקוס אלאנג'ילי (נ"א פי אנג'ילאתכם אלארבעה) אן יסוס בן אללה פתעאלי אללה ען הד'ה אלשהאדה עלוא כבירא.

(68) ושהד לוקא אלאנג'ילי אן אלסמא אנפתחת וקאל אללה ליסוס: אנת אבני וחביבי. וטהרה (נ"א וכאן ד'לך יום אן טהרה) יוחנא אלמעמדאני. וקאל יסוס לפילפוס: מן נט'ר אליי פקד נט'ר אלי אבי ואנא ואבי סוא.

(69) פאכ'תאר אחד אלכ'צלתין: אמא תג'על אלרב עז וגל צאדקא אנה ואחד כמא וצף נפסה ...

(67) 'And David said in the Psalms, in the seventieth (*v.l.* fiftieth) hymn, "Against you alone have I sinned, and I have done that which is evil before you" (Ps 51:6; English 51:4). This, then, is the testimony of David, peace be upon him. And likewise testified all the prophets. And likewise testified Isaiah the prophet, peace be upon him: "The Lord, the king and saviour of Israel, the Lord of Hosts, said: I am the first and I am the last, and there is no other god besides me" (Isaiah 44:6). This is the testimony of the prophet Isaiah, peace be upon him, and of all the prophets, that God is one, and you

claim [that he is] three. God is far exalted above this testimony! Likewise we find in your Gospels [that] Mark the evangelist claimed (*v.l.* in your four Gospels) that Jesus is the son of God. God is far exalted above this testimony!

(68) And Luke the evangelist testified that the heavens opened and God said to Jesus, "You are my son, my beloved one." And (*v.l.* this was on the day that) John the Baptist cleansed him. And Jesus said to Philip, "He who has seen me, has seen my father, for I and my father are the same."

(69) So choose one of two things: Either you say that the Lord was telling the truth when He said about Himself that He is one …'

Lines 14–15: signs of overprinting from the opposite page (3a).

Lines 17–19: a piece is missing from the bottom of the page. It could have accommodated three lines of text.

3a (Gaster Heb. ms. 1623/3-5)

(צדק) אלה ו(א.ב.)[
אלאנגילת אלדי (.)[
ומרקוס ויוחנא וא[
צלאתך אלדי תוצלי פ[
אלאב ואחיד ואלאבן (.)[
ורוח אלקודס פמע[א
תלתה כמא הו מכ[תוב
אלאנגיל פאן קולת (צ)[
צלאתנא וצדקתאנ[א
הום תלתה כמא קאל [
ולוקא פקד אבטל[
ישוע וגעלתוה נק[
מלכות א(ס)מא א(מ)[א
אן ישוע קאל פי (אל)[
ל(ם) אגי אנקוץ מין[
(.)[ ](.) ולא כלא{ם} אלא[
(.)[ ](.)גית אתמהא [
(   ) (א)מין אמין (.)[
]( ) אס(מי) [

Notes

Lines 1–19: cf. Qiṣṣa 69–70:

Parallel text

(69) פאן קלת: צדקו אן אללה ואחד, פקד כד'בת לוקא אלאנג'ילי ומאתיוס ומרקוס ויוחנא ואבטלת צלאתך אלד'י תצלי כל יום.

Base text

(69) פאן קלת: צדק אללה ואנביאה, פאנג'ילאתך אלתי תעתקד עליהא כד'ב, וקד בטל מד'הבך ואעתקאדך אלתי תצלי כל יום: אבא חד ובכל מריא וישוע משיחא ובריך הוא רוחא דקדישא הוא ת'לת'ה אנון.

Parallel text

(70) ואן צדקת אלאנג'יל והם ג' כמא קאל מרקוס ולוקא פקד אבטלת כלאם יסוס וג'עלתה נאקצא פי מלכות אלסמא. אמא תעלם אן יסוס קאל פי אלאנג'יל ליס אג'י אן אנקץ מן תוריה מוסי ולא מן כלאם אלאנביא ולאכן ג'ית אן אתמהא באלחק אקול לכם (נ"פ אמין אמין אקול לכם) תתגיר אלסמאואת ואלארץ' ולא תתגיר כלמה מן תוריה מוסי ומן אבטל כלמה מן אמר מוסי נאקץ ידעא פי מלכות אלסמא.

Parallel text

'(69) But if you say, "It is true that God is one", then you contradict Luke the evangelist, and Matthew and Mark and John, and you negate your prayer which you pray every day.'

Base text

'(69) If you say, "God and His prophets were telling the truth," then your Gospels, in which you believe, are lying, your religion is proven false as is the creed which you repeat daily in your prayer, "The Father is one, and Mary is the virgin, and Jesus is the Messiah. Blessed is the Holy Spirit, they are three."'

Parallel text

'(70) But if the Gospels tell the truth and they are three, as Mark and Luke have said, then you deny what Jesus said and you render him one of those who are called 'deficient' in the Kingdom of Heaven. For you know what Jesus said in the Gospel: I have not come to abolish the Torah of Moses nor the words of the prophets, but to fulfil them in the truth. I say to you (Base text: Amen, Amen, I say to you), heaven and earth will pass away, but not one word will pass away from the Torah of Moses. And whoever abrogates one word of Moses' commands will be called 'deficient' in the Kingdom of Heaven.'

Line 2, אלאנג'ילת for אלאנג'ילאת.

Line 7:, cf. the variant in ms N of the *Qiṣṣa*, ת'לאת'ה אינון כמא מכתוב פי אלאנג'יל (…)

Line 16:,{ם}כלא: the scribe appears to have written לאככ!

Lines 16–18: signs of overprinting from the opposite page (2b). At the beginning and end of these lines the paper has laminated, the top layer peeling off and taking the writing with it.

3b (Gaster Heb. ms. 1623/3-6)

1](..) (יבטו)ל מן
2](..) (.)שיי ו(מן)
3]טרת צגירה או
4 בירה](נ)קיץ יודעא (פי)
5]אסמא פאין כאן
6]צאדיק פאנוה (לם)
7](.) תורת מוסא (פאן)
8](.) בעבו(..)( )
9](ת) יושוע אמו(.)א
10]תוה (נאקי)ץ פי
11](א)סמא ולא נעלם
12](מ)עצ'(ם) ממן יגעל
13](..) תלתה (כ)מא
14](.)ל(..)ו(.) יאעל
15](נ)ט'רת פי אנ(וה)
16 לו]קא ומרקוס[
17](.. .יס י)שהאד(וה)[ ](..)
18][ )(..ל..)[
19] [

Notes

Many of the letters on this page are badly rubbed, with only faint traces remaining.

Lines 1–5: cf. *Qiṣṣa* 70 end (parallel text) quoted in the notes to 3a above.

Lines 5–17: cf. *Qiṣṣa* 71 (parallel text) and 72 (base text):

(71) פאן קלתם אן יסוס כאן צאדק אנה לם יג'י ינקץ מן תוראת מוסי, פמן אמרך בעבאדה אלת'לאת'ה? אן קלת: יסוס, פקד ג'עלתה נאקץ פי מלכות אלסמא. ולא נעלם, נאקץ אן הו אעט'ם, ולא מן יג'על אלאה ואחד ת'לאת'ה כמא וג'דנא פי אנג'ילכם.

(72) ואעלם אני פתשת אנג'ילאת מתא ומרקוס ויוחנא פאד'א פיהם קולא מכ'תלף פי שהאדאתהם עלי אלמסיח.

'(71) And if you say that Jesus was telling the truth, namely, that he did not come to abolish [anything] from the Torah of Moses (cf. Matthew 5:17), then who is it that commanded you to worship three [Gods]? If you say, 'Jesus', then you include him among those who are called 'deficient' in the Kingdom of Heaven. In fact, we do not know whether his rank is deficient or high. Nor [do we know] who it is that makes one God into three, as we find it in your Gospel. (72) You should know that I have examined the Gospels of Matthew, Mark and John, and have found their testimonies about Christ contradictory." The phrase 'deficient in the Kingdom of Heaven' alludes to Matthew 5:19, 'Whoever, therefore, shall break one of the least of these commandments, and shall teach men so, shall be called least in the Kingdom of Heaven: but whoever shall do and teach them, he shall be called great in the Kingdom of Heaven.' Matthew 5:18-19 is an important text in the *Qiṣṣa*. It underpins the argument that Christians by not obeying the Law of Moses are in breach of Christ's own teaching: see *Qiṣṣa* 63, 127–8, 146.

Line 9, יושוע: in context this must be an unusual spelling of ישוע. A reference to Joshua the son of Nun (*Qiṣṣa* 22) is unlikely at this point.

Line 19: a piece is missing from the bottom of the page. It could have accommodated one line of writing.

4a (Gaster Heb. ms. 1623/3–7) + 4b (Gaster Heb. ms. 1623/3–8)

Only a small fragment of this page survives. It has darkened. Faint traces of writing are visible on both sides, but none of it is legible. 3a+3b and 4a+4b together form the outer bifolium of a quire. Assuming there were the same number of bifolia in this quire (B) as in quire C (= 5a–12b), then there were three bifolia = 12 sides missing between 3b and 4a.

5a (Gaster Heb. ms. 1623/3–9)

אלאהא חין יקול]
ואלאהכום ואן קו[לת
הו אלה' ואלה' הו אל[
לאן אלמסיח ל(.)[
לם יסתגית בא[
אלגהד איד קאל (ב)[
לם ודׄעתני(.)[
אנת אלאילה' פ[
צאדקין פקד]
אי(י) [אל](ק)ול מא (ק)[
צ(א. קאל ... ..)[
בש(....)[
(...)
(...)
(...)
(...)

Notes

Lines 1–2: The argument here probably was: How can you say that Christ is God when he himself says, 'I will ascend to my God and your God', with a quotation of John 20:17: cf. *Qiṣṣa* 43 (base text): 'And it is also written that Christ said: “I will ascend to my God and to your God.”’ (ומכתוב איצ'א אן אלמסיח קאל: אצעד אלי אלאהי ואלאהכם).

Line 2, קו]לת. It is tempting to restore קו]לתום, because of the preceding -כום, but that belongs to a quotation. See the parallel in the *Qiṣṣa*, quoted in the previous note.

Lines 2–7: cf. *Qiṣṣa* 45 (base text): ואן קלתם: אללה הו אלמסיח ואלמסיח הו אללה, פקד כד'בתם, לאן אלמסיח לו כאן אלאה לם יסתגית' בגירה ולא באחד חין לחקה אלג'הד ואלמרץ', אד' קאל: אלאהי אלאהי לם תרכתני. פאן כאן אלמסיח אלה פכיף אסתגאת' באלה גירה פי וקת שדתה? (‘And if you say that God is Christ and that Christ is God, then you lie. For if Christ were a God, he would not have appealed to another [God] nor to anyone else to help him when he met with suffering and illness, as he said, “My God, my God, why have you forsaken me.” If Christ were God, how could he appeal to another God to help him when in hardship?’). Note ודעתני in our text as against תרכתני in the *Qiṣṣa*. Psalm 22 is quoted again in *Qiṣṣa* 54 (base text).

Lines 12–16: The bottom part of the opposite page (? 4b) has laminated and stuck to this page. Some of the writing from the opposite page is showing through in reverse, but a few letters from our page are also visible. There is nothing legible.

5b (Gaster Heb. ms. 1623/3–10)

1](מ)עכום ואסלם
2]דאננא וישוע
3 ש]הד פולוס באן
4 אלכ]ומס אלוול מן
4](ה)ומא אתנין קאל
5]תהא תשהד עלי
6]ני אלא אלעאלם ואלה'
7 ישה]ד עלי אן אלה'
8](ע)תוה קט ולא
9](..)[ ](..)מך (..)די
10 (...)
11 (...)
12 (...)
13 (...)
14 (...)
15 (...)

Notes

Lines 1–9: cf. *Qiṣṣa* 48 (parallel text): פקד שהד פולוץ אנהמא ב' (נ"א פקד שהד פולס באנהמא את'נין), פי אלכ'מ[ס] אלאול מן אול אלכתאב יוחנא וקאל: אל[אעמאל] אלדי עמלת מעכם ישהדו עליה (נ"א אלאעמאל אלד'י עמלהא תשהד עליי) באן אלאהא ארסלני אלי אלעאלמין ושהד עליה פי וצייתה מא סמעתמוה קט ולא ראיתמוה באעינכם ובכלמתה אהדאני באנה

לא תת'בת פיה אבצארכם באנכם לא תאמנון באלד'י ארסלני. פאן כאן ארסלהו אלאהא אכ'ר, פהמא את'נין ('Then Paul testified that they are two, in the first fifth at the beginning of the book of John, and he said: "The works which I have done with you testify concerning him [*v.l.* testify concerning me] that God has sent me to the people of the earth [lit. to the worlds]. You have never heard His voice, you have not seen Him with your eyes. He guides me with His word. Your eyes cannot see Him, and you will not believe in Him who has sent me." Now if another God has sent him, then they are two Gods.'). There is some confusion at the beginning of this text. The quotation is clearly from John 5:36, but why should this apparently be given as a testimony of Paul? The confusion, which is even clearer in the *Qiṣṣa* base text appears to have been shared by our text.

Line 4, אלוול = אל{א}וול: The author first wrote אוול, but, noticing his mistake, he added a stroke to convert the א into a ligatured אל. That the final word is אלוול, seemingly leaving the word an א short, is a known feature in early Judaeo-Arabic spelling.[8] For the biblical reference here see 1a.3 note.

Lines 11–16: The bottom part of the opposite page (6a) has laminated and stuck to this page. Some of the writing from the opposite page is showing through in reverse. There is nothing legible.

6a (Gaster Heb. ms. 1623/3-11)

ואזֻבור וקאל בולו[ס
ובזועמכום ות[
ארב לרבי אגליס[
אגעל כול אעד[
וזעמתום קד ול̇[
ינט'ור אלא וגהי[
ואלהואן כמא וג(.)[
אלאנגילאת אלדי [
לוקא ומתיי ומר[קוס
בהואהום וריצ'א[הום
](..)ה' (..)[ ](ת) מ(.)[
](...) א(... .)[
] [
] [
] [
] [

Notes

Lines 1–5, cf. *Qiṣṣa* 50 (parallel text):

8 Cf. Blau and Hopkins 1987: 126/440 ff. (§1.2).

פאן קלתם: ואחד הו, כד'בתם אלאנג'יל ואלזבור וכתאב פולץ, לאנה מכתוב פי אלאנג'יל פי יוחנא בזעמכום ותפסירכם:

קאל אלרב לרבי: אג'לס עלי ימיני חתי אג'על כל אעדאך תחת קדמיך וזעמתם קד צעד ד'אלך אלרב פג'לס עלי ימין אלאכ'ר.

'If you say that He is one, then you deny the Gospel, the Psalms and the book of Paul. For it is written in the Gospel of John, according to your express claim: "The Lord said to my Lord: Sit at my right hand, till I make your enemies your footstool" (Psalm 110:1). You claim, then, that this Lord ascended and sat to the right of the other [Lord].'

Lines 11–12: signs of overprinting from the opposite page (5b).

Lines 13–16: a piece is missing from the bottom of the page. Part of it is stuck on the opposite page (5b). It could have accommodated 4–5 lines of writing.

6b (Gaster Heb. ms. 1623/3-12)

](.)א נצרוה אלה עלי

]אלבשר ולא אקדר

] פעל אלה' במוסא

] ואלקווה ואשרף

]עום אבנוה לם

](ו)אחידה ולם

]כיר שיי פלם

]במיצר ומרה

]מרה בב(י)ת

]והו (.)לא אל(..)[

מכ]תוב (פי א..)[

](....)[

] [

] [

] [

] [

Notes

Lines 1–2: The idea expressed here may have been that if Jesus himself confessed his powerlessness, then it is absurd to claim that he is God.

Line 8: The word 'Egypt' is clear. The flight into Egypt and Jesus' sojourn there is mentioned in *Qiṣṣa* 94.

Lines 10–12: Signs of overprinting from the opposite page (7a).

Lines 13–16: A piece is missing from the bottom of the page. Part of it is stuck to the opposite page (7a). The missing fragment could have accommodated 4–5 lines of writing.

7a (Gaster Heb. ms. 1623/3-13)

אלפסח פי בית אל[מקדס
יסתחל חלל בנ(.)[
חראמהום תום[
תורת מוסא ולא]
נקיץ מן נקץ מ[
צגירה אם כבי[רה
ואן קולתום ב(.)[
פקד כד'יבתום]
מא זאל יסוס (י)[
ובולוס אמרכ]ום
( )(...)ה (.) .. כיף)
(...   )
(...   )
(...   )
(...   )
(...   )

Notes

Line 1: the restoration בית אל]מקדס seems obvious. There may be an allusion here to the story of Jesus and his brothers, going up to Jerusalem to celebrate the Passover: see *Qiṣṣa* 113 (base text): מא תעלם אן ישו ואכ'ותה ואמה צעדו אלי בית אלמקדס ליעידו פיה עיד אלפטיר אלד'י אמר אללה תע' לסי' מוסי ע'ה'. פאקאמו פי אלקדס אלי כמאל עיד אלפטיר ונזלו, 'Do you not know that Jesus, his brothers and his mother made a pilgrimage to the Temple to celebrate Passover, as God had commanded Moses, peace be upon him. They stayed in Jerusalem till the end of Passover, and then went back.' This story is one of the Jesus stories in the *Qiṣṣa* that is not in the Gospels.

Line 2: חלל for חלאל.

Lines 10–11: signs of overprinting from the opposite page (6b).

Lines 12–16: The bottom part of the opposite page (6b) has laminated and stuck to this page. Some of the writing from the opposite page is showing through in reverse. There is nothing legible.

7b (Gaster Heb. ms. 1623/3-14)

]קד צאר נאקיץ
](.) ואנא אוביין לך
אלת]ורה ואלאנגיל פי
] ארב ואחיד לא
] תזעום אן
] הו מכתוב
]עה אלאב ואלאבן

8] פהאדא אוול
9 א](נ)י עמיל לכום
10]איסכום ואפצ'להא
11]מיל מן דהב
12](א) נתכדון לכו[ם
13 (...)
14 (...)
15 (...)
16 (...)
17 (פום להום ולא)

Notes

Line 1, נאקין, 'deficient/least', is probably an allusion to Mark 5:18–19, a passage which plays an important role in the argument of the *Qiṣṣa*. See *Qiṣṣa* 71 (parallel text) quoted in the *Notes* to 3b. See also 7a.5 above.

Lines 10–12: signs of overprinting from the opposite page (8a).

Lines 13–17: The bottom part of the opposite page (8a) has laminated and stuck to this page. Some of the writing from the opposite page is showing through in reverse. There is nothing legible. There is no trace of the words פום להום ולא, but their presence can be inferred from the beginning of the next page.

8a (Gaster Heb. ms. 1623/3-15)

1 יתכלמון ועינין [להום ולא ירון
2 אודנין להום ולא [יסמעון ואנף
3 להון ולא ישתמ[ון וידין להום
4 ולא יבטשון ר(ג)[לין להום ולא
5 ימשון כמתלה[ום
6 ומין יתוכל ע[ליהום
7 אתוכל עלא א[לה
8 ותעלא מכתו[ב
9 פי יום אתמין (.)[
10 תרכהא ס(ו)נה אל[
11 ופי אתורה אחפ[
12 (...)
13 (...)
14 (...)
15 (...)
16 (...)

Notes

Lines 1–8: The long quotation from Psalm 115:5–9 is clear, but cannot be paralleled anywhere that we can find in the existing *Qiṣṣa* manuscripts. It may have been cited here in the context of a critique of Christian veneration of images, and as an example of Christians violating their own Scriptures in defiance of Jesus' affirmation of the Torah.

Line 3: להון for הוםל.

Lines 8–10 seem to have quoted Lev. 12:3, 'And on the eighth day the flesh of his foreskin shall be circumcised.' Again the argument may be that Christians fail to observe a clear Torah prescription. See *Qiṣṣa* 63 and 121–6, especially 121 (parallel text): 'Tell me about Jesus: did he follow his own law or the law of someone else? If you say, "His own law", you lie, for he was circumcised when he was eight days old, as [God] told Moses in the Torah. And if you say, "The law of someone else", then who ordered you to abandon circumcision' (אכ'ברני ען יסוס: בסנה נפסה כאן יעמל או בסנה גירה? פאן קלת: בסנה נפסה, פקד כד'בת, לאנה כ'תן בן ח' איאם כמא קאל למוסי פי אלתוראה. פאן קלת: בסנה גירה, פמן אמרכם בתרך אלכ'תאנה?).

Lines 10–11: signs of overprinting from the opposite page (7b).

Lines 12–16: The bottom part of the page has laminated, taking the writing with it. It is now stuck to the opposite page (7b). There are faint traces of the original writing but nothing is legible.

8b (Gaster Heb. ms. 1623/3-16)

1 צ[גירה אם כבירה
2 [ה תזווגו אניסא
3 אלב[נין ואלבנאת ופי
4 [(.)ו אניסא הד'א
5 [שמאמיסתכום
6 [ניסא אלד'י אמר
7 [ומוסא ובני יש'
8 [מיא ותזווגו באמר
9 [(.)ני ען מוסא
10 [א חית אתזוגו
11 [ם אלבנין ואלבנאת
12 [(...   )
13 [(...   )
14 [(   ) וגמיע ( )
15 [(. יס)וס ושמ(מ..)
16 [( )(.)ס(מ)א לא(.)

Notes

Lines 1–11: The argument here was apparently that the celibacy of the Christian clergy is contrary to the Torah of Moses. Cf. *Qiṣṣa* 135 (base text): 'Do you not know that God, praised and exalted, told Moses son of Amram, and the Children of Israel, and all the prophets and good people to marry and multiply in the earth. But you – your monks, priests and deacons – shun matrimony and do not marry. Now who [would you say] is in the right: God's friends, the prophets, the pure ones and the legatees, or your deacons and monks?' (אליס תעלם אן אללה סב' ותע' אמר מוסי אבן עמראן ובני אסראיל וסאיר אלאנביא ואלאכ'יאר באן יתזוג'ו ויתמ'רו פי אלארץ', ואנתם, רהבאנך וקסיסך ושמאמסתך כ'לוא אלג'וזה ולם יתזוג'א. פאימא אלצואב מע אלאוליא ואלאנביא ואלאצפיא ואלאוציא אם מע קסיסך ורהבאנך?).

Lines 11, 15–16: signs of overprinting from the opposite page (9a).

Lines 12–14: The bottom part of the opposite page (9a) has laminated and stuck on to this page. Some of the writing from the opposite page is showing through in reverse. There is nothing legible.

9a (Gaster Heb. ms. 1623/3-17)

1 יסוס קאל נאקיץ]
2 מוסא ופי אתור[ה
3 אד'בייח תנזל]
4 ותכולה ויגפי(.)]
5 ואנתום קראב[ין
6 יציר רגיע מ(נ)[תן
7 מוכן קֶרבאן]
8 מוסא ~~בנג(..)~~]
9 אלמִית אומין]
10 בשרי או בקב]
11 תאייס ולא ידכ]
12 (.. ואב)וה ויסט.)]
13 [(...   )]
14 (...   )]
15 (...)ת פי א(....)]
16 (ו)תסתשפין בב(.)]
17 אין אלדין (יח...)]

Notes

Line 1: the final letter of the first word is half-way between a *sāmek* and a final *mēm*, but there seems little doubt that the name Jesus was intended. For נאקיץ see 7b.1 above.

Lines 5–6: cf. *Qiṣṣa* 127 (base text), ת'ם אמרכם באכל אלכ'נזיר ואן תקרבו אלכ'בז ואלכ'מר יציר פי אג'ואפכום רג'יע מנתן ('He [Jesus] also ordered you to eat pork and make sacrifice of bread and wine, which becomes smelly dung inside your bodies'). The argument is the absurdity of the body and blood of Christ becoming excrement.

Line 8: the scribe appears to have crossed out the second word.

Line 9: the reference here may be the Christians' practice of burying their dead in their churches, thereby defiling them. Cf. *Qiṣṣa* 128–33, especially 128 (base text), 'You put your dead in your churches, then you anoint the dead bones and claim to cleanse them by so doing' (ותג'עלון פי אלכנאיס אלתי לכם אלמותי. ת'ם אנכם תצבון עלי עט'אם אלמותי אלזית ותזעמון אנה יטהרהם). See further 9b.1 below.

Lines 10–11, 14–17: signs of overprinting from the opposite page (8b).

Lines 13–15: The paper has laminated, taking the writing with it. Part of it is now stuck to the opposite page (8b). Faint traces of writing remain, but none is legible.

9b (Gaster Heb. ms. 1623/3-18)

1]תטפא ודֵכן לא
2]קיאמה ונהא
3](ע)ן אכל אלכנזיר
4]די נאב וקאל
5] טאבת בה נפסך
6 פ](י) אגואפכום הו
7]לכין אלדי יכרוג
8](.)ו אלדי יונגיסכום
9]כום סונה ולא
10](.)לא ביה וקד קאל
11](ן) אלדי(ן) יאכל(ון)
12](ו)אלי רב(..) (.)[
13](.)ק ד(י) ו(...) (....)
14]כום ביום ( )
15](...)
16](...)

Notes

Lines 1–2: cf. *Qiṣṣa* 129-30 (base text), אליס תעלם אן מכתוב פי שריעה מוסי אלנבי ע'ה': אן כל מן דנא במיית או בעט'ם או בקבר ינג'ס סבעה איאם ת'ם יטהר. וקאלוא אלקום אלאכ'ר אן אלד'י יתכ'ד' מסאג'דהם קבור להם נאר לא תטפא ודכ'אן לא יפנא אלי יום אלקיאמה ('[129] Do you not know that it is written in the Law of the prophet Moses, peace be on him: "He who touches a corpse, a bone, or a grave, shall be unclean seven days; then he shall cleanse himself." [130] And other people say[9]: "Those who take their places of worship for their burial grounds, [their] fire shall not be quenched and [their] smoke shall not dissipate until the day of resurrection."'). The logic is that only the general resurrection will remove the defiling bodies from the sacred precincts.

Line 3: The reference must be to the eating of pork in defiance of the Torah of Moses. See *Qiṣṣa* 127, quoted under 9a.5-6 above.

Line 6: פ[(י)אגואפכום, 'in your innards/insides'. For the phrase cf. *Qiṣṣa* 127 quoted in the note to 9a.5-6 above.

Lines 7–8: Is there an echo here of Jesus' words in Matthew 15:11, 'Not that which enters into the mouth defiles the man; but that which proceeds out of the mouth, this defiles the man', which in context is seen as a challenge to the Torah of Moses?

Lines 11–16: Signs of overprinting from the opposite page (10a).

Lines 13–16: Part of the bottom part of the opposite page (10a) has laminated and stuck to this page. Some of the writing from the opposite page is showing through in reverse. Where the present page is overstuck, nothing is legible.

10a (Gaster Heb. ms. 1623/3-19)

1 אלדי כאנת אלאנ(ג)[יל
2 וקד אמר ארב (.)[
3 בני יש' בסת מ[
4 יאמורכום בו[
5 תרכת אלהודא (.)[
6 פתקי אלה' וארגי[
7 אנת עליה מין[
8 אלה' ותעלא בי(ש)[
9 אזור עלא אלה' [
10 ען מא תקולון [
11 תצפון בה מי [
12 יסוס אבן אלה (.)[
13 (לא) (...תח)י ת(.)[
14 (.)לא (...) (....)[
15 (...)[
16 ( )ואנת (...)[
17 (...)[

9 This is the reading of the base text (וקאלוא אלקום אלאכ'ר), but Lasker and Stroumsa prefer the parallel text reading, 'And he also said' (וקאל איצ'א), but it is hard to see why, because the quotation that follows is not from the Torah of Moses, nor from anywhere else in the Bible.

Notes

Lines 1–4: The argument here may have been about Christian violation of the Torah laws regarding Sabbath. Cf. *Qiṣṣa* 127 (base text): 'Do you not know that God, the exalted, created the heaven and the earth and all the various things they contain in six days, and on the seventh He rested from creating? He stipulated that the Children of Israel should keep the Sabbath for all generations to come. They should observe the Sabbath, as should their children, slaves and livestock; whoever desecrates it should be put to death' (אליס תעלם אן אללה תע' כ'לק אלסמאואת ואלארץ' ומא יחויהמא ומא פיהמא מן אלאצנאף ואלאשכאל ואלאג'נאס פי סתה איאם ופי אליום אלסאבע עטל כ'ליקתה. וג'על ד'לך שרטא עלי בני אסראיל, באן יכונוא עלי מר אלאג'יאל יחפט'ון אלסבת ויוג'בונהא עלי נפוסהם ואולאדהם וממאליכהם וסאיר בהאימהם, ואן מן בדלהא ילזמה אלקתל).

Lines 12–16: signs of overprinting from the opposite page (9b).

Lines 16–17: part of the paper has laminated, taking the writing with it. It is stuck to the opposite page (9b). Traces of a few letters are still visible.

10b (Gaster Heb. ms. 1623/3-20)

1]ה מרים אומֶה
2](נ)י אנא ואבוך פי
3]גלך פהדא שהדת
4]ומכתוב איצ'א
5]ד אלאנגיל יסוס
6](.)ן מן בני יש'
7] ותפכר פי קולך
8]ך אמרך יוסוף
9]יסוס אבנוה
10]ין אין הדא אלחיכמה
11]ס תקול אני כופת
12](.)ך פי(הם) שדי(..)
13](...   )
14]אנת א(.)בן(...)
15](   )[ ](..ג   )
16](.)

Notes

Lines 1–2: Cf. *Qiṣṣa* 99 (base text): ואקרת (מרים אם יסוע) איצ'א אנהא וג'דתה פי בית אלמקדס, וקאלת לה: יא יסוע אבני, אני כנת אנא ואבוך פי הם שדיד וחזן מן אג'לך, פאד'א מרים תעזם אן יסוע אבנהא ויוסף אלנג'אר אבוה ('She (Mary the mother of Jesus) stated also that she found him in the Temple, and she said to him: "Jesus, my son, your father and I were very worried and distressed about you." Mary claims, then, that Jesus is her son and that Joseph the carpenter is his father.'). The issue here is the paternity of Jesus: Mary, and the Gospels in general, preserve traditions from unimpeachable sources (his mother and his townsfolk) that he was the natural son of Joseph, and therefore, *pace* Matthew and Luke, he could not have been virgin-born.

Line 10: Cf. *Qiṣṣa* 107 (base text): אמא תעלם אן אהל אלנאצריה אלג'ליל קאלוא: מן אין הד'א אלחכמה להד'א יסוע בן אלנג'אר והוד'א אכ'ותה ענדנא וכ'ואתה ('Do you not know that the people of Nazareth in the Galilee said: "Whence this wisdom of this Jesus, son of the carpenter? His brothers and his sisters are among us!"'). Parallel: *Qiṣṣa* 55 (base text): יבהתו מנה ויעג'בו בעצ'הם לבעץ': מן אין הד'א אלחכם והד'א אלאמור להד'א? אליס הד'א אבן אלנג'אר אלד'י אסם אמה מרים ואכ'ותה סמעאן ויוסף ויעקוב ויהודה? ('They were astonished at him and said to each other in wonder, "Where did that one get this wisdom and these words? Is this not the carpenter's son, whose mother's name is Mary, and whose brothers are Simon, Joseph, Jacob and Judas?"').

Line 11–16: Signs of overprinting from opposite page (11a). In addition part of the opposite page has laminated and stuck to this one, obscuring some of the writing.

11a (Gaster Heb. ms. 1623/3-21)

1 כלמך ולא תגחד]
2 לך אלחק פכתר]
3 אן אחבבת תכ]
4 אבן כמא תזע(.)]
5 אנגר ומרים (.)]
6 תכדבהום והום]
7 מינך אמא תע]
8 פגסל רגלין בט]
9 באלמא פהאדיה]
10 אלא אליום אן תקו]ם
11 תגסיל רגלין ש]
12 יעגב (מנ)כום (מ)]
13 (...) (אן) אלא(..)]
14 (.)ה ל(..)]
15] [
16] [

Notes

Line 5: Joseph is referred to several times in the *Qiṣṣa*, mildly pejoratively, as 'the carpenter': see *Qiṣṣa* 55, 77, 107, 150, 152. The designation is, of course, derived from Matt. 13:53. In the parallel in Mark 6:3, it is Jesus himself who is the carpenter.

Lines 8 and 11 may refer to the story, alluded to several times in the *Qiṣṣa*, about Jesus washing his disciples feet. Peter objects, and his objection calls forth from Jesus the declaration that 'the son of man came not to be served but to serve'. It is this assertion from Jesus' own lips of his humanity ('son of man' not 'son of God'), and of his subordinate status that is the polemical point of the quotation. See *Qiṣṣa* 105, אמא תעלם אן יסוע קאם ליגסל רג'לין פוטרוס באלמא, פקאל יסוע אן לם יג׳י אבן אלבשר ליכ'דם ואנמא ג'א ליכ'דום, פחיניד' יסוע אללאה למא תחכו ענה הד'א אלחכאיה, וכיף תקדר תקול אנה ליס באנסאן ('Do you not know that Jesus got up to wash Peter's feet with water? For Jesus said that the son of man came not to be served but to serve. So Jesus affirms that he is human, while you claim that he is God.'). Cf. also *Qiṣṣa* 106, 150, 153.

Lines 12–14: Signs of overprinting from the opposite page (10b). Part of the paper has laminated, taking the writing with it. It is now stuck to the opposite page (10b).

Lines 15–16: A piece is missing from the bottom of this page. It could have accommodated two lines of text.

11b (Gaster Heb. ms. 1623/3-22)

1]יכון כאדיב או
2]פקד קאל יסוס פי
3]בן אנֶסי יכדום
4] פי יסוס קד
5](.)ה אנוה בן אנאס
6]ה בן אלה' כבירני
7]אנת או הוה פי
8]לם לא אחד
9] מין נפסוה וקאל
10](ע)דתוה אד'הב
11 יהו]דייה לכן אנבי
12](.)ס פי מדינתה
13]עלי נפסוה
14]אנת(...)
15 (...)
16 [ ]

Notes

Line 1: The sense must be: 'Whether he is lying or you'. Cf. line 7 below, and *Qiṣṣa* 112, quoted in the note to lines 11–12.

Lines 5–6: For the title 'son of man' see below 12a.2, with the note *ad loc*; for 'son of God' see *Qiṣṣa* 11, 67, 115, 147b.

Line 7: The sense probably is: 'Who is telling the truth – you or he?' See line 1 above. Note the phonetic spelling הוה.

Lines 11–12: The reference to the Jesus saying that a prophet is not without honour save in his own country and among his own people (Matt. 13:57; Mark 6:4; Luke 4:24; John 4:44) is unmistakable. Cf. *Qiṣṣa* 56, וקאל איצ'א למא אברא אלסקים: אלסמאואת ישהדון אן נבי לא יקבל ולא יכרם פי מדינתה. פהד'א שהאדה אלחואריון פי אכ'ר כתאב לוקא ('And he also said, when he cured the sick person: "The heavens will testify that no prophet is accepted or honoured in his own city." This is the testimony of the apostles at the end of the book of Luke.'). *Qiṣṣa* 112 (base text) quotes the saying in a slightly different form: וקאל לפטרס: אן אלנבי לא יבג'ל ולא ירפע בה ראס פי בלדה, פאד'א יסוע יזעם אנה נבי ואנת תקול אנה רב, פיא לית שערי מן הו אלצאדק פיכם, אנת אם הו? ופי אלחקיקה אנכמא ג'מיעכם כד'אבין, וכמא קאל דאוד ע'אלס': תביד מתכלמו באלכד'ב וד'וי אלמעאצי ('And he said to Peter: "A prophet is never honoured or respected in his own town." Now if Jesus claims that he is a prophet and you say that he is Lord, I wish I knew which one of you is telling the truth, you or he? But in fact you are both liars. It is just as David, peace be on him, said: "You shall destroy those who speak lies and perpetrate sinful acts" [Psalm 5:6]'). Note פי בלדה here as against פי מדינתה in 56. The former is somewhat closer to the wording of the Gospels.

Lines 11–13: Signs of overprinting from the opposite page (12a).

Lines 13–15: Part of the paper has laminated, taking the writing with it. It is now stuck to the opposite page (12a).

Line 16: A piece is missing from the bottom of the page. It could have accommodated one line of writing.

12a (Gaster Heb. ms. 1623/3-23)

1 עלא נפסוה פי ג]
2 אבן אנס ושהיד]
3 ומתי במא קד בינ]
4 שהדתהום ועילמ[הום
5 וגדנאה פי אלאנגיל [
6 אן דאוד קד קאל [
7 תתכלו עלא סולי[מאן
8 אנסאן אלד'י תכרו(ג)]
9 ארצ'וה וקאל דאוד]
10 כאן אלאה יעקוב [
11 עלי אלה' רבנא (אל)]
12 ואלארץ' וקאל ידמ(.)]
13 (.)ן תוכל עלא ב(.)]
14 [(.) אן י(סוס) לי]
15 [(   ) ל(....)]
16]   [
17]   [

Notes

Line 2: אבן אנס must be a reference to the common Gospel title 'son of man' which Jesus applied to himself, thereby implicitly denying, so the author of the *Qiṣṣa* argues, that he was 'Son of God': see *Qiṣṣa* 39, 57, 105, 106. None of these passages, however, uses the exact formula found here, אבן אנס: *Qiṣṣa* 39 has אבן אדם, *Qiṣṣa* 57, אבן אנסאן, and *Qiṣṣa* 105, 106, (א)בן אלבשר. See above 11b.3, [בן אנסי, and 11b.5, בן אנאס.

Lines 6,7,9: Quotations from David (i.e. the Psalms) are common in the *Qiṣṣa* (150, 151, 170, 176), those from Solomon less so, but see *Qiṣṣa* 164 and 177.

Line 10: There is probably a reference here to Psalm 146:5; cf. *Qiṣṣa* 151 (base text): דוד קאל פי אלזבור: (...) ולאכן טובא מן אלאה יעקוב פי עונה וכאן רג'אה מן אללה והו מעינה ונאצרה

('David said in the Psalms: (…) "But happy is he whom the God of Jacob helps, whose hope is in God. He is his help and his saviour"').

Lines 12–14: Signs of overprinting from opposite page (11b).

Lines 14–15: Part of the opposite page (11b) has laminated and stuck to the present page, obscuring the writing.

Lines 16–17: A piece is missing from the bottom of the page. It could have accommodated one, and probably two, lines of text.

12b (Gaster Heb. ms. 1623/3-24)

1 [מתי וא(.) (.)אצדיק
2 [פאין כונת אנת
3 [ך ואערף בה מן
4 [(ע)גב אלעגב ואמא
5 [(ה)ום הו אלה' ואלה' הו
6 [ת אנוה מכתוב
7 [מוסא סאל רבוה
8 ק]אל אלה' למוסא יא
9 [ה לא יקדיר אחד
10 [(ק) כן יסוס אלה' כמא
11 [(.)תום פקד קאל
12 [זור ודאך אנוה
13 [א לם יוצנע
14 [אליה אלבשר ואל(ד)י
15 [(.)אגל יקול למוס]א
16 [(.)יא פתקי אלה' ו(.)]
17 [א וצף נפסוה (..)]
18 [(...) אמ(א) תעלם]
19 [ ]

Notes

Line 4: The reading גב(ע) seems certain. Was there a dittography?

Line 5: Cf. *Qiṣṣa* 33 and 45 (both base text): הו אלמסיח ואלמסיח הו אללה.

Lines 7–9: Cf. *Qiṣṣa* 118 (base text): ומוסי כלים אללה ע'ה' יסל אללה ג'לת קדרתה אן ינט'ר מלאך אללה אלד'י הו וקארה, פקאל לה: יא מוסי עבדי, לם יקדר אחדא ינט'ר אלי וקארי ויעיש ('Moses, peace be on him, to whom God had spoken, asked God, great is His might, to see the angel of God, who is His glory, and God said to him, "O Moses, my servant, no one can see my glory and live"'). Note also the variants in the parallel text of the same passage: אמא תעלם אן מוסי רסול אללה סאל אן ינט'ר אלי אללה פקאל אללה למוסי: לא יטיק אחד מן אלנאס ינט'ר אלי ויעיש.

Lines 15–17: Signs of overprinting from the opposite page.

Lines 18–19: A piece is missing from the bottom of the page. It could have accommodated one line of text. It seems reasonably clear that this cannot have been the conclusion of the text or the manuscript. Further pages are missing, but how many it is impossible to say.

The New Testament Quotations in Rylands Gaster Heb. ms. 1623/3

One of the most remarkable features of Rylands Gaster Heb. ms. 1623/3 in particular, and of the *Qiṣṣa* texts in general, is the number of direct quotations they contain both from the Hebrew Bible and the New Testament. Quotations from the Hebrew Bible are not so surprising, though there are interesting questions to be raised as to what translation or translations are cited, and how much knowledge they display of *Christian* use of the Old Testament. Jews had access to Arabic translations of Tanakh as early as the ninth century. The most popular was Saʿadya's *Tafsīr*, but the text of this was far from fixed, and there were other translations as well. The textual affinities of the *Qiṣṣa's* Tanakh quotations have yet to be thoroughly assessed. As to Christian use of the Old Testament, it is striking how few of the *Qiṣṣa*'s citations from the Hebrew Bible correspond to the classic Christian *testimonia*. There is, astonishingly, next to no reference to the classic prooftexts of the messiahship of Jesus, still less any attempt to refute them. This might suggest a lack of *active* debate with Christians, because it would have been precisely these passages that Christians would have placed at the forefront of any argument with Jews.[10]

10 The messianic *testimonia* had been a central feature of the Christian *kerygma* since the New Testament, and are central to early apologists such as Justin. See Skarsaune 1987. The *Qiṣṣa*'s argument relies

So many quotations from the *New* Testament, however, *is* surprising. Though some of these are a little loose and paraphrastic, and in some cases different passages seem to have been conflated, the majority are so close to the New Testament wording that their sources can easily be identified. It is obvious that some Jews had access to parts of the New Testament in Arabic. But in what form, and in what translation?

Some light may be thrown on this question by Rylands Genizah fragment Ar. 261. This is a single page of light brown, rather course paper measuring 6.3 cm high by 12.5 cm wide. On the recto (Ar. 261-1) is the text of Mark 4:17–24, and on the verso (Ar. 261-2) Mark 4:25–32. The script is Arabic, the hand a rounded, flowing cursive, possibly to be dated to the twelfth century. Diacritics are employed, but the text is effectively written in *scriptio continua*, with no punctuation or gaps between the words. The page was not ruled, and lines tend to slope up towards the end. There are eleven lines of writing on the recto and twelve on the verso. The writing is rubbed and faded in places, and there are several holes, but they have not removed much text. The textual affinities of the fragment are probably with Kashouh's Family K, the so-called 'Alexandrian Vulgate'.[11]

The page probably comes from a copy of a complete Gospel of Mark, or of the four Gospels — an inexpensive production for personal use, rather than a *de luxe* altar copy. The possibility cannot be entirely ruled out that it derives from a lectionary. Copies of Coptic Arabic lectionaries have been discovered in the Genizah (see below) but it is unlikely this leaf was from such a work, because the passage displayed would normally have fallen into two different lections, and one would have expected this to have been marked in the text. More probably it is, as we have suggested, a fragment of a complete copy of a private Gospel book. The significance of the fragment lies not so much in its content as in its reputed provenance: it was, apparently, found in the Cairo Genizah. From a Christian provenance it would barely merit a mention, but it acquires significance if it was once in Jewish hands. Now we cannot be sure that every single item in the so-called Gaster Genizah originated in the Ben Ezra synagogue in Cairo. It is not impossible that Gaster picked this piece up from some other source, or a dealer mistakenly or fraudulently sold it to him as Genizah. But

---

overwhelmingly on claiming that the Christian tradition is self-contradictory and philosophically absurd (incarnation, the Trinity). It has no real exegetical component.

11 See Kashouh 2012: 205–57. The *Vorlage* of the Alexandrian Vulgate probably goes back to the ninth or tenth century, so this form of the text may have been around when the *Qiṣṣa* was first composed. We are deeply grateful to Dr Kashouh, and to Dr Elie Dannaoui, for sharing with us their expert views on our manuscript, and for correcting our initial transcription. Our account of Ar. 261 embodies a number of their insights. Any mistakes, however, remain our own.

scepticism in this case has to be tempered by the fact that a quantity of *other* Christian material has also, apparently, been found in the Cairo Genizah, and the fragment certainly entered the Rylands Library as part of the Gaster Genizah collection.

The rarity of Rylands Gaster Ar. 261, however, even within the reputedly Christian Genizah texts, should not be underestimated. In an article published posthumously in 2009, Friedrich Niessen offered a useful survey of New Testament translations from the Cairo Genizah. These include:

1. Two pages from a printed edition of parts of the New Testament in Judaeo-Arabic published in London in 1847 (T-S NS 267.57 [= Heb. 8:5–9:13], and T-S AS 198.152 [= Matth. 19:23–8 and 20:5–10]).

2. New Testament passages (Acts 7:20-2; Luke 2:39–52; 2 Tim. 1:1–5; 2 Tim. 3:14–15) in Arabic in Arabic script from a printed booklet containing a miscellany of texts, not all of them by any means religious in content (T-S Misc. 10.247).[12]

3. Two manuscript copies of Coptic Arabic lectionaries, one in Arabic script (T-S Ar.52.219), the other in Judaeo-Arabic script (T-S Ar.52.220). Niessen demurs from Szilágyi's view that Jews would have possessed such books for polemical purposes, since 'criticism or mockery of the liturgy was part of the standard repertoire of (...) anti-Christian polemical literature' (2006: 132–3), suggesting as an alternative that the Judaeo-Arabic lectionary, at least, may have belonged to 'a Jewish convert to Coptic Christianity [who] relied on a Judaeo-Arabic version of the biblical readings for Holy Week. The Hebrew characters with which he was more familiar, would have enabled him to follow the readings more easily than a text written in Arabic characters' (2009: 212–13) — though this would still leave a puzzle as to why such a text ended up in the Genizah.

4. Fragments of a text which contained two passages from the letters of Paul in Syriac, viz., Rom. 16:26-7 and 1 Cor. 13:12b–13 (T-S 13J7.8 + T-S NS J390). On the verso of these fragments is a trousseau or dowry-list which would originally have been attached to a *kᵉtubbâ*. This is a clear case of Jewish recycling, purely as writing material, of a Christian text, which happened to contain passages of the New Testament. It argues no interest in the content of the Christian text: quite the reverse. This reuse of Christian texts is attested also in those palimpsests from the Genizah where the underwriting is the Greek or Syriac New Testament, though these do suggest that Jews would have had ready enough access to copies of the New Testament, had they so desired.[13]

---

12 One wonders if this was a Christian Arabic text that served some sort of paedagogic purpose.

13 Taylor 1900; Smith Lewis and Dunlop Gibson 1900. For such a palimpsest in the Rylands Genizah collection see P 49.

Niessen's article supplements Krisztina Szilágyi's slightly earlier study, which does not deal specifically with the New Testament, apart from a reference to the two lectionaries mentioned above. She lists versions of the Bahira legend, fragments of various Christian polemical and theological treatises, homilies, and hagiography – some eight items in all (mostly in Arabic script, but some in Judaeo-Arabic). These are meagre pickings. Szilágyi cautions that more Christian texts may well emerge from among the unidentified Genizah fragments, but the overall picture is unlikely dramatically to change. She suggests that the paucity of Christian texts might not reflect accurately the incidence of Christian Arabic religious writings in Jewish libraries: since these texts would have mostly been written in Arabic script they were much less likely to end up in the Genizah. She bolsters this claim by citing Geoffrey Khan's opinion that 'fragments in Arabic characters found their way into the Genizah by accident and not by design' (Szilágyi 2006: 124 quoting Khan 1986: 59). All that said, the fact remains that neither Niessen nor Szilágyi record from the Genizah a manuscript of the New Testament in Arabic exactly comparable to Gaster Ar. 261.

Whether or not Ar. 261 is from the Genizah, Jews in Cairo unquestionably must have had such manuscripts in their hands. This is a necessary inference from the frequent *verbatim* quotations of New Testament verses in Judaeo-Arabic anti-Christian polemical writings such as the *Qiṣṣa*. These must surely have begun life as transcriptions into Judaeo-Arabic of texts in Arabic script like Ar. 261. We should not assume that the whole Gospels or even the whole New Testament would have been transcribed. Possibly someone extracted from the Gospels and from selected other New Testament writings (such as the letters of Paul) an anthology of verses deemed useful for polemical purposes, and did these into Hebrew script, and it was from this work that the quotations were taken. This might explain, as we noted earlier, the peculiar referencing system for some of the New Testament quotations in the *Qiṣṣa*. These quotations would repay analysis on a number of different levels. The original *Qiṣṣa* seems to have been composed in the ninth century, and, as we have argued, the New Testament quotations are integral to the work from the outset. Though there may have been already in pre-Islamic times parts of the New Testament in Arabic,[14] the

14 Though, if this was the case, it is puzzling that the references to Gospel stories in the Qur'ān don't reflect more closely the canonic Gospels. The same is true for stories from the Hebrew Bible. Though both Jewish and Christian converts to Islam were, reportedly, to be found among the companions of the Prophet, Muhammad does not seem to have started from the versions of the stories found in the New Testament or Tanakh — unless he was applying some sort of 'rewritten Bible' technique to the retelling of them.

ninth century is, nonetheless, rather early for Jews to be directly accessing the New Testament in that language. What are the nature and the textual affinities of the Judaeo-Arabic New Testament translations in the *Qiṣṣa*? The *Qiṣṣa*, of course, evolved and grew as a text. Were further New Testament quotations added, or were those already in the tradition changed in any way, possibly to accord with more recent Arabic versions of the New Testament, or are the same passages simply repeated in the same wording? It should not be assumed that Arabic copies of the New Testament were at all common among the Jews of Cairo. It is perfectly conceivable that once verses from the New Testament got embedded in writings like the *Qiṣṣa*, they would simply have been passed on from one copy to the next, or been recycled into other polemic works, without any reference back to an independent copy of the New Testament. Jews who knew anything about the wording of the New Testament might, for the most part, have derived this knowledge second-hand from quotations in works such as the *Qiṣṣa*, rather than directly from copies of the New Testament itself. But that some Jews at some point in time had access to copies of the Arabic New Testament, and transcribed substantial portions of them into Judaeo-Arabic is indicated by compelling circumstantial evidence, which supports the Genizah provenance of Ar. 261.

The text of Ar. 261 is as follows:[15]

Ar. 261-1

اذا عرض طرد او ضيق بسبب الكلمة فيشكوا للوقت
والذين زرعوا في الشوك هم الذين يسمعون الكلام
فيغلب عليهم هموم هذا الدهر ومحبة الغنى وساير
الشهوات السالكين فيها يخنقوا الكلمة فلا تثمر فيهم
والذي زرع في الارض الجيدة هم الذين يسمعون الكلمة
ويقبلونها ويثمرون واحد ثلثين واخر ستين واخر
(ما)ية وكان يقول لهم هل يوتا بسراج فيوضع تحت
المكيال او سرير لكن على منارة كذلك ليس خفي الا
(سيظهر) ولا مكتوم الا سيعلم من له اذنان سامعتان
فليسمع وقال لهم انظروا (ماذا تسمعون) في الكيل
الذي تكيلون يكال لكم وتزادون ايها السامعين

15 For an image of the text, see the Rylands Genizah database on the University of Manchester Library website http://enriqueta.man.ac.uk/luna/servlet/.

Ar. 261-2

لان من له يعطى ومن ليس له فالذي عنده يوخذ
منه وقال تشبه ملكوت الله انسانا يلقي زرعه
على الارض فينام ويقوم ليلا نهارا والزرع
ينمو ويطول وهو لا يعلم (...) الارض وحدها (تاتي)
بالثمرة اولا عشب وبعده (السنبل) ثم تمتلي
السنبل حتى اذ(ا انتهت الثمرة) حينيذ يضع المنجل
اذ قد دنا الحصاد وقال لهم بماذا تشبه ملكوت
الله وباي مثل امثلها تشبه حبة خردل التي
اذا زرعت على الارض وهي اصغر الحبوب كلها
على الارض واذا زرعت فصعدت (صارت اكبر) من
جميع للحبوب البقولات فتصنع غضونا عظاما حتى
ان طير السما يسكن تحت ظلها و(بمثل) هذه الامثال

Rylands Gaster Heb. 1623/3 and Jewish anti-Christian Polemic in the Early Islamic Period

The extensive quotations from the New Testament in Gaster Heb. ms. 1623/3 and the *Qiṣṣa* provide evidence for more than Jewish-Christian interaction in the medieval Islamic world, or some intriguing footnotes to the history of the Arabic New Testament. They are fundamental to the genre of these two works and help us locate them on the map of Jewish anti-Christian polemic in the early Islamic period. The only other Jewish anti-Christian text which seems to rival the *Qiṣṣa* in popularity among the Genizah manuscripts is the *Tôlᵉdôt Yēšû*.[16] This was originally an Aramaic composition that originated in pre-Islamic times, but, probably in the ninth century, in Egypt, it was translated into Judaeo-Arabic.[17] A number of manuscripts of it have

16 Aramaic versions: Cambridge: T-S Misc. 35.87; T-S Misc. 25.88; T-S NS 298.56; New York: JTS, ENA 2529. Judaeo-Arabic: Cambridge T-S NS 264.24; 298.49; 298.55; 298.57. Eleven other Genizah fragments have been identified in the Firkovich collection and two at the Jewish Theological Seminary Library, New York. The Aramaic versions can hardly be regarded as 'popular'. Aramaic became very much a scholarly language among Arabic-speaking Jews in the Middle Ages, comfortably accessed only by the learned. Though Saᶜadya, Maimonides, and the Qaraites lament the decrease among Jews of a knowledge of Hebrew, it was much more commonly taught and understood than Aramaic.

17 For recent work on the *Tôlᵉdôt* see Schäfer, Meerson and Deutsch 2011. Particularly relevant to the present study is the essay by Alexander 2011b.

been preserved in the Genizah. Lasker and Stroumsa detect in the *Qiṣṣa* a certain 'vulgarity of expression' (1994: 14) which it shares with the *Tôl^{e}dôt*. Indeed they identify the *Tôl^{e}dôt* as one of the sources of the *Qiṣṣa* (1994: 21). While not wanting to deny either of these claims, we would argue that there is more to be gained from stressing the differences between the two works than their similarities, and the key difference is the presence of genuine and extensive quotations from the New Testament in the one, and their total absence in the other. It is true that *Tôl^{e}dôt*-like legends about Jesus are to be found occasionally in the *Qiṣṣa*, such as the claim that Jesus had a wet-nurse called Salome who was a prostitute, but curiously this legendary material is not found in any of the extant versions of the *Tôl^{e}dôt*, and the *Qiṣṣa* focuses overwhelmingly on the canonic Gospels, with little allusion to apocryphal Gospel traditions.[18] The *Tôl^{e}dôt* is totally different from the *Qiṣṣa*: it is a counter-narrative, an anti-Gospel, which retells the story of Jesus in a scurrilous and hostile way. Several episodes in it show some knowledge of episodes in the Gospels, but it has no interest in representing Christianity in its own terms (Alexander 2011a). The *Qiṣṣa*, by way of contrast, is an argument, which while criticizing the Gospels takes care to quote them reasonably fully and accurately, and it does not question their historical veracity, which is the fundamental premise of the *Tôl^{e}dôt*. We have already noted the general absence of the pejorative name Yeshu in the *Qiṣṣa*. Altogether the *Qiṣṣa* is a measured critique of Christianity, which, though hardly on the highest level of rational criticism, does not sink to the scurrility of the *Tôl^{e}dôt*. It shows a genuine attempt to understand Christianity, and to engage it on its own terms.[19]

Both the *Qiṣṣa* and the *Tôl^{e}dôt* belong to the early Islamic period — to a time which saw an upsurge of Jewish polemical writing against Christianity. There were two reasons for this. The first was the stimulus given to religious debate by the rise of Islam, which claimed both Judaism and Christianity as its forerunners. The second

18 There were clearly a number of Jesus legends circulating among Jews in late antiquity and medieval times, not all of which got into the *Tôl^{e}dôt Yēšû* tradition. Interesting is the *lack* of congruence between *Tôl^{e}dôt Yēšû* and the Jesus-traditions of the Talmud — a hint, perhaps, that the *Tôl^{e}dôt* did not originate in a rabbinic milieu. The *Tôl^{e}dôt* has relied at a number of points on apocryphal Gospel traditions.

19 Szilágyi's analysis suggests an interesting stratification of Jewish anti-Christian polemic in the early middle ages into — our terms, not hers! — 'low-brow' (e.g. *Tôl^{e}dôt Yēšû*), 'middle-brow' (e.g. the *Qiṣṣa*) and 'high-brow' (e.g. al-Qirqisani and Saʿadya). The high-brow polemic is characterized by a close exegetical encounter with the opposing tradition, which shows, on the Jewish side, a sometimes deep knowledge and understanding of Christian Bible interpretation, which is not invariably polemical. It focuses precisely on that element which we noted was missing from the *Qiṣṣa* — close engagement with the Christian messianic *testimonia*. The continuities here with pre-Islamic Jewish-Christian debate should not be missed. See Grypeou and Spurling 2009.

was the fact that Islam now held the political ring, and cared little if Jews attacked Christianity. Polemics which Jews would have found dangerous under Byzantine Christian rule carried little or no risk under Islam. Though they no longer held political power, Christians remained numerically dominant and socially powerful in many regions of the Islamic Middle East, including Egypt, in the first few centuries of the Islamic era. Religious polemics are always intended as much for internal as for external consumption – they serve primarily to reassure the faithful, rather than refute opponents and make them see the error of their ways. Arabic-speaking Christians were unlikely ever to have read a word of the *Qiṣṣa* or the *Tôlᵉdôt*: they could not have managed the script. It is not impossible that some Jews may have been tempted to convert to Christianity, and works like the *Qiṣṣa* and the *Tôlᵉdôt* were aimed at deterring them. It is also not impossible that there is an inner-Jewish connection between the *Qiṣṣa* and the *Tôlᵉdôt*. It may be significant that the Vulgate Arabic New Testament, the *Qiṣṣa*, which testifies for the first time to extensive Jewish access to the New Testament itself, and the Arabic *Tôlᵉdôt* all seem to emerge together around the ninth century. The Arabic Vulgate popularized the New Testament among Arabic-speaking Christians, and made it possible for Jews to write a work like the *Qiṣṣa*, which relies so heavily on quoting the New Testament. But this resort to the New Testament did not please all Jews, and to counter its influence someone for the first time did a version into Judaeo-Arabic of the Jewish anti-Gospel, the *Tôlᵉdôt Yēšû*. From the tenth century onwards, however, as, on the one hand, the social condition of Jews in the Muslim world ameliorated, and on the other the Christian communities began to decline, the composition of new Jewish anti-Christian works seems to tail off, and the focus of Jewish intellectuals turns towards anti-Islamic polemic. This anti-Islamic polemic scaled heights never attained in the attacks on Christianity — heights which attest the profound acculturation of many Jews into the Islamic world and thought of their day. The classic anti-Christian polemics, however, continued to be copied, and remained rather popular.[20] From the fourteenth century onwards, however, probably coinciding with concerted and sustained Muslim attacks on the Christian communities of the Middle East which sent Christianity into a precipitous decline (a decline which, despite Christian missionary activity in the nineteenth and twentieth centuries, has continued to the present day), Jewish interest in Christianity seems to have waned. Whether or not we classify Gaster Heb. ms. 1623/3 as a version

20 As Szilágyi points out the evidence of the Genizah suggests that there were only four Jewish anti-Christian texts in circulation among Cairene Jews – the *Tôlᵉdôt*, the *Qiṣṣa*, and two treatises by Ibn Marwan, and they were all composed before the ninth-tenth centuries.

of the *Qiṣṣa*, it is unlikely, given the broad picture we have sketched, to have originated later than the fourteenth century. It should probably be dated much earlier.

Appendix 1: Manuscripts of the *Qiṣṣa* (after Lasker and Stroumsa)

Lasker-Stroumsa Siglum	*Location and Shelfmark*
GENIZAH	
/ה	Cambridge, University Library, T-S Ar. 11.32 = ***Qiṣṣa*** **114-25**.
R/ר	Cambridge, University Library, T-S Ar. 29.187b = ***Qiṣṣa*** **24-8** + **62-8**.
T/ת	Cambridge, University Library, T-S Ar. 44.20 = ***Qiṣṣa*** **156-8**.
A/א	Cambridge, University Library, T-S Ar. 54.34 = ***Qiṣṣa*** **42-61**.
ARA/ארא	Cambridge, University Library, T-S Ar. 52.221 = ***Qiṣṣa*** **101-5** + **112-8**.
ARB*/*ארב ARB/ארב	Cambridge, University Library, T-S Ar. 52.222 = 2 mss (1) fols 1-4 = ***Qiṣṣa*** **1-2** + **33-9**. (2) fols 5-8 = ***Qiṣṣa*** **26-37**.
ARG/ארג	Cambridge, University Library, T-S Ar. 52.223 = ***Qiṣṣa*** **50-8**.
ARD/ארד	Cambridge, University Library, T-S Ar. 52.224 = ***Qiṣṣa*** **115-27**.
ARH/ארה	Cambridge, University Library, T-S Ar. 52.225 = ***Qiṣṣa*** **61-7**.
ARV/ארו	Cambridge, University Library, T-S Ar. 52.226 = ***Qiṣṣa*** **80-93**.
ARZ/ארז	Cambridge, University Library, T-S Ar. 52.227 = ***Qiṣṣa*** **59-64**.
ART/ארט	Cambridge, University Library, T-S Ar. 52.229 = ***Qiṣṣa*** **80-90** + **128-36**.
K/ק	Cambridge, University Library, T-S AS 165.8 = ***Qiṣṣa*** **69-77**.
B/ב	Oxford, Bodleian, Ms Heb. e. 32 (Bodl. 2631, fols 18-25) = ***Qiṣṣa*** **66-80** + **137-54**.
D/ד	Oxford, Bodleian, Ms Heb. d. 68 (Bodl. 2836.7) = ***Qiṣṣa*** **7-12** + **21-7**.
S/ס	Oxford, Bodleian, Ms Heb. d. 57 (Bodl. 2745, fols. 24-25) = ***Qiṣṣa*** **90-9** + **119-28**.
G/ג	Paris, Alliance Israélite Universelle, VA 71 (Schwabe) = ***Qiṣṣa*** **124-8** + **80-90**
GB/גב	New York, Columbia University Library, but cannot now be located. Originally owned by Richard Gottheil, who published it in 1909: 89 = ***Qiṣṣa*** **41-51**.
Y/י	New York, JTS, ENA 3337.31 = ***Qiṣṣa*** **50-5**.
N/נ	New York, JTS, ENA 2594/9-10 = ***Qiṣṣa*** **17-21** + **25-7** and continues directly to **69-73**.
NS/נס	New York, JTS, ENA NS 55/14 – Mic. 10061 = ***Qiṣṣa*** **112-20**.
KR/קר	New York, JTS, Adler Collection, published by Krauss 1912, but original can no longer be located. = ***Qiṣṣa*** **106-12**.
LA/לא	Petersburg, II Firkovich, I, Heb. Ar. 3001 = ***Qiṣṣa*** **1-5** + **25-45** + **111-9**.
LB/לב	Petersburg, II Firkovich, I, Heb. Ar. 3002 = ***Qiṣṣa*** **61-67**.
LG/לג	Petersburg, II Firkovich, I, Heb. Ar. 3003 = ***Qiṣṣa*** **68-80**.
LD/לד	Petersburg, II Firkovich, I, Heb. Ar. 3004 = ***Qiṣṣa*** **102-9** + **112-50**.
LV/לו	Petersburg, II Firkovich, I, Heb. Ar. 3006 = ***Qiṣṣa*** **1-6** + **67-91** + **98-105** + **127-31**.
LZ/לז	Petersburg, II Firkovich, I, Heb. Ar. 3007 = ***Qiṣṣa*** **18-26** + **111-20**.
LIA/ליא	Petersburg, II Firkovich, I, Heb. Ar. 3011 = ***Qiṣṣa*** **1-3** + **123-7**.
LIG/ליג	Petersburg, II Firkovich, I, Heb. Ar. 3013 = ***Qiṣṣa*** **67-78**.
LKV/לכו	Petersburg, II Firkovich, I, Heb. Ar. 2026 = ***Qiṣṣa*** **65-9**.
LO/לע	Petersburg, II Firkovich, II, Heb. Ar. N.S. 76 = ***Qiṣṣa*** **56-8** and continues to sections **111-2**.
Z/צ	Jerusalem, JNUL 4° 577.4.104 (photo, original not located) = ***Qiṣṣa*** **60-8**.
NON-GENIZAH	
M/מ	Moscow, Ginzburg 1893, fols 1-5 and 7-10 = ***Qiṣṣa*** **1-58** + **111-27** + **80-9**, in that order.
P/פ	Paris, Bibliothèque Nationale, héb. 755 = currently the only ms that purports to present a complete text of the ***Qiṣṣa***. But badly garbled in places, 'as if copied from a torn-up page that had been wrongly reassembled' (Lasker and Stroumsa).

Appendix 2: Families of *Qiṣṣa* Manuscripts (after Lasker and Stroumsa)

Round brackets enclose fragments from the same manuscript (A+B+C)
A→B means B is copied from A
A→B/C means B and C are copied from A
Family 1: (H+Z+K) + LD + (ARA+G+KR)→(ART+S) + ARV + B + LKV + LIG + NS + ARH
Family 2: P→M/ARZ + T + ARB + LA + LG + (LV+LB) + LZ + D + LA + LIA
Family 3: (A+ARG) + Y
The affinities of the remaining mss (viz., R, ARB*, ARD, GB, LO) are unclear.
= approximately twenty-nine copies represented by thirty-six manuscripts and fragments of manuscript.

References

Alexander, Philip. 1993. 'Textual Criticism and Rabbinic Literature: The Case of the Targum of the Song of Songs', in Philip Alexander and Alexander Samely (eds), *Artefact and Text* (Manchester). 159–73

—— 2011a. 'Jesus and his Mother in the Jewish Anti-Gospel (the *Toledot Yeshu*)', in C. Clivaz, A. Dettwiler, L. Devillers and E. Norelli (eds), *Infancy Gospels: Stories and Identities* (Wissenschaftliche Untersuchungen zum Neuen Testament 281, Tübingen). 588–616

— 2011b. 'The Toledot Yeshu in the Context of the Jewish-Muslim Debate', in P. Schäfer, M. Meerson and Y. Deutsch (eds), *Toledot Yeshu ("The Life Story of Jesus") Revisited* (Tübingen). 137–58

Alexander, Philip and Alexander Samely (eds). 1993. *Artefact and Text* (*Bulletin of the John Rylands University Library Manchester* 75/3) (Manchester)

Blau, Joshua and Simon Hopkins. 1987. 'Judaeo-Arabic Papyri – Collected, Edited, Translated and Analysed', *Jerusalem Studies in Arabic and Islam* 9, 87–160 (= Blau, Joshua. 1988. *Studies in Middle Arabic and its Judaeo-Arabic Variety* (Jerusalem). 401–74)

Goodman, Martin and Philip Alexander (eds). 2010. *Rabbinic Texts and the History of Late Roman Palestine.* (Proceedings of the British Academy 165. Oxford)

Gottheil, Richard. 1909. 'Some Genizah Gleanings', in: *Mélanges Hartwig Derenbourg* (Paris). 84–104

Grypeou, Emmanouela and Helen Spurling. 2009. *The Exegetical Encounter between Jews and Christians in Late Antiquity.* (Leiden)

Kashouh, Hikmat. 2012. *The Arabic Versions of the Gospels: The Manuscripts and their Families.* (Arbeiten zur Neutestamentlichen Textforschung 42, Berlin/Boston)

Khan, Geoffrey. 1986. 'The Arabic Fragments in the Cambridge Genizah Collections', *Manuscripts of the Middle East* 1, 54–60

Krauss, Samuel. 1912. 'Un fragment polémique de la Gueniza', *Revue des études juives* 63, 63–74

Lasker, Daniel J. and Sarah Stroumsa. 1996. *The Polemic of Nestor the Priest:* Qiṣṣat Mujādalat al-Usquf *and* Sefer Nestor Ha-Komer. 2 vols, (Jerusalem)

Niessen, Friedrich. 2009. 'New Testament Translations from the Cairo Genizah', *Collectanea Christiana Orientalia* 6, 201–22

Skarsaune, Oskar. 1987. *The Proof from Prophecy. A Study of Justin Martyr's Proof-Text Tradition: Text-type, Provenance, Theological Profile.* (Leiden)

Smith Lewis, Agnes and Margaret Dunlop Gibson. 1900. *Palestinian Syriac Texts from Palimpsest Fragments in the Taylor-Schechter Collection.* (London)

Szilágyi, Krisztina. 2006. 'Christian Books in Jewish Libraries: Fragments of Christian Arabic Writings from the Cairo Genizah', *Ginzei Qedem* 2, 107–62

Taylor, Charles. *Hebrew-Greek Genizah Palimpsests from the Taylor-Schechter Collection.* (Cambridge)

Index of Manuscripts

Index of Qumran Fragments

Index of Genizah Fragments

1 Formerly NS 194.114

2 Formerly NS 193.107

3 The Jacques Mosseri Genizah collection is on long-term loan.

A 611 47
A 643 224–31 *Transcrp., Transl., Comm., Pl.*
A 664 64, 77
A 666 162
A 678 162
A 692 162
A 711 64, 78
A 739 158
A 744 162–3, 176
A 767 158
A 855 64–5, 77
A 897 220–4 *Transcrp., Transl., Comm.*, 230–1
A 904 47
A 918 47
A 955 163
A 960 21
A 992 162–3, 176
A 1000 65, 79
A 1015 163
A 1016 47
A 1019 21/nt 69, 163, 176, 177
A 1053 23
A 1062 175
A 1092 47
A 1098 64–5, 77
A 1106 65, 78
A 1108 46
A 1184 47
A 1252 220–4 *Transcrp., Transl., Comm.*, 230–1
A 1295 65, 77
A 1382 164
A 1420 65, 79
A 1466 65, 79
A 1621 65–6, 78
A 1649 66, 78
A 1681 66, 78
A 1718 175
A 1750 175
AF 10 147–50, 152–5 *Transcrp., Pls*
Ar. 83 170
Ar. 103 170–1, 176
Ar. 122 171
Ar. 123 170–1, 176
Ar. 152 172
Ar. 188 172
Ar. 252 172, 176
Ar. 261 280–4 incl. *Transcrp.*
Ar. 311 172, 176
Ar. 320 172–3
Ar. 321 172–3
Ar. 341 173
Ar. 345 22
Ar. 400 22
Ar. 435 173
Ar. 467 170–1, 176
Ar. 475 173
Ar. 479 173–4, 176
Ar. 481 173–4, 176
Ar. 493 175, 177
Ar. 497 174
Ar. 543 174, 176, 190
Ar. 613 172–3
Ar. 615 172–3
Ar. 711 175, 190
Ar. 720 175
Ar. 826 175
B 1010 43/nt 21

4 Bodl. 2776.3

5 Bodl. 2745, fols 24–25

6 Bodl. 2836.7

7 Bodl. 2631, fols 18–25

8 Bodl. 2787.24

General Index

(Names and Topics)